Created and Directed by Hans Höfer

INSIGHT GUIDES

Eastern Europe

Written by Rowlinson Carter

Editorial Director: Brian Bell

HOUGHTON MIFFLIN COMPANY

APA PUBLICATIONS

EasternEurope

First Edition
© 1993 APA PUBLICATIONS (HK) LTD
All Rights Reserved
Printed in Singapore by Höfer Press Pte. Ltd

Distributed in the United States by:
Houghton Mifflin Company
2 Park Street
Boston, Massachusetts 02108
ISBN: 0-395-65770-9

Distributed in Canada by:
Thomas Allen & Son
390 Steelcase Road East
Markham, Ontario L3R 1G2
ISBN: 0-395-65770-9

Distributed in the UK & Ireland by:
GeoCenter International UK Ltd
The Viables Center, Harrow Way
Basingstoke, Hampshire RG22 4BJ
ISBN: 9-62421-159-0

Worldwide distribution enquiries:
Höfer Communications Pte Ltd
38 Joo Koon Road
Singapore 2262
ISBN: 9-62421-159-0

ABOUT THIS BOOK

When this book was first mooted – and so much has happened since that it feels like a century ago – a loose consensus among politicians, academics and journalists defined Eastern Europe as the Communist countries behind the Iron Curtain. It superseded, although it did not quite correspond with, the older notion of Central Europe, which had romantic connotations positively enhanced by the hint of mysterious and, even better, slightly sinister qualities. By comparison, Eastern Europe was austere. Whether Yugoslavia was included in Eastern Europe depended on how far it was deemed to have flown Moscow's coop. By this criterion, Enver Hoxha's Albania had clearly gone to another planet.

Race Against Time

The convulsions which destroyed so many of the Communist world's certainties at the beginning of the 1990s were echoed in the production of this latest addition to the 180-strong Insight Guides series. In Apa Publications' London office, editorial director **Brian Bell** watched daily events rapidly overtaking text and pictures even as they arrived from Bonn-based **Alfred Horn**, who had commissioned them from a wide range of contacts throughout Eastern Europe.

To pull together and update this mass of material, Bell appointed **Rowlinson Carter**, a widely travelled journalist, TV documentary maker and historian firmly committed to the view that history is not about dates and battles but a story about people – their glory, bravery, villainy and greed. His text establishes a firm historical context without which

no account of Eastern Europe today would make sense.

One problem he immediately faced, however, was that Eastern Europe has never been marked as such on any map. Map-makers wisely decline to commit themselves on politically-loaded issues and are in fact reluctant to be specific even on where Europe and Asia meet. While everyone knows about the Hellespont, the "Greek bridge" near Istanbul, the border becomes murky after that, tacking vaguely across the Black and Caspian Seas before picking up the line of the Ural Mountains and heading off towards the Arctic Circle.

The relatively stable definition of Eastern Europe in terms of the Iron Curtain began to crack on the night of 9 November 1989 when a million East Germans poured through the Berlin Wall. Within days, chunks of the wall were on sale on stalls in New York City. Although the Berlin Wall was probably the most familiar stretch of the Iron Curtain, one provided with special platforms which tourists could mount to peer over, there were posts like Checkpoint Charlie, as well as barbed wire and minefields along thousands of miles of a divided continent. The removal of these obstacles, one of the most momentous developments of the 20th century, forced the editors of this book to move fast.

German reunification, which was on the cards that night, meant Germany as a whole either went into or stayed out of a guide to Eastern Europe. That much was easy – out! Not so Czechoslovakia, the heart of the old "Central Europe" and a land forever being tugged backwards and forwards across the East-West axis. The Czech half of Czechoslovakia managed to keep its feet in the Western camp for 1,000 years before the Iron

Carter

Bell

Horn

Sharman

Curtain came down like a guillotine and bundled it into the East. Slovakia, on the other hand, was traditionally part of the East, certainly in the sense of the bad-tempered Habsburg Emperor who once declared that anything east of Vienna was "Asia".

When Czechoslovakia split in 1992, by which time this book was almost completed, it was the earlier German question in reverse: not all-or-nothing, but conceivably one but not the other. In the event, we left both in.

There are powerful historical arguments which would put Poland and Lithuania into Western Europe as well, but at that rate we faced the prospect of a very slim volume. Not for long. The dissolution of the Soviet Union meant separate and expanded chapters on the three Baltic states (Latvia, Lithuania and Estonia), and on Ukraine and Belarus. We also needed to take a fresh look at Russia, detached from the numerous autonomous and semi-autonomous enclaves in the Caucasus, for example, which swell it out to make the Russian Federation. Strictly speaking, Armenia, Georgia and Azerbaijan deserve a chapter each by virtue of their being technically part of Europe, but they will not be on many tourist itineraries until the security situation settles down.

The net result of such deliberations is self-evident on the contents page. What cannot be so easily conveyed is the confusion that accompanied the compilation of the Travel Tips at the back of the book. It is one thing that visas to the newly independent countries of Eastern Europe are officially readily available; quite another that there are as yet very few independent embassies abroad to issue them. A year after independence, one country's ambassador to London had not yet acquired an embassy and was taking all calls on a mobile telephone in his car.

As our deadline approached, the one person who could confirm that the new name for Byelorussia should be spelt with one "s" rather than two (Belarus, not Belaruss) was on holiday and not expected back until after our deadline. The Russian embassy cheerfully confessed that it had no idea. It was impossible to confirm by telephone, almost certainly because the number had been changed, whether a restaurant which impressed us on a recent visit was still trading under the same name (it was a prime candidate for privatisation) and still at the same address (more and more streets are dispensing with the names of heroes of the Soviet Union and taking on new identities).

The process of "all change" nevertheless offers bonuses to visitors. It would be an exaggeration to say that they now have a *carte blanche* to go anywhere they like in Eastern Europe, but there are fewer places where their prying eyes are thought likely to bring the state down in flames. Under the rigour of group tours, visitors used to be steered towards the short list of things they were deemed fit to see. There is still something to be said for joining a group tour – but it no longer invites arrest to break away from the group and march forth independently.

For the moment, and probably for the next few years, there will be all sorts of questions that can be better answered by specialist travel agents who are privy to changes that occur on an almost daily basis. What we have tried to do here is answer the essential question which readers will be asking: "What, I wonder, makes this country tick?"

They Also Served

An impressive team of photographers combined to provide one of the most comprehensive portraits of Eastern Europe ever assembled. Prominent among them were, from English sources, **Tim Sharman**, **Jimmy Holmes**, **Lyle Lawson** and **Tony Souter**, and, from German sources, the **Jürgens Ost + Europa photo agency**.

Thanks go to the many writers who assembled material for this book, including **Zoltan Ivany**, **Ruomi Zlatarowa**, **Jan Jelinek**, **Roman Ainadis**, **Wieland Giebel**, **Sibylle Burkhardt**, **Barbara Kryskiewicz**, **Ivan Ivanji** and **Radu Mendera**. The Travel Tips section was researched by **Jasper Pleydell-Bouverie**, and the book was proofread and indexed by **Carole Mansur**.

Introduction

Russia

Ukraine

Belarus

The Baltic States

Poland

The Czech and Slovak Republics

Hungary

Romania

Bulgaria

Maps

TRAVEL TIPS

Compiled by:
Jasper Pleydell-Bouverie and
Rowlinson Carter

For detailed information
see page 345

PEOPLES OF THE EAST

The Iron Curtain cast a dark shadow over Eastern Europe. Perceived from the West through a haze of Cold War prejudice, the countries behind it were a charmless collage of antiquated tractor factories, collective farms, grim apartment blocks, secret policemen and queues for absolutely anything in the way of consumer goods. For many Westerners, a quick dash behind the curtain was quite enough. They could then say they had been there, and it hardly mattered whether it was to one country or the next because they and the people living in them were presumed to be peas in a pod.

Travellers came back with tales which cast doubt on the efficacy of Communism's great exercise in social engineering, the creation of Soviet Man. The blueprint called for the abolition of undesirable anachronisms like nationalism and God. Soviet Men would be uniformly sincere socialists able to speak Russian and ready to accept what the state recommended in the way of music, literature and art. Visitors got the impression that the system was instead disgorging half-baked malcontents whose first concern was to beg or barter for a decent pair of denim jeans.

The unthinkable happens: On 9 November 1989, a million East Germans flooded through the Berlin Wall. By the end of the year, Bulgaria, Czechoslovakia and Romania had ditched their Communist leaders. Hungary and Poland, which had in many respects shown the way, quickly caught up. Events unfolded at blinding speed. Estonia, Latvia and Lithuania, Russia's Baltic provinces under the Tsars, proclaimed their independence. Finally, in a move which the textbooks had always said was unthinkable, the supposedly monolithic "Russian" core of the empire crumbled with the defection of Ukraine and Belarus ("Little Russia" and "White Russia").

The collapse of the Iron Curtain has driven home the point, frequently lost in the West,

that Russia and the Soviet Union were not one and the same thing. The East European satellites – Poland, Hungary, the Czech and Slovak Republics, Bulgaria and Romania for the purposes of this book – were recognised as being relatively remote from the Soviet Union if only because they had their own seats in the United Nations and fielded their own national teams in international competition. On the other hand, the athletes of Russia, Ukraine, Belarus, Estonia, Latvia, Lithuania and Moldova were lumped under

the Soviet banner together with the citizens of eight other Soviet Republics, a roll-call of less familiar names like Kazakhstan, Kirghizstan and so on. Strangely, Ukraine and Belarus (then Byelorussia) had independent seats at the United Nations, whereas Russia shared its with the rest of the Soviet Union.

The practicalities of tourism in independent Eastern Europe are affected by whether the country concerned was part of what may be called the inner or outer layer of the Soviet Empire. The satellite states tended to have their own airlines and state tourist organisations, and, while these may be undergoing various degrees of privatisation, there is an

Preceding pages: astronomical clock on Prague's Old Town Hall; Bugac horseman, Hungary; Polish priests; Warsaw parade; Russian girl; Lithuanian mother and daughter. <u>Left</u>, watching the birdie in Bucharest. <u>Right</u>, Romanian village girl.

element of continuity missing from inner member states that previously operated under the umbrella of Intourist and Aeroflot, the Soviet travel agency and airline, and are now on their own. An avowed policy of making tourist visas more readily available does not amount to much if there are no embassies abroad to issue them. One year after independence, the Ukrainian "embassy" in London, for example, consisted of one man, the ambassador himself, doing all his business over a mobile telephone in his car.

For the foreseeable future, the tourist infrastructure – certainly within the former states of the Soviet Union, not excluding Russia, and to a lesser degree in the satellite

states – will remain so fluid that there is very little that can confidently go into a guidebook without being overtaken by events before it leaves the printer. Simply to recommend a restaurant is to run the risk of being immediately wrong on its name (if it switches from state to private ownership), its address (if the street was named after a hero of the Soviet Union) and conceivably the name of the town or city (ditto). All of which leaves hanging the fundamental question of whether food which was worth recommending beforehand is still edible afterwards. The one comfort is that, unless the restaurant happens to be in the Metropol Hotel in Moscow or is

a Japanese establishment anywhere, the meal will be very cheap by Western standards.

None of this should deter the prospective visitor. In the old days, the independent traveller who approached a policeman for street directions was likely to be met with an incredulous stare and "Where's your group?" Old habits die hard, and the same thought may still cross his mind, but the inclination to arrest an obvious subversive probably will not. A lot remains to be said for travelling, or rather arriving, with a group, which guarantees transport from the airport to a functioning hotel, instead of a possibly futile search for a taxi which might run out of fuel on its way to a hotel that has run out of food.

Moscow is no longer the hub for flights to all other parts of the Soviet Union. New airlines are being founded and new airports are being built. This book may provide an incentive to visit Eastern Europe and it may help to draw up an itinerary, but the nitty-gritty of what happens on arrival is for the moment best put in the lap of specialist travel agencies who are privy to developments virtually on a daily basis.

Nevertheless, a trip to Eastern Europe now is an opportunity to pick through the detritus of a fallen empire not in any ghoulish sense but to feel a little bit like Edward Gibbon reflecting on the ruins of ancient Rome. First impressions may be of economic and environmental carnage. Recovery is not easy for a national economy which for four decades was devoted almost exclusively to keeping the Soviet Union in light bulbs and cigarette papers, as was the unfortunate fate of one of the Caucasian republics. The economies of Eastern Europe were not as narrow, but the difference was one of degree. A broader range of heavy industry was not an unalloyed blessing if factories were planted in the middle of residential areas.

Positive thinking: The gloomy aftermath of the Soviet Empire has been well-documented and needs no further elaboration here as visitors would not be going to the trouble merely to gloat. The more positive proposition is to turn over the detritus with a view to discovering the things that were lost in the shadow of the Iron Curtain: the forgotten Greek and Roman antiquities of Bulgaria and Romania, the grandeur that made Prague the most glittering capital of medieval Europe, the steppes which produced the legendary Polish cavalry officer, Hungarian hussar and Cossack, and so on. The list is as long as this book, and it goes to show that Eastern Europe is not simply a factory floor, and that the people living in it are not all surly figures standing at a primitive assembly lines with spanners in their hands.

One of the games travellers play is to keep an eye open for the quirks – objects or behaviour, but nothing too blindingly obvious – that most memorably capture the character of a country. In Western Europe it is easy to come up with all sorts of things that distinguish Norway, say, from Spain, but not so Norway from Sweden unless one gets to know both reasonably well. Isolation – and

look rather German, whereas aspects of Lithuania could almost pass as Italian. A good example of the game was the request for an unspecified "traditional breakfast" which produced a large bowl of cold beetroot. This cannot be true of too many countries, one sincerely hopes, but in the spirit of the game we shan't say which it was (although neither Latvia nor Lithuania was responsible).

An earnest version of this innocent pastime was played out at the Paris peace conference after World War I. The Russian Empire of the Tsars had just collapsed, as had those of Prussia, Habsburg Austria and Ottoman Turkey. These empires had between them filled the map of Eastern Europe,

hence unfamiliarity – make the game a real challenge in Eastern Europe. In trying to distinguish between neighbours like Latvia and Lithuania, for example, it would help to know that, while both populations are of Indo-European origin and speak related languages, thus setting themselves apart from surrounding Slavs, the former tend to be Lutherans and the latter Roman Catholics. It would be even more useful to know that the Lithuanians were proudly the last pagans in Europe. The cities in Latvia, as it happens,

and with their departure their clear-cut boundaries were replaced by vague, contradictory and highly controversial historical frontiers. The peace conference was required to produce new boundaries (in the Middle East as well), and one delegate famously asked whether a nation was a piece of real estate or a homogenous group of people. If the latter, which common factor was to be given priority: race, religion or language?

The judges were, in short, looking for the combination of factors, territory being only one, that constituted a single people and the result, whatever it was, had to be compatible with economic common sense. Roads and

Left, family in the southern Carpathian mountains. **Above**, family group near Cracow.

railways were key elements in this respect. The criterion when the empires laid out their roads and railways was the crow's flight. It became apparent in Paris that either roads and railways would have to be reshaped to fit in with the proposed demographic-political boundaries or vice versa. In one instance, a map which scrupulously observed ethnic and cultural contours instead of mountains would have meant an existing railway line crossing national boundaries six times in the space of 26 miles.

These questions are as relevant nowadays as they were then because the boundaries of Eastern Europe after the collapse of the Soviet Empire reverted in close detail to the

In 1919, Poland had not existed on paper for more than 100 years, having been notoriously dismembered by Prussia, Austria and Russia in the 18th century. The overwhelming consensus at the peace conference was that Poland ought to be restored as a nation state, but there were arguments over exactly where to put it. In the event, the decision to leave Vilnius out of Poland and make it the capital of Lithuania was deeply resented – and, in Poland, still is.

While most of the current problems in Eastern Europe can be traced to contentious decisions in 1919, the origins invariably go back much further. To follow the trail back may explain the nature of problems but at the

1919 model – with the ominous difference that the ethnic balance in 1919 has since been altered, in some locations dramatically, by an influx of Russians. The worst scenario was played out in the former Yugoslavia under the sinister term "ethnic cleansing", in part a legacy of 1919. A more peaceful demonstration of the fallibility of the Paris peace conference was given by the separation of the Czechoslovak Federation into its constituent Czech and Slovak parts in 1992. These inherent flaws, compounded in certain cases by later Russian immigration, are bubbling beneath ill-feeling in the Baltic states, Romania, Moldova and other places.

same time it says a great deal about the countries tourists will experience and enjoy in the 1990s. The exercise is certainly full of surprises, and flipping through the pages of early history can provoke neck-snapping double-takes. Stop at one page and it looks as if the Teutonic Knights who founded Prussia were going to settle instead somewhere between Romania and Hungary. A few pages on and Hungary appears poised to move into Italy, with perhaps a suburb or two in Switzerland. Even mighty Russia starts life in Ukraine before disappearing from contemporary maps for two centuries, only to resurface around Moscow, where it was discov-

24

ered by Westerners at roughly the same time and in the same sense that Christopher Columbus discovered America. There is no knowing where Bulgaria might have ended up had a certain Khan Krum not burst a blood vessel in his brain while on the point of pulling off a military master-stroke.

The racial mix: One way of getting to the bottom of Eastern Europe is to imagine a multi-layered jigsaw in which the pieces at various levels are colour-coded according to ethnicity, language, religion and imperial subjection. At the ethnic or racial level, the majority are either Slavic or Germanic, with smaller contingents coloured Indo-European or Finno-Ugrian. In its simplest form, the

cultural purposes Slavs themselves. The Bulgars were Germanic descendants of Attila the Hun who were similarly subsumed by their Slavic conquests, and it is to signify their switch from a Germanic to Slavic identity that they conventionally stop being "Bulgars" and become "Bulgarians".

The East Europeans were, of course, all pagans to begin with, and some remained so until remarkably late in history – the 13th century in the case of the Lithuanians. The presence of Jews pre-dated the conversion to Christianity in many areas, which generally occurred at the turn of the millennium. The broad division was between the influence of Rome from the West and of Byzantium, in

language puzzle corresponds with the original ethnic arrangement because the only workable definition of Slavic, Germanic and so on was that the numerous tribes concerned shared kindred languages and possibly nothing else. The pattern changes as a military caste from one group conquers a much larger number from another with the familiar result that the rulers are actually absorbed by the ruled. The Viking Varangians were foreign interlopers who in conquering Slavs living in modern Ukraine and Russia became for all

Left and **above**, sticking with it in Bulgaria, Romania, the Czech Republic and Poland.

other words Orthodoxy, from the East. The Middle Ages were characterised by the vigorous evangelical activities on behalf of Rome by Poland and the Teutonic Order of Knights, with Russia assuming the mantle of militant Orthodoxy after the fall of Constantinople to the Turks in the 15th century.

Religious patterns were severely disrupted by the spread of empires which tended to insist on their subjects converting to the official faith, typically banning non-conformist clergy and refusing to recognise the validity of marriage according to any other rites. In a hotly contested area, unlucky couples might have had to re-marry two or three times to be left in peace. The original schism between Rome and Byzantium, as divisive in its time as the Iron Curtain in the 20th century, was, of course, complicated by the encroachment of Islam from the East under the aegis of the Ottoman Empire and thrown topsy-turvy by the Reformation. Russia was conspicuously aloof from the pressures of the Reformation and Counter-Reformation, its religious disputes being chiefly over the gradual divergence of Russian Orthodoxy from its Greek roots until, of course, the Communists banned religion of any kind in the interests of Soviet Man.

The following chapters on the individual countries of Eastern Europe show how these section of the former Moravian empire were severely subjugated by the Magyars and spent the following millennium in agrarian serfdom while in the process being led by their overlords in the direction of Rome and, after the Reformation, Roman Catholicism. The Bohemians and Moravians, in other words the Czechs, gravitated instead towards the Germanic world of the Habsburgs, which steered a different religious course and resulted in an urbanised and ultimately industrialised society. Although the language of the Czechs was Germanicised while the Slovak version remained relatively pristine, they remained basically the same language and this, together with the notion of ancient

swirling currents are not merely of academic interest but have a direct bearing on current events and what tourists will see and experience, especially as it is now possible to fraternise and be seen fraternising with locals without the police wanting a word with them in private immediately afterwards. The dissolution of the Czechoslovak Federation in 1992 is a pithy example which bears a summary here.

To begin with, Czechs and Slovaks were indistinguishably part of a group which came to be known as the Western Slavs. They were split by the Finno-Ugrian Magyars in the 9th century. The future Slovaks in the eastern common roots, helped the Paris peace conference to agree that Czechs and Slovaks should once again form a single country. The divorce in 1992 indicated, some 70 years after the marriage, that the partners had in reality drifted too far apart. The decisive factor, it would seem, was an invasion in the year 898.

Ask Czechs and Slovaks today what the problem was and there are jokes about Czechs liking beer and Slovaks preferring wine, a kind of shorthand for their respective German and Hungarian acclimatisation. Of course, it is possible to accept at face value the East European variations in architecture, cuisine, humour and the use of the Cyrillic as opposed to Latin alphabet. It is not absolutely imperative to think hard about Bulgarian churches that appear to have been built in holes in the ground, nor why Russians make consistently jolly drunks, but if only in the interests of the little travellers' game mentioned above, the search for the answers is unfailingly fascinating.

The fostering of Soviet Man had a messianic arrogance which presumed that nothing much of what had happened prior to the Bolshevik revolution was worth preserving. Soviet Man was supposed to supersede the colourful characters produced by conditions on the great plain, or steppes, which domi-

whose military effectiveness on a vast plain with no natural defences depended on speed and superb horsemanship. It is not hard to imagine how months on a featureless plain exposed to fierce elements imbued in the East European plainsman a love of colour and strong drink, the latter perhaps not unconnected with volatile switches between deep melancholy and maniacal dancing.

Modern times: For much of the 20th century, the differences which delineate the peoples of Eastern Europe have been suppressed. The Paris peace conference after World War I drew up the map of Eastern Europe more or less at it exists today, but Hitler sought to redraw it by making a dramatic push to the

nate southern Russia, Ukraine, Poland and, overlapping around the Carpathian mountains, Hungary. An early Russian chronicle spotted the symptoms in a 10th-century prince who "carried with him neither wagons nor kettles, but cut off small strips of horseflesh, game or beef, and ate it after roasting it on the coals. Nor did he have a tent, but he spread out a piece of saddlecloth under him and set his saddles under his head."

This, surely, is the prototype for the Polish cavalry, Hungarian hussars and Cossacks,

east, initially by invading Czechoslovakia and Poland. His ultimate aim was to push Russia right out of Europe, to consign it to Siberia, east of the Ural Mountains. In the event, his advance was checked at Stalingrad and then turned back. It was then the Red Army's turn to resume the old march westwards. The territory occupied by the Red Army was expanded farther west by Communist machinations immediately after the war. The Iron Curtain came crashing down like a guillotine.

The independence of Eastern Europe in 1990 brought extraordinary hope and opened a new chapter in a very long book.

Making music in Prague (left), in Budapest (above, left) and in Zlatica, Bulgaria.

RUSSIA

A certain Sergei Krikalev appreciated one aspect of the split between Russia and the Soviet Union more intimately than Boris Yeltsin or Mikhail Gorbachev. Krikalev was the Soviet cosmonaut rocketed into orbit in January 1991 to set a space endurance record, so he had ample time to peer through the port-hole of Soyuz TM-13 and possibly reflect on the fact that, in sprawling from the Baltic to the Pacific, Russia was bigger than the face of the moon he could see. Krikalev had been in space for some months when he learned that the Soviet Union had ceased to exist. Sooner rather than later, there would be no Soviet seat at the United Nations, no Soviet armed forces – and no Soviet space programme. Sergei Krikalev was entitled to wonder who on earth, if anyone, would bring him down.

In the event, he landed safely, Russia having inherited the space programme among other Soviet assets. The division of the estate in other respects was more contentious. Between Russia and Ukraine, for example, there was disputed ownership of the Soviet arsenal on Ukrainian soil, including inter-continental missiles, and of the Black Sea Fleet in Ukrainian ports. The title deeds to Crimea were compromised because in a blood-rush of Soviet solidarity in 1954, Russia had made a present of Crimea to Ukraine. At the time, it was a symbolic gesture with no real substance. On their parting of ways in 1992, Russia decided that the gift had been outrageously over-generous and sheepishly asked if it could have Crimea back.

The disentanglement of Russia from ties of one kind or another with the other Soviet republics helped to dispel the impression which had long been commonplace in the West that the Soviet Union and Russia were somehow one and the same thing. It became clear that Gorbachev personifed the former and Yeltsin the latter. Gorbachev was eventually resigned to the disintegration of the Soviet Union over which he had presided, but instead of wholesale divorce among its constituent parts, he hoped to keep as many as were willing under the umbrella of a less centralised Common-wealth of Independent States. On the other hand, Yeltsin barely concealed his hurry to dump what he considered Russia's imperial albatross and concentrate on Russia itself.

The opening of Russia's doors to the West through talk of joining NATO and so on was a repetition of Peter the Great's celebrated "Window to the West" which he sought to achieve by, among other things, building St Petersburg on the Baltic at the turn of the 18th century. It was neither the first nor last attempt, but in each case Russia snapped shut before many Westerners could properly exam-ine the contents of the country's cultural and historical treasure chest with their own eyes. The door has now been opened again.

When Russia embarked on detaching its armed forces from the Soviet Union, Boris Yeltsin casually mentioned that Russia might quite like to join NATO. This gave Western strategists something to think about: Russia applying for membership of a military alliance that existed for no other purpose than treating with Russia as the arch enemy. The fact that the idea was not hooted out of court reflected relief that Russia wished to be admitted to the fellowship of the West, thus ending not only the Cold War but a very much older if less familiar isolation, the author of which was not Karl Marx but one Temuchin Bagatur, born 1154 and better known by his assumed name, Genghis Khan.

A race apart: The older isolation, the feeling that Russia was not part of Western civilisation, was manifested by expressions like "Scratch a Russian and you'll catch a Tartar", the implication being that Russians had been indelibly tainted by Genghis Khan's so-called Mongol Yoke. The expression was commonplace in the mid-19th century, three centuries after the lifting of the Mongol Yoke and coincidentally while Marx was working on his *Communist Manifesto*.

It was with a view to winning Russia's acceptance as a bona fide European state that Tsar Nicholas I visited Queen Victoria in England. "His profile is beautiful," the queen noted, but the old prejudice was unshakeable and probably exacerbated by the tsar's insistence on sleeping on straw even in her palace. "His mind," Victoria concluded, "is not civilised."

Peter the Great set a precedent for Nicholas's bid for acceptance in 1697 when he hoped to drum up a Grand European Alliance to drive Turkey out of Europe. He accompanied his Ambassador Extraordinary on a tour of Germany, Austria, Holland, Poland, Venice, the Vatican and England which singularly failed to impress. "The strangers spoke no civilised language," an English historian complained. "Their garb, their gestures, their salutations, had a wild and barbarous character. The ambassador

Left, an 11th-century Varangian prince, one of the founders of Kievan Russ.

and the grandees who accompanied him were so gorgeous that all London crowded to stare at them, and so filthy that nobody dared to touch them. They came to the court balls dropping pearls and vermin."

Curiously, it was not ever thus. In the 11th century, before the pivotal intervention of the Mongol Yoke, the Russian royals were so welcome in the courts of Europe that Yaroslav the Wise married the daughter of the king of Sweden and himself had daughters who became the queens of France, Norway and Hungary. Three of his sons married German princesses, and one of his close successors, Vladimir Monomakh, married the daughter of King Harold of England, the loser to William the Conqueror at the Battle of Hastings in 1066. Clearly, the Mongol Yoke made the important difference because even in those days Russia was culturally alien from, yet acceptable to, the West.

The pre-Mongolian Russia which produced these nubile princesses was actually not in modern Russia at all but centred on Kiev in Ukraine. Kievan Russ is covered in the Ukrainian chapter of this book, but what needs to be said here is that it was doomed when in 1213 Genghis Khan completed his conquest of China, a feat which went unnoticed in a Western Europe then preoccupied with undoing the damage of the disastrous Fourth Crusade, which had looted Christian Constantinople instead of evicting the infidel from the Holy Land. The only intimation of what was going on farther East were garbled reports of a massive army whose shields were adorned with what looked like a cross.

Clerical error: These distant sightings were welcomed as confirmation of the rumoured existence of a Christian nation poised to strike the infidel from the East. This army was tentatively identified first as that of Prester John, then of "King David of India" and finally, through a clerical error, of "King David of Israel", the last creating a completely unprecedented enthusiasm among European Jews for Christian Crusades.

It fell on the Russians to discover the truth of the matter, or some of it. "We know not who they are, nor whence they came," wrote a chronicler of invaders who in 1223 galloped across the Great Northern Plain, destroyed everything in their path, and vanished. "We know not what their language is, or race, or faith. But they are called Tartars." The horrifying experience resulted in a mass exodus from the southern steppes into the shelter of the northern forests in case the Tartars, or Mongols, returned. At least one thing was clear: the "crosses" on the shields of the "Christian" army of the East were pairs of sheeps' shoulder blades, the Mongol motif.

In 1237 three strangers in exotic costume, one a woman, presented themselves at the gates of Riazan, a vassal state of Sudzal, and demanded there and then one tenth of the city's wealth. The princes of Sudzal were apparently still chuckling at their presumption when columns of Mongols trotted into view. With Genghis Khan's grandson, Batu Khan, now giving the orders, all but a few of the population were flayed alive. The exceptions were spared to run away and spread the word that the Mongols were back.

Moscow and Sudzal were razed on the turn, and there was only enough advance warning in Vladimir for the royal family to scramble into the choir loft of a cathedral which quickly filled up with people hoping that its sanctuary would be respected. Although the Mongols were scrupulous on the fine point of not spilling royal blood except in battle, this did not preclude putting a torch to the cathedral, roasting the royals and bringing the roof and walls down on the refugees. Novgorod in the far west was their next objective, but a sudden thaw deprived the Mongols of the frozen rivers which they used as hard roads for their ponies. They retired to western Ukraine for the spring and summer.

Battle on the ice: Spared from the Mongols, Novgorod and its westerly neighbours like Pskov immediately came under attack from entirely different quarters, namely Sweden and the Teutonic Order of Knights, the latter having arrived on the Baltic shores after being expelled from the Holy Land in the Crusader imbroglio which had prompted sightings of "King David of Israel". Defeat of the Swedes in a battle on the Neva River brought great distinction to Prince Alexander of Novgorod, who was granted the honorific "Nevski", or "of the Neva". The Teutonic Order was defeated in an equally famous battle on frozen Lake Peipus.

In spite of the Russian victories, the pres-

ence of these belligerent powers probably helped to persuade the Mongols after a wide-ranging rampage throughout Eastern Europe to limit their imperial yoke to the Russian mesopotamia, the area between the Volga and Oka rivers, which included Moscow and the cities which feature in the "Golden Ring" tours popular with present-day tourists. The Golden Ring was so-named after the Golden Horde, the dominant faction during a Mongol Yoke which lasted 250 years.

Muscovy enjoyed favoured status under the Golden Horde, its annual tribute amounting to 4,000 roubles compared with Vladimir's 85,000. In 1452, however, Basil the Blind, Grand Prince of Muscovy, decided that even 4,000 was too much and refused to pay. When his son Ivan III proved no more compliant, Khan Ahmed felt obliged to act, albeit reluctantly.

Strangled in his tent: With the Muscovite and Tartar armies face to face across the confluence of the Oka and Ugra, Ahmed offered to negotiate the settling of the arrears by instalments. He was actually awaiting the arrival of reinforcements promised by a Polish king no less alarmed by Muscovy's growing power. When their reinforcements did not arrive, Ahmed called off his army and turned for home, near Volgagrad. He was strangled in his tent en route, and his sons died soon afterwards in battles with the Crimea Tartars. That ended the Golden Horde and the Mongol Yoke. The Mongols never tried to re-assume their control over the north.

Western Europe had no idea of what had transpired in Russia under the Mongol Yoke. In reality, Ivan III, later Ivan the Great, exploited the loosening of the Mongol Yoke not only to consolidate under the Grand Duchy of Muscovy the various minor Russian principalities but to regain vast tracts of land which the Lithuanians had seized while Russian hands were tied. Muscovy had in the process become the largest country in Europe. The Holy Roman Emperor got wind of this expansion and sent word to Ivan offering him the title of king. "We have been sovereign in our land from our earliest forefathers," Ivan replied, "and our sovereignty we hold from God." As if to prove the point, Ivan got genealogists busy on his family tree, and they came up with a satisfactory line of descent from a certain Prus, not the most famous person in history but a blood brother of the Roman Emperor Augustus nevertheless. Ivan began to sign himself "Tsar", a derivation from "Caesar".

Enormous sums were invested in making Russia fit for the putative Caesar. The Italian architect Ridolfo Fioravanti was brought in to build the Uspenski and Archangel cathedrals and the Granovitaya Palace. The familiar red brick walls of the Kremlin were added in this period. As news of this activity filtered out, one or two Western ambassadors were sent to investigate. The first was Sigismund von Herberstein, whose account appeared not long after Christopher Columbus's discovery of America and, running into 18 editions, caused not much less excitement.

the army extraordinarily hardy, surviving with evident good cheer on practically nothing. On the debit side, the reigning tsar was clearly a tyrant and the country abounded in "such excess of superstition as the like hath not been heard of".

Chancellor's note of an "excess of superstition" became the conventional view of Russia. It was shorthand for the fact that Russia had not been party to the process in the West which had separated the spiritual authority of a Pope sitting in Rome from the temporal power of kings at home. In Russia, the two were indistinguishable. Cocooned in its Byzantine world, Russia was exposed to none of the forces which were already shap-

In 1553, the English adventurer Richard Chancellor was trying to find a northern sea route to China when he was shipwrecked near Archangel. He was taken inland to meet the ruler and was afterwards able to bring his countrymen up to date on conditions in the land. Russia, he confirmed, was "a very large and spacious country, every way bounded by divers nations". Moscow was larger than London but rough and disorderly. Nevertheless, the Kremlin enclosed nine churches which were "not altogether unhandsome". He thought the population and particularly

Above, in 1223 Mongols wiped out Kievan Russ.

ing Europe. There was never a Russian Reformation nor would there be a Renaissance or anything like the rise of liberal thought which in turn spurred democracy, private economic initiative, industrialisation and of course their attendant internal commotions.

The pattern in Russia was to a very large degree set by the personality of the tsar who occupied the throne, and the incumbent whom Chancellor met was Ivan IV, already known behind his back as Ivan the Terrible. "It would be easy," says one sober history of Russia, "to construct an interpretation of Ivan's reign that would be no more than a case-study in abnormal psychology." Ivan succeeded at the age of three with his mother, the Polish Princess Helen Glinskaya, acting as regent. One of her tasks was to shield the boy from lesser princes, known as boyars, and she was almost certainly poisoned by boyars for her pains. Without her protection, boyars ran riot through the palace, and it is said that young Ivan never got over boyars brawling in his theoretically private apartments and helping themselves to any of his possessions that caught their fancy. Ivan's reign in later years had the characteristics of a private vendetta against these intruders.

Ivan matured fast in the licentious atmosphere of the palace. He lost his virginity at 13 and was reputed to have had hundreds of

however, Ivan ran into stiffer opposition from Germany, Poland-Lithuania, Denmark and Sweden.

Poison or witchcraft was the suspected cause of the "beloved heifer's" sudden death, and either way the grieving Ivan decided that boyars were behind it. He demanded from the government, such as it was, the right to ban, execute or dispossess boyars entirely at his own discretion, and on the same day the power was granted he showed that he meant business by having one eminent boyar impaled on a stake and a further six beheaded. It occurred to him to have a number of judges skinned alive. "If they grow new skins," he said, "their fault shall be forgiven them."

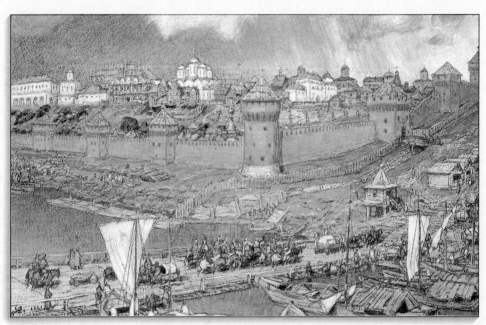

sexual experiences before it was decided that, at 16 years of age, he ought to get married. The wife chosen from a parade of several hundred virgins was Anastasia, a member of the Romanov family. He called her his "beloved heifer".

Ivan's foreign policy was to expand in every direction. He celebrated victory over the Khazars on the Upper Volga by building St Basil's Cathedral, one of the showpieces of modern Moscow. The conquest of Astrakhan made him master of the Volga from Moscow to the Caspian. The Stroganov family of merchant-adventurers were despatched to open up Siberia. In the Baltic region,

Rulers who shirked from using every ounce of power at their disposal, said Ivan, were inviting trouble with their intestines, and to avoid any such complaint himself he formed the *Oprichnina*, literally "a force apart" answerable only to him. These vigilantes wore black, rode black horses and paraded under the symbol of a dog's severed head in case there was any doubt about their purpose. Ivan also created the *pomeshchiki*, in effect blackleg boyars standing by to take over the running of real boyars' estates as he felt inclined to expropriate them. In order to ensure that the *pomeshchiki* had as much (unpaid) labour as they required to fulfil this role, Ivan nailed the existing peasants to the land, the cornerstone of Russian serfdom. Peasants who defied the death penalty by running away did not stop until they reached Ukraine, where they were welcomed to the ranks of outlaws, adventurers and fugitives who constituted the original Cossacks.

The reign of terror attained a new plateau when Ivan got the idea that Novgorod was seething with treachery and sentenced the entire population to death. More than 60,000 were killed in the space of five weeks.

The Archbishop of Novgorod invited Ivan to dinner, hoping to reach some kind of accommodation, especially as Novgorod was virtually an independent state, never having been under the Mongol Yoke. During the meal, Ivan ordered his men to loot the cathedral and turned to the archbishop to tell him his ecclesiastical career was finished. He was going to be married – to a horse – and would in future earn a living as a bagpiper in charge of a dancing bear. "Since he had never learned to play," wrote a sympathetic chronicler, "it may well be imagined how the music sounded."

Great plague: While the country trembled in anticipation of what Ivan would get up to next, he died. Sir Jerome Horsey, the agent of the English-run Muscovy Company, was at hand to record his last days. "The Emperor began grievously to swell in his cods, with which he had most horribly offended above fifty years together, boasting of a thousand virgins he had deflowered and thousands of children of his begetting destroyed." Death came as a choking fit while Ivan was playing chess according to his own set of rules, which dispensed with the king so that the king could never be checked. Sir Jerome was by no means sanguine about the future. Ivan's second son and heir Fyodor was plainly an imbecile. "God hath a great plague in store for this people," he predicted.

Fyodor was totally preoccupied by his hobby, bell-ringing, and content to leave affairs of state to his brother-in-law. Opera lovers will be able to anticipate the difficulties ahead because the brother-in-law in question was Boris Godunov. The end of Moussorgsky's opera, with the stage knee-deep in corpses, is a fair reflection of Russia's "Time

of Troubles". Boris was of Tartar descent and had no personal claim to the throne. As long as the idiot Fyodor was on the throne, he could as regent rule as he pleased, the only fly in the ointment being Fyodor's half-brother by Ivan's seventh wife Maria Nagaya, a boy named Dmitri, the heir presumptive. Boris took the precaution of sending him away with his mother to the little town of Uglich on the Volga.

When Dmitri was nine years old, his mother was alarmed by a scream from the courtyard where he was playing. She found him with his throat cut. The official report into the cause of death said it was probably an accident, possibly self-inflicted. Unofficially,

those responsible "merrily returned to Moscow, hoping to be well rewarded by Boris for a service so willingly rendered. Instead, Boris ordered the murderers slain at once in order that the treachery might remain secret." As conjecture about the death was rife, Boris set Moscow on fire to give the population something else to think about.

In 1603, five years after he was formally proclaimed tsar, Boris was taken aback to learn that someone claiming to be Dmitri, who by then would have been 21, had surfaced and that moreover King Sigismund of Poland was raising an army to put him in his rightful place on the Russian throne. The

Left, Moscow in the 15th century when first discovered by Europeans. Right, Ivan the Terrible.

plot, it transpired, had been hatched by a certain Jerzy Mniszek; "Dmitri" was in reality a disgraced monk named Grishka (or Gregory) Otrepyev. King Sigismund was soon advancing on Moscow at the head of a motley army of Poles, disgruntled Cossacks and runaway serfs and with "Dmitri" and Mniszek in tow.

Boris died "suddenly and unexpectedly" on 13 April 1605 before the army arrived. The Moscow boyars hastily installed Boris's young son Fyodor as tsar but then reconsidered their position. Having "Dmitri" on the throne, they reasoned, would better suit their purposes, and little Fyodor was accordingly strangled. Prince Vasili Shuiski, who may

even have slit the real Dmitri's throat personally, was left to ensure that the imposter was authenticated on arrival, and to that end he had a word with the real Dmitri's mother, who was languishing in a nunnery under the name Marfa. She was duly waiting when the imposter arrived, looked him over, and declared that he was definitely her son.

The False Dmitri, as history calls him, was proclaimed tsar and married Marina, the daughter of Mniszek, the Pole acting as his manager. His bona fides were first questioned by the bath attendants who ran a fresh bath for him every day and could tell whether he used it. They noted that he did not imme-

diately have a bath, as Russian custom required, after consummating his marriage. He had still not had a bath when he next went to church, and to make matters worse he went into the church followed by a pack of dogs. From servants in the kitchen they learned that his favourite food was veal, which no self-respecting Russian would touch.

Of course Prince Shuiski did not need to be told any of these things. He was alarmed not by flaws in the False Dmitri's character but by the army of toughs he had brought into Moscow with him. Shuiski took the extreme measure of making a public announcement that the man he had helped to install in the Kremlin was an imposter. Those who were not privy to talk among the servants in the palace concluded that Shuiski had gone mad and that the best place for him was prison.

The deal struck between the False Dmitri and King Sigismund was that on becoming tsar the former would convert Russia to Roman Catholicism and pave the way for annexation by Poland. Once in office, however, he reneged on the deal, and while Sigismund seethed, stories about the False Dmitri's lax bathing and dietary habits reached a wiser audience. It then occurred to ordinary people that there was very little about Tsar Dmitri that corresponded with memories of the young prince. He certainly did not look like the man the prince would have grown up to be: he was short, stocky, had flaming red hair and an unsightly wart on the side of his nose.

The end of Dmitri: Having betrayed his Polish backers and lost credibility among his putative Russian subjects, the False Dmitri managed to remain in office for all but a year before his luck ran out. A mob burst into the Kremlin and murdered some 1,700 of his hangers-on before they got hold of him. His naked body was dragged through Red Square and left lying for three days on a table "so that everyone might see and damn the imposter". To leave no doubt as to who the real perpetrators of the farrago were seen to be, the body was then burnt and the ashes loaded into a cannon. With pointed deliberation, the cannon was wheeled round into the direction of Poland and discharged.

Prince Shuiski, remorsefully released from prison, personally took the throne and arranged to have the remains of the real little Dmitri brought to Moscow and put on display prior to canonisation. Shuiski might have imagined that he had brought this unsatisfactory business to a conclusion, but he reckoned without Poland. He was engaged in putting down a peasant revolt when he learned that the Poles were on their way again with a new Dmitri in their armoury, history's Second False Dmitri. Shuiski locked himself in the Kremlin and would not come out when they arrived. Undeterred, the Poles established a rival court in the suburb of Tushino and, taking a leaf out of Shuiski's book, sent for the lovely Marina to pronounce again on his authenticity.

Marina must have wondered what she was expected to say. The original Dmitri's bones were on public display, and her late husband's cremated remains had been blasted from a cannon. She looked at the Second False Dmitri and decided he was a bit of both. Her verdict was sufficient pretext for Poland to threaten full-scale war, a prospect which caused the boyars to enquire nervously whether King Sigismund might not prefer to put his son Wladslaw on the throne, forget about the Second False Dmitri, and let them sort out the problem of Shuiski.

Rousing demagogue: Shuiski was forcibly given the tonsure and packed off to a monastery, but the proposal concerning Wladslaw, or Vladislav, stuck on the point of his having to convert to Russian Orthodoxy. Sigismund cut short the debate by saying that he would take over the throne personally, and the problem of the Second False Dmitri dissolved when he was murdered while out hunting. A simple solution was neverthless not yet within reach. While Sigismund pursued a siege of Smolensk, Sweden seized Novgorod and suggested that a Swedish prince would do better on the Russian throne than either Wladslaw or his father. Various factions of boyars saw an opportunity to make their own bids, and at one point the Polish garrison still in Moscow was besieged by one Russian force which was itself besieged by a second. To cap it all, word was received of an uprising in Pskov under a rousing demagogue who claimed to be – by now almost predictably – the true Dmitri.

Eventually the Polish garrison was butchered and the *zemsky sobor*, or assembly, met in Moscow in 1613 to consider the various candidates for tsar, a list which seemed to lengthen every day with the addition of the names of men claiming to be sons of Ivan the Terrible. The assembly ruled out of contention any prince who was not Orthodox and anyone connected with False Dmitris or Marina. Eventually, the name of 15-year-old Michael Fyodorvitch Romanov was mentioned, and it seems he was too insignificant to provoke any strong objections. Thus was Russia's most famous dynasty founded.

Michael himself (1613–45) made no great impact, suffering all his life from trouble with his feet and being mainly interested in clocks and German trumpeters. His son

Alexis, 16 when he succeeded, came to be regarded as the most pious of tsars, Alexis the Gentle, for his indulgence of Nikon, a peasant who had risen to the rank of abbot in a monastery on the White Sea. Nikon believed that it was time to purge the Russian Church of corrupt practices, like building churches with fewer than five domes and making the Sign of the Cross with two fingers instead of three. In steering the Church back to its Greek roots, Nikon grievously offended conservative elements in the Russian Church who declared themselves "Old Believers" and stood four-square against the re-introduction of practices which were in

Left, Tsar Boris Godunov, plagued by Russia's "Time of Troubles". **Right,** the first False Dmitri.

reality and ironically older than their own.

To begin with, Alexis went along with Nikon's reforms, granting him the title Grand Sovereign to augment the traditional one of Russian Patriarch. The most obvious effect of these reforms was to persuade many "Old Believers" to leave their homes and seek remote sanctuaries where they could continue as before, the origin of the pockets of Old Believers still to be found in various parts of Eastern Europe. The monks in the Solovyetski Monastery on the fringe of the Arctic Circle defied an army siege for eight years rather than give in. Nikon was eventually deposed and saw out the rest of his life in a remote monastery.

Tsar consorted with foreign ladies," a censorious boyar noted, "and his first amour was with a merchant's daughter named Anna Ivanova Mons. True, the girl was passable and intelligent. Here in this house began debauchery and drunkenness so great as cannot be described; for three days, shut up in that house, they were drunk, and it befell many to die therefrom."

Peter's exposure to foreign society in Moscow turned his gaze firmly to the West, and hence his desire to see the capitals of Europe in the course of drumming up support for the Grand Alliance with which he proposed to drive Turkey out of Europe and coincidentally seize Constantinople for him-

A significant number of foreign entrepreneurs, craftsmen and mercenaries took up residence in Moscow at this time and a cosmopolitan quarter sprang up on the River Yauza just outside the city. This exotic society beguiled Alexis's son Peter, weaning him away from a childhood which had been devoted to staging war-games with playmates and learning to sail an old English boat on a lake near Yaroslavl.

Peter succeeded at 17 but continued to spend a lot of time in the foreign quarter, particularly in the house of François Lefert, a Swiss mercenary officer. "And there in this house it came to pass that His Majesty the

self. His European tour, as we have seen, failed to impress, but he was initially successful against the Turks and able to capture Azov. This secured his "Window to the East" via the Black Sea, and his next intention was to do the same via the Baltic in the West.

Birth of St Petersburg: Peter's Baltic campaign, which began disastrously at Narva in Estonia and dragged him into war with Charles XII of Sweden, is recounted in the Baltic sections of this book. The outcome was eventual victory over Sweden and the construction of St Petersburg, and although this success was diminished by defeats at the hands of Turkey in the East, Peter assumed the title Emperor of All Russia. After him, the crown went into decline. Catherine, his widow and successor, died of wretched excess, setting a precedent for the appalling Anna who surrounded herself with a German Mafia from Latvia. The Empress Elizabeth collected 15,000 dresses and liked nothing more than having her feet tickled by young men. Peter III was usually drunk, at least half-mad and eventually strangled. Against this run of form, Peter's widow, a German princess who converted to Russian Orthodoxy and took the name Catherine, managed to win the accolade of Catherine the Great.

With a soft spot for the French Enlightenment, Catherine kept up a correspondence his case – which made things even worse – he claimed to be the reincarnation of Peter III, her late and unlamented drunken husband. Suvorov, Russia's most famous and successful general, was unleashed on Pugachev, who was eventually dragged into Red Square and quartered alive. The Cossacks paid for their rebellion by losing their semi-independent status in Ukraine.

Catherine's foreign policy in the West was concentrated against Poland. The Russian army drove into Poland and installed on the Polish throne one of her (many) former lovers, Stanislaw Poniatowski, her pretext being that nothing less would guarantee religious freedom for Orthodox believers in a

with Voltaire and other intellectuals. While she professed a desire to improve the lot of the Russian serf, the power she dispensed to the nobility gave them a greater degree of independent estate management which tended to have the opposite effect. Catherine consequently had to contend with a series of peasant uprisings and one, rather more menacing, by the Cossacks under Emilian Pugachev. To Catherine's consternation, Pugachev seemed to have been influenced by the saga of the False Dmitris, although in

Left, Catherine the Great. <u>Above</u>, Alexander I and Napoleon on the raft at Tilsit in 1807.

notoriously intolerant Roman Catholic Poland. A fuller measure of Catherine's cynical partition of Poland over the course of the 18th century so that it no longer existed is provided in the Polish chapter of this book.

After Catherine, the Russian rulers reverted to what had sadly become type. Her son Paul despised her and set about dismantling anything that bore her imprint. He could not see why aristocrats should be exempt from corporal punishment. He sent off 25,000 Cossacks to conquer British India, apologising for his inability to provide maps and advising them to "Make straight for the Indus and the Ganges." Foreign ambassadors complained that most of the time they could not understand what he was talking about. The Swedish ambassador quoted the tsar as saying that "only he is great with whom I speak, and only while I am speaking to him". The British ambassador gave up. "The fact is," he reported to London, "that the emperor is literally not in his senses."

Alexander I began propitiously. He was able to intercept and bring back the Cossacks when they were about 1,000 miles into their journey to India. His liberal education predisposed him towards the abolition of serfdom and democratic innovations, but his most pressing concern was Napoleon. He was at first inclined to join Austria, Britain

and Prussia against him, but French victories at Ulm and Austerlitz made him reconsider. In the summer of 1807 he and Napoleon met to discuss a separate peace. One thing led to another and they were soon trying to decide how best to carve up Europe between them.

Their meeting took place on a raft in the middle of the Niemen River near Tilsit. Concealed under the raft and listening to every word was Count Simon Vorontsov, a former Russian ambassador to Britain and confirmed Anglophile, who passed on the information to his friends in London. Napoleon proposed to take over Prussia and re-establish Poland on a smaller scale as the Duchy of Warsaw.

Russia should attend to Sweden and Eastern Europe generally.

Russia made the first move by invading Finland and Bessarabia, now Moldova but then part of Romania under the Ottoman Empire. Alexander waited for Napoleon to match his move as planned, but instead he woke up to Napoleon's invasion of Russia in June 1812 with 600,000 men and without so much as a declaration of war. On 26 August the Russian and French armies met at Borodino, about 70 miles west of Moscow, and within a single day lost 100,000 men between them. Nevertheless, on 2 September Napoleon entered Moscow and, having received no reply from Alexander to his offer of negotiations, set it ablaze.

While the smoke was still rising from Moscow, Napoleon realised that he had been drawn into a trap by Russian "defence in depth" which meant sucking the enemy into the Russian heartland. As without Moscow's resources he was unlikely to be able to feed his army during the approaching winter, he decided on a withdrawal to Smolensk and Vilnius, the present capital of Lithuania. Napoleon's Grand Army was harassed throughout its retreat by Russian cavalry and Cossacks and, hopelessly ill-equipped to cope with the early winter, barely 20,000 of the original force of 600,000 reached Vilnius. Leaving the survivors to manage as best they could in a city with little to offer, Napoleon hurried back to Paris.

Extreme reaction: Russia gained the part of Poland which Napoleon had earmarked for the Duchy of Warsaw after the latter's ultimate defeat at Waterloo, but this was inadequate compensation for Alexander's disillusion with the West and in particular with the notion of Liberty, Fraternity and Equality. The tentative liberal reverted to extreme reaction, a legacy which left his successor Nicholas I floundering between the desire to build bridges with the West, as he demonstrated by his visit to Queen Victoria in England, and quirky conservatism.

His insistence on sleeping on straw was matched by a pathological hatred of the smell of tobacco. It was not enough to ask people to refrain from smoking in his presence; he banned smoking anywhere in Russia. He would allow his Imperial Guard officers to wear moustaches only if they were black, although he later bent this rule to allow them to paint them black if necessary.

The revolutions which swept through France, Germany and Hungary in 1848 were anathema to Nicholas. "Revolution stands on the threshold of Russia," he said, "but I swear it will never enter Russia while my breath lasts." He had an army of 400,000 standing by to intervene in France and was willing to do the same in Germany. Neither offer was accepted, but Nicholas did have the satisfaction of helping Austria put down rebels in Hungary. He enjoyed being "The Gendarme of Europe", but when the Russians marched into the Turkish provinces of Moldavia and Wallachia in 1853, the British and French fleets appeared in the Bosporus

the stunned tsar announced, "what consequences we may expect from aspirations and ideals which arrogantly encroach upon everything sacred... My attention is now turned to the education of the youth..." That was it. As a result, thousands of students went abroad to Geneva and Zurich to sit at the feet of revolutionaries preaching anarchy and the thoughts of Karl Marx.

With nihilists in full song, attempts on Alexander's life came so thick and fast that he was moved to ask: "Am I such a wild beast that they must hound me to death?" The last was a bomb aimed at his carriage which left him unscathed but killed the horses and two of the Cossack bodyguard. "Thank God your

to stop him. The result was the Crimean War. He died in 1855 (some months before Sebastopol fell), officially from a lung infection, but some say from suicide by poison.

His son Alexander II breezed into office like a new broom, genuinely committed to the abolition of serfdom and the introduction of liberal reform. These ideals evaporated when a student who had been dismissed from St Petersburg University made a bungled attempt to assassinate him. "Providence has willed to reveal before the eyes of Russia,"

Majesty is safe," said a policeman on the scene. "Rather too early to thank God," shouted a voice. A second bomb landed at Alexander's feet. The injuries were dreadful. "Quickly," he cried as he passed out, "home to the Palace to die."

His successor Nicholas II had to adjust to the realities of an industrialisation process which had been making steady progress throughout the 19th century. By 1900 some three million uprooted peasants had become factory workers – fertile ground for Russia's first Marxist party, founded in 1898.

On Sunday, 22 January 1905, huge crowds of workers carrying icons and singing hymns

Left, boyars at play. **Above**, the Russian court under Alexander II.

converged on the Winter Palace in St Petersburg to petition the tsar. The demonstration was orderly until troops suddenly opened fire and Cossacks staged one of their fearsome charges. Several hundred people were killed. Bloody Sunday, as it was later known, led to a general strike in October and the formation in St Petersburg of a "Soviet" (i.e., workers' council), among whose members was Leon Trotsky.

In no time, peasants throughout the country were evicting their landlords and taking possession of the land. Even military units mutinied, the most famous example being the crew of the battleship Potemkin. Nicholas made a few concessions, but his principal

White Russia. Nicholas assumed supreme command of the Russian forces and things grew progressively worse.

Chronically indecisive, Nicholas became wholly dependent on his German wife Alexandra. She was in turn beholden to all sorts of quacks, especially Grigori Rasputin, who treated her haemophilac son with hypnosis and professed to be a monk "from Siberia". Whether or not the hypnosis worked on the boy, it seems to have given him control over the minds of his royal employers. Rasputin was no ascetic, however. His debaucheries were legendary and, through a little tactical blackmail and other means, he was able to make or break generals and

cure for the revolution was brute force.

When World War I came, Germany's rout of the Russian Second Army at Tannenberg in East Prussia in 1914 was, as chance would have it, exactly where the Teutonic Knights had been defeated by the Slavs in 1410. Apart from one victory in Galicia, the Russians suffered colossal casualties. The troops were as brave and uncomplaining as ever, but the army command was corrupt, incompetent and thought nothing of sending men to the front without rifles. In the summer of 1915, the Austrians and Germans took possession of the whole of Poland, most of the Baltic provinces, and much of Ukraine and

senior government officials. "His gaze," said the French ambassador, "was at once piercing and caressing, naive and cunning, far off and concentrated. When he is in earnest conversation, his pupils seem to radiate magnetism. He carries with him a strong animal smell, like that of a goat."

With the war going worse than ever, a cry went up "to deliver Russia from this filthy, vicious and venal peasant". Prince Yusupov invited Rasputin to his home. On his arrival, he was shown into a room provided with copious quantities of wine and cakes, all poisoned. Yusupov returned after a decent interval and was dumbfounded to find

Rasputin still eating and drinking lustily and evidently enjoying every mouthful.

The exasperated prince drew a revolver and fired a shot which brought Rasputin down to all fours but did not prevent him from crawling up a flight of stairs and making his escape into a courtyard. The prince pursued and put three more bullets into him, but now the sound of the shots alerted police. There was nothing wrong, the prince assured them, he was merely shooting a dog. Rasputin was thrown, still alive, through a hole in the ice of a nearby pond. When later found, the body was frozen stiff – and still clutching at the supports of a bridge.

Three months later, a shortage of bread in

on 14 March a provisional government was formed under Prince Lvov. The following day, under pressure from the army, Tsar Nicholas abdicated. The real Communist revolution was yet to come, but tsarist Russia was toppled quickly and bloodlessly – no more than a few hundred casualties.

The loss of life had started before the war. Although the economic revolution was theoretically aimed at the richer peasants, anyone with a house or a couple of cows was in danger of having them confiscated or destroyed. Anyone who protested was killed out of hand or deported to labour camps. Fields were left untilled, famine was inevitable, and several million people died.

St Petersburg led to riots, demonstrations and strikes. The police who intervened were stoned but, unusually, the Cossacks did nothing. On 9 March 1917, Alexandra said in a letter that there was nothing to worry about. The very next day, two regiments of the Imperial Guard joined the rioters, taking with them the contents of the arsenal. Workers' and soldiers' deputies soon took possession of one wing of the Tauride Palace, and

The first Five-Year Plan was completed and the second was just beginning when in 1933 Hitler came to power in Germany. Russian efforts were switched to defence, and in his mental preparation for a war which Stalin did not want but could see was inevitable, he became paranoid about enemies of the state. The result was a series of purges with a death toll probably higher than the excesses of Ivan the Terrible and all the other tsars put together. It numbered many millions.

The infamous Nazi-Soviet pact of 1939 with its secret protocols, whose existence was not officially admitted by Moscow until 1990, was virtually a replay of the meeting

Left, Nicholas II and Alexandra; itinerant Jewish musicians. **Above**, 1919 poster entitled "To Horse, Workers!"; homage to the leader called "Lenin Points the Way".

between Alexander and Napoleon on a raft at Tilsit with the Anglophile ambassador dangling underneath. The deal was the division of Eastern Europe between the two parties.

Hitler stuck to the pact only as long as it suited him, and that was until June 1941, when he invaded Russia with 175 divisions. By September the German army had reached the outskirts of Leningrad, as it then was, and by October the approaches to Moscow. The Russian capital may well have been saved only by the worst winter in living memory. Leningrad managed to hold out the siege, but the main Red Army kept on retreating until it was ready to take a stand at Stalingrad. The Germans had to break through at Stalingrad

met up in Germany. Russian prestige then stood sky-high in Western eyes, but any hopes of post-war cooperation were dashed when Stalin withdrew into isolation. It was in these circumstances that Winston Churchill made his historic observation about an Iron Curtain descending across Europe.

After Stalin: When Stalin died in 1953, he was succeeded by Nikita Khrushchev who, like Tsar Alexander II, was ready to risk loosening the reins. In 1956, he took the unprecedented step of denouncing Stalin by name. With inside information which showed that the Soviet economic miracle was not all that it was cracked up to be, Khrushchev diverted some of the investment in heavy

in order to reach the oil fields in the Caucasus, but after a siege lasting six months a German army of 100,000 was forced to surrender in what proved to be a turning-point of the war. At more or less the same time, the German thrust across North Africa towards an alternative source of oil in the Middle East was turned back at Alamein.

The defeat of the German army in North Africa opened the way for an Allied invasion through Italy. By summer 1944 the Germans were withdrawing from Russia, and the Allies were ready to open the second front with the D-Day landings in Normandy. In the spring of 1945, the Red and Allied armies

industry into consumer goods. There were limits beyond which Khrushchev would not venture, however, and these were revealed by the crushing response to revolts in Poland and Hungary in 1956. The immutable nature of the Soviet Union and its satellites became an article of faith in the Brezhnev Doctrine as laid down by his successor.

Leonid Brezhnev ruled for 18 years after his peaceful palace coup in 1964. It was another case of Russia taking two steps back having just taken one forward. The only power not kept in his own hands was doled out to a small group of unquestioning henchmen. Nepotism and corruption put the faltering economy into a tail-spin, and the further it fell, the more self-congratulatory the rhetoric of the leadership became.

It was against this economic mismanagement cocooned in hypocrisy and lies that in 1985 Mikhail Gorbachev pitched his campaign for *glasnost* and *perestroika*, the former being for more candour in government, the latter for a market-inclined economy. Gorbachev dared to say aloud and with the full authority of his office what people standing forlornly in queues had been saying for years: that the Soviet economy did not work. He only just stopped short of saying that perhaps the whole intellectual edifice created by Marx, Engels and company did not

new complexion on this line of reasoning. Not only had the cure proved to be worse than the complaint, the cure for the misguided cure, he warned, would amount to severe shock therapy.

And so it proved. Exposed to market forces, the rouble dropped lo less than 1 percent of its previously contrived exchange rate in a matter of weeks. Its domestic purchasing power collapsed too. Wages were so far behind the rate of inflation that they practically dropped out of sight.

While Gorbachev's prestige abroad was undiminished, at home he was held responsible for an economic disaster that wiped the shine off *glasnost* and his achievements on

work either. Factories built in the 1930s out of World War I booty were no longer responding to the desperate measures which had just managed to keep them ticking over.

People who were not necessarily predisposed towards Communism had long said that perhaps there was a case in 1917 for trying it in Russia. The assumption was that Russia had become so sick under the tsars that only a very powerful medicine was likely to have any effect. Gorbachev put a

Left, Nikita Khrushchev extolling the virtues of collectivised agriculture. **Above**, traditional toys updated for the 1990s.

the world stage. It was a predicament adeptly exploited by his rival Boris Yeltsin, who publicly distanced himself from the concept of a Soviet Union in order to mount a campaign which was unashamedly "Russia for the Russians".

The message struck a receptive chord – except, of course, among those who couldn't imagine life (or a livelihood) without a Soviet Union. A farcical coup attempt in 1991 exposed the loneliness of the plotters' position, but it was not long before Gorbachev was forced out anyway. Boris Yeltsin triumphantly inherited what many suspected would be a poisoned chalice.

RUSSIA: WHAT TO SEE

Most visitors, especially those in Russia for the first time, concentrate on Moscow and St Petersburg and only after them on what is known as Moscow's Golden Ring, a chain of city-states which were rich and famous long before Moscow-Muscovy dominated Great Russia. This chapter observes the order of these perfectly sensible priorities.

Moscow: Muscovites are fond of saying that their city is surrounded by seven hills. The listener who then wonders aloud whether the obvious parallel with Rome does not extend to other ennobling qualities would not be contradicted. Cities are entitled to a little poetic licence when it comes to retailing their origins: the story of the baby miraculously suckled by Romulus and Remus, for example, is believed by some to have been cover for a faithless wife's embarrassing pregnancy.

The origin of Moscow, as far as can be ascertained, begins with a certain boyar named Kuchko living a contented and rather isolated existence among pine trees on a hill overlooking the Moscow River in the 12th century. It had probably never crossed his mind that the position he occupied, neatly between the headwaters of four great rivers, the Oka, Volga, Don and Dnieper, had enormous strategic value.

The point was not lost on Prince Yuri Dolgoruki of Rostov and Sudzal who called on Kuchko, killed him on the spot and packed off his beautiful daughter Ulita as a little present for his son Vladimir. The royal celebration of this coup, to which the ancient chronicles give the date 1147, is taken as the founding of Moscow. Eight centuries later, in 1947, the city unveiled an equestrian statue to Prince Yuri.

In the course of the following century, Moscow grew into a little town protected by a wooden stockade which proved pitifully inadequate against the Mongol invasion of 1240 under Batu Khan. Moscow was burned to the ground but, as we saw in the previous section of

this book, the town and the duchy of Muscovy which developed around it ultimately flourished under the Pax Mongolica. The Kremlin, or citadel, at the heart of the town was progressively extended and strengthened, and it was within this stronghold that the modern city took shape, the cornerstones being four stone-built cathedrals. Today it is a city of 8 million, one of the largest in the world but also one of the easiest to get around thanks to the best underground system in existence. Visitors should not be intimidated by the signs being in Cyrillic script. Carry around a piece of paper with a transliteration of the obvious pitfalls (what looks like a backwards "P", for instance, is treated as "R") and, all of a sudden, the signs make sense or can at least be pronounced for the purpose of asking directions.

The **Kremlin** is the logical starting point from which to see Moscow. The first stone walls, built roughly along the lines of the present walls, were useless when the Tartars struck a second time, slaughtering the entire population of

24,000. Ridolfo Fioravanti, an Italian architect imported from Bologna in 1475 principally to build churches for Ivan III, rebuilt the Kremlin's fortifications in the familiar red brick, adding moats and drawbridges on three sides.

Red Square was built on one of these moats when they had outlived their military purpose and were filled in. The **Spasskaya Tower**, one of 20 towers, was added by another Italian architect, Pietro Antonia Solari, in 1491. An Englishman, Christopher Halloway, provided the tower clock in 1625. The latter was employed for four years at 60 roubles a year plus a wagon-load of wood per week. The little look-out near the gate, the **Tsarskaya Bashnia**, was built by Ivan the Terrible to provide a discreet view of what was happening in Red Square – usually executions.

The Kremlin grounds are generally entered through the **Troitskaya** (Trinity Gate). Legend has it that Napoleon entered the city bare-headed, an irreverence which was asking for trouble, which of course he got. The huge glass and steel anachronism in the centre is the **Kremlin Palace of Congresses**, built in 1961. To the left is the Arsenal, built in 1701–36 by Peter the Great and adorned with trophies taken after the defeat of Napoleon's army in 1812.

To the right is the **Armoury**, now a museum of armour and valuables belonging to all the Grand Princes from the Varangian Ruriks to the Romanovs. The double throne, used by Peter the Great and his half-brother Ivan, has a little window built into the back of it. It was used as a peep-hole by their fat sister Sophia.

A bit further on is the **Square of the Cathedrals**. The white-walled **Uspenski (Assumption) Cathedral** in the centre was the work of Fioravanti, who was asked to produce a facsimile of the cathedral in Vladimir. Some of the original icons and frescoes have disappeared, but they have been replaced and the interior remains stunning. The gold iconostasis, or screen, hid the priest from the congregation for much of the service, as was Orthodox practice. "We

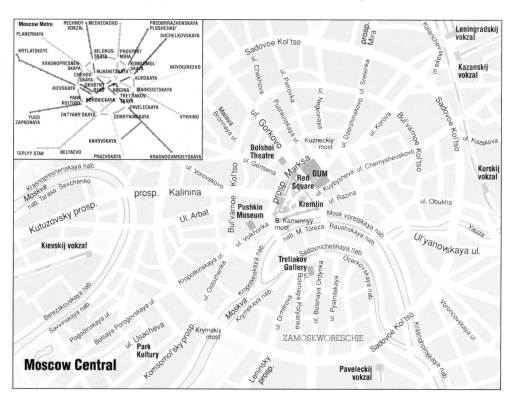

see Heaven!" Ivan III cried on entering the cathedral for the first time. The carved throne originally belonged either to Ivan the Terrible or Vladimir Monomakh of Kiev; in either case it was used for the coronation of all tsars right down to Nicholas II, the last. Napoleon was singularly unimpressed. He used the cathedral as a stable for his cavalry and, on leaving, absconded with five tons of silver and 500 lb (226 kg) of gold.

The **Annunciation Cathedral** was built by masons from Pskov as a private church for the Grand Princes. Its iconostasis was carried over from the Blagoveshensky Church previously on the same site. The paintings are by Theophanes the Greek and Andrei Rubliyov; the floor covered with agate and jasper tiles was the gift of the Shah of Persia. Aristotle, Plutarch and Virgil somehow managed to get themselves included among the portraits of the various Grand Princes.

The Archangel Michael Cathedral was built a century later as a burial place for tsars and Grand Princes until Peter the Great. Later tsars preferred to be buried in the Alexander Nevski Lavra, with the exception of Boris Godunov, who is buried at Zagorsk. The holiest spot in the cathedral, right next to the altar, was given to Ivan the Terrible who, in spite of everything, considered himself a deeply religious man.

The highest building in the Kremlin is the **bell-tower** named after Ivan the Great. It started off, in 1508, at 195 ft (60 metres) but was extended by Boris Godunov to 265 ft (81 metres). It was then decreed that nothing in Russia should be higher, a ruling that has obviously since fallen by the wayside. Boris commissioned the biggest bell in the world to go with the tower, but on being hoisted into position it slipped and all 200 tons of it shattered on the ground.

A century later, the Empress Anna ordered a replacement, but it was engulfed in an accidental fire while still on the ground. Water was poured on it when it was red-hot, and it promptly cracked in two places. It was left where

Easter returns to Red Square.

it was, half-buried, until Tsar Nicholas had it mounted on a special base in 1835. In the light of obvious deficiencies in contemporary iron-foundaries, it is perhaps as well that the colossal 16th-century cannon nearby, the Tsar Pushka, was never fired. The pile of 2-ton cannon balls lying next to it were made only in the 19th century but give a good idea of just how badly things could have gone wrong.

The Kremlin contains a host of buildings. Of the remainder, let brief mention be made of the **Terem Palace**, the residence of Tsar Michael, the first of the Romanovs. There were even more churches inside the Kremlin, but Stalin demolished a number to make room for the offices of the Soviet Union. The oldest surviving secular building is the **Granovitaya Palace,** or Palace of the Facets, so named after the faceted white tiles on the exterior.

This part of the Kremlin was long off-limits to visitors, but Richard Chancellor, an English merchant, left an account of a feast given in the palace by Ivan the Terrible in 1553: "The Emperor, sitting upon a high and stately seat, apparelled with a robe of silver and with another diadem on his head... There dined that day in the Emperor's presence above 500 strangers and 200 Russians, and all they were served in vessels of gold."

Outside the Kremlin in **Red Square** is Lenin's Tomb and a perpetual queue of people waiting for a glimpse of the gaunt features under the transparent sarcophagus. It forms the platform from which Russian big-wigs traditionally watch the May Day military parades. Across the square stands GUM, the gigantic department store which superseded the hundreds of market stalls which used to stand in the square in earlier times. The shelves manage to remain comparatively well-stocked when all others in Russia look distinctly bare. Getting to buy anything requires a robust understanding of how the queues work, but the store is well worth a visit just for the fun of it.

GUM faces the equally-proportioned Historical Museum across the square.

The GUM **department store.**

Together, says Sir Fitzroy Maclean, author and former British diplomat in Moscow, they possess "a sufficiently strong element of the fantastic to make them a not altogether unworthy foil for the medieval fantasies of the Kremlin across the way."

The Cathedral of St Basil, also on the square, is more than a match for the Kremlin in its own right. This extraordinary monument, which incorporates nine churches, was Ivan the Terrible's celebration of victory over the Tartars of Kazan, built in 1555–60 by the Russian architects Barma and Postnik. The nine onion domes were originally white and only later painted in all the colours of the rainbow. In its time the cathedral was what might now be called "state-of-the-art" Russo-Byzantine architecture, and Ivan was so pleased with it that he is reputed to have blinded the architects to prevent them from building anything so beautiful again. This dubious tale is told of churches and mosques all over the world, and while Ivan was the sort of man to do so, it seems that it is not true

Art for art's sake in Moscow's Metro.

in this instance either. At any rate, the French Marquis de Custine was not impressed by St Basil's and said that anyone who could bring himself to pray in it was not a Christian.

About 100 yards from St Basil's is the Lobnoye Mesto which, if the cathedral architects' eyes were not gouged out, has more than enough authenticated bloody history to satisfy the most ghoulish tastes. It is a kind of stone platform on which Ivan experimented personally with new kinds of torture, the least remarkable of which was boiling his subjects alive. The False Dmitri was proclaimed tsar on this stone in 1605, and returned to it a year later as a mutilated corpse before being cremated and fired out of a cannon in the direction of Poland. The bodies of many other convicted public enemies were displayed on this stone.

Almost as sinister in modern times was the Lubyanka, the KGB headquarters close by on Lubyanka Square. Some of the figures scurrying in and out these days are Western scholars taking ad-

vantage of *glasnost* to burrow in the KGB archives. The Foreign Ministry is one of seven identical buildings in Moscow which look almost massive enough to lend credence to the story that only by a whisker do they not plunge through the hard crust of the earth. It came to light at the end of 1992 that these buildings contain lift shafts which provide access to an underground city built to accommodate 30,000 key Soviet personnel for as long as 30 years in the event of a nuclear attack.

Even these monsters are dwarfed by the Hotel Rossiya, which set out to be the biggest hotel in the world with 3,000 rooms on a 30-acre site and two restaurants, of several, capable of seating 1,000 diners at a time. The staff put a brave face on guests who step out of the elevators and call for a taxi to take them to their rooms. For all the hotel's size, it manages to maintain a very respectable standard of service.

The National and Metropol are a different class of hotel altogether, pieces of unashamed tsarist grandeur which give the impression that they were not aware of 70 years of Communism drifting by. They should not be missed, but unfortunately too many people already know that and the prices have gone up accordingly. Only a few years ago it was possible to stay at the Metropol for less than one now expects to pay for laundry. The hotel's better rooms are in the $1,000-a-day league.

Other shades of imperial life in Moscow, the estates which once ringed the city, have been swallowed by its expansion but sympathetically preserved. The village of **Kolomenskoye** on the Moscow River, south of the city on the Tula road, was founded in the 13th century. The royal estate attached to the village was Ivan the Terrible's favourite getaway, and also where Peter the Great was brought as a child to avoid the Streltsi uprising. Ivan's palace has long since gone. The wooden house on the site was actually occupied by Peter the Great but not where it is; it was transported from Archangel.

The **Churches of St George the Victorious** and of **Our Lady of Kazan** add interest, but the Church of the Ascension, with a spire which ascends 230ft (70 metres) like the head-dress once worn by Russian peasant women, borders on the bizarre. The Falcon Tower is where Tsar Alexis kept his hawks and falcons. In recent times several examples of traditional architecture have been assembled here as an open-air museum.

The **Tsaritsino estate** a few miles from Kolomenskoye was once the home of Irina, Boris Godunov's sister, the one married to the half-witted Tsar Fyodor. Catherine the Great bought it in 1775 but could not make up her mind what she wanted to do with it. She pulled down the existing buildings, started a summer residence, stopped that, embarked on a Grand Palace – and ended up with an unfinished building site which remains much as it was when she died. The surrounding park has a number of temples and pavilions left over from the previous owners and nicknamed "Little Versailles".

Back in the city proper, there are any number of galleries and museums of

Yesterday's man, today's reality.

58

international repute. The **Tretyakov Gallery** is one of the world's largest galleries, donated to the city by the brothers of that name and covering nine centuries of Russian painting from icons to the contemporary Soviet schools. The **Museum of Fine Arts**, within walking distance of the Kremlin, has works by Rembrandt, Rubens, Van Dyck, Poussin, a number of French Impressionists and many more.

The **Museum of the Art of the Peoples of the East**, opened in 1918 and made up of former private collections, has some extremely rare Parthian drinking vessels from the 2nd century BC as well as examples of early Persian, Indian and Chinese work. The **Museum of Dramatic Art** has over a million exhibits illustrating, as the name implies, the history of the theatre both in Russia and abroad.

Moscow is also known for its parks and public gardens. **Gorky Park** has become a top tourist attraction after the book and film, aficionados pacing out the scene of what was, of course, a fictional crime. The adjacent **Neskuchnyi Garden** contains summer and bath houses, a shooting box, bridges, pavilions and rotundas, all dating from the 18th century. Miniature trains run visitors to the remoter corners of the park.

Left to the last are three attractions which visitors would almost certainly have decided to see of their own accord. Two – the **Bolshoi Ballet** (which sometimes stages opera) and the **State Circus** – need no introduction.

The **Arbat** (derived from, as well as being an anagram of, the Arabic *rabat*) became almost a symbol of *glasnost* and *perestroika*. It is the pedestrian mall, branching off **Kalininsky Avenue**, where small traders were always a couple of jumps ahead of official private enterprise and political cartoonists mocked the creaking Establishment. The Arbat is actually more than five centuries old. It was the start of the ancient road to Smolensk and, in the 18th century, the aristocratic residential area of the city. It has been called Moscow's St Germain des Prés.

Stepping out on Arbat Street.

Muscovy, the Golden Ring: The logical and most popular excursion from Moscow for visitors with a few days to spare is a tour of the Golden Ring, so-named after the Golden Horde, the Tartar contingent who ruled over Moscow and the surrounding city-states for 250 years after the Mongol conquest in the 13th century. The Golden Ring is a euphemism for the Mongol Yoke.

In flattening the original Russia, Kievan Russ in modern Ukraine, the Mongols depopulated the southern steppes and drove many of the Varangian princes and their subjects into the northern forests where a number of settlements, Moscow included, existed as pale and very much smaller reflections of Kiev although not without lively goings-on, as noted in our introduction to Moscow. The Mongols followed the exodus to the north and, ignoring their conquests over a vast area, concentrated exclusively on exacting tribute from the northern cities.

Moscow was either very much smaller than Vladimir in the early years of the

Mongol Yoke, or perhaps it enjoyed a favoured status. In either case, its annual tribute was only 4,000 roubles per year compared with Vladimir's 85,000 roubles. The other cities, Pereslavl Zalesski, Rostov Veliki, Uglich, Yaroslavl, Kostroma and Sudzal were taxed *pro rata*.

While the Grand Princes of Kiev had secured an illustrious position in the mainstream of European royalty, partly by sending a stream of nubile princesses to marry various crowned heads of state, Russia disappeared from West European consciousness after the Mongol conquest. The growth of a new Russia represented by Muscovy and the Golden Ring was unknown to the outside world, and its "discovery" at the end of the 15th century caused almost as much excitement as, and coincided with, Christopher Columbus's discovery of America.

Pereslavl Zalesski, which is likely to be the first stop on a Golden Ring tour, is on Lake Pleshcheyevo, where Peter the Great learnt to sail as a boy. Yuri Dolgoruki, whom we have previously met murdering poor Kuchko and seizing Moscow, started the Cathedral of the Transfiguration which still stands beneath the ramparts of his fortress. The modern bust in front of the cathedral is of St Alexander Nevsky, who was born here. The town has three monasteries worth visiting, the oldest of which, **Goritski**, is said to date back to Ivan Kalita, known as Moneybags, the first of the local leaders whom the Tartars recognised as a Grand Prince.

About 40 miles (70 km) beyond Pereslavl Zalesski is **Rostov Veliki**, "the Great", which is one way of distinguishing it from Rostov on the Don. This is one of the oldest cities in Russia and may even have existed as a fortified settlement in the time of the Finno-Ugrians. It was united with Sudzal in 1054 under Yaroslav the Wise's son Vsevolod and passed two generations later to Yuri Dolgoruki. Rostov's white limestone walls, Kremlin towers and onion-domed churches are reflected in the waters of Lake Nero.

Andrei Bogolyubski, Yuri Dolgoruki's son and the recipient of the mur-

Moscow's monument to space exploration.

dered Kuchko's daughter Ulita as a present, inherited Rostov but ironically was himself murdered by the very same Ulita. Rostov later had an able and energetic builder in its bishop, a certain Jona, who constructed a large palace for himself and two for his guests. The **Church of the Redeemer** in the square was his private chapel. Jona's palace lost its roof, as did a lot of churches their domes, to a hurricane in 1953 but all have since been replaced.

Medieval Rostov had the distinction of producing three famous women. Princess Maria Rostovskaya, whose husband was tortured to death by the Mongols in 1238, wrote a chronicle which amounted to obituaries of the princes who met their deaths fighting the Mongols. She also founded the **Church of the Saviour on the Sands** a little way out of the city. The Princesses Daria Rostovskaya and Antonina Puzhbolskaya donned suits of armour in order to fight the Tartars at the battle of Kulikovo in 1380.

Fresh fruit from the south.

Visiting **Uglich** necessitates a slight deviation from the main road out of Rostov. Whether it's worth doing so rather depends on one's feelings about the unusual business of the False Dmitris. It was to Uglich that Maria Nagaya, Ivan the Terrible's seventh wife, was despatched with the baby Dmitri to keep them out of the way of Boris Godunov's designs on the imperial throne. Maria lived in the palace situated in the Uglich Kremlin, and it was in the courtyard of the palace that the tsarevich met with his officially accidental slit throat.

The actual spot is marked with the **Church of St Dmitri in the Blood**, built in 1692. If nothing else, this extraordinary story puts into historical perspective the despair shown by Boris Godunov in the opera bearing his name. Uglich's other main attraction is the monastery-fortress of **St Boris and St Gleb** nearby, whose massive walls held off a Polish invasion in the 17th century.

Back on the main road, and 30 miles (50 km) from Rostov, is **Yaroslavl**, founded by Yaroslav the Wise on the spot where he fought off, and killed with

a battle-axe, a bear which the local inhabitants had set on him. The said bear is still on the city's coat of arms. Yaroslavi's original Kremlin has been lost, although it ought to be said that the city has been exceptionally conscientious in its preservation of historic sites. The town's prosperity was based on the Volga trade, so it is no surprise that there are almost a dozen churches named after St Nicholas, the patron saint of trade. One merchant family, the Guryevs, did so well that a port on the Caspian Sea was named after them. Yaroslavl offers several examples of twinned churches, a large one for summer use and a smaller neighbour easier to heat in winter.

West of Yaroslavl is **Kostroma**, originally a strategic fortification at the confluence of the Volga and Kostroma rivers. It was founded in 1152 by the indefatigable Yuri Dolgoruki. The main square is flanked on three sides by shopping arcades, an 18th- or early 19th-century innovation, by which time flax was emerging as Kostroma's main prod-uct. The town has at least two secular points of interest: its **Fire Tower** (the town was all but totally destroyed by fire in 1773) and the palace opposite built by General Borshchov, a hero of the Napoleonic war.

The **Church of the Resurrection in the Valley** (Tserkov Voskresenya na Debre) bears the Royal Arms of Great Britain, a legacy of 17th-century trade between Kostroma and the City of London. Kiril Isakov, a merchant of Kostroma, found a barrel of gold coins in a cargo of indigo shipped from London. On asking what he ought to do with the gold, he was told by the people in London to put it towards a good cause. The virtuous Isakov spent the money on the church, hence the note of thanks in the coat-of-arms.

The Godunov family burial vault is in the **Cathedral of the Trinity**, which they built in 1590. With the Godunov connection, it is not totally surprising that Kostroma was dragged into the False Dmitri farrago. It was seized and held for six months by the Poles on

Springtime comes to the dachas near Moscow.

behalf of the Second False Dmitri. The monument in the main square commemorates Ivan Susasin, who was killed by the Poles because of his loyalty to Tsar Michael, the Romanov given the unenviable job of clearing up "The Time of Troubles".

The "Golden Ring" tour continues to **Sudzal**. Whereas most of the places so far mentioned were fortresses or trading posts which grew up into medium-sized cities, Sudzal is the case of a princely capital that fell on hard times and shrank to the size of a village, albeit one with a wealth of attractions, as befits Kiev's successor as the religious capital of Russia. The remains of a pagan temple show that Sudzal was of some religious significance in pre-Christian times. Having made Sudzal his capital, Yuri Dolgoruki then had to contend in 1107 with an invading army of Bulgars. Efficient as ever, he saw them off.

Of Sudzal's fine monasteries, the **Spasski Monastery** has the most distinguished history. It was used as a prison for heretical priests as well as

Old Russian architecture in Sudzal.

revolutionaries in later times. German Field-Marshal von Paulus of the German army was an unhappy and involuntary guest after the battle of Stalingrad in 1943.

The Convent of the Intercession (Pokrovski Monastir) was one of those to which redundant wives were despatched in the tradition of "Get thee to a nunnery". Tsar Vasili III had his wife Solomonia forcibly enrolled here because he believed she was unable to give him an heir. She evidently arrived at the gates screaming and tearing at her habit in protest. She did not calm down and accept her fate until a sound whipping had been administered by Ivan Shigonia-Podzhogin, her appointed guardian. Vasili went on to marry a certain Helen Glinskaya, whereupon Solomonia discovered in the convent that she was pregant after all.

Officially, the son born to Solomonia died and was buried locally, although there had always been rumours he did not in fact die but was smuggled out of the convent and grew up to become Ivan

the Terrible. It seems that Ivan the Terrible himself entertained doubts that his real mother was Helen Glinskaya, as the record showed. Solomonia was later canonised, and the story was given a new twist in 1934 when the tiny sarcophagus said to hold the body of her infant son was opened up. The contents proved to be not human remains but a dressed-up dummy.

The gates of the convent were opened in the 17th century to admit another unwilling inmate in the person of Eudoxia, the wife whom Peter the Great cast off in order to pursue and eventually marry the Livonian serving wench Martha, the future Catherine I whose career is sketched in the Latvian section of this book.

The last major stop on the Golden Ring is **Vladimir**, about 25 miles/40 km from Sudzal and developed around 1160 by the ill-fated Andrei of Bogolyubovo, murdered by his wife Ulita. He could not wait to show that Vladimir had surpassed Kiev by invading and sacking the southern capital. The **Cathedral of the Assumption** (Uspenski) was intended to be the finest church in all Russia. Andrei brought in master craftsmen from abroad and proposed to install in the cathedral a famous icon he had taken from Kiev, since known as the Virgin of Vladimir.

The cathedral was damaged in a fire 25 years after completion, rebuilt, and burned again in 1238. The second fire was a gruesome affair. Batu Khan's Tartars shepherded the royal family, clergy and most of the leading citizens into the cathedral before setting it alight. . They perished, but the main structure survived surprisingly well and was later repaired. The Virgin of Vladimir, incidentally, was taken to Moscow in 1395 to ward off Tamerlane's Tartars.

As for Andrei of Bogolyubovo's end at the hand of Ulita, he was murdered on the staircase of his palace in the neighbouring village of **Bogolyubovo.** The palace survives as part of the Cathedral of the Resurrection. Ulita and her band of helpers looted the palace and threw Andrei's body to the dogs. The court jester managed to rescue the body, wrap it in a rug and carry it to the nearby church. The murderers were caught and executed, their bodies consigned to tarred coffins in which they have ever since floated around the swamps of Bogolyubovo, making terrible noises at night. This rounds off not only the Golden Ring tour but a chain of events which began with Yuri Dolgoruki's outrage on a nice old boyar and his daughter who were living contentedly among the pine trees on a hill above the future Moscow.

St Petersburg: The site Peter the Great chose in 1703 for his "Window to the West" was a vacant swamp at the mouth of the Neva River. *Ipso facto*, there are older cities in the United States, although St Petersburg overtook many of them thanks to the concerted efforts of slaves, serfs and Swedish prisoners of war. The circumstances in which the name later changed to Leningrad and back to St Petersburg are well-known; not so that Peter himself styled the name in Old Dutch: Sankt Piterburkh.

Peter is generally given the lion's

St Petersburg's Kirov ballet.

share of the credit for building the city. In reality, it ought to be shared with Catherine the Great and to a lesser degree with the Empress Elizabeth. In any case, the result was quite unlike any other city in Russia, most noticeably in the use of colour. Against a background of snow, it takes one's breath away. "The streets," wrote an English visitor at the end of the 18th century, "seem to consist entirely of palaces."

There were indeed palaces galore, too many to be dealt with individually in any detail in this book. As Leningrad, the city took a terrible hammering in World War II, besieged by Hitler's army for 900 days but never taken. The death toll of about 700,000 is perhaps made worse by the fact that all but the 17,000 who were killed by bombs and shells succumbed to starvation. The Piskarevskoye Memorial Cemetery alone holds 600,000 victims. A faint idea of what conditions were like is conveyed by an inscription on No. 14 Nevsky Prospekt: "Citizens, this side is most dangerous during artillery bombardment!"

Most of the sights of St Petersburg can be encompassed on foot. Broadly speaking, the **Neva** forms a semi-circle. The inside, bissected at what might be considered the apex by Nevksy Prospekt, is the interesting part. The Winter Palace and Hermitage stand at the apex, looking across the river at the Fortress of St Peter and Paul, the Menshikov Palace, the University and one or two other exceptions to the general rule that most sights of interest to visitors are on the south bank. The apex of the southern semi-circle is the Winter Palace, and that is where most visitors set out, but in the interest of chronology there is a case for nipping across the river to look at the Fortress first.

Peter's original plan had been to build on the north bank of the Neva only, but the city soon spread to the south bank and to the adjacent Vasilievsky Island. Nevertheless, the Fortress was still the focus when the city was proclaimed capital of the Empire in 1712. Less than ten years earlier, Peter had stood on what Finnish fishermen used to call

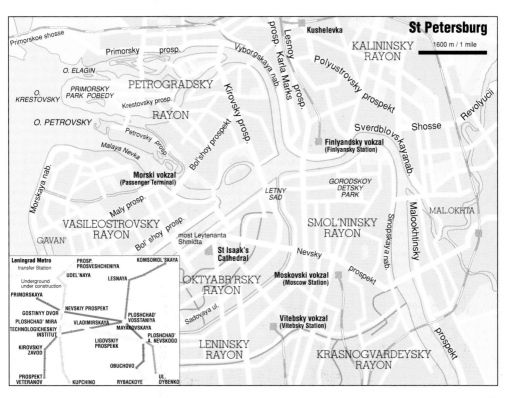

Hare Island, cut two strips of turf with a bayonet, made a cross out of them, and declared grandly: "Here there shall be a town!"

With the Swedes hovering aggressively in the background, the urgent need was for a fort, which grew into the **Fortress of St Peter and St Paul**. He supervised the work from a wooden hut on a neighbouring island; his mistress Catherine was parked in a similarly modest dwelling a short distance away. Personal comfort was evidently a low priority during building works.

Classical and perhaps even a little austere on the outside, the **Cathedral of St Peter and Paul** within the Fortress has a lavish baroque interior. Peter is buried here, as are all his successors with two exceptions. The first is Alexander I, whose tomb was found to be empty. One theory says he did not die while travelling near the Sea of Azov, as official history relates, but faked his death in order to slip away, assume an alias and become a hermit in western Siberia, where he died 40 years later.

The second is Nicholas II, the last of the Romanovs, who also ended up in Siberia, although in his case dead at the bottom of a disused mine-shaft. We shall return north of the river, to Vasilievsky Island, at the end of this section.

The splendid **Winter Palace** at the apex of the southern semi-circle is, chronologically speaking, quite a long way down the line in St Petersburg's development. It was built and rebuilt several times before Bartolomeo Francesco Rastrelli, the Italian architect who had been working non-stop for the tsars since 1732 (when he was just 20), began his final version in 1754 under Catherine the Great's supervision.

The palace is double-sided, the river on one side and the Dvortsovaya (or Palace) Square on the other. The northern and southern facades are similar in design, magnificently proportioned ranges of columns and windows beneath a baroque balustrade of statues and urns. The palace has 1,057 rooms, each one a work of art, and 117 staircases, the main one known as the Jor-

1812 victory chariot on the arch of General Staff Building in Palace Square.

dan **Staircase** or Staircase of the Ambassadors. It was down this staircase and through the entrance leading to the river that on 6 January every year the tsar and his court filed out for the Blessing of the Waters. They were bareheaded and of course the river was frozen, which meant drilling a hole through the ice to draw out water that was supposed to drive away evil spirits and serve other useful purposes.

Newly born babies were lowered through the hole. "A very extraordinary ceremony and very unseasonable…" wrote the wife of a British minister. "It has happened that the shivering priests let the unfortunate little creatures slip through their icy fingers under the ice."

"The more you build," Catherine once wrote, "the more you want to build. It's a disease, like drinking." And build she did. The Winter Palace is flanked by the **Old** and **New Hermitages** and the Admiralty, the overall effect providing a long stretch of the river with an incomparable frontage. "Do not buy any bad pictures," Peter the Great had instructed

his agents. Catherine might have told hers to buy everything they could lay hands on, although they clearly knew what they were doing. The Hermitage probably has the finest collection of pictures in the world, occupying 120 halls: Raphaels, Titians, Leonardos, French Impressionists, everything.The Spanish collection in particular is one of the world's best: its gems include Murillo's *Boy with a Dog* and Goya's *Portrait of the actress Antonia Zarate.*

The collection is said to number some two million items, only a fraction of which are on display in the Hermitage and in the other museums to which they have been loaned. The Hermitage Library alone, one of the world's largest depositories of books on art, runs to 500,000 volumes. Visitors ought to know that the official tours go much too fast. Far better to loaf along independently if possible, perhaps having done an official tour first.

The square behind the palace is formed by Carlo Rossi's 1819 semi-circle housing the Ministries of War, Finance and

The glories of the Hermitage collection.

Foreign Affairs. This square has been the setting for epic moments in Russian history, not least the massacre on Bloody Sunday in 1905 and the crowd bursting into the palace in October 1917.

The **Alexander Column** in the centre of the square was erected in 1834 to celebrate the defeat of Napoleon. The figure on top is a winged angel, but the angel's face has Alexander I's features, the Alexander whom we have seen not only going off (perhaps) to become a hermit in Siberia but also, in the preceding history section of this book, plotting with Napoleon on a raft in the middle of a river with a spy dangling underneath. The double triumphal arch in the middle of Rossi's semi-circle, surmounted by a chariot and winged victory, leads to the Nevksy Prospekt.

It may be as well to stay with the river, however, before going through the arch. To the west is the **Admiralty**, originally the shipyards which, in the year the city was founded, went to work on Peter's ambition to command a Baltic fleet. The golden ship on the spire of the Admiralty commemorates the fleet. The statue in Decembrists' Square at the end of it is of Peter the Great himself. Looming behind is **St Isaac's Cathedral**, an example of church architecture on the most gigantic scale. It was begun under Alexander I in 1818 and took 40 years to complete, the brief calling for a cathedral capable of holding a congregation of 14,000. At midnight on Easter Sunday all the chandeliers and candelabras were set alight more or less simultaneously by lengths of guncotton fuse, while outside 101 cannon roared. The Communists turned St Isaac's into an anti-God museum.

East along the river from the Winter Palace leads to the **Lenin Museum**, built by Catherine as the Marble Palace for one of her countless lovers, in this case Grigori Orlov. Khalturina Street, which runs parallel to the embankment, ends in **Marsovo Polie**, the Field of Mars, the traditional place for military parades. The monument to General Alexander Suvorov was erected in 1801, reputedly the first Russian monument to

Heavenly view from St Isaac's Cathedral.

someone who was not a tsar. Suvorov never lost a battle during a long and busy military career, so perhaps he deserved it.

He is actually buried in the **Church of the Annunciation** near the Monastery of St Alexander Nevsky. The inscription, which he wrote himself, reads: "Here lies Suvorov." The full stop is a solid brass knob, lending the inscription what has aptly been called an "appropriate finality". To the east of his monument, however, is the **Summer Garden**, St Petersburg's finest, and the **Summer Palace**, as built in 1710–14 by Domenico Trezzini. It should be evident by now that old St Petersburg was practically built by Italians.

Before returning to the Winter Palace for the walk down Nevsky Prospekt, it is worth strolling over to the gloomy, dark red **Mikhailov** (or "Engineer's") **Castle** built in 1800 for the paranoid Paul I, son of Catherine the Great, at a cost of 20 million roubles. He built it from scratch in the interest of security. The castle was surrounded by moats and cannon and guarded day and night. It didn't help. Only 40 days after Paul moved in, Count Peter Pahlen, the commander of the Palace Guard and the only man Paul trusted, smuggled in a group who had fortified themselves with drink for the task in hand. While one of the officers tightened a scarf around Paul's neck, another found a heavy malachite paperweight which he brought down on his head.

Paul's son Alexander built the nearby Mikhailov Palace, now known as the **Russian Museum**, for his brother Michael. "Very handsome but nothing extraordinary," wrote the same minister's wife who had deplored the baptism of babies in the frozen river, "a great many naked ladies as handles and pedestals." She didn't think much of the meal she was served either.

Today the Russian Museum is rivalled only by Moscow's Tretiakov Gallery as the world's largest depository of Russian and Soviet art: there are 370,000 items in the collection, and no other museum comes close to its collec-

Crossing the Neva.

tion of graphic and sculptural works. You will also find period furniture, samovars, carved stones, china and Russian gems. The section on old Russian art displays icons, frescoes and mosaics.

Nevsky Prospekt is in two sections. The first runs from the river to the Ploschstschad Vosstania, near the Moscow Railway Station, and is the commercial and cultural centre of the city. The second section is not so interesting, although there is compensation at the very end in the Monastery of Alexander Nevsky. The first part buzzes with activity day and night. Alexander Pushkin lived around the corner on the Moika River, and it was there that he set out for a duel with Baron Georges D'Anthes, a French royalist in the Russian service, over the lovely Natalia Goncharova. Pushkin first met his second at the pastrycook's shop around the corner. He was carried back from the duel fatally wounded.

The "jewel of Nevsky" is the monumental **Kazan Cathedral**, built a few

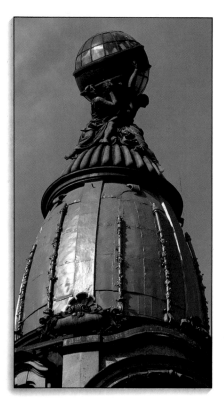

years before St Isaac's (1801–11) and intended to rival St Peter's in Rome. It could not face the street squarely because Orthodox churches are supposed to face west. The architect Alexander Voronikhin, who started out as one of Count Stroganoff's serfs, contrived something of an optical illusion by putting a colonnaded facade on the side of the building. It, too, ended up as an anti-God Museum of Atheism for a while.

In the square in front of the colonnade are **monuments** to the commanders who defeated Napoleon, General Barclay de Tolly and Field Marshal Mikhail Kutuzov. The latter's tomb inside is said to be on the spot where he stood and prayed before leaving to take command at Smolensk in 1812. The tall building opposite the cathedral, with a globe on top, was built for the Singer Sewing Machine Company, whose trademark the globe was. It is now known as the **House of Books**.

Further down the Nevsky is the **Gostiny Dvor**, an 18th-century arcade of some 200 individual shops which was later converted, in the true spirit of collectivism, into a massive emporium like GUM in Moscow. This was the spot where the Provisional Government fired on Bolshevik supporters in July, 1917. The protestors were on their way to the Duma or Parliament, the dark red building with a tall clock tower a little further back, later the headquarters of the Soviet Cultural Foundation.

The square near the Gostiny Dvor is nearly all Carlo Rossi's work, the **Pushkin Drama Theatre** having Apollo's chariot on top. At the end of Nevsky is one of the city's oldest buildings, the **Monastery of St Alexander Nevsky**, built by Peter the Great. St Alexander's bones were brought back from Vladimir to be buried in the Cathedral of the Trinity within the monastery complex, said to be the exact site of his victory over the Swedes and Teutonic Knights in 1241.

To return to the Winter Palace and cross the river by the Palace bridge is to alight on **Vasilyevsky Island**. Two beacons in the square known as the Spit

The Singer symbol above the House of Books.

point to the port that existed here until the middle of the 19th century. The buildings on the square include the **Naval Museum** (the Stock Exchange in pre-revolutionary times and perhaps a stock exchange again one day) and the **Institute of Russian Literature**, said to possess Pushkin's every manuscript. Along the University Embankment is Russia's first museum, built by Peter the Great and now devoted to Anthropology and Ethnography. The **Menshikov Palace**, which now houses some of the overflow from the Hermitage, was built in Peter the Great's time for the pastrycook's assistant who became Peter's right-hand man and was made a prince into the bargain.

Excursions from St Petersburg: It would be a pity when in St Petersburg not to find time to see at least some of the former imperial country residences around the city and two beautiful and historic cities only a couple of hours away, Novgorod and Pskov.

An excursion to Tsarskoye Selo, now called **Pushkin**, along the old coaching road offers the bonus of two astonishing buildings at half-way, the Church and Palace of Chesme. They were built to celebrate Orlov's naval victory over the Turks off Chesme in 1780 and, as if to rub salt into the wound, were built in the Turkish style. The triangular palace was evidently the architect Yuri Veldten's notion of Anatolia, but this is merely a rehearsal for his full flight of fancy on the church. The royals evidently disapproved, and the only record of any ever staying there was when Alexander I's consort escorted his coffin back from the Sea of Azov. As we have just seen above, however, the coffin was almost certainly empty, whether or not his widow knew it.

On the other hand, Pushkin, about 9 miles (14 km) from St Petersburg, was a favourite with the royals. Re-modelling the **Yekaterinsky Palace**, originally designed by the great Rastrelli, became Catherine the Great's passionate hobby, her agent-architect being a slightly dubious Scot named Charles Cameron who had written a book on

Home life is confronting new economic realities.

ancient baths but never built anything. In the circumstances, he seems to have done very well; he certainly delighted Catherine with his fairy-tale interiors. Cameron then decorated the grounds with all sorts of follies.

A glazed gallery was built on to the **Hanging Garden** to house the busts of 54 philosophers and statesmen, the latter subject to dismissal rather as in the waxworks in Madame Tussaud's in London if and when they fell out of Catherine's favour. She erected monuments to one of her younger and more virile lovers, Lanskoi, and to her dogs, one curiously named Sir Tom Anderson. Successive sovereigns filled the park with their own little jokes: a Turkish bath with a dome and minaret, a Chinese village, and so on.

In contrast, the **Alexandrovsky Palace** (built for Catherine's grandson, the future Alexander I) was a Palladian masterpiece. It was popular with the last tsar, Nicholas II, who stayed here with his family after his abdication and before being sent to his death in Siberia.

Pavlovsk, a mile or two from Pushkin, was Catherine's present to her paranoid son Paul, the one simultaneously strangled and clubbed with a paperweight. She threw in a couple of modest wooden houses, but Paul and his wife prevailed on Cameron to build them a Palladian palace with a Temple of Friendship and an Apollo Colonnade. The couple were in two minds about the details, and Cameron was caught in the middle. "My husband consents, though regretfully," the Grand Duchess wrote to him, "to having a vaulted ceiling in the bedroom, but on condition that it takes the least disagreeable form possible…" The palace was severely damaged in World War II but has been carefully restored.

The park, which survived the war well and is all lakes, flowers, temples and pavilions, was largely the Grand Duchess's doing. The advent of railways in the 19th century put the park within easy reach of the city. It became, someone wrote, "the principal place of recreation of the middle classes of St

Dachas still provide an escape from city life.

Petersburg, who resort there daily in such numbers to enjoy the country, to dine and to drink punch and champagne, that they are, in fact, almost the exclusive supporters of the railway."

Splendid as the above palaces are, the most spectacular is **Petrodvorets**, a quick trip up the Gulf of Finland by hydrofoil. Peter the Great discovered the spot while he was turning the island of Kronstadt into a fortress to keep the Swedes at bay and so liked it that he returned a few years later to build a house. It was small, only seven rooms, but the elder Rastrelli was brought in to do it. Peter's man, Prince Menshikov, also liked the area and built himself a palace at Oranienbaum. Never one for half measures, the prince's landing-stage at the bottom of the garden could take a man-of-war.

When Peter returned from his European trip with memories of Versailles, he too wanted a palace. The site was made into a series of three terraces with a Grand Cascade of water which eventually emptied into the sea a quarter of a mile away. The project, designed by Jean-Baptiste Leblond, was abandoned when Peter died. His daughter Elizabeth re-started it on a grander scale than even Peter had envisaged with the help of the younger Rastrelli. Destroyed by the Germans in World War II, the estate was rebuilt by the Soviets. The church presented a bit of a problem. It did not become another anti-God museum, though, but a post office.

Novgorod: Situated about 60 miles (100 km) south of St Petersburg, Novgorod is at the very beginning of Russian history, the place which the Varangian Rurik was "invited" to take under his wing in 862. The name means "New Town" and it was a staging-post on the trade route between the Baltic and the Black Sea. The town was the capital of an independent and powerful republic from the 12th to the 17th centuries, the natural rival to an emerging Muscovy 300 miles (500 km) away and therefore an obstacle which the rulers of Muscovy were bent on removing.

Like most ancient Russian towns,

Live music lives on.

Novgorod has its Kremlin, in this instance called Detinets, on high ground above the Volkhov River. It was once encircled by massive earthworks of which the White Tower is the sole surviving fragment.

St Sophia's Cathedral, dominating the town, is on the site of an earlier oak church of the same name built in 989 by a certain Joachim, who was sent from Kiev by St Vladimir as Novgorod's first bishop. The replacement cathedral, built by the son of Yaroslav the Wise who was made Prince of Novgorod, was meant to compete with its namesake in Kiev. The princes later moved out of the Kremlin to live south of the town. The new Cathedral of St Nicholas was Prince Mstislav's personal church and was meant to be fully the equal of St Sophia's. A few years later Prince Vsevolod did his stuff with the Cathedral of St George and then, to gild the lily, with the Churches of St Ivan and the Assumption. Novgorod does not lack for churches.

The difference between Novgorod and the towns of central Russia, in architecture and perhaps in other ways too, arise because it escaped the worst of the "Tartar yoke" and had a closer relationship with Western Europe through membership of the Hanseatic League. In 1478, however, the state was annexed by Ivan III and, as a grim foretaste of things to come, a large share of the suspect population was deported and replaced by loyal Muscovites. Ivan the Terrible had worse in store: on the flimsiest evidence of rebellion, he had some 60,000 of the population murdered.

The population once stood at 400,000; by the 17th century, it was more like 2,000. When some sort of economic life returned, it was partly because Catherine the Great wanted somewhere to stay when she visited, hence the **Putyevoi Dvorets**, or Travelling Palace. Novgorod was occupied by German forces from 1941 to 1944. As it was almost on the German-Russian front line for much of the time, Novgorod took a fearful pounding. In the circumstances, the restorers have done an amazing job. **New products...**

Pskov: About 120 miles (190 km) away, Pskov has much in common with Novgorod, historically speaking. It, too, faced invasion from the west rather than east, developed influential trading links with the West and was for a long time an independent republic. The town is built around an impressive Kremlin, here called the **Krom**, and lies in the shadow of a cathedral, in this case the 17th-century **Holy Trinity Cathedral**.

The town is extremely well-endowed with churches. Pskov lost its independence to Moscow in 1510 and in 1570 appeared to be in imminent danger of being wiped out by Ivan the Terrible as Novgorod had been. Ivan's mind was changed, it seems, by a monk named Nicholas of Salos, who feigned madness. Nicholas was understandably canonised and buried in the cathedral.

Peter regarded Pskov as a key part of the northern defences against Sweden and accordingly strengthened the fortifications with towers like the surviving **Pokrovskaya Bashnya**, or Tower of the Intercession. Visible from this tower is the **Mirozhsky Monastery** on the far bank of the Velikaya River. It was founded in the 11th century. The **Church of St John the Baptist**, also on the far bank, was once part of the 13th-century Ivanovski Monastery. This church was partly destroyed in World War II, when Pskov was as exposed as Novgorod.

The **Millennary Monument**, so named because it was erected in 1863 to commemorate 1,000 years of Russian history, has a frieze which traces the main points of that history from Rurik to Alexander II. It does not, of course, include a more recent snippet which belongs specifically to Pskov's rather quaint railway station. It was in a train at the station on 15 March 1917 that Nicholas II abdicated as Tsar of All the Russias. A visitor of a few years ago observed that the only change was the Hammer and Sickle, instead of the Imperial Eagle badge, on the station-master's cap. The station-master has presumably, since 1991, rummaged around the office in the hope of replacing it with the old one.

...and old customs.

In 1954 a colossal monument was unveiled in Kiev, the capital of Ukraine, to commemorate the 300th anniversary of the reunion of Russia and Ukraine, once known as Great Russia and Little Russia respectively. For subdued Ukranian nationalists, however, 1654 represented the death of Ukrainian independence and the dawn of their darkest days. In 1991 the ambivalent reunion reached the grand age of 337 years, but it did not see the year through. On 24 August Ukraine declared its independence from the Soviet Union. Although the break was primarily with the Communist order established after World War I, it also wiped clean the slate written in 1654. In so doing it turned the clock back to a fundamental distinction between Russia and Ukraine arising from the Mongol invasions in the 13th century.

The international community was taken aback by Ukraine's 1991 declaration of independence. The republic was such an integral part of the Soviet Union that its defection was of a different order from the independence fever sweeping the relatively remote Eastern European satellite states. Much of the Soviet arsenal, nuclear as well as conventional, was on Ukrainian soil, and most of the Black Sea fleet was in Ukrainian ports. To whom did they now belong? The legal status of Crimea posed another dilemma. It had been Russian territory, but in the rather one-sided euphoria of the 1954 celebrations, the title deeds had been presented to Ukraine as a gift. Russia wanted Crimea back; Ukraine was reluctant to part with it.

Sorting out what properly belongs to Ukraine rather than Russia coincidentally serves notice of an independent Ukraine's potential tourist appeal. The country's assigned role as the engine-room of Soviet heavy industry, coupled with the most adverse publicity imaginable at Chernobyl in 1986, means that it would never be a place for sun and fun. For culturally-minded visitors, however, Ukraine stands out as the cradle of Russian history, the seat of the Kievan Russ founded by Varangian Vikings. The evocative Russian steppes which provide the backdrop to so much folklore and literature are really the Ukrainian steppes, at least within the context of Eastern Europe, and the legendary rider galloping across them, the Cossack, is historically speaking a Ukrainian.

If these are the considerations most likely to shape a visitor's itinerary, there is also the matter of 1654. It is reflected in statues and other references to a certain Bogdan Khmelnitski, the key figure in an extraordinary tale redolent of the Trojan War. It, too, devolves from the abduction of a beautiful woman, whose face in this instance launched not a thousand ships but 8,000 furious Cossacks and whose name, as luck would have it, was also Helen.

Preceding pages: Kiev University. Left, Gate in Kiev's central market.

Cosacco.

The acorn that produced the modern colossus of Russia was planted by Viking Varangians who in the 9th century cornered trade between the Baltic and the Black Sea and in so doing recognised a Slav settlement which, above all others, was the key to guarding the network of rivers which turned what would otherwise have been a frightful overland journey into a viable commercial proposition. Various rivers brought trading vessels in from the Baltic, and it was then a matter of transferring to a main artery which rose in the northern forests and swept south across the steppes to the Black Sea, Byzantium and Constantinople. The main artery was the Dnieper, and the strategic stronghold was the mid-point between the forests and the Black Sea, Kiev.

Ancient chronicles paint a partisan picture of Slav feelings about a Varangian conquest which began with Novgorod being taken by Prince Rurik of South Jutland in 862 and continued with his son Oleg's capture of Smolensk. "Our land is great and rich," they are alleged to have cried, "but there is no order in it. Come and rule over us." On taking Kiev, Oleg proclaimed it his new capital and "the Mother of Russian cities".

New convert: Trade between Kievan Russ and Byzantium boomed. Every spring a flotilla would sail down the Dnieper with its cargo of furs, honey and slaves and return with gold, silk, wines and spices. In 957 Princess Olga of Kiev joined the convoy to see the sights of Constantinople. She returned with rather more than the usual run of souvenirs: she had submitted to baptism at the fountain of the Eastern Orthodox Church.

Olga tried to convert Svyatoslav, the son for whom she was acting as regent, but he was unsympathetic – and fully occupied by a military campaign which in due course netted the Volga region for the Varangians.

The question of Kiev's conversion to Christianity, and whether it would opt for the Roman Catholic Church or Eastern Orthodoxy, was left to Prince Vladimir, who succeeded when Svyatoslav's distinguished military career came to an ignoble end, his head cut off by Pechenegs who lined the skull with gold and used it as a drinking vessel. Vladimir invited not only representatives of Rome and Byzantium to put their cases before him but also spokesmen for Islam and Judaism.

The Volga Bulgars attended on behalf of Islam, which was making some inroads under the influence of the Persian and Arab empires. Islam, they said frankly, required circumcision and abstinence from pork and wine, but the Islamic after-life would cater more than adequately for every carnal desire. Vladimir pricked up his ears on the last point because, the chronicle explains, he was "fond of women and indulgence". On balance, however, the prospect of immediate circumcision and abstinence from pork was disagreeable, and the ruling on alcohol outrageous. "Drinking," he declared, "is the joy of the Russians. We cannot live without it."

The spokesmen for Judaism were a curious choice in as much as they were Khazars, the tribe whose control over the Eastern Slavs the Varangians had usurped. They were not remotely Semitic by race. They had themselves chosen the Jewish religion hoping to emulate the commercial acumen of the Jews with whom they had extensive business dealings. The Khazars repeated the mistake made by the Bulgars by revealing a similar Jewish position on circumcision and pork, although they were more flexible on wine. In Vladimir's mind, this was not sufficient to make up for the inexcusable failure of the Jewish God to prevent his followers from being expelled from the Holy Land.

Fast thinking: The Pope's emissaries, next up, began with the assurance that circumcision, pork and wine were not issues as far as they were concerned, but any advantage gained in this respect evaporated when they mentioned that to further the glory of their God a certain amount of fasting would be required. Vladimir's response was swift and unambiguous: "Depart hence!"

The Byzantine Greeks immediately put Vladimir's mind at rest on the points that were clearly unacceptable to him and launched into a history of the world from the beginning of time, interrupting their flow to

Left, the Cossacks once ruled the Ukraine as an independent state.

field Vladimir's questions on the relative religious merits of various types of headwear and trousers as opposed to skirts. The Greeks saved till last a painting which showed in terrifying detail just what an infidel could expect come the Day of Judgement. Vladimir was suitably alarmed, but he would not commit himself until emissaries could confirm that the Eastern Church brought greater material rewards to its adherents than did the Roman. They visited Rome and Constantinople and of course there was no comparison. The latter's magnificence impressed them as it had Princess Olga: heaven rather than earth, they reported. As far as Vladimir was concerned, that settled the matter.

Vladimir's alignment with Byzantium was formalised by his baptism at Kherson in 990 and cemented by marriage to Anna, the Byzantine Emperor's sister. Not even this illustrious marriage, however, could induce Vladimir to deviate from the one principle which the entire religious debate had so far neglected to address, and that was that he already had several wives and a harem of hundreds of concubines, none of whom he had any intention of surrendering. He was truly, the chronicler sighs, a *"fornicator immensus et crudelis"*. Vladimir's subjects were compulsorily baptised *en masse* in a river running under what is now one of Kiev's main shopping streets.

No fewer than 40 Christian churches sprang up in Kiev during the reign of Vladimir's son Yaroslav the Wise, and of these St Sophia's Cathedral, modelled on its namesake in Constantinople, miraculously survived the almost total destruction of Kiev on more than one occasion in remarkably good order. Others remain in the state of ruin left by the Mongol invasions in the 13th century. The Monastery of the Caves, originally built in 1051, later spawned a whole complex of churches and secular buildings. This rising grandeur of Kiev was matched by sudden esteem in the Western world. Three of Yaroslav's daughters married the kings of France, Hungary and Norway and his successor, Vladimir Monomakh, married the daughter of King Harold of England, defeated by William the Conqueror in 1066.

End of an era: The golden age of Kievan Russ was not destined to last much longer than 150 years. While Vladimir Monomakh was the towering Varangian prince of his era, others were establishing lesser city-states in the north like Moscow, Vladimir, Yaroslavl and Sudzal. The balance of power shifted rapidly in their favour, and in 1169 Prince Andrei Bogolyubovo of Sudzal was able to sack "The Mother of Russian Cities" with apparent ease. Kiev was certainly well past its best when struck by a thunderbolt in 1223, the Mongol invasion.

"No one knows for certain who they are or whence they come," wrote a breathless chronicler, "or what their language is, or race is, or faith. But they are called Tartars." The Prince of Kiev was taken prisoner, a slight predicament for the captors who traditionally did not shed the blood of a ruler except in battle. They solved the problem by stretching him out beneath a platform of boards, "and themselves took seat on the top to have dinner". By the end of the meal he was ethically dead. St Sophia's cathedral survived the sacking of the city, but there were barely 200 houses left standing by the time the Tartars – or Mongols – moved on to their next target. A visitor who arrived on the scene five years later reported that the streets were still a sea of skulls and bones. In the end, it was not merely the city that was destroyed but the whole of Kievan Russ. Feted by European royalty at one moment, it was gone the next.

The Mongols charged across the plain twice in the space of a quarter-century and there was every expectation that they would do so again. It seemed pointless to rebuild anything that lay directly on their invasion route. The chronicles record Kievan princes weighing up their prospects in the south. "Here in the land of Russ," says one, "we have neither an army nor anything; let us depart while it is still warm." They duly joined the exodus to the northern forests and it was there, behind the screen of trees and under what is invariably called the "Mongol Yoke" that a new Russia evolved, eventually to be dominated by Muscovy.

The Mongols were more interested in northern principalities that could afford to pay tribute than the desolate southern plain. It was of little interest to them, therefore, that the void was gradually filled by a rising power in the West, Lithuania. Skirting around the southern limits of the Mongol Yoke, Lithuania carved out an empire which extended tentatively to the Black Sea and in so doing incorporated virtually the whole of modern Ukraine. It was a ramshackle empire without effective administration, however, until Lithuania entered a dynastic union with land-hungry Poland towards the end of the 14th century.

Although the head of the union was a Lithuanian prince, the Polish aristocracy applied the full weight of their inflexible social order to the Ukrainian lands. They pegged out enormous estates, unilaterally consigning to serfdom the sparse population who had either survived the Mongol rampage or trickled back afterwards. This merely triggered atavistic nomadic instincts and a drift to the east where the dispossessed fell

These early Cossack bands lived on the proceeds of banditry or mercenary soldiering, like those who provided protection for the Stroganov family of merchant-adventurers as they opened up Siberia. Unwilling to be tied down by agriculture, the Cossacks lived mainly on a diet of fish from the rivers where they tended to congregate and from which they took their names, hence the Don Cossacks, Volga Cossacks, Dnieper Cossacks and so on. They communicated in Russian and, in so far as they had any religious beliefs, professed to be Eastern Orthodox.

The most famous of these bands was the "Knighthood of the Zaporozhye Host", or Zaporogian Cossacks, who lived on Khortitsa

into league with outlaws and footloose adventurers with their own reasons for staying one jump ahead of any kind of authority. It was therefore a curiously classless collection of high-born black sheep, disgruntled serfs and runaway slaves who were neither a tribe nor a nation. The majority were Slavs of some description, but there were also Germans and more exotic fugitives. They constituted, for lack of a better term, a brotherhood, the genesis of the celebrated Cossacks who ruled over "The Wild Country".

Above, Zaporozhye Cossacks, "the boldest men on earth", at play.

Island "beyond the rapids" on the Dnieper. The island is still there and has a Cossack museum; the rapids which once protected the camp against surprise attack from the north were submerged by the damming of the river in the interests of the now dominant Zaporozhye power station.

The Zaporozhye Host was an exclusively male establishment, the numbers kept up by a more than sufficient stream of new arrivals. Ivan the Terrible added handsomely to their strength. In the early days, Cossacks went around in animal-skins or half-naked, but their military prowess put an end to that. Successful expeditions against the Turks, their favourite targets, saw them transformed into peacocks: colourful baggy trousers, silk cummerbunds, satin caftans, turbans resplendent with ostrich feathers, cloaks and ornate boots. They affected enormous moustaches with a Tartar hairstyle: a completely shaved head with just one long tuft, sometimes tied in a top-knot.

A good raid was, of course, an occasion for a tremendous party. A Zaporogian danced and drank until he collapsed and, on recovering, began all over again. When the serious business of fighting had to be attended to, however, they stopped drinking altogether. They carried in their boats barrels of biscuits, boiled millet, dried fish and water. Any Cossack who broke the no-drinking rule was in danger of being thrown overboard.

The fleet would paddle silently down the river and emerge through the reeds of the estuary into the Black Sea at night, preferably when there was no moon. They would shadow their targets for days if necessary, attacking out of the sun at dawn or at dusk. The raids on Turkish targets were so systematic in the 17th century that the Turks threw a chain across the mouth of the Dnieper to stop them entering the Black Sea, but the Cossacks still got through. When they took the city of Azov, they secured an outlet to the Black Sea which facilitated their piracy.

No fear of death: The most audacious attack was on Constantinople itself, leading a Turkish chronicler to write: "It can be stated with confidence that one cannot find bolder men on earth who care less about life…and fear death less." As mercenaries, Cossacks fought with perfect impartiality. Poland registered individual Cossacks in its service and, by offering land and other privileges, tried to wean them away from their rumbustious comrades back on the island. Muscovy hired Cossack *atamans*, or commanders, who were allowed to choose the men they needed from their own ranks.

At home, Cossacks had an assembly which met once a year to decide matters like the division of plunder. Proposals were adopted or rejected according to cheering or booing, whichever was louder. For the rest of the year, the *ataman* had executive powers which he exercised without all the noise. He had to put himself up for re-election at regular intervals and, if judged grossly incompetent, he was voted out of office and beaten to death.

Laws were not written down, but everyone knew what they were: a slit nose or severed ear for pilfering, a trip to the bottom of the river in a weighted sack for traitors. Murderers were tied to the corpses of their victims and buried alive.

Lawless way of life: As long as the Cossacks were left alone to pursue their idiosyncratic way of life, they were as happy to serve in the Polish army as Poland was to employ them. What Poland could not countenance (and the problem became acute in the early 17th century) was the growing number of Cossack "civilians" who jauntily carried on as if they were above any law apart from their own.

The improbable figure waiting in the wings to emerge as the Cossack hero was Bogdan Khmelnitski, the son of a registered Cossack who had taken advantage of the attendant privileges to send Bogdan (whose name meant "The Gift of God") to school in Kiev and to the Jesuit College in Lvov. Fluency in Latin, thanks to the Jesuits, was not the only characteristic which set Bogdan apart from ordinary Cossacks. He was landed gentry and, in 1648, a recent widower in his early fifties caring for five children on the family estate. The only slight question-mark over a life of perfect propriety was Helen, a young woman whom he had installed in the household following the death of his wife.

Bogdan's gain in this respect was at the expense of a certain Czaplinski, the deputy crown bailiff and a senior member of the Polish imperial service, whose bed the lovely Helen had recently occupied. The enraged Czaplinski organised a posse of horsemen, stormed Bogdan's estate, set fire to the mill, bludgeoned his 10-year-old son to death – and took Helen back. Bogdan summoned 8,000 Cossacks, joined by 4,000 Crimean Tartars, and stated his case: "I have decided to take revenge on the Polish gentry."

Anyone dressed in the Polish style or suspected of being a Roman Catholic, Bogdan's Jesuit education notwithstanding, was strung up, their necks festooned with the severed heads of other members of the family. The rebellion was taken up by serfs in Poland itself and as far afield as White Russia (Belarus), Galicia, and Romania. Jews were slaughtered as the perceived agents and profiteers of the Polish feudal system. In the middle of this mayhem, Bogdan never lost sight of the objective of recovering Helen, and when she was found he married her and sued Poland for peace.

As the Poles were not inclined to settle, a punitive army of 40,000 advanced on Bogdan's position under the Princes Zaslavski, Koniecpolski and Ostrogog. The commanders travelled in a train of gilded carriages, proceeding at a leisurely pace which allowed daily banquets en route. The Polish column drew up at the Pilyavka River in mid-September 1648, and waiting on the other side were Bogdan's combined Cossacks and Crimean Tartars. The ensuing battle lasted two days, and the outcome was decided by the Poles falling for the oldest trick in the Tartar book, a feigned retreat which sucked

mous Cossack state consisting of the provinces of Kiev, Bratslav and Chernigov – in other words, Eastern Ukraine. The Cossacks could then, if they wished, exclude from it Jesuits, Jews, Polish soldiers and Roman Catholic land-owners. In accepting the offer, Bogdan fell to his knees before the Polish king and begged his pardon. It was granted.

The one constraint on Cossack autonomy was a ban on foreign alliances. Although this was aimed mainly at Russia, the discovery in 1650 that Bogdan was exploring the possibility of a confederation with the Romanian provinces was taken as a breach of the treaty and the pretext for renewed hostilities. Bogdan's main reason for seeking an accom-

the pursuing Poles into a prepared killing ground. The remnants of the Polish army withdrew to Lvov that night, leaving behind nearly 100 guns, 120,000 carts and plunder worth 10 million zloty.

Poland offered to increase the Cossack register to 40,000, but the war had so swollen the rebels' ranks that there were at least 10 times that number who regarded themselves as Cossacks and were insistent on equal treatment. The offer was gradually improved so that it eventually envisaged an autono-

Above, the Cossack assembly, where the loudest shouts carried the vote.

modation with the Romanian provinces had been to achieve a level of development in Eastern Ukraine which would enable the Cossacks to defend their independence. Reports of the Polish advance and anything else that might have been going through Bogdan's mind were then banished by the discovery that Helen, the catalyst for so much of what had happened, was having an affair with a younger man. On Bogdan's orders, the hapless lovers were stripped naked, lashed together, hanged and left to dangle from the city gates. A distraught Bogdan took to drink, and when the Polish army at last arrived, the consummate military tactician was in a stupor. Apparently embarrassed by his own condition, Bogdan inexplicably vanished.

In Bogdan's absence, the early stages of the campaign favoured the Poles, but just as it appeared that victory was within their reach, Bogdan resurfaced. He was sober and in tip-top condition, the proverbial new man. With Bogdan demonstrating all his old flair, the Cossacks regained the initiative and were able to secure a satisfactory peace with Poland. Bogdan's seemingly miraculous recovery was widely understood to have been the result of a certain Anna Zolotrenka, an attractive girl he met and married during his otherwise disgraceful sojourn.

The regenerated Bogdan's triumph over

Poland was enhanced in October 1653 by the Zemski Sobor, the assembly of "all free Russians", which offered to extend to the Cossacks the status of a free people under the protection of the tsar. As such they would be released from whatever oaths they might have sworn to the king of Poland. Protocol required Bogdan to put the proposal before the Cossack assembly for its ratification. He appeared before it in 1654 wearing a turban and with an orb and sceptre in either hand. The Cossacks' response to the proposal was to be decided, as custom dictated, by whichever side shouted loudest. According to the chronicles, the cry was unanimous: "We

want to belong to the Eastern, the Orthodox tsar!" This moment is enshrined in the "Reunification Monument" erected in Kiev in 1954 on its 300th anniversary.

The profound difference between Russians and Ukrainians is in their recollection of what happened next. In 1992, when Russia and newly independent Ukraine managed to reach a measure of agreement on the distribution of the defunct Soviet Union's assets, a beaming Boris Yeltsin turned towards his Ukrainian counterparts and said that their agreement was a happy return of 1654. Ukrainian jaws dropped, and one of Yeltsin's more erudite aides hastily whispered in his ear. The advice, it seems, was to steer well clear of 1654.

In short, the Cossacks very soon decided that Russian overlordship was worse than their unhappiest moments under Poland and, as if to prove the point, they appealed to Poland (as well as Sweden) for help in a rebellion against it. The Russian reprisals were merciless, and in the general mêlée of the simultaneous Russian campaigns against the Polish and Swedish armies, the devastation on the Ukrainian and Belarussian battlegrounds was more complete than anything witnessed since the 13th-century Mongols.

In 1667, Poland was largely incapacitated by a civil war of its own, and it was with a view to buying time on the Russian front that the partition of Ukraine was agreed. Poland-Lithuania received Ukraine west of the Dnieper; Russia took everything to the east, plus Smolensk and Kiev. Poland was confident of being able to recover Eastern Ukraine when the time was ripe, but events proved otherwise. Poland was so impoverished by incessant warfare that both it and its possessions, including Western Ukraine, were systematically dismembered in the 18th century by Russia, Prussia and the Habsburgs.

As Ukrainian nationalists see things, the direct result of "reunion" with Russia in 1654 was the progressive fragmentation of their country, the various pieces becoming mere addenda to the larger histories of their respective overlords. Although Cossacks generally were absorbed into the Russian imperial service, some bands retained closely-knit identities. These were notably the Terek Cossacks, who acted as a kind of Russian advance guard in the Caucasus, and the Zaporogians on their island in the Dnieper.

The latter remained largely independent of Moscow and retained old habits, like engaging in what amounted to a private war with Turkey, and it was one such exploit that produced a famous tale in Cossack folklore.

It seems the Zaporogians were sleeping off one of their rowdier parties when the Turks managed to land a force on the island and creep up on their camp. The one Cossack who was not completely unconscious caught sight of the intruders and raised the alarm. Holding aching heads in their hands, the Cossacks staged a successful defence, and in their moment of triumph composed a reply to the Turkish sultan's offer to take them under his protection. Stalin evidently considered

point: "We Cossacks refuse every demand and petition you make us now, or which you may in future invent."

Successive tsars were not unhappy to let the Zaporogians conduct a surrogate war against Turkey, but when Russia itself engineered a major victory which cleared the Turks out of the Crimea and gave Russia control over much of the Black Sea, the Dnieper Cossacks had outlived their usefulness. In 1775 Russian troops surrounded the island and, heavily outnumbered, the Cossacks surrendered without a fight. Every building was flattened, and the last of the Zaporogian *atamans*, one Kalnishevski, spent the rest of his days in the least congenial

the Cossack rendition of diplomatic language hilarious: "Thou Turkish Devil! Brother and Companion of Lucifer himself! Who dares to call himself Lord of Christians, but is not! Babylonian cook! Brewer of Jerusalem! Goat-keeper of the herds of Alexandria! Swineherd of Great and Lesser Egypt! Armenian Sow and Tartar Goat! Insolent! Unbeliever! The Devil take you!" That was the salutation. The text came straight to the

Left, Bogdan Khmelnitski: "I have decided to take revenge on the Polish gentry." **Above**, Cossacks composing their famous reply to the Turkish sultan after he had offered peace.

surroundings imaginable for a Cossack, a monastery within the Arctic circle.

For the bulk of the Ukrainian population, conditions rather depended on whether their overlords were Russian, Habsburg, or Polish, the last retaining their estates after Poland ceased to exist as an independent state. Catherine the Great's supposedly liberal instincts did not carry as far as Russian Ukraine, where the burden of serfdom weighed even more heavily on the local population than it did in Russia itself, and Jews were harrassed to the point of persecution. The writer Vita Sackville-West recorded her impressions of life among the Polish gentry before World

War I: "riding, dancing, laughing, living at a fantastic rate in that fantastic oasis of extravagance and feudalism, 10,000 horses on the state, 80 English hunters, and a pack of English hounds; a park full of dromedaries; another park, walled in, full of wild animals kept for sport; Tokay of 1750 handed round by a giant; cigarettes handed round by dwarfs in 18th-century liveries…"

Although Western perceptions of World War I are generally of trenches in France, Ukraine took a horrific battering in the clash between Russia and the combined armies of Germany and Austria. Matters were made if anything worse by a three-cornered war after the Russian revolution between Bolsheviks,

being that Western Ukraine was parcelled out among Poland, Czechoslovakia and Romania. To begin with, Eastern Ukraine under Russia experienced some genuine reform, with the Ukrainian language given official status in education and government and a marked improvement in the living standards of the peasants. Any grounds for optimism were dashed by Stalin's rise to power. The collectivisation of agriculture was an unspeakable disaster leading to a famine in 1932–33 which cost 7 million lives. Stalin's response to discontent was to order the extermination of the educated classes.

These horrors were compounded by World War II, in which 6 million Ukrainians were

Russian nationalists and Ukrainian nationalists, the anarchy exploited by a resurrected Poland to seize Galicia. Sackville-West returned to the same estate after the war: "Gone, as it deserved to go; the house razed to the ground till it was lower than the wretched hovels of the peasants, the estate parcelled out, cut in half by the new Polish frontier, the owner dead with his brains blown out, and his last penny gambled away in Paris."

In 1922, after three years of civil war and no fewer than 14 changes of government in the same period, Ukraine was divided more or less along the lines agreed between Russia and Poland in 1667, the main difference

killed and the destruction of plant and property was almost total. Nor did the carnage stop with Hitler's defeat. The Red Army moved into Western Ukraine and, fired by revenge for earlier support for Germany, fought a merciless war with nationalist guerrillas. Millions of Ukrainians suspected of disloyalty were deported to Siberia. The combination of wars, famine and purges in the first half of the 20th century is estimated to have killed more than half the male population of Ukraine and a quarter of the female.

Post-war recuperation was long, slow and hard, the occasional voice given to the restitution of civil rights and self-determination being countered with ruthless measures. Ironically, the Soviet leader most bitterly opposed to any loosening of ties between Ukraine and Russia was himself a Ukrainian, Leonid Brezhnev. These ties had served him well enough, and he strengthened them by notoriously packing the Politburo with his old friends and colleagues from Ukraine, leading predictably to taunts about the Little Russian Mafia and hijacking.

Volodymyr Shcherbytsky, a close Brezhnev ally, ruled Ukraine from 1973 until 1989, dispensing long terms in labour camps and psychiatric hospitals to anyone raising a critical voice. Unlike in Russia, the clandestine opposition was not among intellectuals but

with a miners' strike in 1989, the last accelerating his resignation in the same year and his death soon afterwards. His departure opened the field for presidential candidates who read the wind blowing across Eastern Europe and plumped for Ukrainian independence. While Gorbachev and Yeltsin had by then reconciled themselves to the possible secession of the Baltic states, Ukrainian independence was more than they could countenance. Ukraine provided at least a quarter of the Soviet Union's agricultural produce and perhaps 70 per cent of its army officers. Yeltsin growled that he reserved the right to reflect on the borders of any republic that left the union, which led to predictably loud

among workers, especially miners, and it emerged in due course at the Popular Movement of Ukraine for Restructuring, or Rukh. Taking stock of Ukraine's position, they recognised that millions of Ukrainians could no longer speak their own language and that 5 million Ukrainians lived in Russia and 11 million Russians in Ukraine.

Shcherbystky's compounded the unpopularity of his iron rule by trying to whitewash the Chernobyl disaster and failing to cope

Left, deportation to death during World War II. **Above**, the Black Sea Fleet, which Russia *and* the Ukraine claimed after the USSR broke up.

protests about the intentions of "Tsar Boris".

Yeltsin's gauntlet was taken up by Leonid Kravchuk, who called for a bill to be rushed through parliament creating a 400,000-strong Ukrainian army and dual control of the Soviet nuclear weapons on Ukrainian soil. This was in time extended to the Soviet fleet in Ukraine's Black Sea ports. Talk of "adversaries" had risen to "enemies" and "the great Russian onslaught" when, probably to the relief of all parties concerned, Kravchuk and Yeltsin sat down to talk things over. This helped to clear the air and enabled a beaming Yeltsin to make an unwitting reference, as we have seen, to the matter of 1654.

UKRAINE: WHAT TO SEE

Although Ukraine is a vast country, the wishes of most visitors would be met by planning a trip around the Dnieper River. The capital Kiev is the logical starting-point, and thereafter it is possible to follow in the wake of the Vikings, taking in the cities of Dnepropetrovsk and Zaporozhe en route to Kherson on the Black Sea and ports beyond. The most notable omission in this plan of action would be the city of Lvov, or Lviv as Ukrainians call it, hard on the Polish border, and visitors may well decide it warrants a special excursion.

As the Dnieper rises in Russia and has therefore flowed through Ukraine for some considerable distance before reaching Kiev, there is little to attract tourists north of the capital unless the prospect of Chernobyl 60 miles/95 km away is ghoulishly irresistible. In any case, the boat operators plying from Kiev have more or less given up on excursions upstream, and it is important to note that they operate downstream only in summer. The voyage from Kiev to Kherson is 600 miles/950 km, and the time taken depends on whether the boat in question is slow, fast or express. Even the express stops in Dnepropetrovsk and Zaporozhye, although only for an hour or so.

High-speed hydrofoils, among other boat services, radiate from Kherson to Odessa and the Crimean peninsula. At the time of writing, whether Crimea remains part of Ukraine or is returned to Russia is still being negotiated. Whichever way the decision goes, it is to be hoped that Crimea will become more accessible. The area was a honeycomb of sensitive Soviet military installations and operations, including arms shipments to the Middle East, so visitors were barred from many parts, including those associated with Florence Nightingale, the Charge of the Light Brigade and other aspects of the Crimean War. It's also uncertain whether the Crimean Tartars whom Stalin expelled to Siberia will be allowed to return.

Preceding pages: interior of Kiev's opera house. Left, St Sophia's Cathedral, Kiev. Right, central Kiev.

Kiev: The "Mother of Russian Cities" was extensively restored in time for its 1,500th anniversary in 1982, and it is a tribute to this enormous undertaking that visitors may need to remind themselves that the city was almost totally destroyed by the Mongols in the 13th century, in World War II, and on more than one occasion in between. On a dark day in the spring of 1986, just four years after the anniversary, there were fears that the disaster at Chernobyl might wipe out all the good work and more, but of course these were not realised and scientific evidence suggests that visitors need not now be deterred.

The near-disaster brought the population of two million to an unprecedented level of environmental awareness, and the streets are now watered twice daily. Kiev is on the same latitude as Frankfurt, so the climate is much milder than, say, Moscow, and for much of the year the city is noticeably green.

Tradition has it that Kiev was founded in the late 5th century by Kiy, the eldest of three brothers, but as we have seen in

the previous section the city did not really come into its own until it was taken over by the Varangians and in particular after their conversion to Christianity in the reign of Prince Vladimir. The river to which his subjects were led for compulsory baptism – emerging in batches of 1,000 or so at a time with the same Christian name – flowed under Kreschiatik, the street whose name in old Russian means baptism.

The builder who put Kiev into the first rank of European capitals in a remarkably short space of time was Vladmir's son Yaroslav the Wise, and his greatest single achievement was St Sophia's Cathedral, begun in 1037 and modelled on its namesake in Constantinople with 13 domes and gilded cupolas. By then Kiev had more than 40 churches and of course others followed, but only St Sophia's survived the Mongol invasions in the 13th century. In some cases, like the Desyatinnaya Church, the ruins are still to be seen almost as the Mongols left them.

A model inside St Sophia's shows how the original architects made a point of rendering in stone some of the features of earlier wooden churches. A comparison with the cathedral's present appearance indicates which parts were subsequently altered or added, but the interior remains virtually pristine, remarkably so in the case of the mosaic of the Pantocreator in the middle dome. The fresco in the west choir contains portraits of Yaroslav and his family, including the three daughters who were caught up in a sudden royal craze for Kievan brides and ended up married to the kings of Norway, France and Hungary. Yaroslav himself was buried in the cathedral under the marble stone which still exists.

The cathedral, which the Communists turned into a museum, housed Russia's first library, and many of the chronicles quoted in this book were written in it, the first and most famous by Nestor, who is buried not in the cathedral but in the Monastery of the Caves. The bell-tower is much later, having been started in about 1740, the

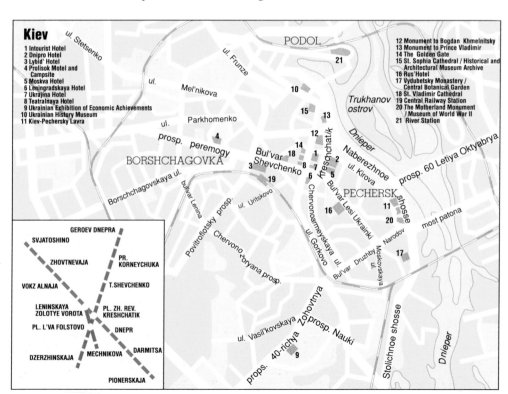

Kiev

1 Intourist Hotel
2 Dnipro Hotel
3 Lybid' Hotel
4 Prolisok Motel and Campsite
5 Moskva Hotel
6 Leningradskaya Hotel
7 Ukrajina Hotel
8 Teatralnaya Hotel
9 Ukrainian Exhibition of Economic Achievements
10 Ukrainian History Museum
11 Kiev-Pechersky Lavra

12 Monument to Bogdan Khmelnitsky
13 Monument to Prince Vladimir
14 The Golden Gate
15 St. Sophia Cathedral / Historical and Architectural Museum Archive
16 Rus'Hotel
17 Vydubetsky Monastery / Central Botanical Garden
18 St. Vladimir Cathedral
19 Central Railway Station
20 The Motherland Monument / Museum of World War II
21 River Station

same time as the wall which encloses the complex was built.

Standing in the square in front of St Sophia's is a statue of Bogdan Khmelnitski, the celebrated Cossack hetman (general). Follow Streletsky and Polupanov streets to the Golden Gate, part of the city's 11th-century fortifications. The gate was fully restored for the 1982 anniversary celebrations and includes a small church built into the arch.

The Central Lenin Museum is likely to be rearranged in time to come, if not already, but the **Museums of Russian Art** and of **Oriental and Western Art** have a timeless quality which is bound to weather any changes in the political climate. The former contains icons from the 12th to 17th centuries as well as outstanding works by 18th- and 19th-century artists. The latter's collection includes paintings from Bellini to Goya and from Hals to Ruisdal.

Relatively modern points of interest locally are the **Opera House**, **Kiev University** (founded 1834), the 19th-century **Vladimir Cathedral**, designed by Beretti and Bernhardt with seven gilded domes and three naves, and the **Ukraine State Department Stores**, Kiev's equivalent of Moscow's GUM.

The next stage of sightseeing is best oriented around the **Monastery of the Caves** (Petscherskaja Lawra), every bit as significant as St Sophia's. The monastery was founded in Yaroslav's time by St Antony, who had visited the great Greek monastery of Mount Athos. The first handful of inmates lived in caves hollowed out of the clay bank of the Dnieper. A tunnel under the river was lined with sealed cells where monks lived, died and were buried in the most sublime celebration of medieval asceticism. Celibate, they divided their time between prayer, literary activities, fasting and what would now be considered serious mortification of the flesh.

The second abbot, the pious aristocrat St Feodosy, moved the monastery to more comfortable quarters on the hilltop. The original monastery became a whole complex of churches, many subsequently converted into museums. The

Monastery of the Caves.

Church of the Redeemer of Beretovo, just outside the complex, was built as a burial place for Kievan princes by Prince Vladimir Monomakh, who married King Harold of England's daughter. It contains the tomb of his son Yuri Dolgoruki, the founder of Moscow. The marble sarcophagus which now stands over Yuri's tomb was added in 1947 by the Soviet authorities to mark the city's 800th anniversary.

The oldest building within the complex is the 11th-century Assumption Cathedral, in ruins now because the Germans blew it up in 1941. The bell-tower was the work of Gottfried Schadel in the 18th century, and the story goes that such was its height (316ft/96m) that the builders had difficulty completing the upper sections. The incomplete edifice obligingly sank into the ground of its own accord to help them, and when they had finished, it rose again under its own steam the following night to its correct height. The Museum of Ukrainian Art in the monastery complex contains the Scythian gold collection.

The sights mentioned above are by no means exhaustive; they constitute merely the "musts". For a taste of contemporary Kiev, the best place is ironically also one of the oldest streets in the city, the **Andreevsky spusk**, or "Descent". In ancient times, the street linked the administrative part of the Upper City with Podol, the commercial quarter. Nowadays, it is a place for fêtes, film festivals and, on public holidays, a throng of dancers, painters and jewellers. The distinguished writer Mikhail Bulgakov (1891–1940) lived here.

Lvov: In January 1990, hundreds of thousands of demonstrators formed a human chain between Lvov and Kiev, 325 miles (540 km) apart. The gesture was in support of Rukh, the Ukrainian nationalist movement, but the physical link between Lvov and the Ukrainian capital might also have been a sly riposte to Poles who still insist that the former is more properly a Polish city. As a glance at the map shows, it is close to the Polish border, and this is a border which moved in leaps and bounds according to Poland's fortunes.

Lvov was unarguably part of a larger, historic Poland for centuries. Towards the end of the 18th century, however, Poland ceased to exist, and Lvov became part of the Austrian Habsburg empire, when it was known by its German name, Lemberg. The city was Polish again when Poland was reconstituted, but it went to Ukraine (or, more realistically, to the Soviet Union) after World War II. Lvov is the Polish name, and universally the most familiar, but Ukrainians call the city Lviv. Either way, it was named after the son (whose name in English would be Leo) of Prince Daniil of Galicia, who founded a fort on the site in the mid-13th century.

This complicated, cosmopolitan background is reflected in the city's marvellous squares, whose buildings between them represent every vagary in European architecture for the past 500 years. In this respect, Lvov is almost another Prague in the way so much is condensed into a confined area.

There is no getting away from politics and their implications, however. **Adam**

Foreign companies come to Kiev.

Mickiewicz, the poet whose **statue** dominates the square of the same name and is something of a city symbol, happened to be a Pole. The baroque **Boim Chapel** in the same square was built at the turn of the 17th century by Hungarians. The **Roman Catholic cathedral**, begun in 1270, has officially never been finished but is still used for services.

Almost every one of the 44 houses in the **Rynok** (Market) **Square** has historical, and therefore political, associations. John Sobieski, the hero of the siege of Vienna and Poland's most dashing king, once owned No. 6, and Peter the Great stayed at No. 24.

Stalin ordered the removal of the trident from the statue of **Neptune** in front of the Town Hall. It was considered politically provocative, and indeed it has since been adopted as a symbol of Ukrainian independence together with the yellow and blue flag.

Down the Dnieper: The **Dnieper**, as we have seen, was "the road from the Varangians to the Greeks", in other words from the Baltic to the Black Sea.

The first stop (in the slow boat) is at **Rzhishchev**, where in 1654 Bogdan negotiated the terms of Russian protection for the Ukraine he had just liberated from Poland. It was at **Grigorovka**, the next stop (about 87 miles/140 km from Kiev) that in 1943 Russian troops fought their way across the river against the Germans. A short distance away is **Kanev**, described in contemporary chronicles as a sturdy outpost of Kievan Russ. The **St George's (Assumption) Cathedral** was built in 1144 and survives to this day. Kanev was the home of the Ukrainian poet Taras Shevchenko (1814–61). He died in St Petersburg but his body was brought back for burial on Taras Hill. A museum celebrates his life and work.

The boat continues through the **Cherkassy** and **Poltava** regions, the latter famous for the climactic battle of life-long rivalry between Peter the Great and Charles XII of Sweden. The river widens into the **Kremenchiug Reservoir**, at one end of which is a huge hydroelectric plant. Cherkassy, more

Out went communism, in came Coke.

than 1,000 years old, is a large industrial centre and important river port but commendably green. The **Museum of Local History** should be on the top of the list for those interested in Tartar and Cossack times.

The first stop after Cherkassy is another must for the historically-minded: this is where the remnants of the Swedish army after the battle of Poltava made their big mistake. Only Charles XII himself and the Cossack hetman Mazeppa made it across.

Dnepropetrovsk, a little way downstream, has twice had close associations with the pinnacle of Russian power. In modern times it produced not only Leonid Brezhnev but the circle of political cronies who ruled the Soviet Union as what was called, not too loudly, the Dnepropetrovsk Mafia. In the 18th century, the town was conceived by Potemkin as a paean to his queen and lover, Catherine the Great. Commissioned by Catherine to develop the newly acquired Russian territories, Potemkin planned hundreds of new villages, most of which never got beyond impressive but flimsy facades, little more than the cardboard cities found on a film set and just enough for Catherine to admire, preferably from a distance.

The original Dnepropetrovsk was named in her honour Ekaterinslav, which would translate as Catherine-ville, and she arrived in 1787 to inspect it in the company of the Habsburg Emperor Joseph II. Potemkin explained his vision of a St Petersburg of the South, a magnificent city complete with a palace, university, law courts, a music conservatory, a cathedral bigger than St Peter's in Rome, and a replica of the Acropolis. Joseph was aware of Potemkin's grandiose follies and could see only a collection of wooden huts, but protocol required him to play along with the charade. "I performed a great deed today," he wrote to a friend. "The Empress laid the first stone of a new church, and I laid – the last." Joseph's cynicism was not quite borne out. The church was eventually completed, albeit not for many years and on a much

Hydroelectric scheme on the Dnieper.

reduced scale. Dnepropetrovsk is today a regional capital and substantial industrial centre, and while there is not much to rivet tourists, they might like to look up the so-called Student Palace, built on the ruins of Potemkin's ill-fated palace.

Another 50 miles (80 km) downstream, a shimmering, reddish cloud gives advance notice of **Zaporozhe**, formerly Fort Alexandrovsk, now a forest of chimneys erected to the cause of modern – well, slightly modern – metallurgy. There are jokes about Zaporozhe being the city of eternal youth because, with chimneys tactically positioned even in the heart of residential areas, nobody has the chance to grow old. A green movement sprang up under *perestroika* and is bravely trying to do something about the problem. To add to the concern, there is just downriver a nuclear power station larger than Chernobyl – and using the same technology.

All of which detracts from the anticipation with which followers of Cossack history would otherwise approach **Khortitsa Island**, the site of the Zaporozhskaya Sech, the most famous band of all. The name meant "beyond the rapids", but the rapids are no more because the dam raised the water level. The consolation is that the island, quite surprisingly big, was turned into a preserve even in Soviet times and has a fascinating Cossack museum.

The last of the reservoir-lakes on the Dnieper is 144 miles (240 km) long and in places 14 miles (23 km) wide. Beyond the lock is **Novaya Kakhovka**, built by workers who put up the power station. A green-fingered lot, they have given the new town a reputation for juicy watermelons, cherries and grapes.

Askania-Nova to the southeast is a steppe nature reserve, home to bison, llama, buffalo, zebra, antelope, ostrich and wild horse. Another 37 miles (60 km) brings up the final stop on the river, **Kherson**, once a Greek colony (Hersones), then a fortress and later a Soviet naval base and shipyard. The Dnieper estuary divides into three channels; the sea proper is still some 50 miles (80 km) away, at Ochakov, the former Turkish

Caring for a monastery garden.

stronghold eventually conquered for Russia by its greatest military hero, Count Alexander Suvorov, in 1788.

Odessa: The switch is made at Kherson from river steamer to hydrofoil for a fast ride to Odessa. The original settlement was also Greek, Odessos, but it disappeared in the 4th century BC and nothing much happened until the new town was founded by the victorious Suvorov. It came into its own under the supervision of, strange to relate, the Duke de Richelieu, who prudently left France during the Revolution.

There was by 1809 a Theatre of Opera and Ballet in which Chaliapin, Tchaikovsky and Caruso subsequently performed. The young Pushkin, exiled to Odessa in 1823, wrote some of his best poetry here.

Odessa and the **Crimean coast** enjoy a fair approximation of a Mediterranean climate and 25 miles (40 km) of beaches. The long, stone stairway leading down to the harbour in Odessa are the **Potemkin Steps**, down which Eisenstein's pram famously rolled. The occasion in the film was the massacre of a crowd responding to the plight of mutineers on the battleship *Potemkin* anchored in the bay.

Less well known, but certainly worth a look, are the labyrinthic catacombs which twist for literally hundreds of miles under and around the city. They were a refugee, not only for criminals and revolutionaries but also for the World War II Resistance fighters, who foiled every German effort to flush them out. A model of the underground headquarters is to be seen in the **Local History Museum**. Both the **Art Museum** and the **Museum of Western and Oriental Art** are worth a visit, but perhaps special mention should be made of the **Archaeological Museum** with its unique relics of the Greek era on the Black Sea, which spawned the legend of Jason and the Argonauts.

Those wishing to pursue the Greek angle further could take a boat to **Ochakov** and make their way from there, about 20 miles (30 km), to the excavated Greek city of **Olvia**.

The Crimea: The boat trip from Odessa to Yalta passes names which still resound to the hooves of the Light Brigade as they made their celebrated charge into the "valley of death" during the Crimean War: Sebastopol and Balaclava. Most organised tours of the Crimea start, however, in **Simferopol**, the regional capital. The city was built on the site of a Tartar settlement.

Neapolis, or **Neapol Skifsky**, in the Valley of Petrovsky, is a Scythian capital of the 2nd century BC. It was destroyed, like virtually everything associated with the Scythians, by the Huns in the 4th century. Excavations at the site began in 1827 and have since uncovered not only a trove of marble and bronze statues but also the richly endowed graves of dozens of Scythian nobles. The Simferopol local library has the priceless Tavrida collection, no fewer than 50,000 books which are by far the single biggest source of knowledge about Crimea.

The winding road along the coast from Simferopol passes military installations which, in Soviet times, were so unutterably secret that visitors were hurried through in closely supervised groups. It is to be hoped that these rules will be relaxed, because it is a magnificent stretch of road with views that invite frequent stops.

The large resort before Yalta is **Alushta**, which boasts the warmest bathing in these parts as well as the remains of a fortress built by the Byzantine Emperor Justinian. It was a Genoese stronghold in the 14th century. The principal attractions around Alushta are the **Suuk Koba** and **Bin-bas Koba** stalactite caves, the **Dzhur-Dzhur** waterfall and the **Crimean State Nature Preserve**, 70,000 acres (28,000 hectares) of flora and fauna.

Roosevelt Avenue, the main thoroughfare through the Old City quarter of **Yalta**, is a memento of the famous wartime conference between the American president, Stalin and Churchill. The conference was actually held just west of the city at Livadia on what used to be an imperial estate, Tsar Nicholas II's **Marble Palace**, built in the Renaissance style in 1911.

The rooms used for the 1945 conference have been preserved exactly as they were then. While the American delegation also stayed at this palace, the British were put up farther down the coast at the **Vorontsov Palace**.

Back in Yalta itself, the visitors seem to divide into those seeking the good life and those ostensibly doing penance for too much of it. The climate is Mediterranean, and indeed Yalta is more or less on the same latitude as Nice. The penitents are to be found in the 100 or so sanitoria dotted along the coast.

The medicinal properties of wine do not appear to be among the top priorities of the **Magarach Central Research Institute of Viticulture and Viniculture**, which works ceaselessly on getting the best out of grape varieties from all over the world. The results are freely available in licensed establishments; the older vintages in the institute's cellars, reputedly going back to the 18th century, are more elusive. It is no great surprise, therefore, that seemingly every well-known Russian in the world of arts and literature has had occasion to spend some time in and around Yalta, so every walking tour is punctuated by "Gorky stayed here", "Chekhov stayed there" and so on. Both of these luminaries, incidentally, have statues commemorating their stays.

Of the other Crimean towns, **Bakhchisarai** is well worth visiting for **Khan Abdul Sahal Girey's Tartar palace** (1519), later destroyed by fire and rebuilt by Catherine the Great in 1787 faithful to some of the original, notably the harem and mosque.

The official list of historic monuments in **Sebastopol** alone runs to some 400 sites, many of them relating to the events and personalities of the Crimean War; the ruined fortifications on Malakhov Hill are worth a visit.

Balaclava, 10 miles (16 km) to the south, has historical associations both with the Scythians and the 14th-century Genoese in addition to being the British base in the Crimean War. The full return of these places to visitors' itineraries is something to look forward to.

Arkadia
Beach,
Odessa.

On declaring independence from the Soviet Union in 1991, the Soviet Republic of Byelorussia quietly let it be known that in future it would rather be called Belarus, the difference being that the old name is in Russian, its replacement in what we must now call "Belarussian". The desired change may have looked like a cosmetic trifle, but in reality it was triumphant confirmation of the survival of a national identity which had been besieged by the Russian tsars, persecuted by Stalin and finally commandeered as a sacrifice to the greater glory of Soviet Man.

"White Russia" should not be confused with the "White Russians" who took up arms against the Communist revolution. The latter, a volunteer army raised by General Denikin, were designated "Whites" because they were opposed to "Reds" – nothing to do with Belarus although there were some Byelorussians coincidentally in the White Russian ranks. "White Russia" in the national sense draws a distinction between it and what used to be called Little Russia and Great Russia, or Ukraine and plain Russia as they are known today.

Delving further unearths other interesting differences between White Russians and the two other varieties. The majority of Belarussians profess, even if they do not practise, Roman Catholicism, an obvious anomaly in what was a sea of Russian Orthodoxy before all religion was banned. The explanation lies back in the Mongol invasions of the 13th century. While most Russians were firmly under the Mongol yoke for 250 years, the White Russians lay beyond the Mongol writ and gravitated instead towards Lithuania and ultimately Poland, thus acquiring the Polish feudal system and an attachment to Roman religion.

As a buffer zone between Poland and a resurgent Great Russia, White Russia was forever being torn apart and distributed piece-meal between them according to the fortunes of war. Although Poland was put out of the reckoning in the 18th century, Byelorussia was still on the road from Western Europe and Russia and thus exposed to the further depredations of Napoleon, Kaiser Wilhelm and Hitler. The accumulative destruction was total.

Ironically, battered Byelorussia came to be regarded as a Soviet success story. Russian, not Byelorussian, was made the sole medium of instruction in most schools. The republic had a positive trade balance with the rest of the Soviet Union, and Byelorussians had 13 billion roubles in their private savings accounts to show for it. The unexpected declaration of independence revealed true feelings about the Soviet system. On the other hand, the 13 billion roubles were suddenly worthless. It is therefore not just in the matter of a new name that Belarus is effectively starting all over again.

Preceding pages: Minsk. **Left**, the ancient face of "White Russia".

Polotsk, the origin of modern Belarus, was once a typical Varangian principality, its destiny separated from that of Moscow and the northern cities by the fact that it remained outside the Mongol Yoke. The Dnieper apart, Polotsk's rivers flowed into the Baltic, and these natural channels of contact meant that the cultural gravitation was towards a Baltic region which came to be dominated by Poland with its firm attachment to the Roman Church rather than Eastern Orthodoxy.

In common with other regions under Polish domination, Polotsk was saddled with a feudal system which saw the indigenous population reduced to serfdom. The Polish-Lithuanian nobility owned the land, and the role of the bourgeoisie was filled by imported foreigners, mostly German-speaking and increasingly Jewish. The absorption of Slavonic influences turned the German dialect of the Jews into Yiddish.

Fight for control: With the emergence of the Grand Duchy of Muscovy and eventually "Great Russia" from beneath the Mongol Yoke, a protracted contest commenced with Poland for control of Polotsk, which lay between them. These wars went on well into the 17th century, and with every short-lived truce between them, bits and pieces of Polotsk were traded backwards and forwards. When Poland surrendered a slice of territory to Russia, the inhabitants were required to switch their allegiance from Roman Catholicism to Russian Orthodoxy, and vice versa. Poland was itself dismembered out of existence during the course of the 18th century, ancient Polotsk being given to Russia.

The terms White Russia and Little Russia became current during this period of Russian ascendancy. "White" was probably chosen simply as a contrast with "Black" or common-land on which peasants could roam or settle in their own right as long as they paid a tax directly to the tsar. The steppes of Little Russia, or Ukraine, were traditionally nomadic black-land, whereas with a Polish tradition of serfs living as vassals on a landlord's estate, the former Polotsk was known

in contrast as "White Russia" or Byelorussia.

The romantic nationalism of the 19th century fell on receptive ears among the dispersed Byelorussians and inspired dreams of a unified state. World War I, however, saw them far apart, with some nationalists pinning their hopes on German support while others put their trust in the tsar. The separate peace between Germany and Russia after the Russian revolution in 1917, negotiated at Brest-Litovsk on the present Polish-Belarussian border, brought the two camps to-

gether. They proclaimed the "Byelorussian National Republic", but this cut no ice at all with bands of renegade German and Polish soldiers still heavily engaged on the territory in question. The Bolsheviks intervened on behalf of the nationalists, but on condition that the independent state would become the "Byelorussian Soviet Republic" – a rather different matter.

The Byelorussian Soviet Republic was actually declared in January 1919, but by then Poland had been reconstituted at the Paris peace conference – and was immediately at war with Russia to regain the formerly Polish land, including Byelorussia,

Left, itinerant holy man. **Right**, 19th-century Belarus was the most backward part of Russia.

which the Paris peace conference had awarded to the Soviet Union. The old protagonists carved up Byelorussia just as they had done in the 17th century, and this time round Poland got the larger share. Reduced to what amounted to little more than the province of Minsk, the Bolsheviks at first tolerated and even encouraged the revival of the Belarussian language and its literature, which had been targets of Russification under the tsars. While these concessions were welcomed by the intelligentsia, the peasants saw little change in the economic conditions which had made Byelorrussia the most wretched part of European Russia.

Even the cultural revival among the elite

time, Byelorussians living in the Polish sector were spared the horrors but were firmly encouraged to banish all thoughts about national independence.

The Nazi-Soviet Pact of 1939 contained secret protocols by which Germany and Russia proposed to scrap many of the independent national boundaries drawn up at the Paris Peace Conference in 1919. The effect would have been to restore the Russian Empire much as it has been under the tsars. By carving up Poland again, the pact intended to restore Byelorussia as a single entity, albeit as part of Russia.

The pact of course collapsed on 22 June 1941 with Hitler's invasion of Russia, and

was doomed with the rise of Stalin. As a Georgian, Stalin was as obsessed about being accepted as a bona fide Russian as the Corsican Napoleon was about being French and the Austrian Hitler about being German. He was utterly opposed to any manifestation of cultural independence in Byelorussia or Ukraine, which he treated as treason. Belarussians were obliged to speak Russian, and the slightest hint of protest was to invite death or deportation to Siberian labour camps. The relatively recent discovery of mass graves at Kurapaty near Minsk has lent substance to the semi-secret programme of extermination waged by Stalin in the 1930s. In the mean-

Byelorussia was again in the firing line. Russian troops and local partisans put up heroic resistance, particularly at Brest on the border, but Hitler had committed 175 divisions to the campaign and by October his troops had swept through Byelorussia and were outside Moscow. Byelorussia remained under Nazi occupation behind Germany's Eastern Front until the tide turned in 1944. Nazi rule had disastrous consequences for the still substantial number of Jews who had not been able to flee.

With the Red Army in control of the entire region at the end of the war, the notoriously fickle matter of a line between Poland and

Russia was perfunctorily settled. Neither the Polish People's Republic nor the equally new Byelorussian Soviet Republic were in any position to argue with the Kremlin's decision in this respect. The illusion of Byelorussian and Ukrainian autonomy was fostered by their admission as founder members of the United Nations, each with its own seat. Russia took its seat in the assembly cloaked as the USSR.

In common with the other Soviet Republics and the countries of Communist Eastern Europe, Byelorussia had an assigned role in the overall Soviet scheme of things. In practice, it did comparatively well out of the arrangement. Unlike smaller regions ordered

was pushed even further into the background. Newspapers were published in Russian, and Byelorussian was no longer used as a medium of instruction in schools. The vestiges of Roman Catholicism were swept under the carpet of Soviet state atheism.

Although we now know that Byelorussians were by no means as acquiescent as was generally supposed, it took a catastrophe outside the republic to trigger a quiet rebellion within. The Chernobyl nuclear reactor is in Ukraine, but the disaster in 1986 sent up a radioactive cloud which, having once circled the globe, dumped its lethal contents even more comprehensively on Byelorussia than on Ukraine. Some 20 per cent of Byelorussia's

to devote their resources almost exclusively to keeping the Soviet Union in, say, light bulbs or cigarette papers, Byelorussia's industries turned out a broad range of products, many under the brand-name "Minsk".

A succession of subservient local Communist Party bosses raised no objection to Byelorussia being used a guinea-pig in the development of Soviet Man: The Byelorussian language, already in a sorry state after Russification under the tsars and Stalin,

agricultural land and 15 per cent of its forests were rendered unusable. Not for the first time did the descendants of ancient Polotsk feel they were carrying the burden of malice or merely misfortune perpetrated beyond their borders and control.

Byelorussia suffered its broken back in silence for another five years, leading Western observers to believe that regardless of what was happening in Eastern Europe generally, the bonds between the three Russias – Great, Little and White – were too tight to be broken. A declaration of independence and an apparently cosmetic change of name put them right.

Left, vast numbers of people were sent to Siberian labour camps after World War I. **Above**, Nazi justice in Minsk, 1941.

BELARUS: WHAT TO SEE

Belarus is, as it ever was, one of the busiest thoroughfares in Eastern Europe. Visitors arriving by road or rail from the West enter Belarus through **Brest** on the Polish border, the city which gave its name to the Brest-Litovsk Treaty by which Germany and revolutionary Russia reached a separate peace in 1917. Railway passengers get scent of Brest's moment of glory in World War II without leaving the station: a plaque commemorates the partisans who tried to resist the first step of Hitler's invasion of Russia in 1941.

An overpass from the station leads to a park with a war memorial over a mass grave. Another heroic action in 1941 took place in the Brest Fortress on the outskirts of the city, where the Russian garrison managed to hold on for six weeks. Their resistance persuaded the German army commanders that the main body of their forces would have to by-pass Brest in order to stick to a time-table whose next objective was Minsk. The tables were turned in 1944 when German defenders were inside the fortress and under attack from the advancing Red Army. The fortress was reduced to rubble, but it has since been partially re-built and contains the Brest Fortress Defence Museum.

On leaving Brest, the road to Moscow passes through the **Belovezhskaya Puscha**, 210,000 preserved acres (85,000 hectares) of the kind of terrain which serves as a backdrop to the migrations from Central Asia. It has a herd of animals said to be the descendants of some ancient mammoth, the East European equivalent of the buffalo which once roamed the North American plain in countless numbers.

Kobrin, was a town in the era of Polotsk, but it tends to be remembered now as the place where the Russian army managed to check Napoleon on 15 July 1812. Alexander Suvorov, the Russian general reputed never to have been

Left, Brest remembers World War II.

beaten, had an estate in the area which is now a municipal park. His house is the **Suvorov Military History Museum**.

Beryoza, about 60 miles (100 km) out of Brest, had one of the monasteries which served as a beacon of Roman Catholicism in Polish times. It later became a prison and, under the Nazis, part of a concentration camp. The journey continues unremarkably through **Ivatsevichi**, **Kossovo** and **Baranovichi**, the last junction for roads going to Vilnius and Rovno. Dzerzhinsk was Koydanovo before being renamed after the Soviet secret police chief. Ironically, Koydan was as feared in his time as was Dzerzhinsky. He was the Mongol commander who was checked, if not beaten, in a battle at this site in 1241. At any rate, the Mongols withdrew to the north and Polotsk, left out on its own, began the cultural drift towards Lithuania, Poland and the Roman Church. Dzerzhinsky was born in the nearby village of Petrivolichi in 1877.

The capital, **Minsk**, important enough to feature on Abu Abdallah Muhammed's map in 1154 and once a contender for the title of the European Jerusalem, has been a massive casualty of war. Anything that looks older than World War II has been heavily restored or totally rebuilt, the exceptions being some 17th-century houses in Bakunina and Ostrovoska streets. The ruins of the 12th-century Zamchische Cathedral are the oldest relics, a memento of Varangian times when Minsk was an outpost of Kievan Russ and at the receiving end of Byzantine influence making its way up the Dnieper River. The Svisloch River flowing through the city made up part of the river grid which linked the Baltic with the Black Sea.

The partially restored **Minsk Cathedral** is 17th-century, built in the city during its Polish period when Poland and Russia were at one another's throats. The capital's other monuments are connected with the world wars, the most prominent being the World War II granite obelisk which acts as a landmark. The monument in Ratomskaya Street commemorates the Jewish dead in that

The Brest Fortress.

war. Whereas Minsk was once a predominantly Jewish city, the Jewish population of all Belarus is now only 1 percent of a total of 10 million and dwindling through emigration to Israel.

Reconstructed Minsk has a number of agreeable parks and avenues. All were named after members of the Soviet pantheon – Marx, Lenin, Engels etc. – and at the time of writing the names are under review and almost certain to be changed. Foreign visitors usually put up at the Hotel Minsk which, for the record, is on what used to be Lenin Prospekt, effectively part of the main Brest-Moscow road.

East of Minsk on the Moscow road is **Zhodino**, a museum-in-the-making. It is quintessential Soviet heavy industry, where standing at antiquated assembly lines the work-force heroically churned out the wheels on which the empire ran. Such Dickensian enterprises enabled Byelorussia to achieve a favourable balance of trade with the other republics. A bit further on, about 60 miles (100 km) east of Minsk, is **Borisov**, so-named after Boris, Prince of Polotsk. It is on the **Berezina River**, where nemesis in the form of the Russian army caught up with Napoleon his retreat from Moscow in 1812. The battle took place on the outskirts of Borisov, near the village of Studenka. Borisov is known today for its tapestries and musical instruments.

Orsha, a total of 350 miles (560 km) from Brest, shares with other Belarussian centres like Vitebsk an ancient history completely masked by an unimposing industrial appearance. There may well be more to such places than meets the eye, but international tourism had no place in Byelorussia's appointed role in the Soviet scheme of things so there was no infrastructure in place when independence was declared. Moreover, the sights which Western visitors might find interesting probably did not correspond with what officialdom thought was worth showing. Left to their own devices, independent Belarussians are bound to produce a different and very much more comprehensive list.

Minsk's sports stadium.

THE BALTIC STATES

One of the most perplexing problems facing the Paris peace conference in 1919 was what to do about the Baltic provinces of tsarist Russia which the Bolsheviks, not without a fight, had consented to let go. Lithuania had once ruled the largest empire in Europe. It was largely overwhelmed by Poland before both were swallowed, almost but not quite whole, by Russia in the 18th century. Estonia and what was put forward to the peace conference as an independent state called Latvia were, by any historical or political criteria, equally elusive.

Nevertheless, three independent states were internationally recognised under these names and lived a precarious existence while first the Bolsheviks and then Stalin made it plain that it was not a situation that could be countenanced forever. Their independence was sentenced to death by the Nazi-Soviet Pact just before World War II. The pact envisaged that the Baltic states would be parcelled out between them, but of course it became academic with Hitler's invasion of Russia. The Red Army came back in force towards the end of the war, and the three states were incorporated in the Soviet Union with ties so close that they were virtually Russian provinces once again.

Ukraine and Byelorussia apart, nowhere did the Soviet mill grind finer than in Estonia, Latvia and Lithuania. They occupied a special place in Soviet strategy, an updated version of Peter the Great's "Window to the West", which began with the founding of St Petersburg but envisaged expansion southwards to maximise Russia's access to the Baltic, often referred to as the "Northern Mediterreanean". Like its southern counterpart, it had a coastline over which the adjacent nations were ready to fight for every inch. Early Russia had been held to ransom by German Balts who controlled the Estonian and Latvian ports, and Peter the Great was determined that it would never happen again, a view with which the Soviet regime totally concurred. Lithuania was regarded in exactly the same light, and it was agents of the tsar, long before any thought of Soviet Man, who vowed to obliterate all signs of national Baltic identities.

The Russification of the Baltic provinces in the 19th century was so thorough that when the matter of their independence came up at the Paris peace conference one of the questions asked was sublimely naive: "Who are these people and whence did they come?" For three nations buried so deep in the history of others that their identities were long presumed to have been lost, they have surprisingly robust tales to tell.

Preceding pages: sports day at Riga; a traditional Baltics folk festival. **Left**, grandfather and granddaughter, Vilnius.

Common knowledge seems to have cottoned on to the fact that the Hungarian and Finnish languages are related but not that there is a third member of the group, Estonian. The kinship explains why, prior to independence, Estonian television aerials were aimed not at transmitters pouring out worthy images from the Soviet state service but out to sea – to Helsinki. The Finns returned the compliment by arriving in droves, the incentive in their case being a quick blackmarket foreign exchange fix to subsidise a weekend binge at bagatelle prices.

Canute's ambition: Finns and Estonians parted company early in their history and moved into different orbits. The Estonians were naturally exposed to developments on their southern flank, but in the event the first intruders arrived by ship, Danish Vikings. Canute, the legendary King of Denmark and England in the 11th century, intended to incorporate Estonia in his expanding empire but died before he could do very much about it. Two centuries later, Valdemar II despatched 1,000 ships to reactivate the plan.

This armada should have been invincible, but the Estonians resisted so fiercely that the Danes were in danger of being routed. They were only saved, so the story goes, by the stirring sight of a red banner with a white cross descending from heaven. It was clearly from God and meant for them as the Estonians were pagans. The Danes charged in with a second wind, captured Tallinn, and of course adopted the miraculous banner as the Danish national flag.

Ridding the Estonians of paganism was a Danish priority. "The simple idolators," says an early history, "had as little relish for the unexplained God of their invaders as for the heavy tribute by which they announced His presence." The Estonians who consented to baptism did so only "after their huts were razed, their land plundered, and their best hunters slain". The Danes appealed for help from German knights who were veterans of the Crusades and had been winning converts around Riga at the points of their uncompromising swords. In 1227, the knights announced that the job in Estonia was done.

The Teutonic Order moved on to other business while the Danes were occupied elsewhere. They transformed the Estonian economy into a model of medieval efficiency. Castles were built at strategic intervals, and towns grew up everywhere. Estonians were not invited to participate in this development. The social order was simple: knights as the nobility, imported lesser Germans as the urban bourgeoisie, and Estonians as serfs. Although the Teutonic Knights were defeated by Russia's Alexander Nevsky on frozen Lake Peipus in 1242, the system survived every political and religious change over the next six centuries. By 1347, the Teutonic Order had Estonia so tightly sewn up that the most the Danish monarchy could retrieve from a lost cause was to sell Tallinn to the Order for cash. That done, the knights renamed the city Reval.

Comfortable as the knights were in Reval, their aggressive expansion in the Baltic region generally brought them into conflict with the Lithuanians, especially when they usurped a chunk of Lithuanian territory called Prussia. Lithuania joined forces with Poland through a dynastic marriage recounted in the Lithuanian chapter of this book, and together they were able to defeat the Teutonic Order at the battle of Tannenberg (or Grunwald) in 1410. This shook the confidence of the knights in Reval but did not dislodge them. They had their separate trading interests in the north centred on the two ports, Reval and Narva, which were nicely positioned to handle Russia's Baltic trade.

Mongol Yoke: Russia's main trade had traditionally been with Constantinople in Byzantium, links which had led Kievan Russ and then Russia proper into the fold of the Eastern Orthodox Church. Relations with Constantinople, trade included, had been severely curtailed by the "Mongol Yoke" which was thrown over Russia in the 13th century, causing much of Russia's foreign trade, limited though it was, to be funnelled through Reval and Narva. Two developments in the latter half of the 15th century pushed Reval, Narva and Estonia in general

Left, Alexander Nevsky and the Teutonic Knights battle on the ice of Lake Peipus in 1242.

on to a higher plain. The first was the Turkish conquest of Constantinople in 1453, which meant Russia's only viable outlet was the Baltic. The second was Ivan III wriggling free of the Mongol Yoke and deciding that Narva, at least, belonged to Russia.

As far as the Teutonic Knights were concerned, Russia freed from Mongol constraints was an alarming enemy, and they turned to Sweden for protection. Sweden's readiness to oblige was reminiscent of the Trojan Horse, and the Germans were soon aghast as the Swedish crown and nobility systematically stripped them of their Estonian estates. With perfect but imprudent impartiality, the Germans eventually did a complete about-face

had other things he wanted to attend to, namely the Patkul business covered in the Latvian section of this book. "There is no glory in winning victories over the Muscovites," he said breezily, "they can be beaten at any time."

While Charles went off in pursuit of the wily Patkul and his conspirators, Peter, who had not been present at Narva, licked his wounds on a Baltic beach, dreamt of building St Petersburg in what was then a malarial swamp, and entrusted the military riposte to a Scot, one Ogilvie. The second assault on the Swedish garrison was successful, the gratified Ogilvie ordering that no prisoners be taken, military or civilian. The most fright-

in asking for Russian help against their misjudged Swedish benefactors. By then Peter the Great had ascended the Russian throne, and he readily agreed. The die was cast for a titanic struggle which came to the known as the Great Northern War.

Peter made the first move by closing on the Swedish garrison in Narva with 35,000 men. Charles XII of Sweden, not yet 20, hurried to its aid with a force of 8,000. The Swedes approached the encircling Russians in a blinding snow storm and plunged straight into battle. The Russians were caught by surprise and cut to pieces. Charles's officers advised him to press on at once to Moscow, but he

ful massacre was going on when Peter showed up. He is said to have stopped the proceedings by cutting down some of the crazed executioners with his own sword.

With Narva under his belt, Peter turned to the Swedish garrison in Reval. The defenders fought valiantly before succumbing to thirst and an untimely outbreak of plague. Their last act before surrendering was to send an apology to their distant king for so doing. The first round of the Great Northern War therefore ended with Russia in control

Above, "divine intervention" assists the Danish invasion of Estonia in the 13th century.

of the two Estonian strongholds, but there was more and worse to come. The campaign became a personal duel between Charles and Peter which swept across the breadth of Europe. They developed a high degree of mutual admiration, but in the process the Baltic states were devastated, the aftermath of battle compounded by rampant plague. By the Peace of Nystad in 1721, Sweden formally renounced all claims to the Baltic lands, and Estonia among others awaited a first taste of Russian rule destined to last into the 20th century.

Cunning evasion: As previouly intimated, the German nobility and urban bourgeoisie managed to survive the Russian regime with their privileges intact, the latter if only because there was no Russian bourgeoisie who could have replaced them. The Estonian serf, on the other hand, was no better off than his counterpart in Russia. They lived and died "like beasts", according to one account, "happy if they could subsist on dusty bread and water". This assessment was echoed by a 19th-century visitor who said of the Estonian peasant that "we can find but little interesting in his character; nor indeed is it fair to look for any, excepting perhaps that of a servile obedience or cunning evasion, among a people so long oppressed".

Reval was a decidedly exotic city for the large numbers of Russians who made a summer pilgrimage from St Petersburg. For them it was the South of France with perhaps a dash of Lourdes thrown in. "I have seen delicate creatures," wrote an English visitor in 1841, "who at first were lifted from the carriage to the bathing-house, restored day by day, and in a fortnight's time bathing with a zest that seemed to renew all their energies." Lady Eastlake, the visitor in question, also detected a high level of police surveillance. Tsar Nicholas I was on the throne, the mood of the 1848 revolutions was in the air, and official paranoia was rife. If nothing else, police activity suppressed the level of general crime. There had been only 87 disdemeanours among Reval's population of 300,000 over a whole year, she discovered, "and five of these consist merely in travelling without a passport".

The wave of romantic nationalism which swept through Europe after the 1848 revolutions manifested itself in Estonia through the formation of a group known as the Young Estonians. Their immediate discontent was against what touched them most closely, German economic domination, but being anti-German did not make them pro-Russian, and certainly not pro-tsar. The entire structure of the status quo repelled them, and that made Marxism attractive.

In this mood, World War I confronted Young Estonians with a Hobson's choice of supporting Germany or Russia when, in truth, they were implacably opposed to both. Nevertheless, thousands found themselves in Russian uniform whether they liked it or not. Their plea for specifically Estonian units under Estonian officers fell on deaf ears. At the same time, there was no doubt about where the sympathies of the large and powerful Germanic population lay.

The Russian revolution in 1917 and the subsequent separate peace between Germany and Russia looked as if it might ease the dilemma. An Estonian national army was formed and 170,000 volunteers immediately signed up, but at the same time a smaller though still substantial number joined the so-called international brigades established by the Bolsheviks. Heedless of various exiled politicians calling for Estonian unity and independence, the two camps went at one another's throats.

Fierce battles were fought over Tallinn between local Bolsheviks backed by Red Guards against nationalist irregulars who included schoolboys and the Tallinn fire brigade. The tide at first went in favour of the Bolsheviks. By the end of 1918, they held Narva and Tartu, and Russian comrades had advanced to within 20 miles (32 km) of Tallinn. It amounted to civil war and it was fought with all the savagery traditionally associated with one.

Estonia triumphs: The tide eventually turned, although not without considerable clandestine help given to the nationalists by the British Navy. The final battle was at Narva, and resulted in the nationalist coalition driving some 18,000 Bolsheviks across the Russian border. One year later, with the Bolsheviks still engaged in heavy fighting elsewhere, Russia renounced its sovereignty over Estonia "voluntarily and for ever".

Victory for independent Estonia brought problems of a different kind, the most awkward being with Latvia over the border town of Valka. The two countries, which had so recently been closely linked in the struggle against the Bolsheviks, came to the brink of war over who should have Valka, an important rail junction. A British colonel was the reluctant arbitrator. He listened to both sides for a while, said he had heard enough, and unrolled a bale of barbed wire down the middle of the main street. One side was in Estonia, the other in Latvia. Both parties were dissatisfied.

A visitor to Valka a couple of years later reported that the wire had been removed but it was necessary to have police permission to cross the road. History repeated itself in 1992 when, with Estonia and Latvia again independent, the divided citizens of Valka, it

was reported, set about building a wall down the middle of the main street.

While all minds in Valka were on the wire down the middle of the road, Communists elsewhere in Estonia were not inclined to accept the new government. There was an attempted putsch in 1924 which resulted in street fighting in Tallinn. Numerous other disturbances were countered by authoritarian measures, amounting to dictatorship.

Before the war, more than half of Estonia had belonged to 200 German-Balt families. An Agrarian Reform Law passed after independence took over all baronial and feudal estates, plus those belonging to the Church and the former Russian Crown lands, and redistributed them as 30,000 new farms. The peasant's lot was further improved by the right to engage in trade.

Estonia was still struggling to find its feet when any gains were put in jeopardy by the secret protocol of the 1939 Nazi-Soviet Pact. Stalin and Hitler agreed between them that the Soviet Union would annex Estonia together with Finland and Latvia, and Germany could help itself to Lithuania, although this was later amended to give Lithuania to Russia as well. On 28 September 1939, the day after the amendment had been agreed, Estonia was forced to sign a non-aggression pact with the USSR which provided for the stationing of 25,000 troops in the country. A blatantly rigged election set the stage for an outright annexation on 6 August 1940, and almost immediately 60,000 Estonians were forcibly conscripted into the Soviet army, deported to labour camps or executed.

The collapse of the Nazi-Soviet Pact naturally changed everything. German forces invaded in July 1941, meeting determined resistance in Estonia where large numbers of Soviet troops were cut off. Estonia had only about 1,000 Jewish families, nothing like the numbers in Latvia and Lithuania, but 90 per cent of them were murdered as Germany set about incorporating the country into the Third Reich. By the end of the war, however, some 70,000 Estonians had fled to the West and the population had dropped from its pre-war level of 1.13 million to 850,000.

The educated classes had not waited to find out what would happen when the German forces in Tallinn surrendered to the Red Army on 22 September 1944. Tens of thousands of those who did not flee were consigned to Soviet labour camps, and into the vacuum thus created were introduced comparable numbers of Russians with the dual purpose of manning heavy industry and completing the Russification programme begun by the tsars.

After the war: Post-war Estonia inched along the familiar Soviet groove – including, of course, an economy under Moscow's remote command. A programme of heavy industrialisation was pursued with extraordinary insensitivity even by Soviet standards. Unlovely factories right in the middle of long-established residential areas and poisonous levels of pollution were tailor-made for the environmental lobby which raised a nervous voice in the late 1980s and soon became a cloak for more radical change.

The voices suddenly shed their nervousness with an astonishing outburst in 1988. A political rally ended with 10,000 voices raised in song. It was a patriotic Estonian song unheard in public for years and one which in Stalin's time would have been a one-way ticket to Siberia. Spontaneous massed singing went on all summer and coaxed out of hiding a forest of banned national flags. The Estonian Communist Party was knocked off balance by what became known as the Singing Revolution and desperately tried to recover by lending its name to national causes,

disingenuous message was sent to Moscow to the effect that there were Estonians ready "to accept parliamentary responsibility should the need arise". There were anxious moments wondering whether the Red Army would intervene as it had in Czechoslovakia in 1968, but by then the Soviet Union was under siege on all sides and, moreover, the decision rested with the altogether more benign figure of Mikhail Gorbachev.

The technicalities of independence were attended to by the Estonian Supreme Soviet's blithe conclusion that as the existing constitution was invalid, and had been ever since its inception in 1919, there was really nothing that needed to be abolished. This

including the restoration of Christmas celebrations and turning clocks back an hour so that they were on Estonian, not Russian, time. These developments were monitored with the gravest misgivings by the ethnic Russians who made up about 25 per cent of the 1 million population. In Narva, 96 per cent of the population was Russian.

With the momentum towards independence gaining speed, only 1 in 20 of the resident Russians took advantage of, or qualified for, the offer to Estonian citizenship. A

happened to correspond with the view of Western governments which still recognised the republican constitution of 1918. The Russian connection, forged in the noise of the Great Northern War between Peter the Great and Charles XII of Sweden, thus ended, to everyone's relief, in the proverbial whimper, but one which demands a somewhat sinister postscript. The criterion for citizenship in independent Estonia, aimed at excluding Russians, was the ability to speak, read and write Estonian up to standards so high that not even the Finno-Ugrian cousins in Finland could have hoped to meet them, had they chosen to try.

Left, Estonia's singing revolution, 1988. **Above**, independence seekers unfurl suppressed flags.

ESTONIA: WHAT TO SEE

In the days when Western visitors travelled to Estonia by sea, their first sight was invariably of the capital Tallinn rising above the port, and the standard reaction, as recorded in a number of travel books, was of surprise at quaint houses with steeply peaked roofs set among ancient ruins.

As may be gleaned from the preceding history, Eastonian towns were and to some degree still are decidedly German in appearance and atmosphere. The influence can be traced to the Teutonic Order in the 13th century but, as our history also shows, the Danes had already left their mark by then and there were Swedes and Russians to follow.

Estonia's size is such that any two points are, if necessary, within a comfortable day's driving of one another. After Tallinn's historical sights and medieval architecture, the cities of most likely interest are Narva, if only because it triggered the Great Northern War, and Tartu, the university city which was known in German times as Dorpat and in Russian as Yuriev.

Tallinn: The Estonian capital has a long tradition of playing host to visitors with a particular reason to be there. In the 19th century, as we have seen, special transport was laid on for the annual summer influx from St Petersburg. Between the world wars, it was the favourite haunt of Western diplomats based in Moscow and feeling the need to get away from the reigning austerity. References to weekends spent in Tallinn crop up in diplomatic memoirs and give the impression of a Little Paris.

In more recent times, while Estonia was part of the Soviet Union, the restaurants and nightlife in Tallinn were the best within reach of Russians who had neither documents nor the foreign currency to venture abroad. For them, Tallinn was a slice of Olde Europe. For pre-war Finns, it was an oasis because Finland was dry. Finland is no longer

Left, Tallinn, showing St Olav's spire.

dry, but it is still extremely expensive, and the flow of thirsty Finns continues unabated.

Tallinn is a compact city and has prominent landmarks which enable you to take a chronological tour. An Arab traveller and geographer, Abu Abdullah Mohammed Idris, left the earliest written account of the future capital. It was then, he wrote in the 12th century, "a small town resembling a large fortress". King Eric IV of Denmark had laid its foundations in the 11th century with a fortress on Castle Hill, which the Danes knew as Toompea and the Germans later called Dombeg.

The fortress itself was Lindanisse, but the peasants knew it as Dani-Linna, or Danish town, which in due course became Tallinna and then shrank to Tallinn. Valdemar II, whom we met in the preceding chapter, came along in 1219, pulled down Eric's fortress and built a new one. It was at this stage that "Reval" came into currency. The origins are not absolutely certain, but the name may have been derived from the Danish "Refwell", in which case it was probably a reference to the "reef" of stone which formed the natural perimeter of the city.

Valdemar's 1219 creation was the "Small Castle" on Castle Hill. Parts of the 60-ft (19-metre) wall and three bastions survive, the most conspicuous of which is "**Long Hermann**". The Teutonic knights made some improvements to the Small Castle, which became their stronghold. During the Middle Ages, it functioned as the seat of government, at times the *hated* seat of government, and with the "Great Castle" growing up alongside, it became a castle within a castle, rather like the Vatican as a city within Rome.

The moat was filled in and the east wall knocked down in the reign of Catherine the Great to make room for the baroque building which is still used as government offices. Much of the Great Castle was destroyed by fire in 1684. The grand houses built on the site were the prized residences of the German-Balt barons.

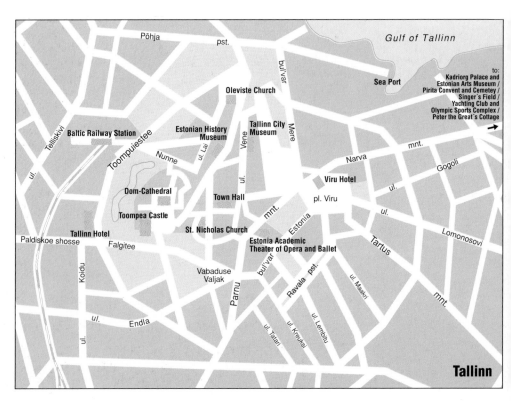

The imposing Gothic **cathedral** on Castle Hill – the **Toomkirk** or, to the Germans, the Domkirk – was begun in the 13th century by the Teutonic Knights. They made their peace with God here before setting out to do battle with Alexander Nevsky, the Russian prince, on frozen Lake Peipus. They were heavily defeated, and when the Russians built their Orthodox cathedral in Tallinn in 1894, was it pure coincidence that they named it after their victorious forebear? The Toomkirk has several interesting tombs, including a rather surprising one, by Giacomo Quarenghi, containing the remains of the Scottish admiral Samuel Greig who was serving in Catherine the Great's fleet when it smashed the Turkish navy at Chesme in 1780.

The **Upper** and **Lower Towns** were once linked only by Pikk Jalg Street, very steep and evidently very dangerous. While horse-drawn traffic struggled uphill, those coming down were almost out of control. With blind corners, head-on collisions were inevitable. "To obviate this," a 19th-century visitor wrote, "all postilions and coachmen descending the hill are bound to give notice of their approach by a loud whoop, which a sentinel stationed in the archway repeats with all his strength for the benefit of those approaching from the town." Pedestrians simply had to take their chances.

The same visitor reported that the Upper Town had no proper drainage. The spring thaw therefore discharged a torrent of dirty ice water into the town. "For several days the householders contemplate with perfect equanimity the spectacle of the stream of running water, while deep puddles of a black, merging into an orange, hue settle at the foundations of their houses, particularly embosoming the house door, and ooze into their cellar grates."

Before descending to the Lower Town, it is worth identifying the 400-ft (120-metre) steeple of the so-called **Oleviste Church**, actually a commemoration of St Olav, Norway's first serious Christian and among those who made the trip to these Baltic shores to

drum the faith into unimpressed local pagans. Old Tallinn had its own wall and towers, two of which still stand out. One was nicknamed Kiek-in-de-Kok, apparently because it afforded a view into people's kitchens. The second is "Stout Margaret", named after the formidable queen who united the three Scandinavian crowns, guarding the Coast Gate. Stout Margaret houses a museum covering local history since the 17th century; the preceding centuries are dealt with by the museum in the Town Hall.

A notable building at No. 26 Pikk Street is now the **House of Culture** but was formerly the local seat of the Blackheads (Schwarzhaupterhaus), a society with houses in a number of Baltic cities. The Blackheads were a quasi-military order and the Tallinn Blackheads, in particular, were a notable cavalry unit whose name lived on as long as World War II. Next door is the home of the Olaf Guild, curiously a medieval guild for specifically non-German craftsmen.

On the other side of Pikk Street is another and the most exclusive guild, the **Great Guild**, whose members were not only hugely rich but also enjoyed the sole right to supply the city with its councillors. This early 15th-century house, graced with the city's coat-of-arms, has a magnificent ceremonial hall where the good burghers let their hair down. The prize for the winner of an annual beauty contest was, strangely, the right to free one convict in the city jail. As the present **Historical Museum of the Estonian Academy of Sciences**, it may not be as lively as it once was, but the scholarly value of the collection of documents, coins and archaeological finds is incalculable.

The old market square, now **Town Hall Square**, produced many of the finds which ended up in the museum. It holds the secret to what existed here before the Danes, Teutonic Knights *et al*. In view of the unsavoury mess caused by the absence of drains in the Upper Town even in the 19th century, it is curious that the lower town had a well-engineered sewerage system in the 12th

Flower market in Tallinn.

century. The town hall, still used as such, is in almost its pristine Gothic form. The city stalwart serving as a weather-vane on top of the building is a replica of the original Old Toomas who has since been removed to graceful retirement in the museum.

Perhaps it ought to be remembered that until the end of the 19th century, ethnic Estonians had no part in the business that was conducted in this square. When the German burgher monopoly on commerce was relaxed, it was only to admit other foreigners.

A vivid picture survives of life in the square in tsarist times: "With the standing colony of army and navy is come also the long-bearded Russian Kupetz, or merchant, who is seen pacing gravely before his open shop, where neither fire nor candle is permitted, his hands drawn deep within his ample sleeves, his face nestled between his warm cap and beard, but who, at the moment a customer approaches, retires behind his counter and asks what the Sudarina, or signora, requires… These are the shops whence the Wirthschaft is provided wholesale with tea, coffee, and all the items of grocery; including the Pastello, or Russian bonbon, the dried sweetmeats from Kieff, etc."

There were a few Estonian peasants to be seen – "long-haired and long-coated" – and also Swedes "who sledge over the smooth ocean-track and sell their commodities of coarse linen and lace from door to door, or practise contraband acts with greater caution."

It is not possible in the space available here to do justice to Tallinn, and visitors must be left to make their own discoveries. In winding alleys barely wide enough to roll a barrel, and with history dripping out of the brickwork, it is a challenge which ought to be relished.

Kadriorg, or Kateriyna Org (Catherine's Valley), is only a tram-ride from Tallinn and should on no account be missed. The background to the baroque palace which is now the **Fine Arts Museum** was Peter the Great's preoccupation with turning Russia into a maritime power. He was a frequent visi-

Tallinn: the Lower Town.

tor when his fleet was moored here. Peter was content to stay in a modest house himself, but was struck by the idea of building a palace for Martha, the buxom Latvian serving wench who had first become his mistress and then, changing her name to Catherine, his wife. A fuller version of this story is given in the Latvian section of this book. He took two architects, Zemtsov and Michetti, off the job of building Petersburg to run up a palace for her while he progressively bought up the surrounding land to the tune of several million roubles.

The palace became a favourite with his successors, and Catherine the Great (not to be confused with Catherine, *née* Martha) invited Maria Theresa of Austria here to sign a peace treaty over Silesia. Much of the land was sold off over the years, but there is still a substantial park attached to the palace. Meanwhile, the little house which Peter had previously stayed in still stands and is kept just as it was in his day.

As the Fine Arts Museum, the palace

now houses a comprehensive collection of the Estonian realist school as well as 20th-century art and sculpture. The modern building in the park is a gigantic open-air stage and auditorium, built in 1960 for the Tallinn Song Festival. The "stage" is large enough for 30,000 singers to entertain an audience of 100,000. A bronze angel in the park commemorates the crew of *Rusalka*, a Russian battleship which sank with all hands in the Gulf of Finland in 1893. A second monument honours Yevgeni Nikonov, a Russian sailor who was taken prisoner by the Germans in 1941. Resisting all their ways of making him talk, he was strapped to a tree and burnt alive, thus becoming a posthumous Hero of the Soviet Union.

Pirita, not far from Kadriorg, is Tallinn's beach and water sports centre and includes – a rare bird in Eastern Europe – a motor-racing circuit. The huge yachting marina was built for the 1980 Olympics and has its own highway link with Tallinn, or it is possible to catch buses Nos. 1, 8 or 34. Near the beach are the ruins of the **nunnery of St Brigit**, built in 1407 by three members of the Reval Town Council. It was destroyed in 1577 during the siege of Tallinn by Ivan the Terrible.

Narva: The twin fortresses of Narva, glowering at one another across the Narva River, the border with Russia, are the symbols of a medieval arms race between Russia and what amounted to the Western world. The one known as Hermannstadt, first built by the Danes and sold to the Teutonic Order in 1347, safeguarded the early Baltic trade route with Russia.

When Russia threw off the Mongol Yoke, this Baltic outlet was considered too strategic to be left any longer in the exclusive hands of the German Balts, and in 1492 Ivan III moved in to secure the river port by building his fortress opposite. The knights responded by enlarging their fortress so that it overlooked Ivan's, and he in turn called in Italian engineers to redress the situation. Legend has it that in their haste the Italians forgot to include a church in their extension. An enraged Ivan gave

Yachting centre at Pirita.

them just 24 hours to make amends and, with the help of St Nicholas, they narrowly met the deadline.

The Teutonic Knights, as we have seen, took fright at Russia's growing power and called for the assistance of Sweden. Swedish engineers added the bastions along the river front and dug the network of underground passages which have since sprouted stalactites. Once the Swedes had installed themselves in the fortress – and expropriated German estates all over Estonia – they proved impossible to budge, and the Germans turned a full circle by then calling on the Russians for help, a request which Peter the Great was all too ready to grant. The Russian siege of the fortress and Charles XII's hasty arrival with Swedish reinforcement resulted in a battle in a raging snowstorm which saw the Russians cut to pieces. Peter's second attempt, commanded by the Scot Ogilvie, was successful and is commemorated by the plaque on the Victoria bastion.

The battles at Narva triggered the Great Northern War which eventually devastated the entire Baltic region, but in the meantime Peter built a palace in Narva (in Ruutli tan) and gave the house opposite, No. 20, to his friend Prince Menshikov. The scene of the second battle, after which a massacre of Narva's civilian population was only averted by Peter's personal intervention, is a little distance outside the city in the Priska woods, almost precisely the same spot where in 1918 the Estonian nationalists defeated their Bolshevik compatriates, driving them across the border with their Red supporters.

After Estonia's annexation by Russia in 1940, however, the Russians came back as job-seekers in Soviet industry, and after independence only 4,500 out of Narva's population of 82,000 qualified by the language criterion as ethnic Estonians.

Tartu: Known to the Germans as Dorpat and to the Russians as Yuriev, Tartu is said to be the oldest settlement in all the Baltic states – founded by Yaroslav of Kiev in 1030. "Tar" refers

Narva Fort, in Estonia, and Ivan's Fort, across the border in Russia.

to the supreme god of Estonian mythology, a name obviously not far removed from the Scandinavia Tor.

It is famous for its **university**, founded by Gustavus Adolphus of Sweden in 1632 to encourage the spread of Lutheranism not only in his new Baltic conquests but where he thought it was really needed, across the border in Russia. When Russia took the country over from Sweden, the university was turned around, as it were, to broadcast Russian propaganda, thus anticipating modern coups in which rebels make a bee-line for the radio and television station. That aside, the university has powerful intellectual traditions and has produced a great number of distinguished scholars in many disciplines. The magnificent library is the sacristy of the **Cathedral of Tartu Castle**.

The university later became the repository of Estonian folk culture when it was in danger of being lost. This work was done in conjunction with the National Museum in Tartu: the final tally was 45,000 songs, 10,000 fairy tales and sayings, 52,000 proverbs, 40,000 riddles and 60,000 superstitions. Some of the riddles seem to lose something in translation – "How many stars in the sky?" "Two million, and if you don't believe me, count them" – but perhaps it is not for outsiders to pass judgement.

The town has an unusual stone **bridge** built by Catherine the Great across a river which flows not into the sea but into Lake Peipus. The pagan legend attached to the river concerns a god, Wanemuine, who was responsible for teaching men to speak and animals and birds to make their various sounds. Being stupid, fish did not surface to hear what was going on. Beneath the water, they could only watch what appeared to be a mime, hence their inability to sing – although they do their best by going through mouthing motions. This story is, of course, logged among the 10,000 tales mentioned above.

Unfortunately, most of Tartu's medieval monuments have been destroyed by fire or war, including a Swedish fortress which once stood on the Dom, the hill in the city centre. There remains in the surrounding park a large stone said to have been used for sacrifices in pagan times.

Lakes Peipus and Chud: Peipus, the second largest lake in Europe, is a natural buffer between Russia and the Baltic States, forcing armies to make long detours to the north or south of it, with one very famous exception when Alexander Nevski and the Teutonic knights advanced across the frozen ice to meet in the middle. With a plentiful supply of fish, the lake attracted settlement in the earliest days, and indeed the ancestral home of Estonia is an ancient fortress at Irboska.

The fortress, however, is no longer in Estonia, the Soviets having adjusted the border, which used to run down the middle of Lake Peipus, to absorb not only Irboska but Petseri, or Pechora, the principal shrine of a colony of Old Believers, together with many of the Old Believers themselves.

A much reduced colony of Old Believers is still to be found near **Lake Chud** in Estonia. One of the reasons they are here is that in 1705 Peter the Great imposed a tax on men's beards. Although clearly an unusual tax, it appeared to be even-handed in that the tax rate was adjusted to the social status of the wearer and peasants were exempt if they stayed at home and did not show their beards in public.

This was only one measure among many designed to weed out certain Russian religious practices which were thought to corrupt the true precepts of Eastern Orthodoxy. These included the local habit of making the sign of the cross with only two fingers instead of three, the failure to build churches with five domes, the way "Jesus" was spelt, and an extra word which had crept into the Creed.

These reforms appalled the traditionalists who thereupon scattered, some to the Ukraine, some to Turkey and some to the southwestern shores of Lake Peipus, which were then in the state of Pskov, as opposed to Muscovy. This group became known as the Setu, and "Setumaa" was within Estonia when independence was declared in 1918.

The Setu were of course different from Estonians: they spoke Russian, the women wore a long, tight-fitting, white serge coat reaching to their ankles, the men had blue eyes – and enormous, untrimmed beards.

The religious fervour of the Setu had continued undiminished in their remote exile. It was their custom to chant funeral dirges appropriate to the manner of death, age, occupation and position of the deceased. One old woman was found to have committed to memory no fewer than 20,000 lines of song. The population was almost uniformly illiterate. The only education a woman needed, it was said, was to be able to sing her own wedding-songs.

The shrine of the Setu was the golden-domed fortified **Monastery of Pechori**. It is said that towards the end of the 15th century a hunter in the woods was mystified by the sound of singing issuing from the ground. All became clear when he uncovered some holy men in a cave, and it was around this cave that a monk named Cornelius built the monastery with walls of such impregnable design that Ivan the Terrible had him killed before he was commissioned to build any more for Ivan's enemies. Ivan is reputed to have regretted the killing and to atone for it he had Cornelius's body brought back to the church and buried there. Peter the Great later strengthened the walls even further.

The **Uspenski Cathedral** built over the cave was refurbished in Russian baroque at a later date, and there are still monks who spend their lives and are buried in the catacombs.

Pechori was a major Estonian tourist attraction during inter-war independence, but of course that changed when the Soviets moved the border on the grounds that the Setu were clearly Russians and had no business being in Estonia. It remains to be seen whether border formalities will one day be relaxed to enable people to nip across the frontier to pick up this detached bit of Estonian history. At the time of writing, Russian visas are not issued at the border, but the situation is nothing if not fluid.

Festival of medieval customs.

Latvia's capital, Riga, caught the imagination of the writer Graham Greene and, judging by his comments, might have joined the third man's Vienna, the quiet American's Saigon and our man's Havana as a "Greeneland" setting for one of his novels. "There was something decayed, 'Parisian', rather shocking in an old-fashioned way about the place," he observed between the world wars. "All the lights in Riga were dimmed by ten: the public gardens were quite dark and full of whispers, giggles from hidden seats, excited rustles in the bushes. One had the sense of a whole town on the tiles. It was fascinating, it appealed immensely to the historical imagination, but it certainly wasn't something new, lovely and happy."

Greene's novel would have captured, one imagines, the pathetic urgency with which Latvian nationalists tried during 20 years of unprecedented independence between the world wars to prove, perhaps even to themselves, that there actually was a Latvian nation and that they were not, as had often been said, a people "without history".

Common culture: The Paris peace conference after World War I agreed to recognise a Latvian state on little more than the strength of a shared language among the peasant populations of parts of historic Livonia and the Duchy of Courland. The Lett-speaking Latvians had painstakingly collected 2,300,000 items of "common knowledge" to show that they shared more than a language: 775,000 folk songs, 301,000 tales, 48,000 legends, 450,000 riddles, 244,000 proverbs, 334,000 beliefs, 48,000 incantations, 65,000 examples of folk medicine, and so on.

Attempts to scrape together a Latvian identity had begun before World War I under the disdainful noses of an alien landed gentry and urban bourgeoisie whose presence could be traced to 13th-century German knights and immigrants. When the Teutonic Order of Knights was no longer a military force, the German hold on the constituent parts of the future Latvia had been retained under the

guise of the Hanseatic League. Just before World War I, Riga was the apotheosis of a social and economic order which had endured for seven centuries: 90 percent of the city's population was German.

After occupation by the Nazis during World War II, the Red Army invaded in 1944 and Latvia was swept into the Soviet Union. The German Balts were replaced by Russian immigrants, and by 1989 the Latvians had been reduced to a bare majority of 51.8 percent in the country as a whole. Independence from the Soviet Union was a race against the loss of this 1.8 percent margin, and what has happened in Latvia since is a replay of this tortured national awakening.

Beginnings: Latvia simply means "the land of the Lett-speakers", an allusion to the ancient Indo-European Baltic settlements which pre-dated the arrival of the Slavs in Eastern Europe. They led an isolated existence and were still pagan when in 1180 Meinhard of Bremen began to preach Christianity around the mouth of the Daugava River, where Riga now stands. Meinhard managed to win a fair number of converts until he broke the news that being a Christian meant paying a tithe.

With freshly-minted converts deserting the cause fast and threatening to kill him, Meinhard appealed to the Pope for help. The Pope, as it happened, had just the men for the job, German Crusaders who had been conspicuously out of work since their expulsion from the Holy Land by Saladin, the conqueror of Acre. In 1200, 500 heavily-armed Knights of the Sword under the command of Bishop Albrecht von Buxhoerden sailed up the Daugava estuary in 23 ships and disembarked. Meinhard, they discovered, was dead, albeit from natural causes. Still, his Christian mission had to continue, and the hardened Crusaders were not to be trifled with. One chronicle tells how they went about it: "All the places and roads were red with blood."

Bishop Albrecht was nothing if not industrious. He threw a defensive wall around Riga and built within it a fortress and church. By 1211, he was ready to begin a cathedral. German civilians were imported to speed up the construction of what became a city state. The so-called Livonian Knights of the

Preceding pages: Riga Old Town. Left, a window in Riga's Dom Cathedral depicts the 1525 move from Catholic to Lutheran worship.

Sword were subsequently amalgamated with the Teutonic Order, and although defeated as a military force by Poland and Lithuania at the battle of Tannenberg in 1410, the German political and economic imprint was unassailable. It led in due course to the introduction of Lutheranism, an intolerable provocation to staunchly Roman Catholic Poland. As the dominant political power in the region, Poland's answer was to despatch Jesuits to root out the heresy.

Polish power in the Baltic region had mixed implications. The German economic system was designed for no other purpose than to serve German interests, and in this the Lett-speaking Latvians had been allowed no part

ter of 1601 which left 40,000 dead from hunger and cold. King Gustavus Adolphus of Sweden succeeded 20 years later where his predecessor had failed, but the German land barons who had instigated Swedish intervention were mortified when Sweden made it plain that their estates were considered the legitimate spoils of the wars. A similar pattern of events was unfolding elsewhere in the Baltic, and the embattled barons felt their only recourse was Russia.

The Great Northern War between Peter the Great of Russia and Charles XII of Sweden is covered in the Estonian chapters. Peter the Great's ultimate victory resulted in Russian domination of the Baltic generally.

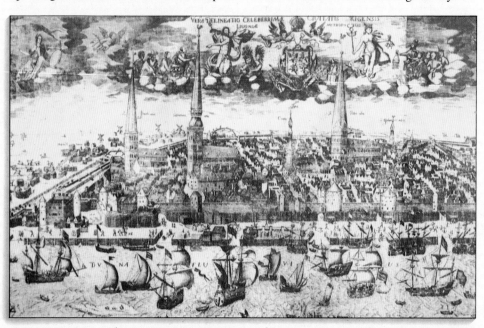

except at the rock-bottom level of agrarian serfdom. For them, Poland meant Jesuits, and Jesuits meant compulsory conversion to Roman Catholicism. For Riga's merchants, the Polish connection was a blessing because Riga became a conduit for Polish trade. The most troubled group was the German land barons who, if they did not actually lose their land to the Polish nobility, saw their serfs being alienated by the Jesuits. They saw their salvation in a friendly Protestant power; the obvious candidate was Sweden.

Poland resisted Swedish intervention to the hilt, and the bloody war fought largely on Latvian soil was followed by the bitter win-

Peter's Baltic blueprint was considerably influenced by a Livonian or Latvian serving wench known as Martha. She had married a Swedish army officer when Sweden held sway in the region but later caught Peter's eye when she appeared at his court on the arm of one of his ministers. She was, as portraits reveal, strikingly buxom. Nothing developed until she began appearing at court on the arms of several different ministers and finally on that of Peter's great friend, Prince Menshikov. In the interest of friendship, or perhaps because Menshikov knew what was

Above, Riga as it looked in the 1500s.

good for him, Martha was soon on Peter's arm and accompanying him on his travels. This went on for some years until Martha embraced Russian Orthodoxy, changed her name to Catherine and became Peter's wife. He personally crowned her in 1724.

The marriage was not perfect. Peter discovered after her coronation that Catherine was having an affair with one of his chamberlains. He apparently said nothing, but not long afterwards Catherine noticed an unfamiliar jar next to her bed as she prepared to retire. Curiosity caused her to lift the lid and peer in. The jar contained, swimming in a pickle solution, the head of the indiscreet chamberlain. With that little joke off his chest, Peter's marriage settled down until cut off less than a year later by his death.

Imperial potential: Succession to the throne was highly contentious, but nimble manipulation by Menshikov, Catherine's lover while she was still Martha, resulted in the previously unthinkable scenario of a Latvian serving wench ascending the Russian throne in her own right as Empress Catherine I. She seemed to have had genuine imperial potential but there was barely time to find out: at liberty to apply the authority and resources of office to her pursuit of strenuous pleasures, she was dead within two years.

Far from ending Latvian influence behind the Russian throne, Catherine's death elevated Peter's niece Anna, the widow of the Duke of Courland (the Duchy was later incorporated in Latvia). The more generous assessments of Anna's character are couched in terms like "monstrous". Beheaded or at least exiled, the Russian boyars who had backed Anna's bid for the throne were replaced by her German Balt cronies from Riga, quite the worst of whom was a certain Ernst-Johann Buhren, "a worthless and second-rate character, whose cruelty and boundless rapacity astounded even the Russians". The influence of the German-Balt Mafia extended beyond Anna's 10-year reign – death from debauchery – through Peter III (a feeble-minded drunk) and into that of Catherine the Great, herself of German origin although not from Latvia.

With the Mafia element capable of reaching into the heart of Russian power, it is not surprising that the Germans in Latvia were more than able to look after their local interests under Russian overlordship. The towns, especially Riga, continued to prosper, but if anything the lives of Latvian serfs got even worse. A peasant uprising in 1802 led to talk of its leader in terms of "the Lettish Bonaparte", but after his capture and excruciating death he was fittingly just "Poor Conrad".

Peasants viewed the Lutheran Church as the agent of their misery, a tendency which fell into the lap of a Russian Orthodox church struggling to make headway. The Orthodox catechism was translated into the Lett language and distributed free. The German establishment understood perfectly what was going on and retaliated by refusing to release land for any more Orthodox churches. In the end, Bismarck was prevailed upon to say something on behalf of the Lutherans, to which Tsar Alexander III responded by locking up some Lutheran pastors, sending others to Siberia, and telling 30,000 of their flock that they were thenceforth Orthodox.

Religious disputes aside, Latvian peasants drew some benefits from Russian overlordship, most notably the extension of the Russian railways to the Baltic coast, which invigorated previously barren areas and created supplementary jobs.

Connection by railway to Russia put Riga in a position potentially more lucrative than its previous role as a "Polish" port, and the German interests running the port were accordingly overjoyed. Their problem lay not in Russian domination but in liberated Latvian serfs making their way up the economic ladder. Having climbed a rung or two they found they could go no further, and the barrier was perceived to be German, although not without the Russian tsar lurking menacingly in the background. The easiest answers to their dilemma were to be found in the newly published writings of Karl Marx.

The Baltic Revolution of 1905 coincided with the uprising in St Petersburg and was aimed with equal venom at all things German and Russian. The Russian Imperial Guard was needed to restore order in Riga, and the tsar had no qualms about letting the outraged Germans join in the reprisals. Although many Germans left Latvia over the next few years as the clouds of World War I gathered and they faced the prospect of being trapped in Russian territory, the population of Riga was still not less than 50 per cent German when the war broke out.

The early stages of the war largely bypassed Latvia, which had units of the Russian army drawn up in defensive positions alongside a national army whose formation was not without certain Russian misgivings. In any case, the joint defensive strategy was made redundant by the Russian revolution, which resulted in the withdrawal of the Russian forces. Germany did not need reminding of Riga's strategic value, and the ill-trained national army was all that stood between it and the Kaiser's advancing forces. The Latvians put up a spirited defence of the port and lost 32,000 men before it fell. For some of the German troops, the march into Riga was something of a home-coming, and a most welcome one for the German Balts

over, the Kaiser accepted. The Allied victory in November 1918 killed the idea stone dead.

An *ad hoc* Latvian state council anticipated the Paris peace conference by proclaiming an independent state of Lett-speakers, i.e., Latvia, which would grant citizenship to all existing residents except Bolsheviks, whether or not they spoke Lett, and German unionists, with the same proviso. The testing moment came when the last 45,000 German troops were withdrawn. The Bolsheviks, a mixture of Lett-speaking exiles and Russians, charged in and summarily declared a Latvian Soviet Republic. An almost identical situation arose in Estonia, but the Estonian national forces were better or-

who had managed to remain in the city. The prize was a disappointment: the port had been stripped of its machinery and was all but useless. The machinery, and not a few of the population, had been shipped to Russia.

With Latvia under German occupation, nationalists were split, as they were in Estonia, between cooperating with the Germans to ensure that their Russian imperial masters never came back and taking at face value the solemn Bolshevik assurance that the new Russia would bear no resemblance to the old. German Balts managed to garner support for the idea of creating a Baltic monarchy and offered the crown to Kaiser Wilhelm. More-

ganised. They first expelled the Bolsheviks from their soil, and then crossed into Latvia to lend a hand there.

Independent Latvia was in a sorry state. The population was a third below pre-war levels, industrial output was virtually nil, and many children had never been to school. A land reform programme expropriated the German baronial estates and redistributed them in parcels to Latvian peasants. Agrarian reform was supplemented by a take-over of the remnants of industry and commerce. The Lett language was of course given official status, and there was a general revival of Latvian culture. Perhaps the most significant statistics were the changing population ratios. By 1939, Latvians were in a commanding majority, as high as 75 percent.

Steady if unspectacular progress came to a jarring halt in 1939. The Nazi-Soviet Pact was short-lived, and in June 1941 the German army drove out the Soviet forces. Latvia, with Estonia and Lithuania, was made part of Hitler's Ostland, and an estimated 90 percent of Latvia's 100,000 Jews were killed. Riga was reconquered by the Soviet Army on 8 August 1944, and 320,000 people out of a population of just 2 million were deported to the east; most never returned.

More executions and deportations followed in the purge of so-called bourgeoisie nation-

alists in 1949–53, and all the time Russians were surging in ostensibly to man the industrial machinery of the Five-Year Plans. Khrushchev purged 2,000 influential locals who raised their voices in protest, replacing them either with Russians or so-called Latovichi, Russians who purported to be Latvians on the strength of a few years' residence. The Communist Party of Latvia was packed with Khrushchev nominees.

Left, **Russians and Germans united against Latvia's 1905 uprising. Above**, **World War I German propaganda mocked the prospect of outside help from Scandinavia.**

New hope: Signs of a quiet revival of Latvian culture surfaced in the 1980s. First there was an unobtrusive restoration of derelict churches, then the odd historical monument. Poets and folk groups performed discreetly. The catalyst was the Green Movement. Environmental concern served as cover for the formation of nationalist pressure groups, and before long the underground press was addressing such taboo subjects as the activities of the secret police and human rights. The break-through occurred in 1986 when public protest stopped the construction of a hydro-electric scheme on the Daugava River.

With a softer line on public protest emanating from Moscow, the protest movement began to talk of national sovereignty within a Soviet Federation. The possibility of total independence was still too fanciful. The Popular Front, one of the emergent organisations, tended to favour reform within the status quo. But the National Independence Movement of Latvia (NIML), founded in June 1988 largely by victims of earlier purges, was more radical. They maintained that the illegal annexation of 1940 invalidated the Soviet regime, and a 1989 census which revealed that Latvians represented just 51.8 percent of the population lent an air of urgency to the campaign. The Russian minority rallied in opposition under the colours of an organisation called Interfront.

The Soviet Union eventually collapsed so quickly and so passively that it is easy to forget how bravely Latvians stuck their heads above the parapet with escalating demands for a free-market economy and a multi-party political system. No one could have ruled out the possibility, or even probability, of a Soviet invasion to put a stop to it. The pressure for a complete change eventually boiled down to a straight fight between nationalists lumped together as the "Democratic Bloc" and the pro-Russian Interfront.

Elections gave the nationalists a two-thirds majority. Anatalijs Gorbunovs was elected president, Ivars Godmanis became prime minister, and the country was renamed the "Republic of Latvia". Would the Kremlin let them get away with it? Presumably it will one day be known what the contingency plans in Moscow were. As things turned out, the Soviet Union was no more, and Russian nationalists were a pot neither in a position, nor inclined, to call the kettle black.

Riga: "This city of spires has the true air of a metropolis," wrote an appreciative visitor who went to see how Riga had recovered from the ravages of World War I.

His observations neatly complement those of Graham Greene. "She has traded so long; the clash of steel within her walls has been heard for so many centuries… Riga smells of sea salt and old timber, of incense and roasting coffee beans, of musk and sunflower seeds, of leather and lime-trees, of new-cut wood and limewash; all blended together into a pleasant, indistinguishable whole. You can wander along its narrow, twisting streets for days together and yet continually find some new thing to enjoy, here an ancient gateway, leading into the courtyard of an even more ancient monastery; there a sculptured window niche set high in a wall, or a quaint bas-relief on the blank face of a warehouse; or an engaging primitive carving on a house front tucked away behind a modern café…"

Visitors are inclined to enter the capital reborn after independence from the Soviet Union with the same kind of curiosity. They will find a city of nearly 1 million people spread out along both banks of the **Daugava River**. Most of it is new, but on an island created by a semi-circular canal fed by the river, they will find the old town, known as Vestriga, in a remarkable state of preservation given Riga's history of sieges and bombardment.

There is nothing left of the fortress which Bishop Albrecht von Buxhoerden built on his arrival with the German Crusaders in 1200, but there are traces of the old walls. The canal which cordons off the old city from the new used to be the moat, and Bastion Hill (Bastejkalns) Park just inside the canal had traces of ancient fortifications. **Marstalu Street** is now notable for 17th-century mansions built by prosperous German

<u>Left</u>, Riga, a mixture of old and new.

merchants, but it is evidently where the bishop's men stabled their chargers.

The cathedral which Bishop Albrecht started in 1211 took 500 years to complete and went through several transformations to become the Lutheran Cathedral, or **Domkirk**, in Junija Square, the largest church in the Baltic States. Among a number of interesting tombs is that of Bishop Meinhard, whose remains were transferred to Riga from his original grave at Iksile. The Domkirk organ, once the biggest in the world with its 6,768 pipes, was built by German craftsmen in 1884. The Soviets turned the cathedral into a concert hall and museums of navigation and local history, although the convent next door continued to function as such. In October 1988, the first religious service in the church for over 30 years was held.

The old city has three 13th-century churches in and around **Skarnu Street**, the most conspicuous being **St Peter's** with a steeple which was, until the Latvia Hotel went up, the tallest structure in the city. Its contemporaries are **St George's**, which later became a poorhouse and then a warehouse, and **St John's**, which has been rebuilt several times, hence the Renaissance features and baroque altar. It is said that the wall above the street contains the skull of a monk who murdered his bishop rather than hear him preach again.

The building next door with crow-step gables was founded in 1435 as lodgings for "homeless travellers and pilgrims" and later became a home for poor widows. The plaque outside commemorates Mayor Ek, the benefactor.

The yellowish castle was built in 1330 as the headquarters of the Teutonic Knights and now houses the **Riga Pioneer Palace** and museums devoted to Latvia's history, foreign art and literature respectively. The 19th-century **Arsenal** around the corner from **Pioneer Square** includes a bastion and parts of the old city wall. It will be noticed that the 13th-century **St Jacob's** (Yekaba) Church was built outside the wall for the benefit of Latvians as opposed to the privileged caste living

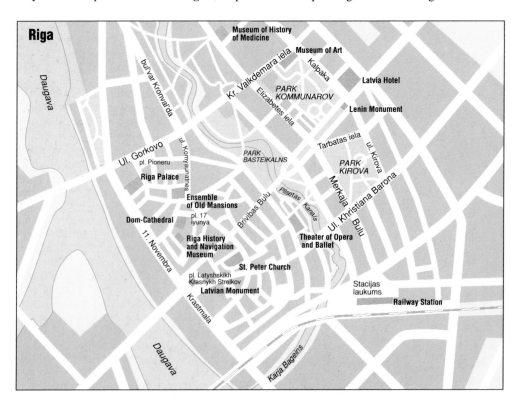

within. In the 16th century this church became Latvia's first school.

Maza Pils Street has fine examples of 15th-century architecture in the so-called Three Brothers ("Tris Brali"), one of them a house with holes cut in the floors to accommodate a small goods lift. A 1935 description of this part of town reads: "You may buy all manner of things from the wooden booths with their awnings, and be jostled by a wonderful variety of types: fair-haired country boys holding each other by the hand as they listen open-mouthed to the Jewish pedlar crying his wares; brown-faced peasant women, chaffering over a coloured handkerchief; bearded Russians who have come down from the forests with the timber rafts; long-haired priests with trailing black robes and high hats, and sailors from the ships along the quays."

There are a number of sites associated with the Swedish period in Latvia's history. Gustavus Adolphus entered the city in 1621 through the city gate which is still standing. It was subsequently rebuilt by the Swedes and is now known, together with the adjoining buildings, as the **Swedish Gate** (Zviedru Varti). They also rebuilt the **Powder Tower**, originally erected in 1330 and converted by the Communists into the Latvian Museum of the Revolution.

The mansion and coach-house near the corner of Lenin Street and the river promenade is the residence built by Peter the Great after beating Sweden in the Great Northern War. His first visit was in 1711, four years after his secret marriage to Martha, the future Empress Catherine, but a year before the official one. Peter did not particularly like Riga – "that confounded city", he called it – and for a while thought of rebuilding it nearer the sea.

Modern Riga, which picks up from Vestriga across the canal, is a curved grid of boulevards and streets interspersed with parks as neat as any American city. Bividas (Independence) Boulevard is the main thoroughfare linking the two. The **Museum of Art**, the **Museum of the History of Medicine** and

All smiles in Riga's Central Market.

the **Latvia Hotel** can all be found here.

Outside town, the **Mezaparks** is at 500 acres (200 hectares) or so Riga's largest. It has a zoo, amusement park, and a miniature railway run for and by children. There are also open-air theatres and boats. For a change of pace, it is sometimes possible in summertime to get to Mezaparks by the river boat service from the centre of town. The area contains the mass grave of some of the 3,600-odd people murdered by the Bolsheviks during their occupation of Riga in 1919. In the same period about 20,000 prisoners were kept in camps on various islands in the river.

Jurmala, west of Riga, is a string of small villages along miles of sandy beaches. It was popularised as a resort area by Russian officers after the Napoleonic Wars and became a major holiday destination for their compatriots.

The individual villages tend to have their specialities: **Dzintari**, for example, is for music lovers and has a philharmonic orchestra. Otherwise, there are all sorts of recreational facilities as well as the many and varied forms of therapy which East Europeans tend to regard as an integral part of a happy holiday. This is the place, apparently, for fixing high blood pressure. Trains run backwards and forwards at regular intervals between city and beach.

About 11 miles (17 km) from Riga in the direction of Salaspils is **Iskile** with the ruins of the oldest castle in the country. This is where the monk Meinhard first began his missionary activities among the pagan Latvians in 1180. It was his difficulty in exacting a tithe from his somewhat reluctant converts that led to the intervention of the German Crusaders. Meinhard was originally buried here after his death in 1196; his body was later transferred to the Domkirk in Riga. Iskile was the scene of some of the most bitter fighting between Latvians and Germans because it held the key to Riga. The area changed hands several times during 1915. The small peninusula formed by the bank of the river was called the "Island of Death".

Salaspils, a few miles further on, has the unwanted distinction of being the site of a Nazi concentration camp in which more than 100,000 people from the Soviet Union, Czechoslovakia, Poland, Austria, the Netherlands, Belgium and France were murdered.

Well worth seeing is the sumptuously restored **Rundale Castle**, 6 miles (10 km) west of Bauska and about an hour's drive south from Riga. Designed by the noted Russian/Italian architect Bartholomeo Francesco Rastrelli, it was built between 1736 and 1768, becoming the summer residence for the Dukes of Courland. Catherine II later gained control of the palace and in 1920 it became the people's property. After years of benign neglect, restoration began in 1972 and craftsmen from all over the former Soviet Union laboured to recreate the elegance of the mid-1700s. Today two-thirds of the rooms in the U-shaped building have been finished; those on view include the Gilded and White Halls, several state apartments filled with period furnishings, and a permanent exhibit of Latvian, Russian and Western European decorative arts.

Left, art nouveau in modern Riga. **Right**, Rundale Castle.

LAURYNAS
STUOKA-GUCEVIČIUS

THE MAKING OF LITHUANIA

No country in Eastern Europe has suffered swings of fortune as outrageous as those of Lithuania. Having arrived very early in the migrations across the Northern Plain, the Indo-European Lithuanians at first spread expansively across western Russia, Ukraine, Belarus and Poland. They were progressively evicted by new arrivals until they were concentrated along the Baltic shoreline. Obdurate Lithuanian paganism inflamed the pious wrath of the Christian Teutonic Knights, who conquered a slice of Lithuanian territory which they kept for themselves while retaining its former name, Prussia.

In the 12th century, Mindaugus feigned Christian baptism in the hope of winning Pope Innocent's sympathy and recognition as Prince of Lithuania, but his conversion was pure expediency as he immediately demonstrated by sacrificing a number of captured Christians to Perkunas, the Lithuanian God of Thunder. Imperial expansion was mainly the work of Prince Gedimnas (1315–41), and it developed so fast that the imperial subjects, who for the most part spoke Russian and were Orthodox by religion, far outnumbered the rulers. Russia under the Mongol Yoke was in no position to resist the spread of the Lithuanian empire.

History might well have provided another case of the rulers being absorbed by the ruled but for the fact that Poland was then experiencing difficulties and had been tacked on to the Hungarian kingdom under King Louis of Anjou. Not certain what to do with Poland, Louis had nominated his daughter Jadwiga as its queen in the knowledge that whomever she married would become king. When Jadwiga turned 12, arrangements were made for her to marry young Wilhelm von Habsburg in Cracow, then the Polish capital.

As matters stood, Lithuania seemed likely to become a genuine Russian state, and Poland was poised to go into the Habsburg bag. This fate was averted by the arrival in Cracow of a delegation of Lithuanian nobles who went into urgent conference with their Polish counterparts. Among other things,

both parties were concerned about the aggressive Teutonic Order. The outcome of the conference was that the archbishop was sent to have a word with little Jadwiga in Cracow castle. She learned that the wedding was off and, subject to one or two conditions, she would be marrying instead Prince Jagiello of Lithuania, who was three times her age and had the fresh blood of his uncle on his hands. Jadwiga watched helplessly as the castellan led the downcast Habsburg boy out of the castle and banished him from the kingdom.

The marriage of Jagiello and Jadwiga took place in 1385, which made the bridegroom King Ladislaus V of Poland. He fulfilled the preconditions to the marriage by submitting to baptism, smashing the statue of Perkunas, and ordering the mass conversion of his Lithuanian subjects. To begin with, and for the better part of two centuries afterwards, a large section of the empire remained under a separate line of Lithuanian princes, but the core under the Polish-Lithuanian dynastic union was from the outset thoroughly Polonised. Vilnius, founded by Prince Gedimnas, took the Polish name Wilno.

The combined strength of Poland and Lithuania was sufficient to defeat the Teutonic Order at the battle of Tannenberg (Grunwald) in 1410. With this danger removed and Russia still out of commission under the Mongol Yoke, Poland put its cultural stamp on Lithuania. Instead of acquiring, as once seemed likely, all the characteristics of a Russian state, including religion, language and the Cyrillic script, Lithuania followed the Polish model in all respects. This was particularly true of the Lithuanian nobility, who were quick to appreciate what they gained personally from Poland's rigid but efficent social and political order. The union between the two countries was tightened at Lublin in 1569 so that there was little to tell between them by the time they were jointly dismembered during the 18th century by Russia, Prussia and Austria.

The torso of Lithuania was bequeathed to Russia – Prussia got "Little Lithuania" – which set in motion a conflict between Polonised Lithuanians who were Roman Catholics and successive tsars who wished to Russify them, including the imposition of Russian Orthodoxy. Russian tactics wavered between the carrot, which offered Lithuanian peasants 120 acres (50 hectares) of land each, an offer which Russian peasants would have seized had it ever been made, and the stick, which reserved jobs in the state service for members of the Orthodox church.

Intransigence, a luxury more available to educated Lithuanians than peasants, hardened Russian attitudes. The university was closed down, only Russians were entitled to an education above the elementary level, the Lithuanian language could not be used for official purposes, and possession of a prayer book in the Latin alphabet (rather than

were almost immediately under attack by the German army and, in conducting a scorched-earth retreat, marched the Lithuanian men of military age back to Russia with them. The approaching German troops were greeted as liberators, but it was soon apparent that they, too, regarded Lithuania as a source of free labour. German policy was not to entertain any idea of Lithuanian independence but to re-incorporate the country administratively into Poland, which Germany occupied.

While the post-war Paris peace conference convened to consider claims for independence, including one by Lithuania, the unresolved Bolshevik revolution in Russia overflowed into the Baltic region. While

Cyrillic) was a punishable offence.

In the unsettled conditions in Russia in 1905 following the St Petersburg uprising, Lithuanians put in a hasty bid for an autonomous state with a "Sjem" or National Assembly. They followed this up with a campaign of passive resistance which won concessions like the reintroduction of the Lithuanian language in schools. Vilnius was recognised as a limited capital, Lithuanian literature began to flourish and, one way or another, it looked as if the country might be making some progress. The optimism died with the outbreak of World War I.

The Russian troops stationed in Lithuania

Estonians, Latvians, Lithuanians and indeed some Poles were heavily engaged in driving the Russian and Baltic Bolsheviks back into Russia, a separate Polish force managed to seize Vilnius. Rather than surrender the city to Lithuanians, the Polish occupiers held their positions until a Bolshevik force was available to take the city over.

The Polish argument on this intractable question includes a Russian census of 1910 which showed a population of 97,800 Poles, 75,500 Jews and only 2,200 Lithuanians. The conclusion drawn is that Vilnius may have been a Lithuanian city five centuries ago, but as Wilno it long ceased to be one.

The Lithuanian position is that this and a subsequent German census used a person's everyday language as the criterion for nationality. At the time, Polish was the language of the urban population regardless of ethnic origin, and after generations or even centuries of linguistic discrimination, Lithuanians did not commonly speak Lithuanian again until some years after the war. In any case, the Red Army's return of Vilnius to Lithuania in 1940 was mourned in Poland as a national tragedy.

The Red Army's presence in Lithuania in 1940 after independence between the world wars, as eventually provided by the Paris peace conference, was not by invitation.

man army entered Lithuania (and Latvia and Estonia) in June 1941, the death warrant for Lithuania's 150,000 Jews. The horrors mounted with re-occupation by the Red Army in 1944, or at least with Stalin's subsequent purge in which 200,000 Lithuanians were killed or disappeared. By 1950 Lithuania, in common with Estonia and Latvia, had been minced into the Soviet machine with a thoroughness meant to ensure that the question of independence would never again arise.

Credit is given to the Sajudis, an underground organisation drawn largely from the Philosophy department of the Lithuanian Academy of Science, for providing the lead which put independence back on the agenda

"Whether you agree or not is irrelevant," Molotov told its government after the Nazi-Soviet Pact had secretly agreed to partition the Baltics, "because the Red Army is going in tomorrow anyway." The army brought in its baggage train a new "government" for Lithuania. The existing parties were dissolved and those leaders who had not already fled were sent to Siberia. A "vote" purported to show that "99.1 percent" of Lithuanians approved annexation by the Soviet Union.

The annexation lasted only until the German army entered Lithuania (and Latvia and

Left, Luthuania and Poland unite at Lublin in 1569. **Above**, Vilnius as drawn in Polish times.

in the late 1980s. There was no need to apply to the Soviet Union for independence, they argued, as the "vote" in 1940 was fraudulent. This was too provocative even for Gorbachev, and on the day parliament planned a unilateral declaration of independence, Soviet tanks drew up outside the parliament building. Television coverage of the crisis was memorable for the stoical determination of Vytgautas Landsbergis, a musician who had been elected president. The stalemate was ended by circumstances beyond even the Kremlin's control. Indeed, Lithuania's slate had not been so clean since, well, the marriage of Jagiello and Jadwiga in 1385.

LITHUANIA: WHAT TO SEE

Lithuania consists of fertile lowlands punctuated by hundreds of lakes, many of them feeding the Nemunas River and its tributaries. It is so flat that the highest hills, the Telsiai Heights, barely reach 1,000 ft (305 metres). It was once almost entirely forested and a paradise for hunters.

Vilnius: It will be immediately apparent to visitors that Vilnius is quite different from other major Baltic cities, a port in spite of being 200 miles (320 km) inland. The cities of Estonia and Latvia retain a strong German flavour because of the historical pre-eminence of the German-Balt burghers, whereas Vilnius bears the stamp of its long and controversial Polish and Roman Catholic connections, hence the predominance of Italian architecture. The population of Vilnius is about 700,000. The city is divided by the **Neris River**, the southern bank being of principal interest to visitors and easily explored on foot.

The most striking feature to be seen is the **Upper Castle** and in particular the **Tower of Gedimnas**, the prince who founded Vilnius in response to a howling wolf which appeared to him in a dream. The tower contains an exhibition of Vilnius's history.

Nothing remains of his Lower Castle, which excavations suggest was on the site of the neoclassical building, formerly the Roman Catholic cathedral, in **Gedimnas Square** in the city centre. This would seem to have been built on the site of a pagan shrine to Perkunas, the God of Thunder, presumably the one Jagiello dutifully smashed to fulfil the terms of his marriage to young Jadwiga. The shrine incorporated a snake pit, and if the evidence elsewhere is anything to go by, early Christians were thrown to the snakes in the same way as Romans threw them to the lions. Jagiello, or King Ladislaus V, replaced the shrine with a cathedral in which St Casimir, Lithuania's only saint, was buried. The

Right, Vilnius, built on the Neris River.

156

saint's remains were later removed to the Church of St Peter and St Paul to join its collection of 2,000 statues and reliefs. All that remains of the 13th-century cathedral is the bell-tower.

The old quarter stretches south from Gedimnas Square and is dissected by **Gorky Street** (Great Castle Street), the main thoroughfare of medieval Vilnius. The street is flanked by a number of interesting houses and churches, the latter including the Jesuit church of **St Casimir** (turned into an anti-God museum by the Communists), the Orthodox **Church of the Holy Ghost** and the **Monastery of St Basil**. The street ends at the Gothic-Renaissance **Medininkai Gate** in a 16th-century wall that was once well over a mile long. The chapel above the gate contains an icon of Our Lady of Vilnius, which is credited with miracle-working properties.

Vilnius University, originally a Jesuit College on the site of an early Christian church, was given its charter in 1579. The old church, rebuilt in 1737 after a fire, forms one side of the main court-yard. The university was forever in trouble in Russian times and was closed down more than once for a suspected role in fomenting anti-Russian activities. Ironically, one of its alumni went on to become the Kremlin's expert on putting down anti-Russian activities, namely Feliks Dzierzynski, the founder of Lenin's secret police.

The former KGB headquarters in Vilnius, incidentally, are in Lenin Square at the end of Lenin Prospekt, names which must be due for a change. The building is said to extend under the square itself with three floors of cells. The prison in tsarist times was the Dominican Monastery and Church of the Holy Ghost in Garelio Street.

The palace on **Kutuzov Square** was the residence of the bishops of Vilnius before it was taken over by the Russian governors like Muraviev who, as we saw in earlier pages, vowed to wipe every trace of Lithuania and Lithuanians off the map. It was occupied by Napoleon in 1812 when he planned his march on Moscow; it also served as his

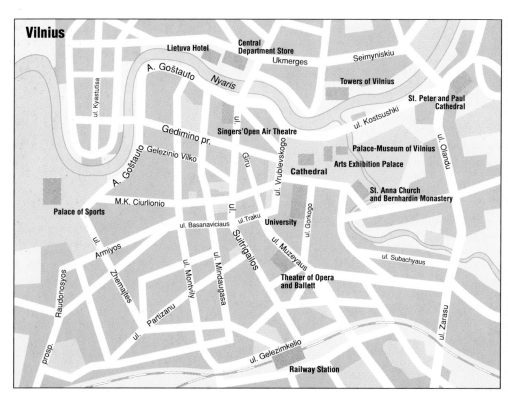

bolt-hole when the invasion failed. General Kutuzov, Napoleon's nemesis, moved in after him, and in 1824 the palace was reconstructed in what can only be called the Russian imperial style.

Trakai: Today a small town, Trakai was the capital of the Lithuanian Grand Princes before the founding of Vilnius. It is about 18 miles (25 km) west of Vilnius on **Lake Galve**, the venue for local and international boating events. The castle situated on an island in the lake has been restored to its 14th-century appearance when it was a bastion of Lithuanian paganism against the Teutonic Knights. Among the restored buildings are a synagogue and houses built and occupied by Tartar mercenaries whom the Grand Princes employed as bodyguards. When its military usefulness was over, the castle became a royal residence but it fell into disuse in the 17th century.

Kaunas (or Kovno), about 40 miles (60 km) west of Trakai, was propelled to the status of Lithuania's capital while Vilnius was officially part of Poland between the world wars. It was described as a "filthy, overgrown Russian village" when fame was suddenly thrust on it. Kaunas has the unenviable record of having been largely destroyed 13 times by war and at least once, in 1732, by fire. Its sorry state after World War I, which saw the ring of 12 Russian forts around the town flattened, may have reflected a certain sense of resignation. Today it is an important industrial centre, and while most of the city is necessarily new-ish, there are fascinating older parts which have somehow survived.

The Teutonic Order attacked the town in 1317 and Gedimnas had to pay a large ransom to save the occupants of the fortress, the ruins of which may be seen at the confluence of the two rivers. A second castle, known as "New Kaunas" was built, and it was here that peace terms after the historic defeat of the Teutonic Order at the battle of Tannenberg were negotiated.

The **St Peter and Paul Cathedral** is on the site of a church built by Vytautas, Jagiello's cousin, to commemorate a

Freedom Allee, Kaunas.

victory over the Tartars. It is the largest Roman Catholic church in Lithuania with an interior by the Italian master Andriolli. The church is on the river which Napoleon crossed on four pontoon bridges in 1812 on his way to Russia. He is said to have fallen from his horse while crossing, and this was taken as a bad omen. He requisitioned the church to stable horses, while he personally stayed first in the Carmelite monastery and then in a house in Kantas. Napoleon gave himself a grand send-off with a ball in the town hall. There was later a very different scene when his army returned ragged and starving from Moscow.

The **Ciurlionis Museum** houses the work of Mikalous Ciurlionis (1875–1911), Lithuania's most famous artist. He began his career as a musician and composer and only later took up painting in the belief that there were certain feelings and emotions that were better expressed in shapes and colours than in musical notes. The synthesis of music and painting produced pictures in musical forms like sonatas with three or four movements. A more light-hearted museum is devoted to devils. The devils, from all over the world, come in clay, bronze, rags; in fact, in every conceivable material. There is also a collection of painted aprons, a local art form.

The main shopping area of the city is closed to traffic, which makes an interesting comparison with a 1922 description which asserted that "in Kaunas there is no traffic problem, for one rarely sees a motor-car; the clatter of hoofs and drosky wheels over the cobbles takes the place of humming engines and the only other public conveyances are dilapidated and overcrowded (horse-drawn) trams."

Not far from Kaunas is the baroque church and convent of the Sisters of St Casimir at **Pazaislis**. It was planned and decorated by Italians who were brought in by the founder, Chancellor Christopher Pac, between 1631 and 1684. The cost is said to have been eight barrels of gold pieces. It is hexagonal in form; the great copper roof was re-

Lithuanian artist Rimas-Zigmas Biciunas.

160

moved in World War I, and the frescoes were badly damaged in the fighting. The Germans carted off the marble mosaic floor and the sarcophagus of Pac and his wife. The unfortunate bodies were left lying around in open coffins. Napoleon had previously taken the ivory statuettes of the Apostles, and Russian vandals wrecked seven altars.

A few miles outside the city is **Fort IX**, the Nazi death-camp in which tens of thousands of Lithuanian Jews and Resistance fighters were exterminated between 1941 and 1944. There is now a museum and a monument to the victims on the spot.

Along the river from Kaunas is the **Zapyskiai church**, the first Christian church in Lithuania. According to legend, the roofs were not supposed to slope quite so steeply. Perkunas so resented the presence of a Christian church that he engulfed it in a storm which caused the building to subside. A brass icon was supposedly delivered by a stag which swam across with the icon between its antlers.

The lake district: Siauliai is the most practical hub from which to explore the lakes of **Samagitia**, one of the most picturesque areas of the country. The town achieved fame in the fighting after World War I as the place where the renegade Bermondt was finally defeated. The town was almost totally destroyed in the process but has subsequently been rebuilt. Something to look out for in this region is the particular kind of cross outside houses. The origins are pre-Christian and are possibly connected with the worship of the sun, as in Egypt.

Kraziai has a gory episode in relatively recent history. In 1893 the Russian governor ordered the church closed. The townsmen took him prisoner and kept him in the loft. He managed by some treachery to get a message to the Cossacks, who duly arrived and drove the population on to the thin ice of the lake. Those who didn't fall through and drown were butchered. The locals used to say that this single action meant that Tsar Alexander, then reigning, would never get to heaven.

Hill of Crosses, Siauliai.

POLAND

Poland, an exasperated President Franklin D. Roosevelt once remarked, "has been causing trouble for 500 years." Trying to introduce Communism in Poland, said Stalin in tacit agreement, would be like trying to put a saddle on a cow. Poland is that kind of country: charismatic, unpredictable and able to get along in a language which appears to have hardly any vowels.

Even in the drabbest days of Soviet conformity, when Poles were supposed to be in overalls and getting on with the current Five-Year Plan, the ghosts of Copernicus, Chopin, Conrad and dashing cavalry officers in ostentatious outfits were never quite eclipsed. Conrad was writing novels in English, with typical Polish panache, before he had ever heard English from the lips of a native speaker. "There are certain things in this world that are at once intensely loved and intensely hated," wrote G. K. Chesterton. "They are naturally things of a strong character and either very good or very bad. They generally give a good deal of trouble to everybody; and a special sort of trouble to those who try to destroy them. But they give most trouble of all to those who try to ignore them." Poland was an example in his mind.

Poland seems never to have done anything by halves. Once the joint master of the largest empire in Europe, it contrived – not without a little help from its enemies – to disappear off the map altogether for the whole of the 19th century. On being reconstituted after World War I, it was immediately at war with Russia again, picking up the threads of a dispute they had been having in 1792 as if after a break for lunch. "It is impossible to identify any fixed territorial base which has been permanently, exclusively, and inalienably Polish," concludes Norman Davies, the foremost Western authority on Polish history. "At various times in Eastern Europe, the Polish state has been everywhere and nowhere."

Poland's peripeteia – here today, gone tomorrow – has inspired Polish artists to preserve the nation's history on canvas in minute detail. They seem to have combed every page of every book to make sure that no event of any consequence is left unrecorded on canvas. After Warsaw was pulverised in World War II, it was therefore completely in character that the Poles did not take the easy option of sweeping away the wreckage and starting all over again but began to reassemble as much as they could of the city piece by piece, a painstaking process immeasurably helped by the mountain of historical paintings. For this modern tourists have much to be grateful, the towering Palace of Culture giving an impression of the city the easier concrete-slab option might otherwise have produced.

Preceding pages: the park of Warsaw's presidential palace; Malbork Castle, one of Europe's largest castles. **Left**, Rynek Old Town, Warsaw.

THE MAKING OF POLAND

In July 1980, Poland's Communist government decreed that the better cuts of meat would in future be sold only through "commercial" butchers. Workers in the Huta Warszawa steelworks and Ursus tractor factory read between the lines, suspected a general increase in prices and downed tools.

The protests spread and on 14 August reached the Lenin Shipyard in Gdansk. The director of the yard climbed on to an excavator to say that he was willing to discuss the workers' demands but they must first go back to work. He appeared to be winning the day when a small man with a large moustache climbed on to the excavator beside him. The two men needed no introduction. Lech Walesa, once an electrician at the shipyard, had been sacked for his part in an acrimonious dispute 10 years earlier. Walesa butted in with a rousing speech and the mood of the workers changed. When he called not merely for a strike but an occupation of the yard as well, a roar of approval went up.

One of the 21 demands presented by the Gdansk workers was for a trade union independent of the Communist Party. This was heresy: the Communist Party was in theory nothing if not the champion of labour. Nevertheless, Solidarity was born and, by signing up 10 million Poles, registered a vote of no-confidence in the system. Faced with a *de facto* opposition party in a one-party state, General Wojcich Jaruzelski declared martial law on 13 December. Hundreds of Solidarity activists, Walesa included, were arrested.

Solidarity was banned in October 1982, but by then the world was watching. Walesa became an international figure and was awarded the Nobel Peace Prize in 1983. Jaruzelski cut a slightly incongruous figure in the circumstances. He was a Pole of the old school: the scion of a distinguished family, educated by Jesuits and incorruptible. He had once been deported to a Soviet labour camp for his Polish nationalism and he was opposed to using military force against fellow Poles. "I think he's all right," Walesa once said, "he's a good Pole." Many Poles

believed that he was their best protection against a Soviet invasion as had been ordered into Czechoslovakia in 1968.

Jaruzelski's room for manoeuvre was limited by Poland's horrendous foreign debt and complicated by the fact that the former Cardinal Wojtyla of Cracow had become Pope John Paul II. The fear was that Poland as the standard bearer of Catholicism would pit itself against Soviet Communism.

Beginnings: The background to these momentous events begins in 991 when Mieszko I, Prince of Poland, decided to become a Christian, not least because this would pacify the Teutonic Knights who would otherwise stop at nothing to root out paganism. While Mieszko's conversion bought temporary peace on the German front, his successor, Boleslaw the Brave, courted trouble with Kievan Russ in the east by meddling in a disputed succession to the throne and backing the wrong horse in the person of Svyatpolk the Accursed against Yaroslav the Wise.

The Russian threat evaporated when Kiev was destroyed by the Mongol invasions in the 13th century and the northern cities like Moscow were put out of commission for 250 years by the Mongol Yoke. Poland felt the Mongol "Scourge of God" too, and its arrival at the gates of the capital Cracow is still observed by the daily trumpet call sounded from St Mary's church. The call breaks off in mid-note, just as it did when a Mongol arrow pierced the original trumpeter's throat as he sounded the alarm. Despite this scare, Poland prospered during the 14th century under the Piast dynasty, and in 1364 its most illustrious member, King Casimir III, founded a university in Cracow. Only Prague already had a university in this part of Europe.

Although the Bohemians of Prague were regarded as rivals, Poland's more immediate concern was the pagan Lithuanians who stoutly resisted every attempt to convert them to Christianity. Having tried and failed, Poland invited the Teutonic Order to have a go. The knights were successful in ridding one part of the Lithuanian lands of paganism by slaughtering its inhabitants, the Prussians, whose territory and name they promptly took on themselves. With a firm territorial base, the Teutonic Order represented a greater threat to Poland than did Lithuania, which was immediately apparent when they demanded – and Poland was forced to cede – the province of Pomerania and the port of Gdansk, which the knights renamed Danzig.

Casimir's death without a suitable heir in 1370 put Poland's future in peril, and in fact it became a mere appendage to the Hungarian Kingdom under King Louis of Anjou. Poland might then even have passed to the early Habsburgs, but a sudden change in the wedding plans of Poland's young Queen Jadwiga, as described in the preceding Lithuanian chapter, resulted in a dynastic union with Lithuania and the combined strength to

feat of the Teutonic Order was Poland's Golden Age. The size of the combined empire grew to colossal proportions. In 1492 it stretched from the Baltic to the Black Sea and was twice the size of modern France. The spread of Polish rule was good news for the Roman Church, which was not only about to be engulfed by the Hussite religious revolt in Bohemia, the forerunner of the Reformation, but was also nervous of increasing Russian influence over Eastern Orthodoxy. Poland could be relied on to do its utmost to safeguard Rome's interest.

The Renaissance which accompanied the Polish-Lithuanian Empire was not so much in art and architecture (mostly the work of

take on and defeat the Teutonic Order at the battle of Grunwald (or Tannenberg) in 1410.

Jan Matejko's painting of the battle is probably the best-loved picture in the Warsaw National Gallery. The knights are mounted on heavy chargers while the Poles and Lithuanians are on foot, hacking away at them with an armoury of grim weapons. The painting leaves the outcome of the battle in no doubt. The Order was not quite finished yet, however, and another major battle was fought in 1466 with another victory for the allies. Poland regained Danzig and switched its name back to Gdansk.

The Jagiellonian period following the de-

imported talent) but in science and literature. The greatest name is that of Copernicus (1473–1543), whose most famous discovery was of the earth's movement around the sun.

The Polish social order had more in common with the Indian caste system than the feudalism which prevailed in other parts of Europe. The "five estates" were defined by birth and intransmutable. There was no question of upward mobility – or downward either. It was said that that the Crown was intended to rule, the clergyman to pray, the burgher to trade, the Jew to be a Jew, and the peasant to till the fields.

"A landless noble family," says the historian Norman Davies, "might well have sustained an existence which by any economic yardstick was indistinguishable from, or even inferior to, that of their peasant neighbours; but their poverty in no way impaired the fiscal, legal, and political privileges to which their inherited noble status entitled them. Similarly, a prosperous Jewish family might easily exceed many of its Gentile neighbours in wealth and affluence; but nothing short of conversion to Christianity could gain them access to the ranks of the Burghers or the Nobility."

The clerical estate was the oldest established and its members had fixed positions within the church's own hierarchy. The burghers were invented, so to speak, to run the towns which sprang up in the early Middle Ages. The burghers ran municipal governments by royal charter, dividing commercial activities among specific guilds.

The peasants naturally represented the single largest estate, although their proportion might have been exaggerated by the number of people who lived as peasants but were actually failed burghers.

The nobles did not have it easy either. They were given generous estates and were exempted from taxation, but the *quid pro quo* was that they kept themselves and perhaps a body of men permanently available for military service. The distressed noble could not opt out of the system in order to go off and earn a living. Indeed, until 1550 they were not allowed to own houses in town.

The Jews were a panacea. Polish Jews were joined by others who, having been expelled by the Germans, arrived with the skills and commercial aptitude which could make the estates pay. They facilitated cottage industries on the estates and ran the distilleries as well as plying their traditional roles as brokers and money-lenders. Mortgages and loans went into default, and the Jewish lenders ended up as the *de facto* owners of large tracts of land, regardless of what the law said.

The successful Jew (many remained wretchedly poor) dared not flaunt his wealth. He could not wear a sword or live on an estate he might secretly own. Jews were supposed to live in special streets, the ghettos. Later on, the rules were relaxed to enable them to buy certain privileges, a process made easier if they were prepared to change their religion and names.

The pedigree of the Polish nobility was obscure and not nearly so grand as its members liked to think. Whatever was lacking in quality, however, was made up by numbers. Some 25,000 families (500,000 persons or nearly 7 percent of the population) qualified as nobles. Writing in England, where the figure was 2 percent, Daniel Defoe took a snooty view of the Polish gentry: "They are the most haughty, imperious, insulting people in the world... They think they are above being tied to the rules of honour... and ex-

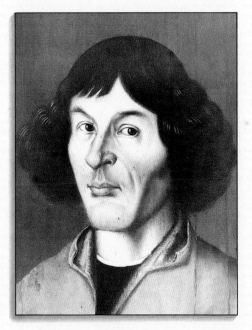

pect allowance even from Heaven itself on account of their birth and quality." On one point Defoe did admire them: the Polish nobility spoke excellent Latin.

Curiously, the nobility insisted on absolute equality among themselves and there were even moves to abolish titles. In the army, portentously, everyone was called "Towarzysz", or "Comrade". The greatest importance was invested in mutual respect and submission, so that noblemen greeted one another with kisses. Children greeted their parents on their knees.

Dress was no less important. Men wore thigh-length leather boots, sleeveless waist-

Left, defeat of the Teutonic Order at Grunwald (Tannenberg) in 1410. **Right**, Copernicus.

coats, and enormous overcoats; they kept daggers in their belts indoors but otherwise carried sabres. Women wore floor-length robes. Both sexes favoured sable fur.

It was the defeat of the Teutonic Order that made Poland a world power. If anyone was likely to challenge that status, it would be the Russian princes, so it suited Poland to have them in the grip of the Golden Horde. When there were signs that the grip might be slipping, King Casimir IV had no scruples about offering military assistance to Ahmed Khan to strengthen it.

In 1500, however, the Muscovites rose and in remarkably short order not only drove out the Golden Horde but annihilated a great

number of Poles and Lithuanians in the farther reaches of the empire. Ivan III was soon hammering at prized Polish possessions like Smolensk.

While a full-scale confrontation with Russia was clearly developing, Poland could be forgiven smug satisfaction at the fate of its *bête noire*, the Teutonic Order. Although no longer a military threat, the Order still existed. It was finished off by the Reformation, when German princes were no longer inclined to subsidise knights whose *raison d'être* was to fight for a Pope whose authority they no longer recognised.

With no army left, the Grand Master of the Order begged Sigismund I of Poland to take over Prussia and install him as its hereditary duke. The act of submission was duly performed in the Market Square at Cracow on 10 April 1525, and ex-Grand Master Albrecht von Hohenzollern became a Polish subject.

Poland showed few signs of wavering from Catholicism, and the problem in imperial parts like Ukraine was not so much Lutheranism as a longing for closer links with Orthodox Russia.

Lutheranism was a much more important issue in the Baltic states, where the middle and commercial classes were German and therefore susceptible. As Orthodox irredentists and Baltic Lutherans between them looked threatening, the old dynastic union between Poland and Lithuania was put on a formal constitutional footing by the Union of Lublin in 1569.

Poland made several attempts to conquer Russia, using a succession of False Dmitris (*see pages 39–41*) as pretexts for invasion. For a while, a Polish garrison occupied the Kremlin, but in the end the Polish king accepted 200,000 roubles to forget about his dubious claims to the Russian throne.

By then Poland had over-reached itself. East Prussia fell to the Elector George William of Brandenburg in 1624 and at the same time Moscow applied relentless pressure. Smolensk was recaptured and Moscow's Swedish allies entered Cracow and Warsaw. Swedish military successes alarmed Russia as much as Poland, however, so the two of them reached a temporary settlement of their differences at Vilna (Vilius) in 1656.

On another front, Poland was being harassed by the Ottoman Turks. A famous action in which a besieged Polish force hung on until its last barrel of gunpowder and then, rather than surrender, sent out the cavalry to win a remarkable victory over the Turkish besiegers, is the subject of Poland's most celebrated epic poem, *The War of Chocim*, by Waclaw Potocki. Nevertheless, Poland was in mortal danger.

"All the existing strands of internal and external conflict were suddenly twisted together into a web of strangulating complexity," says Norman Davies. "Cossacks, Tartars, Muscovites, Swedes, Prussians, and Transylvanians were drawn one by one into a tightening mesh involving traitorous magnates, rebellious soldiers, religious dissenters, and international plotters." The machinery of government was made ludicrous by the so-called Liberum Veto, which enabled any single member of parliament to veto any bill for any or conceivably no reason.

The Ottomans brought all these crises to a head with their siege of Vienna in 1683. The Habsburg emperor and his court fled, the fall of the capital seemed imminent, and it was feared that the Turks would not stop until they reached Rome.

This darkest hour was the making of one of Poland's greatest heroes, the soldier-king John Sobieski. He was the descendant of three great Polish families and already had a substantial military career behind him. He

emperor, who had taken care to be well out of harm's way, insisted on being the first to enter the city "for I fancy that otherwise the love of my subjects for me would be diminished and their affection for others increase". The "others" were Sobieski in particular, and he became the hero of all Europe.

The glory gained at Vienna was soon dissipated by the Polish nobility being unable to agree on Sobieski's successor. The crown went to August II of Saxony, an unwise choice resulting in a succession of Saxon kings and what has been called "the most wretched and the most humiliating (period) in the whole of Polish history". Thomas Carlyle described the state of Poland under

had beaten the Cossacks in 1671 and crushed an earlier Turkish army at Podolia in southeast Poland in 1673, a victory which had won him the Polish crown (the kingdom was elective, not hereditary) but had nevertheless not prevented Turkey from taking Podolia.

The Polish cavalry under Sobieski made up only a small part of the army which forced the lifting of the siege of Vienna, but they managed to steal the limelight with one of their magnificent charges. The Habsburg

Left, the last Teutonic Grand Master swears allegiance to Poland in 1525. **Above**, Polish hero John Sobieski at the siege of Vienna, 1683.

the various Saxons as a "beautifully phosphorescent rot-heap", but if Poles thought things could only get better when they saw the last of the Saxons out in 1763, they had reckoned without Catherine II of Russia.

Stanislaw-August Poniatowski, a former Polish plenipotentiary in St Petersburg, replaced the Saxons (as Augustus IV) on the strength of having been one of Catherine's more satisfactory lovers. Did Catherine have an ulterior motive, like annexing parts of Poland? She denied this "completely baseless rumour" but that is exactly what she had in mind.

In the meantime, Frederick of Prussia,

short of money, restless and ambitious, had managed to steal Silesia from Austria in 1740. Prussia was not yet a contiguous whole. The two largest fragments were Brandenburg and Ducal (East) Prussia, separated by the Polish province of Royal (West) Prussia. In fact, it was Polish territory which generally stood between the bits and pieces of Prussia. Frederick was more frank about his intentions than Catherine. He described the Polish corridors dividing Prussia as an artichoke which he proposed to consume "leaf by leaf".

Despite earlier differences, Frederick gained the support of the Empress Maria Theresa of Austria as well as that of Catherine. The only flaw in his plot was the assumption

that Augustus IV, Catherine's former lover, would do as he was told. He turned out to be something of a Polish patriot and shared the feelings of a Polish nobility disgusted by Russia's manifest designs on their country. Moves against Russia in 1768 brought the most savage reprisals imaginable against the Polish presence in Ukraine. Cossacks and Ukrainian peasants turned on Poles and Jews with the cry of "Pole-Jew-Dog: all of one Faith". The Polish and Jewish death toll in just three weeks reached 200,000.

These atrocities in turn fuelled anti-Russian uprisings by Poles and Lithuanians. Catherine was by then also embroiled in war

with Turkey, and Frederick proposed that between them they could carve up some of Poland. The morsels he earmarked for himself just happened to remove most of the impediments standing in the way of a unified Prussia. Maria Theresa was asked if there were any bits of Poland that appealed to her. In February 1772, she provided a list.

Poland was made to surrender more than a quarter of its territory and nearly half its population. Prussia took Pomerania, Austria got Galicia, Russia took most of White Russia, the future Belarus. It all went so smoothly that by 1792 Russia and Prussia saw no reason not to repeat the exercise. This time a Russian army occupied Warsaw and Prussia seized western Poland. The Second Partition provoked a Polish rebellion under Tadeusz Kosciuzko which managed to drive the Russians out of Warsaw, but not for long. General Suvorov, Russia's greatest military hero, regained the city, and in so doing massacred a large part of its population.

After two successful partitions, why not a third? Russia and Prussia invited Maria Theresa to rejoin them. "The more she wept for Poland," Frederick quipped, "the more she took of it." Prussia now took the land between the Niemen and the Vistula, including Warsaw. Austria took Cracow and Lublin. Russia received the largest share of all, which included Lithuania. After the Third Partition, there was nothing left of Poland at all. It had ceased to exist.

"There is no other instance," Davies comments, "when [victorious powers] deliberately annihilated one of Europe's historic states in cold blood. Poland was the victim of political vivisection – by mutilation, amputation, and in the end total dismemberment; and the only excuse given was that the patient had not been feeling well."

In the event, Poland was not reconstituted until after World War I, but there was a moment in 1806 when a partial restoration was on the cards. Napoleon had just defeated Prussia, and on a raft in the middle of the Niemen River, he and the Tsar Alexander sat down to discuss how they would carve up Europe. The short-lived "Duchy of Warsaw" was dismantled at the Congress of Vienna in 1815. Posen went to the King of Prussia, Galicia to Austria, and Russia got the rest.

The Poles hung on to their national identity tenaciously while there was no Poland *per se* and the Polish people were dispersed among Prussian, Russian and Austrian overlords. Heinrich Heine, the German poet and essayist, reported on the condition of Poles under the Prussians in this period. "It is almost laughable," he wrote, "to see how among the Poles everything has to do with the fatherland. 'Fatherland' is their first word, 'freedom' only the second."

Heine, a revolutionary, thought the Polish peasants were too ready to tug their forelocks to a nobility who were hardly better off than they were. For all his revolutionary feelings, however, Heine did not think the Polish peasant was ready for emancipation: "He is so improvident that he would fritter away and lose everything he possessed."

Nostalgia for the fatherland was no less pronounced in the parts of Poland taken over by Russia, and in 1831 and 1836 there were uprisings which took an army of 150,000 men more than a year to put down. The Poles in Austrian-administered Galicia seem to have been more content.

The larger part of Poland was still Russian territory at the outbreak of World War I. By the summer of 1915, however, the German and Austrian allies had taken it over together with much of the Baltic provinces, Ukraine and Byelorussia. Under the combined incompetence of Tsar Nicholas and Alexandra, not to mention the hypnotic influence of Grigori Rasputin, the war went disastrously for Russia. The revolutions of 1917 led to a separate peace with Germany.

The peace terms after the war established a Polish republic under Jozef Pilsudski, a veteran socialist who had gone into the war in the Austrian army and later transferred his allegiance to the goal of a completely independent Poland. The so-called Curzon Line was a tentative frontier for a reconstituted post-war Poland, but by then Polish sights were set on recovering parts of the old empire as well, especially in the Ukraine. Moreover, Poland was ready to go to war for them.

Pilsudski, now Marshal of the Polish army, led his forces as far as Kiev before being turned back by the Russians. Nevertheless, the Poles managed to hang on to a frontier which was considerably east of the Curzon

Line and did include some of the Ukraine, including Lvov (Lviv), and some of Lithuania, including Vilnius (Wilno). The dispute over the border with Germany went all the way to a private war between them in 1921. Poland emerged with greater gains in the east than in the west, but the latter did include a corridor to the Baltic which drove a wedge between Germany and East Prussia. Gdansk-Danzig was declared a Free City.

Poland was back in existence but not a happy place. The country divided into hostile political camps. The National Democrats, known locally as the "Endeks", were middle-class, intensely nationalistic, conservative, pro-Catholic and anti-Semitic. The

Socialists were split between the Rosa Luxembourg faction, who had traditionally put social revolution before national independence (and later became the Polish Communist Party), and Pilsudski's larger faction, who were patriotic revolutionaries.

A constitution was adopted in 1921 which limited the authority of the president, causing Pilsudski to retire with the comment that he had no wish to become a cipher. He was back in 1926, however, via a peaceful *coup d'état*, but the powers he felt were necessary to combat the chaos – there were by then 26 Polish and 33 minority parties – gradually amounted to a dictatorship which lasted until

Left, Stanislaw Poniatowski, the last king of Poland. **Right**, detail from Jan Matejko's painting depicting the 1773 partition of Poland.

his death in 1935. If nothing else, he is credited with "disinterested patriotism and his personal integrity". With his passing, Polish politics degenerated into a contest over which gang of unprincipled politicians should rule the rest.

World War II began with the German attack on the Polish garrison outside Gdansk on 1 September 1939. Only a week earlier, the Nazis and Soviets had concluded the infamous secret pact which proposed a new partition of Poland. Accordingly, on 1 November, Russia annexed Eastern Poland and Germany occupied the rest. Only weeks before, the Poles had forcibly removed 50,000 Germans who lived near the German border

ing ground in central Poland. According to Nazi experts on race, fewer than 5 percent of Poles were pure enough to be considered suitable for Germanisation and the right to remain in those parts of the country which were to be absorbed into the Reich. The rest were ranked as third-class humans, along with Byelorussians, Ukrainians, Jews and gypsies. The grand scheme was that 12 million Poles would be removed to make space for 4 to 5 million German immigrants.

The horrors are too familiar, and almost too nauseating, to bear detailed repetition. The bare facts are that in the first phase of the war, Stalin actually killed more Poles in Russian Poland than did Hitler in the Ger-

and sent them east. Five thousand members of the German minority were murdered by mobs as they were rounded up.

When the German armies eventually arrived, they were accompanied by Heydrich's Einsatzgruppen bearing a sinister list of names. These consisted of key members of the nobility, professional classes and the Jewish population. They were to be exterminated, and the population as a whole reduced to the lowest level of subsistence.

The sorting out of the undesirables began that winter. They were given one hour's notice of departure times in overcrowded, unheated cattle trucks taking them to a dump-

man sector. Some 750,000 Poles, including 100,000 Jews, died from starvation or were murdered by the Russians. In addition, the Soviets executed 15,000 Polish army officers in the notorious Katyn massacre and hid their bodies near Smolensk. The large number of Polish troops which managed to escape eventually reached Allied lines and served with great distinction.

The Germans killed in all about 6 million Poles, or 20 per cent of the population, half of them Jews. While the Nazi-Soviet alliance lasted, the two sides rounded up one another's enemies in the areas they controlled and swapped them. When the Red Army drove out the Germans in 1945, they collected other Poles suspected of anti-Communist sympathies, including the very substantial anti-German "Home Army", and continued the execution of these political undesirables. Such killings went on for three years after the war. The total number of Russian victims can only be guessed at.

During the course of the war Stalin decided against absorbing Poland into the USSR. He preferred a buffer state between Russia and post-war Germany under close Soviet supervision, and for this he required a Polish government-in-waiting as an alternative to the government-in-exile based in London. Stalin's "Provisional Government of the Polish Republic" was proclaimed a month before the Yalta conference at which the future of Europe was to be plotted. The announcement was made in Lublin where, in 1569, the constitutional union between Poland and Lithuania had been enacted.

The preliminary talks at Yalta were carried over to the Potsdam conference in 1945. The non-Communist Poles were adamant that the eastern frontier should continue to envelop Lvov (Lviv) and Vilnius (Wilno), which had both been part of an older Poland.

The eventual agreement was a reversal of the settlement after World War I. Poland lost in the East but gained in the West, the frontier with the future East Germany being pushed back to the Oder-Neisse line. Instead of merely a narrow corridor to the sea, Poland enjoyed a stretch of Baltic coastline as it had known in the Middle Ages.

Stalin was able to see his pet government installed in Poland and even the most fiercely patriotic Poles were too weakened by the war to do anything about it. Stalin delighted in reminding the Polish Communists that it was by his grace they were in power and that without him they would be shot by their fellow Poles "like partridges". Eager to impress him, the Polish Communists abolished private property, collectivised agriculture and obediently fell into line with the grand Soviet economic strategy. That meant surrendering the countryside and even the ancient cities to the most insensitive industrialisation.

There were occasional popular protests in which demonstrators were killed, but the

ruthless Soviet clampdown in Hungary in 1956 and in Czechoslovakia in 1968 enabled the local Communist leadership to say that only loyal adherence to Soviet policies would spare Poland the same fate.

Jaruzelski used the same argument in the 1980s, but in 1988 Mikhail Gorbachev announced that the Soviet Union was withdrawing from Afghanistan. In the new climate of *perestroika*, that was virtually a signal that the Soviet Union would think twice about invading an independently-minded Poland. With another wave of strikes that year, Jaruzelski invited Solidarity to join him in round-table talks. The events which followed the lifting of the ban on Solidarity

proved why, from the Communist Party's point of view, it had been necessary in the first place. Solidarity moved swiftly from glorified trade union to opposition party to government. On 28 January 1990 the Communist Party voted itself out of existence "because of the impossibility of the party regaining the public's confidence".

Walesa, the man who not long before had climbed on to an excavator to address the work-force at the Gdansk shipyard, found himself leading the country. Yet, as elsewhere in Eastern Europe, the silver lining of freedom was soon to be tinged by dark economic thunderclouds.

Left, German menace in World War II. **Right**, Solidarity celebrations in the late 1980s.

POLAND: WHAT TO SEE

Warsaw: By the end of World War II, 700,000 inhabitants of Warsaw were dead and the city was almost as devastated as Hiroshima. The easiest course of action would have been to flatten the remains and start all over again, but that would have been considered an unspeakable desecration in Poland.

Instead, Polish architects undertook a real-life jigsaw puzzle. They assembled a picture of Warsaw as it had been before the war using paintings, sketches, snap-shots, anything. They allowed themselves a little licence to brush out the more obvious blemishes, moved a building this way or that as they saw fit – and began to put it all together. Within a few years, the paint had faded on schedule to produce the desired effect and historic Warsaw was reborn. Wide boulevards, parks and new suburbs were added with an eye to future needs.

Warsaw is divided by the **River Vistula**, and it is the meticulously re-created left bank that is of most interest to visitors. According to legend, the Warsaw siren – the part-woman, part-fish who graces the city's coat-of-arms – once lived here. At any rate **Old Market** (Rynek Starego Miasta) was thriving on this site in the 13th century.

It is still a picturesque spot where artists sell their work on the street and numerous antique shops and galleries operate out of old patrician houses. Café umbrellas lend a dash of colour; the sound effects are provided by horse-drawn cabs on cobblestones. The Bazyliszek, Swietoszek and Rycerska restaurants are perennial local favourites, and there is also loyal support for the Kaminne Schodki coffee house, the Krokodyl café and the U Fukere wine bar. The area is floodlit at night so, as the saying goes, it stays up late.

The **Warsaw Historical Museum** in this quarter has regular showings of a short documentary which shows the city

Preceding pages: the university city of Lublin. **Left**, old Warsaw.

in the "before-and-after" process mentioned above. Ironically, these film shows are in a row of buildings, including the "Negro House", which actually survived the destruction they portray. The other museum in the immediate area is of Literature and named after Adam Mickiewicz, the romantic poet.

The **Cathedral of St John**, just off the Old Market, is Warsaw's oldest and most important church. Rebuilding this from scratch after World War II was an opportunity to revert to its original 14th-century form without the subsequent "improvements" of the kind which churches everywhere accumulated with the passage of time. Two of the Polish kings are buried here, as is Henryk Sienkiewicz who won a Nobel Prize in 1905 for writing, among other things, *Quo Vadis*. The figure of Christ in one of the chapels supposedly grows hair that has to be cut every year by a Warsaw virgin, the source of any number of rather predictable jokes.

Marie Curie, the discoverer of radium, was born around the corner at 16 Freta Street, now a museum dedicated to her life and work. Also worth looking out for is the **Church and Convent of the Blessed Sacrament Sisters**, founded in 1688 by the wife (and queen) of John Sobieski, the hero of the siege of Vienna.

The passage between the cathedral and the Royal Castle, along **Dziekania Street**, was roofed over as a precaution after an attempt on the life of King Sigismund III Vasa. The culprit was first ripped in half by horses which were whipped into a gallop in opposite directions. His remains were chopped into smaller pieces, cremated, and the ashes fired out of a cannon, all of this to ensure that he would not be inclined to make a second attempt. It is worth doubling back along Swietojanska Street, which runs parallel with Dziekania and is equally picturesque.

Sigismund III, the assassin's intended victim, stands defiantly in the square in front of the castle. It was he who was responsible for moving the Polish capital from Cracow to Warsaw, and fit-

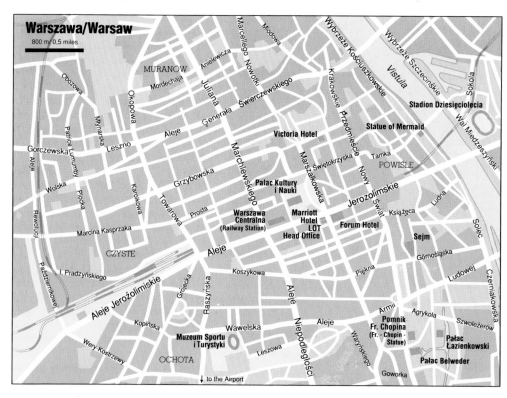

182

tingly his statue was the first monument to be restored after the war. The pieces of the original column are on display in the **Mariensztat Market Square**.

The **Royal Castle** was destroyed in 1944. Communism, naturally, had more urgent priorities, so rebuilding it did not commence until 1971. The scale of the job was such that it was not completed until 1984. Many of the works removed for safe-keeping at the outbreak of war are now back where they belong. Canaletto's views of Warsaw in the 18th century were closely consulted by architects while Warsaw was being reconstructed. So, incidentally, were the works of his nephew Bernardo Bellotto. An urn in the chapel contains the heart of Tadeusz Kosciuszko, who led the Polish assault on the Russians in an early bid for independence.

Before leaving this corner of the city, walk down **Dluga Street** to a newish-looking monument. It stands above the manhole into which, in the Warsaw uprising of September 1944, no fewer than 5,300 insurgents lowered themselves to make their way through the sewers to the city centre.

The logical way to leave the castle is down **Trakt Krolewski**, the King's Way. On leaving the castle square, the royal route begins by following Krakowskie Przedmiescie, in some respects the most historic street in the city. There are statues or references of one kind or another to a long roll-call of Polish dignitaries and heroes.

There is a statue of Copernicus by the Dane, Bertel Thorvaldsen, and the route has close associations with Frederick Chopin, whose heart was repatriated after his death and placed in a pillar of the Holy Cross Church. Chopin gave his first concert in the Radziwill Palace, which is also where the Warsaw Pact was signed in 1955. Meetings between government ministers and Solidarity leaders in the same place in 1989 were conducted in a rather different atmosphere. **Warsaw University** is on the same stretch.

Before following the royal route through the change from Krakowskie

The Zygmunt Pillar at the entrance to Warsaw's old city.

Przedmiescie to Nowy Swiat (New World Street), it may be worth diverting to some of the other sights down side-streets. It will be necessary to back-track a short distance to pick up, in **Teatralny Square**, the colossal **Grand Theatre of Opera and Ballet** and the **Monument to the Heroes of Warsaw**. The theatre was a total wreck after the war; the monument is to the civilians who died in it.

The **Saxon Gardens**, a little further down, were Warsaw's first park, laid out in 1727 according to the principles of French garden symmetry. The chang-ing of the guard ceremony at the **Tomb of the Unknown Soldier** (1925) takes place at noon on Sundays.

Nowy Swiat, to resume the royal route, has two claims to fame. The first is No. 45, the **birthplace of Joseph Conrad** (Korzeniowski), who wrote the first of his famous novels in English before he had ever heard the language from the lips of native-speakers. The second is **Blikle**, confectioners and pur-veyors (particularly) of widely admired doughnuts. Blikle bags are flaunted in much the same way as the Harrods equivalent in London. The former Polish Communist Party Headquarters on Nowy Swiat are straight out of the Sta-lin school of architecture. Comparisons can be made with the Palace of Culture and Science visible on the right down Al. Jerozolimskie.

The **National Museum** is a vast place filled with classical and contemporary art, although pride of place is given to the Faras frescoes discovered in the Sudan by Polish archaeologists. The attraction of the adjacent **Polish Army Museum** for military-minded Western-ers is the array of Warsaw Pact kit, often seen on TV but seldom in the flesh.

The continuation of Nowy Swiat is **Al. Ujazdowskie**, probably Warsaw's most elegant street. Most of the embas-sies are along here, as are the **Polish Parliament** (Sjem) and **Senate**. People now stroll where in earlier times they rode and swanked about in carriages.

Beyond the Trasa Lazienkowska is the **Ujazdowski Palace**, now a museum

Left, help line. **Right**, typical small shop.

but previously the summer residence of the Wasa kings. The **Lazienki**, or Palace on the Lake, on the other hand, was the private residence of Poland's last king, Stanislaw August Poniatowski. He, it may be recalled, was given the job on the strength of being one of Catherine the Great's more satisfactory lovers. Against all expectations, he proved to be an able and patriotic ruler.

The **Orangery** is an authentic 18th-century court theatre. Regular piano recitals are given in summer at the foot of the Chopin Memorial. **Belveder**, at the edge of the lake, is the official residence of the present President of Poland.

Ul. Belwederska takes the royal route out of town to **Wilanow**, the so-called Versailles of Poland and the home of the dashing King John Sobieski, the previously mentioned hero of the siege of Vienna. His life is the subject of a *son et lumière* show – in Polish, naturally, although tape-recorded translations are available. Wilanow was heavily looted by the Germans in the war and there was not much left of the gardens or parkland.

All is well again, and the palace is still used regularly for state purposes. The collection of posters in the museum is unusual and fascinating.

Having come this far, visitors may like to know that three good restaurants are at hand: Wilanow, Kuznia Krolewska and the Café Hetmanskaya.

Until World War II, Warsaw had the world's largest Jewish community. The Monument to the Heroes of the Ghetto is a simple slab of dark granite on **ul. Zamenhofa** in the Muranow district, where the ghetto used to be. Muranow was completely flattened in retaliation for the uprising in April 1943. The site is now occupied by unremarkable high-rise blocks of flats. The only synagogue to have survived the war is situated in **Okopowa Street**.

A contemporary point of pilgrimage is the grave of Father Jerzy Popieluszko, the priest who was murdered by the Polish secret service in 1984. He is buried at the **Church of St Stanislaw Kostka** in Krasinski Street in the Zoliborz area.

One piece of history made in 1989 was Poland's victory in the Miss World contest.

Excursions from Warsaw: The Mazovian plain which stretches endlessly from Warsaw gives a clear impression of Poland's historic vulnerability to invaders. In spite of the apparently unrelenting flatness, there are some attractive stretches of river and pleasure steamers that ply them. The **Kampinowski Park Narodowy** north-west of the capital is at 80,000 acres (35,000 hectares) Poland's largest national park and the natural habitat of elk and other wildlife.

One of the most popular excursions from Warsaw is to **Zelazowa Wola**, Chopin's birthplace. The house in which he grew up (he was born in 1810) is now an inn-cum-museum. On most summer evenings, a piano recital is laid on in the adjoining park. Chopin's baptism certificate is preserved in the church at **Brochowo** were his parents were married. This is one of the fortified churches which are quite common in Transylvania and other parts of Eastern Europe but rare in Poland.

Napoleon built a huge citadel at the confluence of the Narew, Bug and Vistula Rivers. In their time, the barracks at **Modlin** were the largest building in Europe, or so it is said. In any event, they could hold 26,000 men.

In 1806, the army based at Modlin met the Russians in battle at **Pultusk**, an old town built on an island in the Narew. This same island was in the news once again in 1868 when an enormous meteorite landed on it. The former episcopal palace is now the headquarters of the Polonia Society, which is responsible for preserving Poland's cultural heritage. Much of Pultusk's old town wall survives, as do a number of interesting churches.

Day trips are also available from Warsaw to the Nazi death-camp at **Treblinka**, a journey of some 60 miles (100 km). The horror is too well-known to need recounting here. The number of victims was 800,000 and would have been higher but for mechanical limitations which put a ceiling of 2,400 on the number of people who could be murdered per day.

Cracow: Every hour on the hour, a

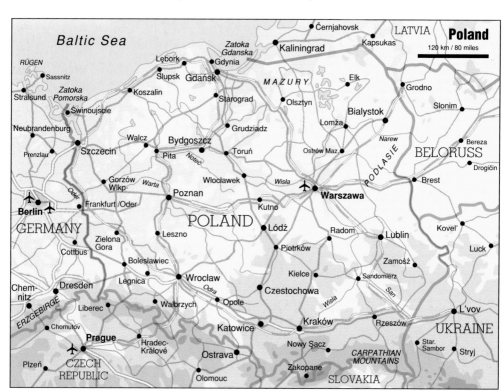

186

bugle call from the spire of the **Church of the Virgin Mary** in Cracow peters out after four short notes, just as it did one day in the 13th century when the city look-out attempted to blow a warning that the Mongols were about to attack and, while doing so, took an arrow in the throat. The city was ransacked on that occasion but significantly, bearing in mind what happened in Warsaw, it survived World War II relatively unscathed, the Germans having been driven out before they could wreak their worst destruction.

Cracow had been a busy trading settlement on the River Vistula for some 300 years before the Mongol attack in 1241. In the year 1000 it became a bishopric and from 1083 the Polish kings used Wawel Castle as their residence. The population reached 30,000 in the Middle Ages, and what became the Jagiellonian University was founded in 1364. The city's prestige received a blow in 1611 when King Sigismund III transferred his capital to Warsaw and it suffered considerable physical damage in the wars of the 17th and 18th centuries. Today, Cracow is Poland's third largest city, and its well-preserved medieval centre has earned a place on UNESCO's list of 12 top cultural centres.

The pride of Cracow is its marketplace, **Rynek Glowny**, which has at its centre a 100-yard long Gothic **Draper's Hall**, originally built in the 14th century but subsequently modified by Italian Renaissance architects. The ground floor still functions as a market, but the upstairs section has been converted into a gallery of Polish painting.

The tower of the **Town Hall** is also 14th-century, but the hall itself was unfortunately demolished in 1820. The replacement building is now one section of the **Cracow History Museum**. It is from the tower of the church on the market square that the bugler does his stuff each hour. The altarpiece inside is quite extraordinary: a gilded and painted polyptych 36 ft (11 metres) high and 42ft (13 metres) wide, the work of Wit Stwosz in the 15th century.

Wawel Castle and **Cathedral** are on

Cracow's market square and Draper's Hall.

a limestone hill above the Vistula. The heart of the castle, started in the 10th century, is a rectangular Renaissance building with 71 halls and a courtyard surrounded by beautiful arcades. The state rooms, adorned with Flemish tapestries, the crown jewels and the armoury, as well as a collection of oriental art, are open to visitors. Two of the prize exhibits are the jagged "Szczerbiec" sword held by the kings at their coronations and some fancy Turkish tents captured by King John Sobieksi at the siege of Vienna.

The cathedral opposite the castle was begun in the 14th century, and this is where the Polish kings were crowned and buried. No fewer than 18 chapels open on to the nave, the most renowned being the Sigismund Chapel with its perfect gilt dome. The **Holy Cross Chapel** contains the tombs of King Casimir and Poland's patron saint, the unlucky St Stanislaw. The cathedral bell, known as Sigismund, was cast out of enemy cannon captured in 1520 and is reserved for special occasions. The most special occasion in living memory was in 1983 when the former Cardinal Wojtyla of Cracow returned as Pope John Paul II, not only the first Polish Pope but the first foreigner to break the Italian monopoly on the job for well over 400 years.

Small streets at the foot of **Castle Hill** contain some of Cracow's finest architecture. Kazimierz, further out, was originally the Jewish quarter governed by a separate set of by-laws. It was a thriving place until 1941 when the inhabitants were rounded up, as elsewhere in Poland, and driven to the extermination camps. They left behind seven synagogues and two Jewish cemeteries. **Boznica Stara** (the Old Synagogue) has been restored and now contains a small Jewish museum.

Except for the **Barbican** and **St Florian Gate**, Cracow's medieval fortifications were removed in the 19th century and replaced by the "Planty" green belt. **Ul. Florianska** was part of the royal route from the castle. The museum in this street has paintings of **Hunting for a bargain.**

188

many scenes in Polish history by the artist Jan Matejko (1839–93) while the nearby Czartoryski in Sw. Jana boasts nothing less than a Leonardo da Vinci – *The Lady with the Ermine* – and Rembrandt's *Landscape with the Good Samaritan*. The Café Jama Michalika seems to attract a bohemian crowd and is worth looking into.

The **Jagiellonian University**, to which the lovely Princess Jadwiga left all her money (see the chapter on Lithuania), produced Copernicus, whose statue is in the park opposite the **Collegium Novum**. There is a special point of interest to the Jagiellonion Globe in the museum which occupies part of the university's arcaded courtyard. It was made in 1510 and, as far as anyone knows, was the first globe ever to show the American continent.

Nowa Huta (New Mine) is the newest part of Cracow and has the dubious distinction in many people's minds of demonstrating just how bad the school of Socialist Realism can be. To make matters worse, Nowa Huta produces about half Poland's iron and steel by means which seem designed to produce a maximum of pollution. It may be worth visiting for no other reason, although the Polish Ecological Club has taken note and things may improve gradually. Reflecting what was happening all over Eastern Europe, a statue of Lenin which stood on the Aleja Roz was removed in 1990 at the insistence of local residents.

The monumental **Church of Our Lady at Bienczyce** is built like a ship and was used as a refuge by those who fell foul of martial law in 1981–89. There is at least a joke attached to the area, even if it is not universally appreciated. The Wanda Mound was apparently named after a certain Wanda who drowned herself in the Vistula rather than marry a German. This gesture met with such local approval (in the 9th century) that a cult formed around the memory of it.

Cracow's oldest mine, on the other hand, is at **Wieliczka**, and it was in business (producing salt) more than

1,000 years ago. This is definitely worth seeing. The salt has been worked in passages more than a mile long and at a depth of nearly 500ft (150 metres). One chamber, some 180 ft (50 metres) long serves as a chapel and is illuminated by chandeliers made out of salt and decorated with statues, also of salt.

At a lower level there is a chamber where in World War II the Germans made aircraft parts and, of all things, a sort of sports hall for miners complete with a stage and bar. At a lower level still is a museum of salt mining with exhibits which suggest that mining operations did not after all begin in the 11th century but possibly in 3500 BC.

North of Wieliczka, albeit at some distance, is the **Djcowski National Park**, a landscape of somewhat bizarre stone formations. Botanists will head for the part that follows the **Prudnik River** because it produces a number of plants that are found nowhere else. **Pieskowa Skala** at the northern end of the park has a late-Gothic castle with a museum and restaurant. For other ruined

castles, try the **Szlak Orlich Gniazd**, or "Way to the Eagle Nests".

Until displaced by Wadowice, the birthplace of Pope John Paul II, the holiest shrine in Roman Catholic Poland was the **Jasna Gora** (Hill of Light) in **Czestochowa**, built as a Pauline monastery in 1382 but converted into a fortress in the 17th century just in time to arrest the advance of the Swedish army. It seems that in the 13th century one of the Mongols attempted to steal the monastery's prized portrait of the Black Madonna. The Mongol thief was brought to his knees as the painting mysteriously grew heavier and heavier, and in the end he turned on it in a rage and slashed the Madonna's cheek in two places.

The Madonna has worked miracles on a fairly regular basis ever since, and Poles converge in their tens of thousands on Assumption Day to seek forgiveness for sins and other considerations. The high point of the ceremony is when the cover is lifted momentarily to give the faithful a sight of the painting underneath.

An altogether unhappier place about 35 miles (55 km) from Cracow is **Auschwitz**, whose Polish name is Oswiecim. The death toll here and at nearby Birkenau was very much worse than at Treblinka – four million people, 29 nationalities, either gassed or shot. The camp is now a museum.

Gdansk: More familiar to previous generations as Danzig, this swashbuckling Baltic port had much the same kind of reputation as Marseille in the Mediterranean. It smelt of salt and sail, and one could imagine Joseph Conrad in some seamen's haunt regaling his companions with tales of recent difficulties on a frustrating voyage up the Congo River into the heart of darkness.

Until the past 20 years or so, Gdansk's whole existence was wrapped up in Baltic turbulence, beginning with the Teutonic Knights, whose exploits are dealt with in the Baltic sections of this book, and on through the saga of Prussia and East Pomerania. Gdansk was a "Free City" between the world wars and only became officially part of Poland after **The symbol of Solidarity.**

the second. Solidarnosc (Solidarity) was born and nurtured in Gdansk.

Like Warsaw, Gdansk suffered irreparable damage in World War II and the question afterwards was whether to build a completely new city or try to reproduce at least some of the old. Unlike Warsaw, there was very little surviving archive material showing the old city in sufficient detail for restoration purposes. In the event, a miraculous job was done with the slimmest resources. **Ul. Mariacka**, for instance, one of Gdansk's most romantic streets, was resurrected from memory, the only hard evidence available being a single surviving staircase.

The most splendid of the restored buildings are in **Dluga** and **Dlugi Targ streets**, part of the "royal route" which is a feature of every Polish city. In this case, it was the route into the city when royalty visited. The length of Dluga Street stretches out from the 17th-century **Golden Gate**, and the slender tower is that of the 14th-century **Town Hall**. It now contains the city museum, an es-

sential port of call for an insight into Gdansk's long history.

The **Neptune Fountain** and the Renaissance **Artus Court**, once the headquarters of the Guild of Merchants, are landmarks. The finest example of a patrician house of the same period is **Zlota Kamienica** with a facade of gilded reliefs. Dlugi Targ Street ends at the **Zielona Brama** (Green Gate), the entrance to the **Motlava quays** which were once the heart of the port. The island opposite, formerly full of warehouses, is being turned into small shops and galleries, but the huge 15th-century wooden crane remains as a reminder of earlier times. It is possible to watch the comings-and-goings of pleasure boats from the terrace of the Pod Zuravien restaurant.

Mariacka Street, the one reconstructed around a staircase, runs parallel to the Long Market, and at the end is the church from which it takes its name. This **Church of the Virgin Mary** took 159 years to build – from 1343 to 1502 – and with a capacity of 25,000 is re-

Gdansk's shipyards.

puted to be the sixth biggest church in the world, not an easy claim to verify but does it matter? The medieval Dominican Fair, an annual event, has been revived and now occupies the heart of the old city in early August.

The **Westerplatte Peninsula** is 3 miles (5 km) from the centre of the city at the mouth of the Vistula. The first shots of World War II were fired here on 1 September 1939, and the Polish garrison of just 180 men commanded by Major Henryk Sucharski managed to hold on for a whole week.

To the north, **Oliva**, Gdansk's prettiest suburb, has a 13th- to 15th-century cathedral with an 18th-century organ and a supporting ensemble of articulated wooden angels. This amazing contraption is kept busy with daily recitals and is the focus of an annual organ festival held in August.

Sopot was a popular resort since the early 19th century, and while the wide sandy beaches are still inviting, the water certainly is not. In fact, bathing is sensibly banned. With that reservation, the recently restored Grand Hotel is evocative of an elegant past with its daily tea dances and so forth. The food is good and the casino is probably the smartest in Poland.

The water clears up and is fit for swimming farther north where the coast is peppered with charming fishing villages with plenty of cheap accommodation in private houses and on campsites. The place to aim for is the forested **Polwesep Helski Peninsula**, which curves out into the Gulf of Gdansk for 25 miles (40 km). **Jastarnia** is the arty village, **Jurata** the more fashionable.

The inland town of **Elblag** has a history reaching back to the 9th century and achieved the height of its prosperity in the 16th and 17th. The date on the Market Gate is 1319 and some of the walls from the same period are still standing. The older part of the town has been well preserved. The two churches of note are St Michael's, with its 300-ft (90-metre) spire and St Mary's, which today houses an art gallery.

Malbork, on the Nogat River south-

The High Tatras near Morskie Oko.

west of Elblag, has a massive castle which was once used by the Grand Master of the Teutonic Knights, whose exploits are covered in the Baltic sections of this book. The castle has been restored with particular attention to the Grand Master's personal palace within it. There is little else in Malbork, but the castle is worth the trip. There is another Teutonic castle with a "Crooked Tower" at **Torun**, a Hanseatic town and the birthplace of Copernicus in 1473. The house in question has a collection of astronomical instruments of the period.

Mansurian Lakes: These lakes, Poland's playground, are neatly positioned between Warsaw and Gdansk. There are reputed to be 1,000 of them, although there are so many interconnecting rivers and canals it is somewhat hard to tell where one ends and the next begins. The net result, however, is a concentration of 90 nature reserves with several species found nowhere else, like a particular type of European bison (in the Borecka Forest reserve) and some tiny tarpan ponies (at Popielno).

The **Puszcza Augustowska** and the **Puszcza Piska** are the best bets for a wider sample of wildlife. Roe deer and red deer, wild boar, elk, bison, storks and eagles exist in an almost primeval world of pine and fir forests, while swans, herons, cormorants, cranes and ducks nest around the edges of the lakes. Gulls follow the boats on lakes and rivers which still abound in eels, pike and salmon-trout. There is selective shooting of geese, duck, and grouse on production of a permit obtainable locally. One of the more unusual local activities is hunting for crayfish by torchlight.

The largest town in the region is **Olsztyn**, a town which once belonged to the Teutonic Order and subsequently passed through the hands of Poland and Prussia before reverting to Poland in 1945. It was once occupied by French troops and then by Russians. All becomes clear on visiting the museum in the **Warmia Castle**.

It was while working here between 1516 and 1521 that Copernicus began *De revolutionibus orbium coelestium* – in other words, his startling idea that the

earth revolved around the sun and not the other way round. Parts of the astronomical charts actually used by him are on the wall of the museum devoted to his work. The tradition is maintained by a planetarium which was opened in 1973, the 500th anniversary of his birth, and a more recent observatory.

At **Gierloz** near Ketrzyn are the ruins of the headquarters which Hitler occupied for two years, the Wolfsschanze. In 1940–42 there were some 80 buildings on the site, many with walls 25 ft (8 metres) thick. It was here that the ill-starred Stauffenberg assassination attempt took place on 20 July 1944.

Justice cannot be done in the space available here to all the places of interest in Poland. It is simply as a reminder, therefore, that reference is made to **Lublin** which, with its five universities, is entitled to claim status as Poland's intellectual centre, and to **Poznan**, a fine historic city which was occasionally the capital of Poland in the Middle Ages. Visits to either would be well rewarded.

Riding high at Zakopane in the Tatras.

THE CZECH AND SLOVAK REPUBLICS

The Sword of Damocles swinging ominously over agitation for independence in Eastern Europe in the late 1980s was the memory of Czechoslovakia in 1968, when 400,000 Soviet troops led by tanks swarmed over its borders to stamp out the gentle Dubcek liberalisation known as the Prague Spring. The fear was that a false move by Solidarity in Poland or its counterparts elsewhere would bring in the tanks again, regardless of the Soviet Union's own progress into the era of *glasnost*.

Czechoslovakia had been quiet for 20 years following the aborted Prague Spring, but it had not been forgotten when Mikhail Gorbachev paid a hugely popular visit in 1988. A loaded question was put to the Soviet leader and commander-in-chief: "What is the difference between *glasnost* and the Prague Spring?" The simple reply was in retrospect a green light not only for Czechoslovakia but the whole of Eastern Europe: "Twenty years."

The subsequent Czechoslovak drive for independence led by the playwright Vaclav Havel was remarkably smooth even next to the generally peaceful international revolution which surged forward under Gorbachev's green light. The tanks did not return, no one was killed and only Hungary among the newly independent nations had economic prospects as promising as Czechoslovakia's. Westerners poured into Prague by tens of thousands to soak up its magnificent architectural heritage and to welcome back a city which had always looked distinctly out of place east of the Iron Curtain.

The euphoria dimmed with the announcement in 1992 that the Czechoslovak Federation was breaking up into Czech and Slovak republics. The first instinct was to recall Communist jibes at the time that the Prague Spring was a disguised plot by the Slovak Dubcek to split the federation, especially as the Slovaks had never concealed their resentment at what they considered the overweening Czech chauvinism of the current Communist leadership. Slovaks always coughed politely when "Czech" was used as a short-form of "Czechoslovak". One of the jokes explaining why Czechs were not Slovaks was that the former liked beer while the latter preferred wine. This was itself a very short form indeed for all the implications of a nation which had once been cut in half, the Czechs growing up in a Germanicised world and hence their supposed liking for beer, while the Slovaks were attached to Hungary and accordingly acquired their taste for wine.

The enforced separation of Czechs from Slovaks occurred, as we shall see, in the year 896, and when the two halves reunited in 1918 under the auspices of the Paris peace conference, the hope was that their common origins would overcome the effects of living apart over the intervening 1,000-plus years. The divorce in 1992 implied that the differences were, for the moment at least, irreconcilable.

Preceding pages: busking in Prague; the capital's Tyn Church, seen from the old town hall. **Left**, St Vitus's Cathedral, Prague.

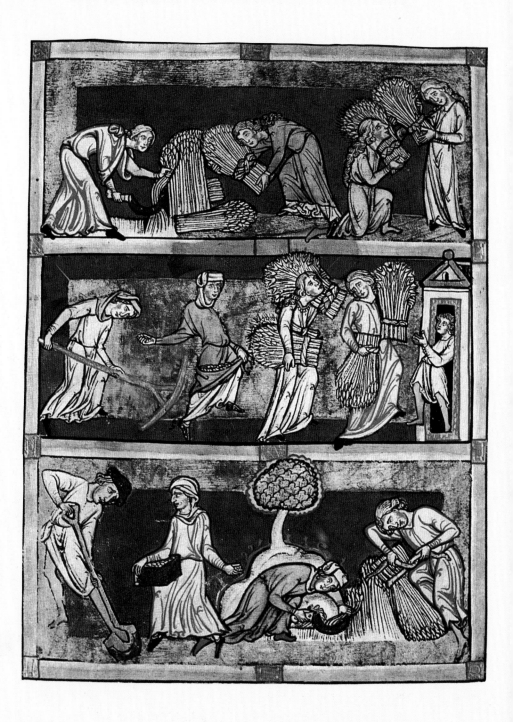

THE MAKING (AND UNMAKING) OF CZECHOSLOVAKIA

The Czech and Slovak Republics are divided into three parts: Bohemia in the west, Moravia in the middle and Slovakia in the east. The rolling hills of Bohemia flatten seamlessly into the Moravian Plain, but where the two so-called Czech lands meet Slovakia, the plain rears up into mountains to make the break clear and unequivocal. The 9th-century Great Moravian Empire embraced all three regions, and it seems there was little to distinguish the so-called Western Slavs who inhabited them. In 896, however, the alien Magyars invaded from Hungary and a decisive battle was fought near Bratislava, the present capital of Slovakia. Svatopluk, the last of the Great Moravian Emperors, saw his forces summarily defeated and retired to spend the rest of his life as a hermit.

The Magyar conquest divided the stricken empire along its natural fault line, the border between the Czech lands and Slovakia, so the three components were to all intents and purposes reduced to two. The eastern half, or Slovakia, was for more than a thousand years afterwards a mere annex of Hungary, and the story of the Slovak people is of an uninterrupted struggle for existence. They were assimilated to the extent of following Hungary's lead into Roman Catholicism and euphemistically acquiring a taste for wine, but there were few avenues of escape from peasantry bordering on serfdom well into the 19th century.

The unconquered westerners took an entirely different route which put them into the mainstream of Western European culture with a strong Germanic flavour and hence a proverbial liking for beer. While the Slovaks disappeared into agrarian obscurity, the early Bohemians bound on to the stage of European history. The brothers Methodius and Cyril, inventors of the Cyrillic script, are seen converting Prince Borivoj and his wife Ludmila to Christianity, although the cause was immediately set back when their son Vratislav married a virulent pagan named Drahomira who insisted on bringing up one of their two sons according to her beliefs. He ended up branded as Boleslav the Cruel,

while his brother became a model of Christian piety, the Good Prince Wenceslas. He earned an unwarranted promotion to "King" in the Christmas carol because an English scholar misread an early Bohemian text.

The historical Prince Wenceslas was bent on making Bohemia more German and less Slavic, which is why Czech Nazis of the 20th century adopted him as a kind of patron saint. He was a good but weak Christian, unable to prevent his formidable mother Drahomira from closing down all Christian churches and ordering a massacre of the faithful. While brave in battle, he was handicapped in other respects by what an early historian called "an excessive zeal for preserving his virginity". He was eventually butchered by his brother, Boleslav the Cruel, who assumed his title and won their mother's admiration by executing all Christian priests.

Like Wenceslas, Boleslav cultivated friendly relations with the Germans, and he was at Otto the Great's side at the battle of Lechfeld in 955 which checked Magyar expansion into Germany and Italy. Thereafter the Magyars were confined more or less to modern Hungary, Transylvania and Slovakia. His son, also Boleslav, was such a pleasant contrast to his father that he was known as Boleslav the Pious. He, too, got on well with the Germans and was rewarded in 973 with the right to have a bishop in Prague. The first incumbent was Detmar, a Saxon monk.

The Bohemian line was carried through 31 members of the Premyslid dynasty, among whom Ottokar I distinguished himself by extracting from the German Holy Roman Emperor in 1212 a Golden Bull which recognised a hereditary Bohemian kingdom. His son Wenceslas I (1230–53) and grandson Ottokar II (1253–78) steered the young kingdom of Bohemia through incessant difficulties, first with Frederick the Quarrelsome of Austria – he personally preferred the nickname "Wonder of the World" – and then with Rudolf, who was the founder of the Habsburg dynasty.

Ottokar II was scandalised by Rudolf's election as Emperor, a position for which he thought his own qualifications were eminently more suitable. Despite a double marriage between the two families, Ottokar was not appeased. In 1278 he marched on Vienna ranting about "the insatiable lusts of the Germans". Rudolf had in the meantime assembled a formidable collection of supporters, Slavic as well as German, and in a battle at Durnkrut on the Marchfeld that year, the German heavy cavalry crushed the Bohemian forces. Ottokar was killed, eventually to be succeeded at Rudolf's instigation by young Wenceslas II.

The Habsburgs thus put shackles on Bohemia which were to remain in place until World War I. The Premyslid dynasty was on its way out, but Wenceslas was able to engineer a final if modest blaze of glory. The

married a sister of the last Premyslid king and was crowned king of Bohemia in 1311 at the age of 15. He was an indefatigable warrior and, evidently finding life in Bohemia too tame, spent all his time fighting other people's wars even after losing his sight completely. A groom led him into the battle of Crécy between France and England in 1346 and he conducted himself with conspicuous gallantry before falling in a last hopeless charge. Edward the Black Prince retrieved his shield emblazoned with three feathers from the battlefield and adopted it together with John's motto *Ich Dien* ("I serve"). They are still used in Britain by the Prince of Wales.

Poles had got themselves into such a mess that they offered him the Polish crown as well. Wenceslas was duly crowned king of Poland in 1300.

The very next year the Hungarians offered him their crown. He passed it to his son who in due course and as Wenceslas III therefore wore the triple crowns of Bohemia, Poland and Hungary. Alas, he fell victim to "dissipation and profligacy" and was murdered in 1306 in unexplained circumstances. That was the end of both the Premyslids and the United Kingdom of Bohemia, Poland and Hungary.

John, son of Henry III of Luxembourg,

In Charles, John's son, Bohemia acquired its most famous king. He could speak Latin, French, German, Czech and Italian with equal fluency. Unlike his father, he felt deeply about his kingdom. "I found Bohemia desolate," he wrote in his autobiography, "not a castle free that was not pledged, so I had nowhere to lodge except in cities like any other citizen. Prague had been desolated and destroyed since the days of King Ottokar. So I decided to build a new palace which should be large and handsome."

The new palace was the signal for what has since been acknowledged as Prague's Golden Age. The mark Charles left on Prague is almost as conspicuous today as it was six centuries ago. He was King Charles I of Bohemia, but he is usually remembered as Charles IV, the title he assumed as Holy Roman Emperor.

Charles started the Cathedral of St Vitus, restored the ruined Hradcany Castle, and built the Karlstein Castle just outside Prague. He founded the University of Prague, which sooned joined the universities at Paris, Oxford and Bologna as a pre-eminent seat of medieval learning. The influx of university people caused townsmen to complain about a shortage of accommodation and rent increases, and it was partly to satisfy them that Charles ordered the construction of a new town across the river and the famous stone bridge leading to it, which bears his name.

Charles died just as schism in the church was coming to a head, and his son and successor to both thrones, Wenceslas IV, lacked the same moderating influence. Historians are not now inclined to accept stories that Wenceslas once roasted an incompetent cook on his own spit or literally went hunting for monks, but there is no doubt that he drank heavily and that the habit "sometimes vented itself in ferocious outbursts".

With Christendom split between three candidates each for the Papacy and Holy Roman Empire, Bohemia produced John Huss, who lent his voice to a campaign by John Wycliffe and the Lollards in England complaining about abuses in the church and suggesting that Christianity would be better served with neither Pope nor Holy Roman Emperor. Huss was born in about 1369 of peasant parents in the village of Husinec, and rose to become Rector of Prague University in 1403. As such, he defended Wycliffe against vilification and was eventually excommunicated by Pope John XXIII, a man once described as combining the worst qualities of a pirate and a gangster.

Huss was summoned to appear before the Council of the Church at Constance, where he put up a masterful defence but to no avail. He was burnt at the stake and his ashes scattered so that no part of him could be returned to Bohemia as the relic of a martyr.

The execution caused rioting in Bohemia, during which Hussites occupied most of the

churches. Protestors stormed the Council House in Prague and, seizing the royalist mayor and a number of councillors, threw them out of a window, thus setting the precedent for the peculiarly Czech practice of defenestration. Some of the protestors fled from the inevitable reprisals to settle outside the city and name their number after nearby Mount Tabor.

Taborites pooled their possessions in what later Communists like to think of as spontaneous socialism. While the Taborites are generally remembered for a strict moral code that banned fighting, theft, alcohol and gambling, there were off-shoots of their movement like the Nicolaitans on a river island

near Vesely who believed that no natural urge could be sinful. Their natural urges included sharing their women and running around naked, which earned them the nickname "Adamists". The stern Taborite John Zizka would have none of it ordered them to be consigned to the flames. The incorrigible Adamists evidently went to their deaths saying that they were fully confident of reigning in heaven that day with Christ. In contrast, the Ultraquists among the Hussites were scarcely distinguishable from Roman Catholics in most respects.

"Fool that I am," wrote Martin Luther after first thinking that Hussites were arch-heretics, "without knowing it, I have taught and held all the teachings of John Huss." He was soon advising the Hussites to sever all links with the Roman Church. This put the Czech Protestants on a collision course with their Catholic Habsburg kings and the Jesuits. When the Jesuits urged the Habsburgs to ban all Protestants from the kingdom, the Protestant nobility countered by establishing a rebel government.

In 1618 an attempt by the Catholic authorities to stop the construction of two Protestant churches resulted in more than 100 Protestant nobles making their way to Hradcany Castle to remonstrate with the Catholic councillors. During the violent altercation which

The war raged across the breadth of Europe – it pitted the forces of the Reformation against those of the Counter-Reformation – but within the context of Bohemia it was focussed primarily on the battle of White Mountain a few miles outside Prague. For all its fame, the battle was decided in the first few minutes and the Protestants were roundly beaten. The statistics relating to the condition of Bohemia afterwards make grim reading: the population fell from 3 million to 800,000; 782 towns and 36,000 villages before the war were reduced to 230 and 6,000, the nobility were wiped out and were replaced by Habsburg favourites and adventurers. Ferdinand III removed the imperial

ensued, two councillors wearing full ceremonial regalia were flung out of the window in the second and more famous "Defenestration of Prague". Their 50-ft (15-metre) fall was broken by a pile of dung and they staggered off, covered in filth, to report the outrage to their Habsburg masters. Defenestration, according to a Czech chronicle, was "in accordance with the ancient custom of the realm and the example of the Bible and Roman history". Whatever the case may be, it resulted in this instance in the Thirty Years' War with devastation more widespread than anything Europe was to experience until the Napoleonic wars.

capital to Vienna and put Bohemia under the special tutelage of the Virgin Mary in theory and the Jesuits in practice.

The last traces of Protestantism were wiped out by forced conversion although, by the Jesuits' own calculation, about two-thirds of the population remained secretly attached to one or other of the old religions. All books in vernacular Czech, and any in German that looked at all suspicious, were destroyed. Literature dried up completely and did not resume until 150 years later when the Jesuits

Above, the 1618 defenestration of Prague, which triggered the Thirty Years' War.

were expelled. The Czech language became nothing more than the patois of serfs.

The other side of the coin would not have comforted contemporary peasants, but it was certainly a boon for the tourist industry in years ahead. The expropriated estates turned their new owners into overnight millionaires, and they spent the money with an abandon which might not have been the case had they actually earned it. Architects, sculptors, artists and craftsmen were brought in from all over Europe to engage in an immense building programme which produced palaces, churches and manorial halls dripping with the frescoes and sculpture which were the hallmarks of baroque Italy, the dominant influence of the time.

In 1775, the peasants rebelled. They had heard and believed rumours that the corvée, which is to say their compulsory unpaid labour on estates, was to be abolished. When this proved to be untrue, their disappointment boiled over into attacks on the country estates. Within a few weeks, 15,000 rebels were converging on Prague. The uprising was put down without too much trouble and only three rebels were executed, but the affair made the Empress Maria Theresa wonder whether the whole system of serfdom ought to be reviewed or even abolished. The estate barons assured her that to tinker with the system would bring the whole economy to an immediate halt.

Maria Theresa's son Joseph II was more determined to press ahead with reforms. He prepared no fewer than 11,000 new laws relating to serfdom, and peasants could look forward to the day when they were no longer tied to a particular estate, could marry at will, change jobs and even own property. They would no longer be required to kiss the hand of the landlord or his agent, nor bow to the ground before them.

All this was supposed to happen on All Saints' Day 1790. Instead, Joseph died before the great day and all his reforms were pushed under the carpet. The corvée was not abolished for another 50 years.

The intellectuals were getting restless, too, and their particular cause was the restoration of the Czech language. Significantly, an eloquent "Plea for the Czech Language and Literature" by the custodian of the Brno library was written in German. The Czech aspirations mirrored the nationalist interests of the romantic movement then springing up all over Europe. The founding of the Narodni Museum in Prague was a manifestation of these sentiments, which also reached the almost forgotten Slovaks still under their Magyar overlords. Some thought their interests would be best served in alliance with the Czechs; others preferred an entirely independent effort.

The French Revolution represented precisely what Joseph had sought to avoid by his reforms. His successor, Francis II, was born within a year of Napoleon, and Europe was simply not big enough to contain their respective imperial ambitions. The Czechs' incidental role in the Napoleonic wars was to provide a convenient battleground for the main combatants. The battle of Austerlitz was fought at Slavkov, to use the local name, in Moravia. It was this stunning French victory over the Austrian army that emboldened Napoleon to declare himself Holy Roman Emperor.

Francis, the reigning emperor, was in no position to argue. He laid down his imperial crown and said he would be satisfied to be plain Francis I of Austria. Napoleon entertained thoughts of creating an "Empire of Bohemia" for himself, but he first had to attend to the matter of invading Russia. That, of course, was that.

The Congress of Vienna, after Napoleon's ultimate downfall, went a long way towards restoring Austria's prestige and Francis felt confident enough to scorn any talk of further liberalisation in Bohemia or anywhere else. "I won't have any innovations," he said in 1831. "Let the laws be justly applied: our laws are good and adequate. This is no time for reforms. The people are, as it were, badly wounded. One must avoid irritating these wounds by touching them."

The 1848 revolutions in France, Hungary and elsewhere raised Czech nationalist expectations to unprecedented levels. "I am a Czech of Slav race," declared Palacky, the author of a 10-volume history of Bohemia. The Slovaks joined in the chorus with variations to suit their own circumstances. Their aim was to divorce Slovakia from Hungary and bring the country into a "Czechoslav" federation with Bohemia and Moravia which would be independent of Austria. When broadsheets appeared in Slovakia calling for a Slovak uprising against Hungary, gallows were ostentatiously erected in villages as a hint to would-be rebels.

In spite of high levels of nationalist feelings throughout Europe in the late 19th century, none of the Czech leaders pursued separatist aims before World War I. The most they dared hope for was autonomy within an Austrian federalist structure.

On the outbreak of the war the majority of Czech politicians, if not of the population as a whole, believed that Russian manpower would steamroller the armies of Germany and Austria-Hungary and arrive at the gates of Prague to establish some kind of Pan-Slavic unity. Thomas Masaryk, on the other hand, preferred an accommodation with the British and French opposition and hoped that an Allied victory would lead to the creation of an independent state consisting not only of Bohemia and Moravia but also of the Slovak districts of Hungary.

Masaryk envisaged a kingdom with a Danish or Belgian prince on the throne. Pro-German Prague was no place to propagate such views, so Masaryk was forced into exile for the duration of hostilities. Before leaving he helped to establish a Czech underground, and in so doing made the acquaintance of Eduard Benes, the future Foreign Minister of Czechoslovakia, its second president and the other great figure of Czechoslovak independence.

After the Russian revolution of 1917, Masaryk lobbied for the creation of a Czech national army made up of Czechs who had been taken prisoner by the Russians while fighting in the Austro-Hungarian army. Some 5,000 such prisoners were being held in Kiev and the majority were not at all keen on re-entering the fray.

Masaryk was strongly anti-Bolshevik and on his instructions the nascent Czech army remained neutral in the war between the Russian factions. When Kiev fell to the Red Army in 1918, all but 2,000 of the Czechs were still there and he wanted them out. But how? The only idea anyone could come up with sounded fantastic: they were to be taken from Kiev across Siberia to Vladivostok and thence via the Far East to France. This exodus, or anabasis as it came to be called, provided one of the most extraordinary sideshows of the war.

Partly under German prompting, the Bolsheviks refused to let the Czechs go and instead demanded the surrender of all arms and equipment. Trotsky, as Foreign Commissar, gave orders to shoot any Czech caught with a weapon in his hands. Nevertheless the great railway odyssey began. The Czech troops found themselves dotted along 5,000 miles of railway between Samara on the Volga and Vladivostok. Ignoring Masaryk's orders, the majority joined in the fighting on the side of the White Russians, although a few sided with the Reds.

These Czech freebooters were on the loose in Russia for two years. Fantastic tales of their exploits reached the West, and the likes of Lloyd George, the British Prime Minister, hailed them as heroes. They were not evacuated from Siberia until November 1920. The affair was deeply embarrassing to Czech communists, who passed a resolution saying that Czechoslovak opposition to the great Russian people and the revolution was "an historical misunderstanding".

A Soviet government came to power in Hungary in March 1919, and by spring a considerable number of Czech troops were in action against the Communists in Slovakia. While the fighting was going on, the peace conference in Paris concerned itself with setting Czechoslovakia's borders. The Germans of Bohemia and Moravia were punished, as it were, for cheering on the "wrong" side in the war, while Masaryk was given the benefit of any doubt because of his loyalty to the Allies.

Discussions on the future of Slovakia acknowledged potential problems arising from the fact that Czechs and Slovaks had effectively lived in different civilisations for centuries, the Czechs having industrialised while the Slovaks remained almost exclusively agricultural. The Czechs had been culturally and psychologically part of the West, the Slovaks of the East.

The Czechslovak state which emerged from these negotiations was divided over which political direction it ought to take. The Social Democrats, who emerged as the dominant party, were themselves split between the nationalist old guard who did not like the prospect of a Bolshevik Russia and a left wing which rejected bourgeois values and wished to embark on socialist, proletarian policies, namely the expropriation of large estates and the nationalisation of the mines, railways, and armament factories.

Left-wing policies were a mixture of idealism and vengeance. The expropriation of the estates had less to do with making agriculture more efficient than with punishing those families who, three centuries before, had been given the land in return for loyalty to Catholicism and the Habsburgs.

Masaryk tried to distance himself from the wranglings within the party although it was clear where his feelings lay. "I know Bolshevik Russia well," he said on a tour of industrial and mining centres, "I observed the Bolshevik revolution very carefully. I say here, according to my best knowledge and conscience that the Russian example is unsuitable for us, the Czechs... In Bohemia we own state and the rights of the ethnic minorities. The German minority, by far the largest at nearly one-quarter of the population, was hostile to the idea of a Czech-run state and, to them, conciliation meant submission. Then came the Depression and, in Germany, the rise of Hitler to power.

In 1934 Czechoslovakia had its own fascist National Union and, at the other end of the spectrum, an increasingly strident Communist Party led by Klement Gottwald. "Real peace and order," Gottwald told parliament, "the kind of peace and order which we are fighting for, will be achieved only when you hang from the lamp-posts."

Not long afterwards and with a warrant out

need a way, a method of work, a method of social changes, according to our own customs and according to our own needs."

The socialist left were not to be placated, however, and a general strike was declared in December 1920. It was put down with some severity and in May the following year the Communist Party was founded. By 1925 it was the second largest party in parliament.

In 1928 the Czechoslovak republic celebrated its 10th anniversary. Masaryk was 78 years old and still trying to reconcile the desire of the "pure" Czechoslavs to run their

Above, Masaryk seeks support in the US in 1918.

for his arrest, Gottwald went into exile in Moscow. Masaryk was caught in the crossfire from right and left. In 1935 he resigned as president in favour of his chosen successor Benes and was soon dead. It was said that he timed his death to avoid seeing the destruction of the state he had created.

Less than a month after Masaryk's funeral, Konrad Henlein, leader of the Nazis in Czechoslovakia, was in London telling British diplomats that 90 per cent of the country's Germans were in favour of complete annexation to Hitler's Reich. In Berlin, he advised Hitler to incorporate all the Czech areas as well as the German into Germany.

On 11 March 1938 Hitler occupied Austria and at Munich later that year, Britain and France gave him the green light to detach the German border areas from Czechoslovakia.

"How horrible, fantastic, incredible it is," said the British Prime Minister Neville Chamberlain, "that we should be digging trenches and trying on gas masks here (in Britain) because of a quarrel in a far away country between people of whom we know nothing." Benes and the government chose not to defend the border territories and the army was pulled back. In March 1939, whether or not on Henlein's recommendation, Hitler's troops marched into Prague and Czechoslovakia ceased to exist. Hitler knew how to get

of the government which he served as Foreign Minister. Were the Czech airmen, he asked, "provisionally dead?" Churchill agreed and fired off one of his famously terse notes: "I do not see why the Czechs should not be put on the same footing as other Allied governments. They have deserved it." Full recognition followed.

In the "Protectorate of Bohemia and Moravia", however, the population seemed strangely resigned to the German occupation. Even when General Elias, the prime minister, was sentenced to death for treason (partly because he had been in touch with Benes in London), he accepted the verdict gladly, he said, if it would make the Czechs

the Slovaks on his side: he gave them their separate state.

Masaryk's son Jan became a public figure at home because of his war-time broadcasts through the BBC. "By the name I bear," he told listeners who risked the death penalty for tuning in, "I declare to you that we shall win this fight and that truth will prevail." In due course, the National Committee which grew around Benes and Masaryk in London was recognised as a provisional government. Meanwhile, many of Czechs had joined the Allied forces and more than 500 Czech airmen were killed in the Battle of Britain.

Masaryk resented the "provisional" status

cooperate sincerely with the German occupation forces. Benes was embarrassed by the passivity of his countrymen and the calm "in which the continuous humming of the Czech armaments industry was the only clearly audible sound".

Plans for something that would shake them up began to form around the sinister figure of Reinhard Heydrich, the chief of Nazi security who was in Prague to sort out which Czechs were qualified to join the German master race. Two volunteers in Britain, one Czech and one Slovak, were trained by the

Above, Hitler crosses the Czech border in 1939.

British Special Operations Executive for a parachute drop, and on 27 May 1942 they blew up Heydrich. The assassination attracted worldwide publicity but failed to stimulate resistance, and the Germans destroyed the village of Lidice in reprisal.

The Czech government in London had its parallel in Moscow where Klement Gottwald had been joined by many members of the Czech Communist Party. Benes was far more amenable towards these Communists than was Masaryk and, during a visit to Moscow, invited them to join his government. The invitation was refused, however, probably on principle but also because the Communist line was that the Czechs and Slovaks were separate peoples and ought to be treated as such after the war.

It was in fact among the Slovaks in 1944 that the most significant uprising against the Germans took place. When it became clear a few months later that the Red Army would reach Czechoslovak territory first, the Moscow contingent of Czechs appeared to have a head-start over their London counterparts.

The future of Czechoslovakia was not specifically discussed at Yalta. The serious bargaining began when the London Czechs arrived in Moscow in March 1945 to be met by Gottwald and the other Czech Communist leaders. Benes was to be president, but the ministries of the interior, education, information and agriculture were to be filled by Communists, as would be the posts of Prime Minister and Deputy Prime Minister, by Zdenek Fierlinger and Gottwald respectively. Masaryk was to be Foreign Minister. This government set off by train for Prague, which had recently been liberated by the Red Army. Masaryk did not travel with them.

The Czechoslovakia to which Masaryk eventually returned in the summer of 1945 was different from the country his father had known. Ruthenia had been incorporated in the Ukrainian Soviet Republic and enormous demographic changes were under way. It had been decided that the more than 3 million German occupants of the Czech lands, almost one-third of the population, were to be expelled, as were the Hungarians of Slovakia. The Jews had either died in concentration camps or left. At Benes's insistence, there were to be no minorities in Czechoslovakia, thereby dispensing with the question of minority rights.

The Red Army left Czechoslovakia in November 1945 but it only went as far as the Elbe River in Germany. Other army units were stationed all around – in Poland and Hungary, in Romania and Bulgaria. In the parliamentary election in May 1946 the Communists emerged as the single most powerful organisation in the country with 40 per cent of the votes in Bohemia and Moravia and 30 per cent in Slovakia. Gottwald, who was Moscow's man, moved up a notch to become Prime Minister in place of Fierlinger.

In 1947, George Marshall unveiled in a speech at Harvard University his plan to achieve a lasting peace in Europe through the injection of massive economic aid. This was something Moscow could not match and therefore was seen as a threat to its plans for Eastern Europe. Pressure was applied through Communist Party channels. Poland was the first to announce that it would have nothing to do with the Marshall Plan. The next day the Czechoslovaks learned from Stalin himself that their participation would be regarded as a hostile act.

Communist demonstrations brought the country to a halt on 24 February 1948 and Benes, who was ill and appeared to have lost the will to resist, called on the Communist Gottwald to form a new government replacing the non-Communists with his own people. The only exception was Masaryk, who was to remain as Foreign Minister although he, too, seemed to have lost his appetite for the job. Two weeks later the last obstacle between the Communists and a complete sweep was removed when Masaryk was found dead beneath a high window in the courtyard of the Foreign Ministry. Whether it was suicide or yet another Prague defenestration has never been settled, although the consensus in recent years has moved towards the latter.

The Czechoslovaks buckled down to life under the egomaniacal Gottwald and his Communist colleagues with very little protest. The arrests, tortures and executions which did occur were principally purges within the Communist Party aimed at eliminating "Trotskyite, Titoite, Zionist and bourgeois-nationalist" tendencies. The accused in one trial was made to confess that in 1927, which is to say 25 years earlier, he had once shouted "Long live Trotsky" in public. Stalin and Gottwald, his fervent Czech admirer, died within a few weeks of one another in 1953. The inflexibility of Gottwald's heir, Antonin Novotny, was demonstrated by the regime's warm endorsement of the Soviet's Union's savage response to the Hungarian uprising in 1956.

Alexander Dubcek, whose father had been one of the founders of the Communist Party in Slovakia and who himself grew up in the Soviet Union, emerged in the 1960s as the mild-mannered spokesman for Slovakian misgivings about the blatant Czech bias of the Novotny regime. A succession of economic crises weakened Novotny's personal position, and in October 1967 Dubcek summoned the nerve to attack him openly, de-

manding that he surrender either the presidency or his position as first secretary of the Party. Novotny appealed to the Soviet leader, Leonid Brezhnev, but to no avail. He stepped down as first secretary on 5 January 1968 and was succeeded by Dubcek.

Dubcek, whose loyalty to the Soviet Union was unquestioned, declared his intention of putting "a human face" on Communism, not getting rid of it, but part of the human face that most mattered was an unprecedented level of press freedom which allowed journalists to say things that Dubcek would probably not have gone as far as saying himself. Novotny, still president, was accused of cor-

ruption and expelled from the party. Brezhnev, it seems, was now genuinely alarmed, especially after a manifesto signed by 70 leading writers, intellectuals and public figures pledged support for further reforms. Dubcek declined an invitation to attend a summit in Warsaw and clarify his intentions. He was then upbraided by Brezhnev personally but refused to recant. On the night of 20 August, 400,000 Soviet troops with tanks invaded from neighbouring Warsaw Pact countries. "Responding to the request for help from leading party and state leaders of Czechoslovakia who have remained faithful to socialism," said a radio broadcast, "we instructed our armed forces to go to the support of the working class…"

In complete contrast with their acquiescence over the previous 20 years, Czechs and Slovaks put up a bold resistance, but over the next few months Dubcek was beaten into submission, eventually to be replaced as party leader by Gustav Husak. Thus was the Prague Spring ended, and Dubcek supporters found themselves out of jobs and forced to resort to menial work like window-cleaning. Dubcek himself became a forestry officer near Bratislava in his native Slovakia. With a few notable exceptions, Czechs and Slovaks were acquiescent again for another 20 years, the memory of what had happened enshrined in the self-immolation of a young student, Jan Palach, in Wenceslas Square.

The cause of Czechoslovak independence during these 20 years was pursued by the country's non-Communist intellectuals under the banner of democratic rights as laid out in the Helsinki Final Act of 1975. Under constant official harassment – which saw them also reduced to window-cleaning, if not jailed – they produced a statement of principles, "Charter 77", largely written by the playwright Vaclav Havel. For his part in the protest, Havel served a total of five years in prison.

Husak retired as party secretary in 1987, to be replaced by Milos Jakes, one of the party leaders who had welcomed the invasion in 1968. The following year, the Soviet leader Mikhail Gorbachev visited Prague, intimating that his policy of *glasnost* could accommodate the kinds of demands which had been made during the Prague Spring and been taken up by Charter 77. By suggesting that the Soviet Union would not intervene to counter any new uprising, Gorbachev was all but inviting the dissidents to do just that.

This did not impress the Prague regime. A small demonstration commemorating the 20th anniversary of the 1968 invasion swelled into a march of 20,000 but was then stopped by the police. The organisers arranged another demonstration five weeks later, the pretence on this occasion being the 70th anniversary of Czechoslovakia's independence from the Habsburg empire. The police again stepped in. On 10 December, however, a third demonstration – International Human Rights Day – was allowed to continue unmolested. Havel scented a change in the air. "Our government," he said, "has finally rec-

Within days, Dubcek had reappeared in public to address a rally in Bratislava. A few days later, he stood next to Havel before a crowd of 750,000 in Prague. By the end of the year, the Czechoslovak Communist Party had packed its bags and gone.

The subsequent election of Havel as president, with Dubcek beside him as parliamentary chairman, was a pointed symbol of Czech and Slovak solidarity. But there was an indication of separatist sentiments elsewhere when, in dropping the name "Socialist Republic of Czechoslovakia", the Slovaks let it be known that they favoured insertion of a hyphen in the new name. It ought to be, they said, the "Republic of Czecho-Slovakia".

ognised that it has to be more tolerant."

The level of protest rose through 1989, the people taking enormous heart from Poland's termination of the Communist Party's monopoly on power and from Hungary's preparations for free elections. The Czechoslovak government remained so firmly in control, however, that Havel and Charter 77 advised students to keep their powder dry. The signal to begin in earnest came from Berlin on 9 November, the night the Wall was breached.

Left, Alexander Dubcek, brushed aside by the Russians in 1968. Above, Vaclav Havel expresses solidarity with Polish leader Lech Walesa.

Parliament went further: it voted for the "Czech and Slovak Federative Republic".

The subsequent decision to break up the Federation completely meant that none of these names fitted the bill. Slovaks, who traditionally winced when foreigners innocently used "Czech" when they should have said "Czechoslovakian" had nothing to worry about. "Slovakia" was self-evident. It was then up to the Czechs either to stick to "the Czech Republic" or come up with something snappier but satisfying both Bohemia and Moravia. Alexander Dubcek did not live to see the outcome: he died in the autumn of 1992, a few months before the final split.

THE CZECH AND SLOVAK REPUBLICS: WHAT TO SEE

Prague: "I can see a great city, whose fame will reach the stars," declared Princess Libussa as she stood with outstretched arms on a precipice above the Vltava River. She was the mythical beauty who was reputed to have summoned an unsuspecting plough-hand, still wearing his boots, to found Bohemia's Premyslid dynasty. This version of events overlooks the fact that the shadowy historical figure of one Samo, the victor over the Avars in about 620, established his capital at Vysehrad a short distance away, but in any case by the 14th-century Prague was the grandest city in Europe, a marvel of Gothic architecture. Three centuries later, having acquired a certain notoriety for defenestration, the fancy term for the basic business of throwing people out of windows, Prague was embellished with the finest baroque building of the age.

In spite of the city's position at the centre of all the religious and political convulsions which have surged across Europe's east-west axis, including World War II and the Soviet invasion in 1968, Prague survives in an almost pristine condition, a cross-section of all the grand themes of Western civilisation.

Removed from the mainstream of tourism for four decades, Prague proved irresistible to tens of thousands of Westerners as soon as the Iron Curtain lifted, and within weeks there was hardly a hotel room to be had. Demand is likely to overstretch facilities for several years to come, so there is something to be said for adopting the view that there is no gain to be had by waiting.

A journey through Prague's crowded history is much simplified by a grasp of its basic geography, and the best place to sort out bearings is the celebrated **Charles IV Bridge**. High on the west bank is **Hradcany Castle**, Prague's

Preceding pages: Prague's Old City. <u>Left</u>, Charles Bridge, Prague, by night.

Acropolis and the throne of political power from the 12th century onwards. Beneath it on the same side of the river is **Mala Strana**, which means "Lesser Town"; it originally caught the civilian overflow from the castle but, after a fire in 1541, it was rebuilt in full Renaissance splendour. On the east bank just opposite the castle is **Stare Mesto**, or Old Town, whose walls enclosed the first phase of Charles IV's bold building programme.

It was obvious even then that space in the old town was limited, so Charles planned the adjacent **Nove Mesto**, or New Town, to the south as a separate district. These plans were not fully realised until the construction of modern Prague in the 19th and early 20th centuries. We shall here track down the sights of Prague in that order.

The St Charles Bridge was thrown across the river at what was a traditional crossing point. Archaeological finds confirm human settlement along the banks as early as the 4th century BC, which predates the shadowy Samo with his settlement at Vysehrad. Whether or not Princess Libussa and her ploughman husband existed, there is no doubt about the Premyslids developing the Hradcany site or Charles IV building his castle, modelled on the Louvre, on top of an older one.

The king's principal architects were Master Matthew of Arras, whom Pope Clement recommended, and after his death in 1352 a young Swabian named Peter Parler, who was not only an architect but a sculptor and wood-carver. Together they produced St Vitus's Cathedral and the Charles Bridge. The other great works of Charles's reign were the Castle of Karlstein outside Prague and the Benedictine Monastery of Emmaus.

Much of their work was destroyed or damaged in 1541 in a fire which began in the Mala Strana and worked up the hill. Legend has it that the fire was started deliberately by Ferdinand I, the first Habsburg king of Bohemia, as a massively indiscriminate way of destroying some embarrassing public

The Teyn Church; artist at work.

records. In any case, a large part of Prague had to be rebuilt afterwards.

The main entrance to the castle complex is on **Hradcanske Namesti**, or Castle Square. Entry through the gate, guarded by Titans which are 1912 copies of 1768 originals, leads to a series of courtyards. Off the second of these is the **Castle Gallery** with a collection of Rubens, Titian, Tintoretto and others which once belonged to Charles I of England and were acquired by Rudolf II. They were presumed lost until found by accident in 1962.

The third courtyard is dominated by the towering Gothic spires of the **St Vitus's Cathedral**. Construction started in 1344 on top of the remains of 10th- and 11th-century churches. It was again interrupted by the Hussite rebellion, again by the 1541 fire and the Turkish wars, and eventually finished only in 1929. The Wenzel chapel with walls studded with semi-precious stones and ancient frescoes survived the fire. The ring on the door is reputed to be from an earlier church in which St Wenceslas

was murdered by his brother Boleslav in 935. It is said he clung to this ring as life ebbed away. His tomb and relics are in the chapel; his statue, by Peter Parler's nephew, is dated 1373.

The adjoining Martinic chapel contains the remains of one of the councillors defenestrated in 1618, while the Sternbeck chapel has the tombs of Ottokar I (1230–53) and II (1253–78). The principal royal mausoleum, however, is in the centre of the Cathedral (before the high altar).

To one side of the cathedral behind a deceptively modest entrance is the great **Vladislav Hall**, built at the end of the 15th century as an indoor arena for tournaments. The hall gives access to the Statthalterei (council room) where the Protestant nobles gathered in 1618 to remonstrate with Catholic councillors. A certain Count Thurni suggested that the two Catholic ringleaders, Councillors Martinic and Slavata, be thrown out of the window.

The 17th-century historian Skala Ze Zhore describes the scene: "No mercy

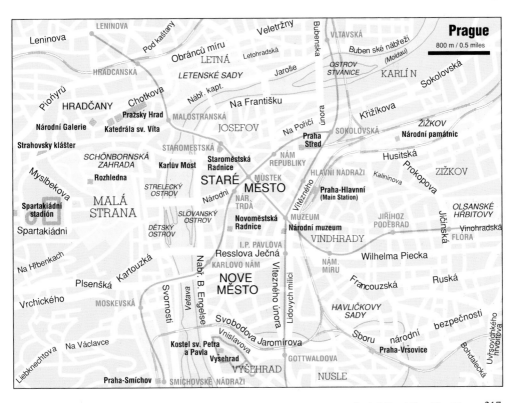

was granted them and they were both thrown dressed in their cloaks with their rapiers and decorations head-first out of the western window into a moat beneath the palace. They loudly screamed 'Ach, ach oweh!' and attempted to hold on to the narrow window-ledge, but Thurni beat their knuckles with the hilt of his sword until they were both obliged to let go." They landed in a dung-heap and made good their escape. Their report of this outrage to the Emperor in Vienna precipitated the Thirty Years' War. The attendant in the council room will point out the window in question.

Across the square behind the cathedral is the **St George's Church and Monastery** whose towers are relics of 970. It contains early and baroque Bohemian art. Beyond is the **Zlata Ulicka** (Golden Lane), a row of small houses built into the castle walls after the 1541 fire. These were generally occupied by palace craftsmen, and they were joined for a while by Kafka.

The **castle keep** at the end of the lane was named after an unfortunate knight who was locked up in the dungeon below, Dalibor of Kozojed. At the end of Jirska street, which runs parallel with Zlata Ulicka, are the **palace gardens** where there is an astounding collection of marble garden architecture culminating in a flight of stairs with a water basin at the bottom.

Although it is possible to leave the Hradcany via the Old Castle Staircase, it is worth returning to the square at the main entrance for the baroque **Archbishop's Palace**, the **National Gallery** in the Sternbeck Palace and the **Museum of Military History** in the Schwarzengberg (formerly Lobkovic) Palace. The summer tournaments in the courtyard of the military museum are thoroughly good entertainment.

A narrow lane leads to the **Loretto Square** with the **Loretto Church** and shrine on one side and the **Cernin Palace** on the other. The church was the gift of a Czech noblewoman who knew that the miraculous transfer of the Holy House of Nazareth, Christ's birthplace, to Loretto in the 13th century saved the **Old Town Square.**

Italian town from the infidel. She felt Prague needed a copy and commissioned the younger Dienzenhofer. The church contains a monstrance, the "Sun of Prague", set with 6,222 diamonds.

The main road through Mala Strana down to the Charles Bridge is **Mostecka** (Bridge Street), flanked by winding streets and small houses which survived the 1541 fire and by the mansions (many now embassies and diplomatic residences) which replaced those that did not. The most impressive of the latter is the **Wallenstein Palace** (1623–45) with its art gallery and the gardens in which concerts are sometimes staged. The **Church of the Infant of Prague** (Prazskeho Jezulatko) has a wax effigy figurine of the infant Jesus which receives a change of costume according to the Christian calendar. When the infant started performing miracles, replica churches sprang up all over the world.

The **Charles Bridge** which links the Castle and Lesser Town to the Old Town is in the same company of Tower Bridge in London and the Golden Gate in San Francisco as a tourist attraction. The statues lining either side were not in Parler's original 1357 design; most were added in the early 18th century. That of St John Nepomuk, Bohemia's patron saint, is particularly fitting as he was the victim of a variation on Prague's tradition of defenestration, which was depontification, in other words throwing people off bridges instead. A marble slab and cross mark the spot where Nepomuk plunged on the orders of King Wenceslas IV on 20 March 1393.

The other notable depontification concerned Jaroslav Hasek, the hell-raising creator of *The Good Soldier Schweik*. His was actually a faked suicide to throw creditors off his scent.

The most famous landmark on the east bank of the river, **Wenceslas Square**, is a broad and sloping boulevard that links Old Town and New Town. Charles IV planned it as the horse market. **Na prikope**, which runs at right-angles across the bottom, follows the line of the old city moat, and the 1475 **Powder Tower,** rebuilt in the

Old wheels in front of Pauline Monastery; Prague's distinctive rooftops.

19th century, is part of the fortifications.

Celetna Street, running past the tower, was once on the royal processional route which filed through the Old Town and across the Charles Bridge up to the Hradcany. Celetna Street is now closed to traffic and its buildings restored, so visitors could do worse than follow the old route. It is generously lined with specialist shops, coffee bars and wine cellars.

Celetna Street enters the delightful Old Town Square and its adjacent Little Square, the latter famous for the astronomical clock on the **Old Town Hall** (Staromestská radnice). Nikolaus von Kadan made the original clock in 1410 and, although it has been restored several times, the Gothic detailing is 15th- and 16th-century. The clock consists of three parts: in the middle is the actual clock, which also shows the movement of the sun and moon through the zodiac; underneath is th calendar, with signs from the zodiac and scenes depicting country life for each month of the year; in the upper part, at the striking of the hour, Christ and the 12 Apostles put in an appearance at two little windows while the Grim Reaper does the tolling. The fact that the clock often broke down between the aborted Prague Spring and Havel's Velvet Revolution was regarded as heavily symbolic.

The Old Town Hall was built in 1338 on the proceeds of a wine tax: the Gothic pointing around the door is thought to be a later addition by Matej Rejsek, one of the masons working on the St Vitus Cathedral. Part of the building was destroyed in World War II.

The groups of statues in the centre of the square were erected in 1915 to commemorate the 500th anniversary of the death of John Huss. The setting is appropriate because the **Teyn Church** on the square was the symbol of the Hussites. The two black towers are pure Prague Gothic. George Podiebrad, the pro-Hussite king of Bohemia, had the symbolic Hussite chalice added to the facade. This was replaced after the battle of the White Mountain by an image of the Virgin. The interior of the church is highly baroque. The sombre figure with a globe in one hand and a sword in the other is Tycho Brahe (1546–1601), the Danish scientist and astronomer who worked at the court of Rudolf II. The nearby **Kinsky Palace** is the work of the famous Fisher von Erlach.

It is worth backtracking to the left from the Old Town Square in order to see the **Carolinum**, or Charles University. The main part of the modern university has been moved elsewhere, but a few faculties remain here where, in one of the lecture rooms, John Huss conducted his "disputations" of current religious orthodoxy. (His most famous sermons were delivered in the Bethlehem Chapel, a short walk away.) Huss was the rector of the university in 1402. The furore caused by his teachings a century before Martin Luther led, as we have seen in the previous section of this book, to his trial at the Council of Constance in 1415 and burning at the stake. The result was civil war.

Resuming at the Old Town Square, either Parizska or Maislova streets leads to the **Prague ghetto**, the oldest in Eu-

Goldsmith's shop.

rope. It dates back to at least the 10th century, in other words to the time of St Wenceslas and some four centuries before Prague took on its recognisable form under Charles IV. The synagogue was built about 1270 and the old cemetery presents the extraordinary sight of more than 12,000 graves crammed into layers one on top of another. One of these tombs is of the scholar Rabbi Low who died in 1609.

The walls which separated the ghetto from the rest of the city were pulled down in the reign of Joseph II. Its history is told in the **Jewish State Museum**; the **Pinkas Synagogue** contains the names of the 77,000 Bohemian and Moravian Jews who were murdered by the Nazis.

The former Red Army Square between the ghetto and the river is now named after Jan Palach, the student who burnt himself to death in Wenceslas Square in protest against the 1968 Soviet invasion. Further along the river, just beyond the Charles Bridge, is the highly impressive **Krizovnicke Nam-**

The National Museum from Wenceslas Square.

esti, or Square of the Knights of the Cross, which its bastion of Catholicism, the Clementinum. This was the Jesuit headquarters and is now the **State Library**. The more modest baroque church is that of St Frances, also known and the **Church of the Crusaders**.

To climb the hill of **Wenceslas Square** towards the statue of St Wenceslas and the National Museum is to enter the New Town. The square is an entertainment in itself. This is where everyone congregates and people-watching is accordingly fruitful. Of the numerous vantage points, the **Hotel Europa** is incomparably the best. Seating on the terrace is limited, but the art nouveau interior is adequate compensation for the loss of viewing.

The **Thomas Masaryk statue** is a timely vindication of this modern Czech hero's contribution. All statues of him were removed by the Communists in 1948. This one was restored in 1990.

The main museums, theatres, shops and hotels are in the New Town. As previously noted, Charles IV's plans for

a new town were never quite realised and most of the buildings are 19th- and 20th-century, but no apologies are necessary for the likes of the magnificently restored **National Theatre** on the river. Coach parties are invariably dropped off at U **Kalicha**, the inn associated with that wonderful man, the Good Soldier Schweik. His admirers will feel obliged to look in, although there are any number of other bars and inns.

Visitors interested in Prague's earliest history ought to consider walking along the river bank a couple of miles upstream to **Vysehrad**, the castle built by Samo before Hradcany. The site rises sheer above the river. Neither the original castle nor a subsequent one built by Charles IV survives, apart from the walls. The later castle was destroyed by the Hussites. On the opposite bank of the river, although some distance away, is the Bertramka villa where Mozart stayed when he was in Prague. It is now the **Mozart Museum**.

Elsewhere in Bohemia: Bohemia has such an embarrassment of tourist riches that simply to list them would exhaust the space available. We shall therefore concentrate on a cross-section of sights which ought to cover most tastes beginning with Karlstein, probably the most famous of scores of castles.

Of the scores of castles that litter Bohemia, two are worthy of special note. **Konopiste**, south of Prague, was originally built in the 13th century but is best remembered for its role in the early 20th century when it provided no fewer than 300,000 game trophies for the tireless Archduke Franz Ferdinand, the target of assassins at Sarajevo in 1914. Shooting and collecting were the two passions of the Archduke's life. He was extremely keen on weapons and anything that depicted St George and the Dragon – a bath towel, a button, absolutely anything. Konopiste contains his incomparable collection of 16th- to 18th-century weapons.

An hour's drive west of Prague is the **Castle of Krivoklat**, another royal shooting estate which serves as an appetiser for the castle of Karlstein further

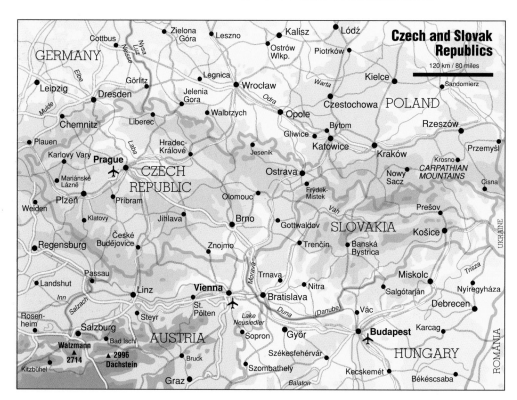

along the Berounka River. It was built on a towering precipice in 1348–65 by Charles IV, another avid collector, who used it to store his holy relics as well as the crown jewels and Bohemian regalia. It came under siege in the 15th century and a succession of similar actions meant that it was in ruins by the end of the 19th century. It has since been restored but the earlier collections have been lost to museums in Prague and elsewhere.

The castle has three chapels, one of which, where Charles used to meditate in private, being little more than a cubicle. The larger chapels, where the collections were kept, have 14th-century wall panels and paintings depicting the Apocalypse and a gilded triptych by Tommaso da Modena. The castle has a reasonable restaurant with fine views.

Tabor, about 50 miles (80 km) south of Prague, was established as a Hussite stronghold when the Emperor Sigismund was saying that he could "hardly await the day" when he drowned the lot of them. In 1419 the Hussites marched on Prague and, on being pelted with stones from the New Town Hall, forced their way in and perpetrated the first defenestration of Prague. Retaliation came in the form of a massive attack on Tabor the following year which was repulsed by the clever use of armed wagons. The use of wagons both in defence and attack was devised by the Hussite leader John Zizka and anticipated the principle of tank warfare.

The Taborites had to fight like tigers to defend their pacifist principles, as may be gauged from the exhibits in the local museum and the underground fortifications of the old town.

The countryside around Tabor and nearby **Trebon** is dotted with ponds for the breeding of carp, a feature of Czech cuisine. The craze for breeding carp caught on in the 14th century and never looked back. One theory after another added to the repertoire of magical benefits supposedly to be had from eating carp. The observation that carp lived to a mighty age encouraged the belief that the secret of longevity was somewhere in the carps' innards, and they were

Karlstein Castle.

thereupon swallowed whole in prodigious numbers by every geriatric aristocrat in the land. Anyway, the ponds are still there and the carp are both breeding and selling briskly. The Rozmberk family were the most energetic pond-diggers in these parts and their crowning glory, big enough to qualify as a lake, is named after them.

The said Rozmberks had their family seat at **Cesky Krumlov**, a very attractive town in a part of the country made lovely by the Vlada snaking through high wooded banks. Getting around Cesky Krumlov is a matter of climbing steps from one level to the next. This Rozmberk castle has a theatre and a superbly decorated Masquerade Hall. The other Rozmberk castle is in a little town nearby called, unsurprisingly, **Rozmberk**.

Charles IV is credited with having opened Bohemia's first spa in the village of **Vary** in 1347, hence Karlovy Vary or the more familiar Karlsbad. Its near neighbour is **Marianske Lazne**, or Marienbad, familiar to film buffs from

Last Year in Marienbad. The heyday of these spas was at the end of the 19th century and until World War I.

Marienbad tended to be preferred by the British crowd, notably Edward VII, and some telling letters were written there by Sir Henry Campbell-Bannerman, a future prime minister. "I do not know how it comes to pass," he wrote to a colleague, "but in this small society of English people, quite half the ladies either have already been, or are qualifying themselves for being, divorced, and a considerable number of the men are helping."

The following year things were even worse. "The English and American society here has contained an extraordinary number of tainted ladies – including five divorcees and about 10 others of various degrees of doubtfulness," he reported. "The decent people were almost in a minority, and we thought of wearing our marriage certificates as a sort of order outside our coats." The former Hotel Weimar where Edward VII used to stay is now the **Kafka** and it is hard to imagine from present appearances what it must once have been like.

The ingredients of the spring water in the various spas differ. At Karlsbad they are sulphate of soda, carbonate of soda and salt. The town is built on a crust over a vast underground reservoir of this water, and it rushes up wherever the crust is broken. The industry thus created has sprouted colonnades, sanatoria and hotels. Some of the springs are in vast halls, others at various points along a promenade. The drill is to stroll from one to another wearing a suitably solemn expression and taking the occasional sip with a special kind of cup. It is also customary to nibble at a local biscuit called an oplatky.

Moravia: Bohemia and Moravia together make up the Czech half of Czechoslovakia, and Moravians are keen to be recognised as fully equal in the partnership. Because there are no physical barriers between the two entities and they share a language and religion, the Moravian tendency is to make the most of such subtle distinctions as do exist. They contend, for example, that the

Marrachon Glassworks in North Bohemia.

specifically Moravian Empire of the 9th century was the true progenitor of the Czech nation. Lest anyone forget, Moravians slip into their bright ethnic costumes rather more readily than their neighbours.

Moravia's agricultural and later industrial wealth has been the proverbial mixed blessing, the disadvantage being that it attracted predators. While Hitler talked loudly about protecting the rights of ethnic Germans in the region, he never took his eye off its highly developed industries, not least armaments. The name of the famous Bren gun significantly combined the first two letters respectively of Brno, the capital of Moravia, and the Enfield arms factory in England. The protracted tussle between the Austrian Habsburgs and Prussia over Silesia, the northern part of Moravia which is rich in coal, was hotly contested between Habsburg Austria and Prussia.

Mention of coalfields and arms factories does not mean that Moravia is bereft of more conventional tourist attrac-

tions. If castles are the criterion, there are probably more per square inch in Moravia than anywhere else, Bohemia excepted. Some of the towns are an architectural delight, and much of the countryside is given over to scenic river valleys and vineyards. Even **Brno** with its unhappy pallor of industrial smoke has sights of note.

The capital lies at the foot of the Spilberk, and the ring-road follows the line of ancient fortifications. While the dungeons of **Spilberk Castle** have not produced the happiest memories in Moravian history, they do have a certain macabre fascination. They were the Black Hole of the Habsburg Empire where in 1749, to quote just one example, a Colonel Trenck of Pandour infamy died in misery. Count Silvio Pellico, an Italian poet, provided such a horrific account of the time he spent in the dungeons (1822–30) that they were put out of commission, only to be reinstated by the Nazis. An extensive restoration programme means that some parts of the castle will be out of bounds to visi-

tors for a while. In the meantime, there is still the **Cathedral of Saints Peter and Paul** on the hill.

As might be expected, the castle and cathedral were the hub of historic Brno. Below them is the market square with the former Dietrichstein Palace, now the **Moravian Museum**, and the Gothic **Old Town Hall** whose mascot, the "Brno Dragon", is a crocodile skin dangling in the main corridor.

While the castle dungeons remain closed, the ghosts of the past are most accessible in the subterranean complex of the **Capuchin Monastery** with its collection of mummified aristocrats and monks. An elaborate system of ventilation shafts created the climatic conditions which kept the mummies in good order. The trouble taken over them in death is all the more ironic because many had died in the castle dungeons. The wretched Colonel Trenck is among their number.

Brno has several interesting churches, most notably those of St James (1314–1480) with a 300-ft (90-metre) tower, St

Thomas and the Jesuits, and two theatres, one a Helmer and Fellner creation and the other named after Leos Janacek (1854–1928), the composer and a native son.

Austerlitz, the scene of the monumental battle between Napoleon and the combined armies of Francis I of Austria and Alexander I of Russia, is just a few miles outside Brno. The local name is **Slavkov**. A museum and chapel are on the battleground, while memorabilia of the battle are on display in a converted chateau in Slavkov itself. Another attraction near the capital – although north rather than east – is **Pernstejn Castle**. If accommodation is hard to find in Brno during trade exhibitions, alternatives are available in the villages around the Pernstejn.

Travelling east again leads into the area around **Strilky** where the House of Liechtenstein gave full vent to its architectural aspirations. They were the biggest and richest land-owners in Moravia in the 17th century, and they believed their money served no other purpose than to erect glorious memorials. Their most compulsive builder was Prince Charles Eusebius, and he evidently gave his architects a hard time. Giovanni Tencala suffered most of all because all too often his domes were majestic in conception but prone to collapse.

Kromeriz is the Liechtensteins' greatest achievement, a restoration project undertaken after the town had been sacked by the Swedes during the Thirty Years' War. The castle was rebuilt with an immense colonnade running through the gardens, a Roman bust in each of the 46 Doric arches. The castle now contains a collection of Old Masters and the family library.

The Liechtensteins are also credited with introducing viticulture in the **Znojmo** area. While the town proper was founded by Ottokar I in 1226 and retains sections of the medieval ramparts, there is an early (11th-century) rotunda of St Catherine in which frescoes give a rare glimpse of what the various Presylids actually looked like. Evidence is to be seen everywhere of the Liechensteins' relentless mission to

Fine carving at Lednice, South Moravia.

build yet more castles. The results never disappoint.

A few miles from **Mikulov**, which of course has a Liechtenstein castle, is the site of the discovery of the oldest clay figure known to man, the fetching Venus of Vestonice. The original is in Brno, but a copy is in the museum at Dolni Vestonice. Archaeologists are putting together a picture of human settlement in this region which begins with hunters of 20,000 years ago and moves through Iron Age Celts and Germanic tribes to the arrival of the Slavs in the 6th century. Traces of the elusive 9th-century Moravian Empire turn up in the Morava valley some distance away.

The excavations have a long way to go, but they have already produced the remains of a fortress, palace, churches and graves near Hodonin, Breclav and Uherske Hradiste. A new museum at **Hodonin** receives the finds as and when they are made.

Slovakia: Czechs and Slovaks parted company early in the 10th century when the Magyars conquered the Moravian empire and lopped off Slovakia for themselves. Although separated physically only by the Morava River, these two Slavic groups effectively spent the following 1,000 years on different planets. Bohemia and Moravia attached themselves to the Holy Roman Empire, whereas the Slovaks were overwhelmed by their Magyar masters. The three groups rose reunited as Czechoslovakia after the World War I only to sink together under the Soviet Union after World War II. In 1992, by which time Czechoslovakia was again free, it seemed that Czechs and Slovaks might choose to again go their own ways.

In 1991, **Bratislava**, the capital of Slovakia, celebrated the 2,000th anniversary of its first settlement, although it did not assume its present name until the arrival of Slav settlers under a certain Bretislav in the 5th century. The Hungarians called it Pozsony, but to the Germans who were encouraged to settle by the Hungarians, it was Pressburg. It became Bratislava again in 1918.

Glory was thrust on Bratislava by the

Left, Kromeriz. Right, Krasna Morka, Slovakia.

defeat of Hungary by the Turks at the battle of Mohacs in 1526. King Louis drowned as he fled from the battlefield and was succeeded by his brother-in-law, the Archduke Ferdinand of Austria, who, under different crowns, became King of Bohemia and King of Hungary. The rump of Hungary was retained by the Turks while the Hungarian nobility ruled over Transylvania under their sufferance. A third fragment, which became "Royal Hungary", was actually a slice of Slovakia.

It was in these circumstances that Bratislava in 1536 became the capital of the "Hungary" over which Ferdinand was elected to reign. He was duly crowned in the cathedral of St Martin, opposite the 15th-century university. Bratislava remained the seat of the Hungarian Diet until 1848.

Modern Bratislava is a grey, sad place, but there is considerable charm attached to the old town around the castle with towers visible from miles around. The Hungarian crown jewels were once stored in the south-east tower. The cas-tle was destroyed by fire in 1811 and restored after World War II as government offices and a very impressive museum. While the Habsburgs generally preferred to live in Vienna or Prague, Maria Theresa had a soft spot for her "Hungarian" subjects (for reasons recounted in the Hungarian section of this book) and was a frequent visitor to Bratislava. This signal of royal approval led to some appropriately regal building like the **Archbishop's Palace** and the **Town Hall**. The hall of mirrors was the setting for the Peace of Pressburg which Napoleon and Francis I signed after the battle of Austerlitz in 1805.

The **Michalska** is a pedestrian promenade leading to the Michael Gate, the surviving remnant of the medieval fortifications. This would be one of the most pleasingly timeless parts of the old town with its row of bookshops, cafés and so on were it not for a modern flyover which sends traffic roaring past, a fate shared by the cathedral. The narrow streets beyond the **Michael Gate** are more sheltered and good value.

Bratislava has a long musical tradition having been host to performances by Liszt and Mozart among many others. An international music festival is still staged here annually, opera and ballet being performed in the 19th-century Slovak National Theatre. The home of the Slovak Philharmonic is the **Redoute Palace**.

While Bratislava became the secular capital of Royal Hungary after the conquest of Hungary proper in 1526, the ecclesiastical see of the Archbishop of Esztergom was transferred to **Trnava**, which duly came to be known as the Slovak Rome. The 14th-century cathedral was thereupon given a baroque interior; the two towers are 18th-century and aesthetically somewhat controversial. In 1635 Trnava was elevated to the status of a university town and given the University Church of St John. The town has several interesting Renaissance houses and a Biedermeier theatre but, generally speaking, has not worn particularly well.

Cultural stagnation under Hungarians who preferred Transylvania means that

The old mining town of Banska Stiannica.

Slovakia cannot really compete in this respect with Bohemia or Moravia, but it does have a strong draw-card in the High Tatra mountains. The gateway is **Poprad**. It is possible to fly there but the last 100 miles (160 km) or so of the railway journey from Zilina has much to recommend it. This follows a winding course through the low Tatras until, beyond **Ruzomberok**, it crosses the watershed between the Baltic and the Black Sea and offers a dramatic view of the High Tatras ahead. The highest station on the main line is **Strba**, and from here funiculars and cog-wheel railways radiate to a number of smaller resorts.

These highlands were settled in the Middle Ages by "Saxons" brought in to work the mines. The best-preserved of these old mining towns is **Roznava**, about 30 miles (50 km) south of Poprad, but in fact all the towns, mining or otherwise, were almost exclusively the work of German settlers. Virtually all of the descendants of these settlers were expelled after World War II. Roznava has a cathedral in which scenes from

Spis Castle.

mining times decorate the altarpiece, and there is also a mining museum.

Most of the 27 highland towns are well preserved. The pattern is a central square surrounded by grand houses and at least one Gothic church with Renaissance additions. The richness of the interiors, and especially the wood carvings, suggest that the craftsmen concerned felt they were in competition. If time is short, **Spisska Kapitula**, now virtually a suburb of Poprad, is a fine example which offers the bonus of the ruins of **Spis Castle**, Spis being the name given to the region as a whole.

The area offers a wide choice of wood-panelled hotels strongly reminiscent of Bohemia. The best is probably the Grand Hotel in **Stary Smokovec**. Most visitors come to these parts for the exercise, and all hotels have sign-posted walks requiring varying levels of exertion. It is possible – indeed advisable – to hire a professional guide for the more difficult ascents: although the Tatras may not appear to be as awesome as, say, the Alps, they are not to be trifled with.

After a brave but futile rebellion against the Soviet Union in 1956, Hungary did what seemed to be the next best thing by pretending that Communism did not exist. Shops were full of luxury goods unheard of anywhere else in the Eastern bloc, gypsy violinists ambled through restaurants serving excellent food with their instruments locked under their chins, and no one was addressed as "comrade" outside the Communist cabal which was supposed to run the country but quite patently did not. The common form of greeting, as it had always been, was "*Kezet cokolom*", pronounced *chocolom* and meaning "I kiss your hand".

This casual disregard of Hungary's official position in the Communist world was reciprocated by foreign visitors, who arrived in numbers which even before the Iron Curtain fell reached 25 million a year. As Hungary has borders with Austria, Slovakia, Ukraine, Romania, Croatia and Slovenia, many were themselves living in the Eastern bloc and therefore had extra reason to be grateful for Hungary's blockade-running role within the system. A background in clandestine enterprise gave Hungary a head-start over the rest of Eastern Europe when the Iron Curtain came down, and it generally maintains a lead in the race towards economic recovery.

Hungary is enveloped in mystique, beginning with its name. The founders of Hungary were the Magyars, a Finno-Ugrian tribe from the foothills of the Ural Mountains. The Magyars have always been the dominant group in Hungarian – the ethnic minorities have been "Magyarised", never "Hungarianised" – and it seems that the Onogurs (hence "Hungarians") were a sub-group of tribes. Whatever the case, the tribes who invaded Europe in the 9th century were exceptionally ferocious, and the story was that they were Hungarians because they were literally – and insatiably – hungry. It was said that they would eat anything at anytime, including human babies, reptiles and wolf-meat. Their present diet is characterised in many minds by paprika and Bull's Blood. This red wine is reputed to have got its name from the solemn assurance given to suspicious Turkish officials, when Hungary was part of the Moslem Ottoman Empire, that the red fluid in the glass under scrutiny was just that, bull's blood, and nothing whatever to do with grapes.

The Northern Plain, perhaps more familiar as the steppes, laps around the Carpathian mountains to give Hungary its *puszta*, vast open spaces which put a premium on horses and horsemanship and contributed to the legend of Hungarian men as gallant hussars. Lower on the scale were ordinary cowboys who lived in the saddle and drove their herds in the Middle Ages to markets in Paris, Hamburg and Milan. Mechanised agriculture has changed the nature of the plain, as it has in America, but many traditions live on.

Preceding pages: Vajda-Hunyadi Castle, Budapest; summer comes to Eger. **Left**, dressed to kill for the harvest festival.

So ich nun auff die zeitt Otto des kaysers pin ko
men so wil ich von den dingen sagen die zu sei
nen zeytten zu auspurg gestherhen send Do sub d
kayser otto beraytet wider berengancium den künig vo
lamparden als wider ain wietrich vnd geitigen vn
der alle gerechtikait vmb gelt gab Doch so forcht
in der selb wietrich wan er die machtikait des kay
sers wol wisset vnd durch ratt des herzogen vo Luth
ringen kom er zu dem kayser vnd begeret frid Do

In the cold light of contemporary East European politics, it is worth reflecting on the Hungarian students who took to the streets in 1956 to demand the overthrow of the Communist system. Soviet tanks rumbled in, blood flowed, and 200,000 Hungarians fled to asylum abroad. Together with simultaneous unrest in Poland, this gave the outside world a clear signal that genuine opinion behind the Iron Curtain was not reflected by the kind of election result in which Communist leaders routinely romped home with 99.9 percent of the vote.

Curiously, no further revolution was necessary in the twilight of the old order. Sensing after 1956 that there was no future in direct confrontation, Hungarians resorted to the passive resistance they had used against the Habsburgs in the 19th century when, for example, "everybody was seized by an inability to pay their taxes".

The Soviet-backed cabal which took over after the 1956 uprising preached Communism until they were blue in the face – to perfect popular indifference. Showpiece agricultural collectives were still on display but the only serious work was done on private plots whose produce, like goods and services generally, were bought and sold in the old-fashioned way. The Communist white elephants sank to their knees and, when there was no one left in Moscow to prop up the old Khrushchev gang, they simply shrugged their shoulders and shuffled off the stage.

No sudden switch in Hungary, therefore, from state to private enterprise. In no time the subversive system which had developed in Hungary was capable of handling 25 million foreign visitors a year, rather more than double the population. The compelling attraction was that Hungary has a character which is entirely its own, and its robust health is all the more remarkable because of the sustained pressure from so many quarters over so many centuries to eradicate it.

It is not a case of Hungary sheltering in a natural fortress. On the contrary, it is bissected by the Danube, as busy as any thoroughfare in European history, and the Alfold is effectively a lay-by on the Great Northern Plain which carried the great migrations from Asia into the heart of Europe. The Hungarians were exposed and, as we shall see, they were pushed off territory they would dearly have liked to hold. Modern Hungary is a fraction of what it once was, but Hungarians are not too bothered, apart from a lingering desire to recover Transylvania from Romania. Their patriotism, they say, is more sublime than real estate; it is the love of freedom.

Frequent patriotic calls have been addressed to "Magyars" rather than "Hungarians", with the implication that the terms amount to one and the same thing. But this is not true. There are loyal Hungarians who would definitely not consider themselves Magyars, just as there are people of Magyar descent who are quite happy to consider themselves citizens of neighbouring states.

The Magyarisation of Hungary has an uneven history. The 11th-century Magyars positively welcomed non-Magyar immigrants: "Guests and immigrants are so useful that they well deserve their position as the sixth element of royal dignity," declared the magnanimous King Stephen (Istvan) I.

On the other hand, the descendants of these useful guests and immigrants and other non-Magyars roped in behind Hungary's frontiers were later Magyarised with a zeal that was at times tantamount to persecution. This curious case of compulsory assimilation, the opposite of exclusive Nazi racial purity or apartheid, produced an aristocracy which at the beginning of the 20th century contained families of lightly-disguised German, Jewish, Czech, Slovak, Croat, Italian, Serb, Romanian, Greek, French, Irish and Turkish origin.

The Magyars were part of a Finno-Ugrian speaking people living on the slopes of the Ural Mountains. Some of these tribes began migrating westward in the third millennium BC, two groups eventually settling along the Baltic coast as the future Finns and Estonians, which of course explains the otherwise incongruous kinship between their languages and Hungarian.

The Magyars started later, or perhaps chose not to travel so far. Either way, they were to

Left, the Magyars halted at Lechfeld in AD 955.

be found between the Danube, the Don and the Black Sea by about AD 600. One of the first recorded sightings of them was by a 9th-century Arab trader who had gone to the Caspian steppes in search of ermine and sable fur to sell in Baghdad.

"The Magyars," he wrote, "are a race of Turks and their leader rides out with 20,000 horsemen. They have a plain which is all dry herbage and a wide territory... They have completely subjugated the Slavs, and they always order them to provide food for them and consider them as slaves... These Magyars are a handsome people and of good appearance, and their clothes are of silk brocade, and their weapons of silver encrusted with gold. They constantly plunder the Slavs."

In the Danube basin about this time, the Avars, a Turkish tribe who had been dominant for the previous 250 years or so, had been squeezed out of the west by Franks who tended to rule through native Slav princes. The east was vaguely under the suzerainty of the Bulgars, while the north was a Slavonic state embracing roughly modern Czechoslovakia. All of these were preoccupied by other matters when, in the winter of 895–96, the Magyars, led by King Arpad, crossed the Carpathians and dropped on to the Alfold. Within a few years they were the undisputed masters of the Middle Danube Basin.

To Europe, the Magyars were savages, barely human in character and interested only in rape and plunder. They were the abominable peoples of Gog and Magog and their arrival was interpreted as a sign that the Day of Judgement was at hand. The name the Western chroniclers latched on to was "Hungarians" and the connection was made not just with hunger but hunger of a particularly virulent kind, insatiable for human flesh (as well as a bit of fox and wolf). All sorts of theories have since been advanced to explain the name, but none quite so graphic.

It was the raids by which they attempted to expand their territory that brought them into conflict with neighbours. The Magyars were defeated first by Henry the Fowler in 933 and then by Emperor Otto I at Lechfeld in 955. They ceased to be the terror of Europe and were confined to territory, hemmed in by powerful neighbours. The survival of their idiosyncratic language is proof of the ferocious defence of their culture. While other tribes in comparable circumstances were assimilated by more populous neighbours, the Magyars were determined that their role would be active, not passive.

"Their history has been one unremitting struggle," says C.A. Macartney, "not only against the fresh invaders from the East who followed in their own footsteps, but against the more prolonged, more insidious, and ultimately even more dangerous pressure of German and Slav. They have never been able to relax, even for a moment, their defence of their nationality."

The greatest single threat to the Hungarians in the 10th century was their attachment to paganism when all around had become Christian. The vicious antipathy of Christian kings towards the godless was intensified by a three-way competition for new converts between the Pope in Rome, the Eastern Emperor in Constantinople, and the German Holy Roman Emperor.

Arpad's grandson Geza converted to Christianity in 975, and his successor Stephen was won over to Rome by Pope Sylvester II, who offered Stephen an extraordinarily generous package. He would personally confer the title of king, establish a special relationship between the crown and the Holy See to circumvent the Emperor's temporal authority, and he would allow Stephen to appoint his own bishops. In case Stephen still had any doubts, he also agreed to recognise him as an Apostle.

The importance of this offer and its acceptance on the future of Hungary could hardly be exaggerated. It brought the country firmly into the fold of Western civilisation and its eastern border would henceforth be the dividing-line between the spiritual life of East and West. In the lofty matter of precedence among European royalty, the privileges bestowed on the Hungarian Crown, especially the Apostolic tag, would make it highly coveted for centuries. Stephen was duly anointed king on these terms in 1001 and took his royal seat at Gran (Esztergom).

The most lasting aspect of Stephen's reign – the repercussions of which were still being felt in the 20th century – was his internal political organisation. He established the freedom and rank of even the poorest Magyar above the considerable non-Magyar population. Not counting slaves (whom a master could kill with impunity but in no circumstances marry), the non-Magyars fell into two classes, those who were already living in Hungary when the Magyars arrived, and those who were subsequently brought in as "guests and immigrants".

Just who the existing inhabitants were is the burning question in the unresolved dispute over Hungarian and Romanian claims to Transylvania. It is dealt with in some detail in the Romanian section of this book. It must suffice here to say that Hungarians insist that they were few in number and were not the Latin-speaking proto-Romanians who, they say, only drifted back from wherever they had been at a rather later date. In any case, the non-Magyars generally lived on the king's land and enjoyed rights roughly invariably given the equivalent Hungarian rank and status. Where there were concentrations of the middle-ranking immigrants – in other words, in towns – they were given almost complete self-government. "What Greek would rule Latins by Greek laws," wrote Stephen, "or what Latin would rule Greeks by Latin laws?" In all essentials, this structure remained the basis of the Hungarian state into modern times.

These principles were codified in the Golden Bull of 1222 after a revolt caused by the proligacy of Andrew II. By selling off crown lands to pay for his excesses, he jeopardised the security of the *servientes regis* who lived on them. The bull dealt with the

commensurate with those of freed slaves. According to a 13th-century writer, Hungary was "almost filled" with this class.

The second category were the "hospites" or privileged immigrants who were invited. Many were Germans (lumped together misleadingly as "Saxons"), a mixture of knights, miners, artisans and town-dwellers. There were also Jewish merchants ("Ishmaelites"), Moslem Bulgars (in charge of the royal mint) and Slavs who were often invited to settle in waste land or forest and bring on cultivation.

Foreign nobels who entered Hungary were

Above, the Apostolic Crown of St Stephen.

rights of nearly all classes of society but the key clauses concerned the rights of Magyars regarding punishments, taxes and military service. These rights were slightly amended by subsequent bulls, but they remained fundamentally a body of privileges for which the minor Magyar nobility fought tooth and nail when Hungary and Austria were joined under the Habsburgs.

Three centuries or so after the Magyars had themselves terrified Europe with their invasion, calumny on an undreamt of scale materialised in the form of the Mongols. They entered Hungary in 1241. The army sent to engage them at Mohi at the confluence of the Hernad and Sajo rivers was ripped to pieces, King Bela IV only just managing to escape across the Danube. With Pope Gregory IX and Emperor Frederick II fully occupied by a private squabble, Hungary bore the invasion almost alone.

But as suddenly as they had descended, the Mongols were gone. The Supreme Khan had died, and Batu Khan, the Mongol commander, was needed at home. Bela surveyed the wreckage of Pest, his capital, and decided to relocate it on the more easily defended west bank of the Danube, the present site of Buda.

The Mongol invasion brought home that Hungary could not afford the luxury of isolation. Bela married off two daughters to by the Magyar nobles. Deeply suspicious of one another, they resorted to a device which was to become common practice throughout Europe: they looked for a suitable foreign candidate, preferably one who could be manipulated and would not presume to curb their own powers and privileges. Wenceslas of Bohemia was taken on for a trial period of four years, rejected, and replaced first by Otto of Bavaria and then, after consultations with the Pope, Charles Robert of Anjou.

Reigning as Charles I, the French prince brought together the most able nobles and commercial magnates in profitable partnership as a kind of centralised government. And by not convening parliament, he left the

Ingressus tartaroz in hungariã temporibus regis Bele quarti

Ruthenian princes and one to a Pole. The hand of his son was deployed to contain the Cumans, a wild tribe who had arrived in the Alfold as refugees from the Mongols and threatened to overwhelm it. "In the interests of protecting Christianity," Bela advised the Pope, "we married our first born son to a Cuman girl... to secure the possibility of converting these people to Christianity."

Unfortunately, the child of the marriage, Laszlo IV, favoured the pagan side of the family. Anxious nobles hired a Cuman killer to get rid of him and on this inglorious note the Arpad dynasty petered out. The subsequent vacuum signalled a scramble for power provincial nobility with almost unfettered independence in their own areas.

In the meantime, the gold mines of northern Hungary and Transylvania produced enormous revenues, a magnet for entrepreneurs, artists and scholars from all over Eastern Europe. It also gave the king the means to create and maintain a professional army whose loyalty was exclusively to the crown.

The power and prestige of Charles and later his son Louis I were such that they were seen as just the ticket for countries in the same rudderless quandary as Hungary. Louis' baby daughter Jadwiga became Queen-designate of Poland and Hungary's influence became predominant in Bosnia, Serbia, Bulgaria and the two Romanian principalities, Wallachia and Moldavia.

The pomp and wealth of the Hungarian Court were dazzling – but there were setbacks. Three attempts to conquer Naples failed, and a distinct danger was growing in the east in the form of the Ottoman Empire. Louis defeated Sultan Murad in 1377, but that was far from the end of the matter.

Significant changes occurred in Eastern Europe between this first encounter with the Turks and their pivotal victory over the Magyars at Mohacs in 1526. The Poles grafted themselves on to the mighty Lithuanian empire. Bohemia and Venice went from strength to strength and the relatively minor House of Habsburg surprised everyone by acquiring the throne of the Holy Roman Empire. And all the time the Turks were encroaching. They destroyed the Serbian army on the Field of Blackbirds at Kossovo in 1389 and by the end of the century they had overrun all of Bulgaria.

The gathering storm produced two of Hungary's most illustrious heroes, the father-and-son combination of John Hunyadi and Mathias Corvinus. The father, a Romanian by descent and birth, was the elected regent for the boy king Ladislaus (Laszlo). Hunyadi's distinguished career ended as the result of an illness contracted at the historic lifting of the Turkish siege of Belgrade in 1456, and his predators moved in after some devious dealings involving the mysterious deaths of Ladislaus and one of Hunyadi's sons. The other son, Mathias, became king. He took his name from the crow on his emblem (crow in Latin is *corvinus*), hence Mathias Corvinus.

After six years spent fighting the claims of the Habsburg Frederick III to his throne, Mathias consolidated his position and by the time of his death in 1490 – a case of suspected poisoning – Hungary had acquired Lower Austria, Moravia and Silesia.

Without Mathias Corvinus's strong leadership, the country fell apart. A long-running duel ensued between the Habsburgs and the Magyar nobility, led by the "national party" and Janos Zapolya. These wrangles were eclipsed by the arrival on the scene of Sulei-

man the Magnificent. Louis II, now locked into marriage with a Habsburg woman, appealed to the Christian world for help against the looming Turkish tide. He was wasting his breath on Francis I of France, who was more than hoping that the Turks would get rid of the Habsburgs. Louis advanced alone at the head of an army of fewer than 20,000 men.

On 29 August 1526 they came face to face with Suleiman's army at Mohacs with catastrophic results. The cream of the Hungarian nobility was wiped out and Louis himself drowned while crossing a swollen stream. There was no Hungarian army left to prevent the Turks from entering Buda and Pest.

Such was the Hungarian despair that there

were some who were willing to see a Habsburg on the throne if that would give Austria the incentive to take up arms against the Turks. They ended up with Ferdinand I ruling over a strip of land called "Royal Hungary" – now part of Slovakia – but no Austrian support of any consequence.

The Turks kept for themselves what is roughly modern Hungary, but they effectively leased out Transylvania (now part of Romania) to the Zapolya faction. The Turks uncannily anticipated the punitive borders which were mapped out for Hungary at the Paris peace conference after World War I.

The three sectors went their different ways.

Left, the Mongol invasion of 1241. **Right**, Mathias Corvinus, a famous Hungarian hero.

Hungary proper, over which the Turks maintained direct administration, was deserted by the nobility and middle classes who went to either Royal Hungary or Transylvania. Contrary to myth, the peasants who stayed behind were probably no worse off under the Turks than they had been under Magyar masters. Royal Hungary, with its capital at Bratislava (then Pressburg), became a faceless part of the Habsburg empire, remarkable only in that a resentful mood made the nobility and educated classes receptive to anti-establishment Protestantism.

Defeat at the gates of Vienna in 1683 signalled the end of Turkish military invincibility in Eastern Europe. They were driven

The legitimacy of Habsburg sovereignty over Hungary was the essence of a dispute that reverberated into the 20th century. To begin with, the clause in the Golden Bull which gave Magyars the exclusive right to the Crown was cancelled.

The Habsburgs then ran out of male heirs and it was necessary to pass the Pragmatic Sanction of 1723 in order to make provision for the accession of the redoubtable Maria Theresa. "I found myself," she said, "without money, without credit, without an army, without experience and knowledge..." In short, she was extremely vulnerable and there were predators about, notably the future Frederick the Great of Prussia, the Elector of

out of Buda in 1686 and ceded virtually the whole of the former Hungarian kingdom by the Peace of Karlovic in 1699. The Habsburg emperor was the new master. Redistributing the land to its rightful owners and settling various other claims after 150 years of occupation would have been difficult even in the best of times and under the best possible administration. In the circumstances, it was all but impossible. Corruption, extortion, unusually high taxes, the sale of land and property to foreign speculators and a violent spate of Counter-Reformation measures brought the population to an open rebellion which lasted from 1703 to 1711.

Bavaria and the King of France.

Imminent invasion by France and Bavaria led to one of the most celebrated cameos in Hungarian history. With no one else to turn to, Maria Theresa mounted a white charger and, clutching her new-born son to her breast, appealed to the ingrained chivalry of her Hungarian subjects with a passionate speech delivered in Latin. They voted her six regiments, sufficient to repel the Bavarians and persuade the French to sue for peace. The bond between empress and Hungarian nobility lasted throughout her reign, and she took particular pride in wearing the Apostolic Crown of St Stephen.

Joseph II, the infant at Maria Theresa's breast on that fateful day, grew up to be less sentimental about Hungary and Hungarians. The Apostolic Crown was put into mothballs in Vienna, he made German the official language throughout the empire and took steps to abolish serfdom.

Any one of these measures would have been sufficient to end his mother's special relationship, but the ulimate heresy was his attempt to tax the Hungarian nobility. Joseph retracted many of his reforms on his death-bed, but that still left his heir Leopold II with a mountain of resentment. Latin was reinstated as the official language, the crown was returned to Buda and, in theory if not in practice, the Diet again elected its own king.

Attempts to find a compromise which would satisfy Hungarian aspirations within the fold of the Habsburg empire were severely tested by the mood of the French Revolution and by Napoleon's call to Hungarians in 1809 to sever their Habsburg ties. While the call went unanswered, there was a distinct linguistic and literary movement to restore the Magyar language and create a literature worthy of the nation's past.

The torch-bearer of this movement was Count Stephen Szechenyi, whose father had founded the National Museum in 1802. His enthusiasm spilled over into all sorts of economic enterprises, not least the construction of the bridge over the Danube between Buda and Pest. The bridge had a hidden significance. By handing over a few coins like everyone else to cross it, the nobles conceded the first breach of their cherished privilege of never paying tax of any kind.

Vienna's lofty amusement at these goings-on was brought down to earth when Szechenyi's shoes were filled by the fiery lawyer and journalist, Lajos Kossuth. His adversary was the equally formidable Prince Clemens von Metternich who, with the amiable but half-witted Ferdinand on the Habsburg throne, ran the empire as he saw fit, and that meant as a police state.

The Paris revolution of 1848 lit powder kegs all over Europe, and Hungary was no exception. Kossuth's rousing rhetoric in the Hungarian Diet was aimed not only at Austria *per se* but also at the system it shored up

in Hungary. He demanded an end to the privileges of the nobility (especially tax exemption), a universal franchise, press freedom and reunification with Transylvania.

In the heat of the 1848 revolution, Metternich fled to England, reputedly hidden in a laundry basket, leaving the harmless but hopeless Ferdinand to sort things out so inevitably they got worse. Kossuth was himself caught off-balance when the cry for freedom was taken up minorities, like the Romanians, Ruthenes, Croats and Slovaks against Hungary itself. Ferdinand was forced to abdicate in favour of his 18-year-old nephew Franz Joseph who, made of sterner stuff, was determined by any means to put

down the independent Republic of Hungary which Kossuth had proclaimed in December.

Incapable of ending the rebellion alone, Franz Joseph needed an ally who was no less threatened by the wave of revolution. He did not have to look beyond Tsar Nicholas I of Russia. The Russian army poured across the Carpathian Basin, Kossuth took flight to Turkey, and the Hungarian revolution was crushed with the utmost severity.

His authority restored, Franz Joseph mixed the stamp of absolutism with attempts to reach a *modus vivendi* with Hungary, initially by proposing a federation and then, in 1867, with the compromise which saw him

Left, Bratislava is declared captial of royal Hungary, 1641. **Right**, Maria Theresa.

crowned king of Hungary in a capacity supposedly independent of his position as emperor, the so-called Dual Monarchy.

While the emperor-king had cause to be satisfied, the sentiment was not shared by the lower strata of Hungarian society. Rigorous Magyarisation of the population left no room for the nationalist aspirations which the various minorities felt no less keenly. While the growing number of Jews, for example, were ready to adopt Hungarian as a mother tongue and assume Hungarian names, the Romanians who constituted the largest majority in Romania were emphatically opposed.

The outbreak of hostilities in 1914 was almost a welcome diversion from Hungary's internal strife. Hungary was drawn in on Austria's side as resolutely as Austria was on Germany's, but the initial Magyar enthusiasm for the war soon gave way to reality. By 1916, the minorities, reluctant conscripts in the Hungarian army to begin with, were deserting in droves. Charles I who succeeded Franz Joseph on his death in 1916 put out peace feelers to the Anglo-French Entente, but these were rejected.

The Paris peace conference after the war dismantled all the empires represented in Eastern Europe, including Habsburg Austria. The various minorities in Hungary all had ethnic homes they could return to if necessary but of course the Magyars were simply themselves in a sea of Slavs and Germans.

The prospect of isolation was tailor-made for the Communists who preached international brotherhood and were delighted to extend a welcoming hand to the Magyars. The Hungarian Communist leader Bela Kun was there to accept it.

The Hungarian Soviet was declared on 22 March 1919, and within three days the Communists had control of the army and the police. Edict followed edict in rapid fire: nationalisation of the banks and industries, land reform, curbs on the church, and so on.

Alarmed by a Communist state mushrooming before their eyes, the Western powers were ready to turn a blind eye when the Czechs and Romanians invaded Hungary. On 3 August, the Romanian army entered Budapest and the Hungarian experiment with Communist government came to an abrupt end. It was seen as a time for settling old scores. The Romanians looted, "Whites" murdered "Reds", and the Jews faced a barrage of anti-Semitism. The Romanians withdrew, and a measure of order was restored on the creation of a pro-Western government under Admiral Miklos Horthy, an admiral who no longer had a fleet in a country which no longer had a coastline.

Hungary was effectively tried and found guilty by the Treaty of Trianon. Its territory was cut by two-thirds, the bulk of the loss being the transfer of Transylvania to Romania. The population, 21 million before the war, shrank to 7.5 million. The Hungarian reaction to all this was summed up in the chant "Nem, nem, soha!" (No, no, never!) but there was nothing they could do. The insult added to the injury was the news that Charles, the deposed Habsburg emperor, had gathered an army and was hoping to revive the dynasty's fortunes by starting a new empire around Budapest. Swift military action put an end to that.

Hitler sensed that a Hungary still groaning under the punitive Treaty of Trianon and economically crippled by the Depression would be fertile ground for his Nazi doctrine. He courted Hungarians by investing heavily in their industry and providing a market for their agricultural produce. He also rearmed a Hungarian army which had been reduced to a militia and denied heavy weapons since World War I.

Successive Hungarian governments were not sure how to react, but there were powerful forces like the Arrow Cross movement who were more than receptive. Hitler gave Hungary a slice of its old Slovakian territory as a reward for a set of "Jewish Laws" which corresponded with his general philosophy.

When Pal Teleki, prime minister at the outbreak of World War II, tried to prevent the Wehrmacht from crossing Hungarian territory, Hitler sweetened the pill by promising to give Transylvania back as soon as he occupied Romania. When he needed to cross a second time to invade Yugoslavia, it helped by itself occupying Croatia. This was too much for Teleki and in April 1941 he committed suicide. His successor Bardossy, however, had no reservations about sending troops to fight alongside the Germans in Russia. In December, Britain declared war on Hungary, and Hitler demanded total Hungarian mobilisation.

While the old Admiral Horthy hoped to reach some kind of understanding with the

Allies, the Nazis took over Hungary completely in 1944. This had dire consequences for the Jewish population in spite of the heroic rescue campaign mounted by the Swedish diplomatic attaché Raoul Wallenberg, later to disappear in circumstances which have never been fully explained.

The battle of Stalingrad turned the tide of battle in Eastern Europe, and Admiral Horthy directed his efforts to an armistice with the USSR. He was promptly kidnapped by the Germans and for the Jews and other "undesirables" in Hungary the war moved into its most terrible phase.

After a grim battle to hold Budapest against the invading Red Army, the Germans evacu-

By mid-1949, the Communists had achieved power by the means which were to become a familiar story all over Eastern Europe. The imprisonment of Cardinal Josef Mindszenty was singled out for international protest from the normal pattern of treason trials and purges. There was a brief ray of hope when the avuncular Imre Nagy seemed willing to challenge Communist orthodoxy after the death of Stalin in 1953, but this was eclipsed by the hard-liner Mathias Rakosi and his henchman Erno Gero.

On 23 October 1956, student demonstrators marched on parliament demanding reforms. The government response was the use of force. Two days later, the entire country

ated Hungary in February 1945, withdrawing across the border to Austria. In the wake of the Red Army came loyal Hungarian Communists who had seen out the war in Moscow. They filled all the important positions in the government established by the Soviet Army. Nevertheless, when the first elections were held, the Communists recorded only 17 percent of the votes against 57 percent for an alliance of various groups campaigning as the "Smallholders". The monarchy was abolished and a republic proclaimed on 1 February 1946.

Above, Soviet tanks in Budapest in 1956.

was up in arms, and the ensuing events were a dress rehearsal for what would happen elsewhere in Eastern Europe.

Hungarian flags appeared everywhere with the red star cut out of the middle. A statue of Stalin in Budapest was blow-torched off its pedestal and dragged through the streets. Cardinal Mindszenty was freed and Imre Nagy came out of retirement to side with the revolution. Orders flowed in from Moscow but the Hungarian army under General Pal Maleter declined to carry them out. With that, the Soviet tanks rolled in and what transpired afterwards is of course where this brief history began.

HUNGARY: WHAT TO SEE

Budapest: The Romans built bridges across the Danube in the 2nd century AD, yet Buda on the west bank and Pest on the east did not get one until William Tierney Clark designed and Adam Clark built the great **Chain Bridge** in the 1840s. The problem, it seems, was that the river flowed very fast and frequently flooded at this point so that there was no reliable hard ground on either side.

The first bridge cost £500,000 and was regarded as an engineering wonder of the age. The two principals were British – Clark also did the Hammersmith Bridge in London – as were many of the work force, together with Italians from Trieste and Slavs. The Hungarian nobility put up the money.

Buda, Obuda (Old Buda) and Pest became a single city in 1872, and other bridges followed. They were all blown up during World War II as the Germans prepared their last stand on Castle Hill, and the rebuilding afterwards was a long process. The Chain Bridge reopened in 1949, exactly 100 years after its completion, but the single-span Elizabeth Bridge was not ready until 1964. The latter was named after a Habsburg royal who was genuinely popular in these parts: the Empress Elizabeth who married Franz Joseph and was universally known as Sissy. Franz Joseph had his bridge, too, but it was later renamed Szabadsaghid, or **Liberty Bridge**.

Although Buda looks older than Pest, it was in fact started only after the destruction of Pest by the Mongols in 1241. While the east bank was flat, the steep limestone hill opposite had natural defensive possibilities and moreover had the Danube between it and the direction from which these terrifying oriental horsemen on their piebald ponies were likely to return. They had come out of the blue and no one had the faintest idea who they were. They disappeared abruptly – trouble at home, it transpired

Preceding pages: Budapest market. **Left**, the capital's parliament building.

– but it was prudent to assume that they would one day be back. People went back to live in Pest but it was always vulnerable and more than once destroyed by other enemies.

The present boulevards and ring-roads were mostly laid out at the beginning of the 20th century. They cope with modern traffic reasonably well but the older parts of the capital do not. This will not bother tourists. The interesting parts of the city are in concentrated clusters and public transport, including a metro, is more than adequate.

It was on one of the hills on the Buda west bank that in 1046 the worthy Swiss Bishop Gellert presumed to preach Christianity to unreceptive locals and for his pains was stuffed into a barrel studded with nails and launched down the hill into the river. If nothing else, he had the posthumous honour of having the hill named after him. It provides an excellent panorama, one that conveys the vastness of the plain beyond the city and the way the Danube arcs through it. **Margaret Island** in the heart of Bu-

dapest is a recreational oasis with its park, restaurants, swimming pools and so forth. **Csepel Island** to the south proclaims by its forest of chimneys the presence of the Csepel Iron and Steel Works. **Gellert Hill** itself has an old citadel and the Liberation Memorial to the dead in the siege of 1944–45.

Bela IV's plans for the new town of Buda in the 13th century began with a fortress on **Castle Hill** to protect the civilian quarter to the north. A very stormy future lay ahead. The city got off lightly in the Turkish conquest of 1526 – the decisive battle was fought at Mohacs – but not in the subsequent recapture in 1686. The Turks then turned the churches into mosques and gave the city a certain oriental air.

Odd touches survive in some of the houses and the baths to which the Turks were so partial. The grave of Abdurrahman Ali, the last Turkish pasha to rule Buda, is in Uri Street on Castle Hill. Below the hill is the tomb of the versatile Gul Baba, a Dervish, a poet and the "Father of the Roses".

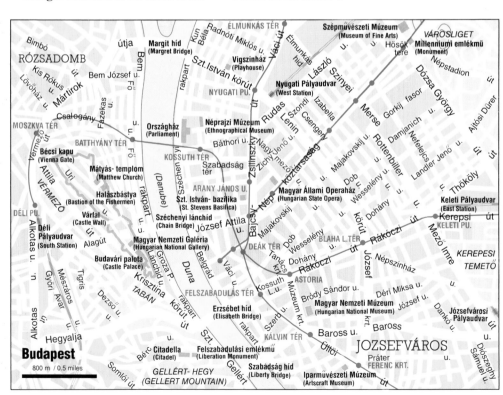

The ruined city was rebuilt after the Turks in the late-baroque fashion of the times, the best examples of which are the University Church, the Zichy Manor and Silk Factory in Obuda, and St Anne's Church in Batthyany Square. The restoration of the monarchy in 1867 led to a second wave of celebratory building in which the fortress was transformed into a royal palace. The enthusiasm carried across the river to Pest as the Hungarians entertained the unashamed ambition of building a capital that would outshine Vienna.

This rebuilding program patched up much of the damage done by the Austrians and Russians in putting down the 1848 revolution, but there was more trouble in store. The Romanians went on the rampage in 1919, the Germans did their worst in 1944, and of course the Russians were back again in 1956. The guides who show visitors around the city seem remarkably confident about which bullet holes in the masonry belong to which army.

The destruction of almost everything that stood on Castle Hill as the Germans made their last stand in 1944 at least gave archaeologists a chance to poke about in the rubble, and this brought to light evidence of the great names of Hungarian history: the Arpads, Angevins, Mathias Corvinus and all. These remains were cleverly integrated in the reconstruction of the palace, which now houses the **Museum of Modern Hungarian History**, the **Hungarian National Gallery**, the **Budapest History Museum** and the **National Library**.

The most extraordinary example of mixing old and new is the **Hilton Hotel**, which combines elements of a medieval tower and an 18th-century monastery with a top which looks like some kind of space rocket. Excavations have also produced dozens of Gothic statues decapitated in what appears to have been a wave of frenetic vandalism. Hungarians tend to blame Turkish religious maniacs for it.

Castle Hill, which has a tunnel through its bowels, can be reached by a funicular railway from **Clark Adam Square** at

Budapest's spa hotels are a big attraction.

the end of the Chain Bridge. The "Furul" statue at the funicular is of the mythical eagle which guided the Magyars from the Ural Mountains in Russia across the Carpathians and into Hungary. The several streets along the plateau, linked by narrow passages, are now closed to private cars and have a fairground atmosphere, especially those around the **Mathias Church**.

Strictly speaking, this is the Church of Our Lady (and for a while an important Turkish mosque) but it is generally known by the name of the hero Mathias Corvinus who was married here (twice) and remodelled it. The church was badly damaged in 1686 and was completely rebuilt in the 19th century. Franz Joseph and Charles IV, the last kings of Hungary, were both crowned here. Not much light comes through the dark windows, but as one's eyes adjust a magnificent interior of decorated pillars, walls and ceilings emerges from the gloom. The murals depict the lives of the Hungarian saints and among the sarcophagi are those of Bela III (1173–96) and his wife Anne of Chatillon, transferred from Szekesfehervar.

A short distance from the church is the **Fishermen's Bastion**, a rather weird building of winding passages and staircases which looks Gothic or Romanesque, or perhaps a bit of both, but was in fact built at the beginning of the 20th century. It is named after the medieval fishermen's town which stood below. Photographers will instantly recognise the potential of the various columns and arches as frames for wide shots of the city. It is customary for lenses to turn next to the equestrian statue of St Stephen outside.

Dwarfed by the museums in the palace complex is the curious little **Museum of Catering** in **Fortuna utca**, not far from the Hilton Hotel. Do not be misled by the name; this is no paean to sensible nutrition or works canteens. Several rooms are each designed to resemble the entrance halls of Budapest hotels when they were the soul of aristocratic high-living. The collection of old menus and photographs of the

Left, stall in Deak Square. **Right,** Fishermen's Bastion.

Magyar chef's art are enough to give anyone a ripping appetite.

For another glimpse of Magyar nostalgia try the **War Museum**, in particular the 19th-century cavalry uniforms which were a large part of the swashbuckling image of the Hungarian officer class. The exhibits are mostly concerned with the Hungarian uprising of 1848 against the Austrians and Russians. The Communists made sure that the Austrians, not the Russians, were portrayed as the arch-villains.

The arch near the War Museum is one way of getting to the newer part of Buda. The main thoroughfare is known as **Fo utca**, and at the northern end is the statue of General Joseph Bemand, a hero of 1848. It was around this statue that the demonstrations of 1956 began.

At No. 72 Fo utca are the **Kiraly baths**. The 120 or so thermal springs lining the Danube are reputed to disgorge 16 million gallons of medicinal water per day. The Romans may have founded Aquincum here for no other reason, and in the Middle Ages all hospitals were built around a medicinal spring. Baths serve much the same purpose in Budapest as coffee-houses in Vienna or pubs in English villages, and if male visitors are inclined to try one, the mosque-like Kiraly baths are probably the best bet.

While women will have to settle for female or unisex bathing – try **Gellert** or **Czaszar baths** – privileged males can luxuriate in dark medieval masonry under a coloured glass ceiling more than 600 years old. The water springs from an amazing depth – some say a mile or so – and reaches the surface rich in radioactive salts capable of snatching the most forlorn wreck back from the brink of the grave.

The fitting way to enter Pest is to walk the 600 yards across the Chain Bridge: there is a pedestrian path. **Roosevelt Square** with its statues of Count Stephen Szechenyi and Lajos Kossuth is on the other side, the neo-Renaissance **Academy of Sciences** having been founded by the former. The **Corzo** running south is a pedestrian promenade leading to

Left, Szechenyi thermal pool. Right, gypsy fiddler.

Vigado Square where, in the **Concert Hall**, all the musical giants seem to have performed at one time or another. The roll-call begins with Brahms and Liszt.

Parallel with the Corso is **Vaci ut**, Budapest's smartest shopping street which even in the 1970s and 1980s was full of luxuries unobtainable anywhere else in Eastern Europe. This was equally true of the **Budapest market** (at the other end of Vaci ut), an amazing 19th-century building with soaring metal columns, high walkways and ramps. It is a busy place with live fish in tanks and long tables of every conceivable kind of mushroom. Red peppers by the thousand are, of course, the fabled paprikas.

Much of Pest's shopping district is now car-free, which greatly enhances the pleasure of strolling about. **Vorosmarty Square** is always a hive of activity, and it is almost obligatory to make at least one call at Gerbeaud's, the esteemed confectioners, established 1857. Most of the airline offices are in this area, as is the bus terminus.

Near the Inter-Continental Hotel is

the **Inner City Parish Church** (*Belvarosi plebania templom*) whose origins pre-date the Mongol invasion. Liszt played the organ in this church regularly; in fact he lived just around the corner in a house where Wagner was a regular guest at his Sunday soirées.

The huge **Parliament** imitated the British model in both its constitution and the way it is mirrored in the Danube as the British one is in the Thames. It was built between 1880 and 1902 to a design by Imre Steindl which required special concrete foundations because of the proximity of the river. The scenes enacted under the vast dome have been strong on rousing Hungarian oratory, and it was an object of considerable pride even when it housed puppet Communist governments. There are 10 courtyards, 29 staircases and 27 gates behind the 300-yard (280-metre) facade with its 88 statues of Hungarian leaders and generals. Tours of the magnificent interior are available on mornings of certain days of the week, which tend to vary.

The **National Museum** is a must for the Apostolic Crown of St Stephen alone. This most potent symbol in the land is apparently 12th-century Byzantine art and, while obviously a masterpiece, cannot therefore be the actual crown which Pope Sylvester II gave to Stephen in the year 1000. The cross on the top was bent, and remains bent, as the result of being hastily hidden during some crisis in medieval times. The Hungarian army handed over the crown and the rest of the royal regalia to the Americans when the Red Army was on the point of entering Budapest at the end of World War II. The United States relented and gave them all back only in 1978.

The museum also has a fine collection of objects related to the Great Migrations as well as Iron Age, Bronze Age and Roman antiquities. The later pieces include a sword presented by Pope Julius II to King Wenceslas, who, during his more celebrated reign in Bohemia, was for a brief period also King of Hungary. Some miniature pistols are said to have belonged to John Sobieski, the dashing Polish hero of the siege of Vienna.

The Chain Bridge.

The **Hary Borozo tavern** nearby at 30 Brody Sandor has sadly lost its star, a gypsy violinist of the old school, "with a penetrating gaze and superb musicianship". It is an unpretentious place with fair food and better wine and, even without its maestro, a comfortable haunt. Far more pretentious – perhaps too much so – is the Café-Restaurant Hungaria near the Opera, an art-nouveau establishment once called the Café New York. Tickets to the opera are scarce, and it is worth getting in even between performances to marvel at the mirrored and varnished interior.

The **Millennary Monument** in **Heroes Square** commemorates the 1,000th anniversary of the Magyar conquest and has an appropriate equestrian statue of Arpad in front of the seven lesser-known Magyar chieftains who accompanied him. It was designed by Albert Schickedanz in 1896. The buildings dominating the square are the **Museum of Fine Arts** and the **Artists' House**, the former containing one of the most important collections in Eastern Europe

and the latter a changing exhibition of contemporary work.

That still leaves the equally impressive **Museum of Applied Arts**, which is out on its own in the south of the city and may require a taxi. The building is an attraction in its own right, the work of Odon Lechner in the 1890s.

Oboda, or "Old Buda", is a little distance from the centre but can be reached by the HEV train from Batthyany Square. It is mostly apartment buildings now, but there is a historic centre with the ruins of a Roman amphitheatre capable of accommodating 15,000 spectators. An 18th-century baroque mansion built by the Zichy family is the local cultural centre.

Danube Bend: A glance at the map will explain why the Danube Bend is so called. After flowing almost due east from Vienna and along the Czech-Hungarian border, the river executes a right-angled turn to the south around the Budapest Mountains. The inside of the corner is the scenic historical heartland of Hungary. It is easily accessible from

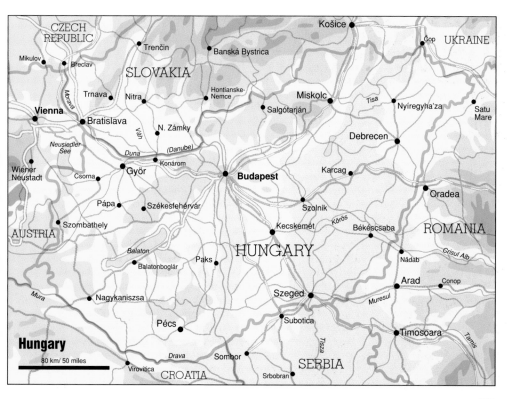

the capital by boat, rail or road, and while the round trip by road is only about 75 miles (120 km) there is more than enough to warrant a night or two away in one of three picturesque towns, Szentendre, Visegrad or Esztergom, preferably the last.

The Danube Bend was a salient of the Roman Empire, and this is evident soon after leaving Budapest with the ruins of **Aquinium**, the capital of the Roman province of Pannonia. The site of the old Roman baths is now one of Budapest's main campsites and bathing areas. The most notable historic remains are the basilica, forum and the Villa Hercules.

Szentendre is a charming baroque town of cobbled streets which was largely settled by Greeks and Serbs fleeing from the Turks. They built imposing Greek Orthodox and Serbian Orthodox churches, and both denominations have ecclesiastical museums. There are still restaurants serving their respective national dishes.

A short bus ride from Szentendre is the ancient settlement of **Visegrad**, an-

other Roman stronghold where the river emerges dramatically from the mountains. The town now has fewer than 3,000 inhabitants, but in the 14th century it was the seat of the Angevin kings who built the citadel crowning the hill of Varhegy.

In the 15th century Mathias Corvinus built a palace on the river bank and turned Visegrad into a Renaissance capital described by one who saw it as "an earthly paradise". In an all too familiar story, it was levelled by the Turks but excavations have revealed enough to give a fair impression of what it once was, especially the red marble fountain. The entrance is in **Fo utca**. A stiffish but rewarding walk up the hill behind the citadel reaches the Solomon Tower with a café attached.

To arrive in **Esztergom** on the river is to come upon the wonderful sight of the domed cathedral, the largest church in the country with eight giant Corinthian columns. It is the seat of the Cardinal-Primate of Hungary. The Romans knew the town as Strigonium, and it is said that the Emperor Marcus Aurelius was inspired to compose his 12 volumes of *Meditations* here. According to tradition, Geza, the father of St Stephen, was born here and it was here that Stephen was crowned king in 1000. When Buda became the political capital in the 14th century, Esztergom remained the ecclesiastical capital.

The **cathedral** was built between 1822 and 1869 on the site of a 16th-century church which was razed during successive sieges in the 1590s. The cathedral retains the earlier altar of white marble by Andrea Ferrucci of Fiesole, and the crypt contains the tombs of a number of medieval bishops. Its treasury is the richest in the land with, among other treasures, the so-called crucifix of Mathias Corvinus of about 1480 and the "Coffin of Our Lord". The library, generally open only to scholars, contains 40,000 volumes, the oldest dated 1187.

Next to the cathedral are the remains of the **Royal Palace** – destroyed, predictably one might say, by the Turks. The excavated chapel contains frescoes by 15th-century Burgundian artists.

Dressed for the occasion.

A bit beyond the bend proper, a few miles south of Gyor, is **Pannonhalma**, the oldest monastery in Hungary, founded by Geza, Hungry's first Christian prince. It is situated high on **St Martin's Hill**, the St Martin in question being the patron saint of France, geese and beggars. The oldest surviving part of the original Benedictine abbey is the crypt with an abbot's throne, popularly but dubiously known as the throne of Stephen I. The Gothic cloisters were built by Mathias Corvinus, the abbey complex in its present form dating from the 19th century.

The crypt also contains the tomb of Princess Stephanie of Belgium, the wife of the Habsburg Crown Prince Rudolf who died scandalously in the company of his young mistress in the hunting lodge at Mayerling in 1889. Stephanie married a second time to the Hungarian Count Lonyay and lived until 1949.

Lake Balaton: Hungarians call Lake Balaton the "Sea of Hungary" and, with tongue in cheek, the half-dozen armed motor launches on it the "Hungarian Navy". It is about 50 miles (80 km) long and has a circumference of about 120 miles (190 km). The average depth of the lake is only about 12 ft (3.5 metres), which means that it quickly warms up under the sun but even more quickly turns violent when the wind comes up. Under these conditions, the officers and men of the Hungarian Navy would be more comfortable riding out a storm in mid-Atlantic.

The southern and northern shores are quite different in character. The former is flat, sandy and, these days, an almost uninterrupted stretch of resorts apt to be packed out in summer. Some of these have Roman origins and others retain the faded charm of what made them very fashionable in the 19th and early 20th century, but the capitulation to mass tourism is more or less complete. The facilities for families with young children are no doubt entirely satisfactory, but it is unlikely that independent travellers would be sufficiently rewarded by the odd Roman site, lace factory or wine press to put up with the crush. A

Country pleasures.

railway line encircles the lake and with the train stopping at a station every few miles there is the chance for a half-lap to satisfy any curiosity about the south.

The northern shore is a different proposition. It also has good beaches, but the topography is enlivened by the spurs of extinct volcanoes and lush vegetation. Neither **Balatonkenese** nor **Balatonuzfo** on the approach from Budapest has much to recommend it, but between them are two peculiarities. The first is a white honey-scented flower, crame tataria, with thick roots that grow 5 ft (1.5 metres) long. It is called "Tartar Bread" because during the Mongol invasion the locals are reputed to have dug them up, baked and eaten them in the absence of anything else. Look out, too, for the warren of dark holes in hillsides. These are the "Tartar caves", home to refugees during both the Mongol and Turkish invasions.

Balatonalmadi was a bathing resort and health spa in the 19th century. The Kneipp form of hydrotherapy used to be administered in the little wooden houses

still to be seen; nowadays patients occupy 12 floors of the Hotel Aurora. The church on a hill in the Vorosbereny district is one of the fortified examples commonplace in Transylvania but less so in these parts.

The stretch of coast around **Felsoors** and **Alsoors** is sometimes called the Balaton Riviera. The vegetation is lush and narrow paths up the hills lead to vineyards which produce some of Hungary's most popular white wines. Alsoors also goes in for fish farming by rather unorthodox means. Bunches of pine and juniper twigs are attached to long lines across the water. When pike and perch have laid their eggs on the twigs, they are drawn in and transferred to pools. When the young hatch, they are at liberty to return to the lake via a special channel.

The oldest spa on the north shore and in many ways the most interesting is **Balatonfured**, which has a picturesque and protective setting in a ring of hills. It was a resort in Roman times and there are the remains of a Roman villa behind

The blue line near the ground traditionally indicated the presence of an unmarried woman.

the Calvinist church. French and British travellers cottoned on to the medicinal properties of the springs as early as the 17th century, and their fame grew steadily thereafter. It earned recommendation in a 19th-century Baedeker as "a pleasing bath with springs impregnated with carbonic acid, beneficial in female complaints and frequented by the country's aristocracy". Delegates to the Congress of Vienna in 1815 used to nip across on visits.

By the end of July the patients are presumed to have regained sufficient heartiness to take part in the annual St Anne's day celebrations around the Sanatorium on the northern side of the square. The arcades have plaques commemorating distinguished visitors; the greatest accolade, however, is to be invited to plant a tree in the park running down to the shore. Rabindranath Tagore, the Indian poet and Nobel Prize winner, recovered from a heart attack to plant a lime tree and dash off a grateful poem which is inscribed in a marble slab in English with a Hungarian translation.

Waiting for a catch.

Not his best verse, true, but here it is anyway:
When I am no longer in this earth,
  my tree,
Let the ever renewed leaves of spring
Murmur to the wayfarer
The poet did love while he lived.

Quasimodo, the Italian poet – not his unlovely namesake – also left a tree.

Nagyvazsony is one of two interesting excursions from Balatonfured, and in either case there is a chance to stop at one of a number of country inns or *csardas*. The drill is to descend to the cellar in order to sample and buy the house wines or *barack*, a hair-raising Hungarian schnapps. In most cases there will be food served from a grill and a gypsy band.

At Nagyvazsony itself is the medieval castle built by Pal Kinizsi, one of Mathias Corvinus's men famed for his brutish strength but at the same time a deeply religious patron of the arts who built the Gothic church in the village. His castle, built in the 15th century, has an exhibition of the wars which reduced

it to ruins. The former Zichy Mansion is now a country house hotel which has received favourable reports.

Tihany, the second excursion from Nagyvazsony, is the peninsula jutting into the lake and crowned by the twin towers of a baroque abbey beneath which ferries from the other side of the lake moor. It is a geological rarity with petrified geyser mounds otherwise found only in Iceland and Yellowstone Park in the United States. The most spectacular of these is near Harmas-hegy and ought to be seen at sunset when it assumes a golden glow.

Tihany is also very old ground, historically speaking. The walls of the **Ovar** (Old Castle) are Celtic, the watchtower on **Csucshegy** (Mount Peak) is Roman, and the traces of early churches are from the time of Arpad. The abbey was founded in 1055 by King Andrew I whose crypt is intact: "The only royal tomb in the 1,000-year-old kingdom of Hungary that was passed down to us in its original form," says an inscription. The tombstone is of white limestone,

with a twisted staff and simple cross chiselled out at one end.

The Abbey's charter, a curious mixture of Latin with some Hungarian words, is a priceless document which is kept at Pannonhalma. King Andrew spent part of his youth at the court of Yaroslav the Wise at Kiev (see the Ukrainian section of this book), married his daughter Anastasia, and brought back some Kievan monks who lived in cells carved out of the basalt-tufa cliffs east of the church.

The vain bid to save the Habsburg Empire after World War I ended here. Charles had hoped to restore the kingdom of Hungary with himself as monarch. His campaign ended when the train he was using as mobile headquarters literally ended up against the buffers of a dead-end. Charles surrendered and was interned at Tihany until, on 31 October 1921, he was transferred to the Danube harbour of Baja where a British warship, *HMS Glowworm*, was waiting to take him into exile on Madeira.

Some 19 miles (30km) west of Tihany, the hill of **Badacsony** stands like a sentinel at the entrance to the plain of Tapolca. These volcanic slopes produce Hungary's best known Sylvaners and Rieslings, and there are any number of cellars and taverns selling them. On the top of the mountain is the **Kisfaludy House**, once the property of the Hungarian poet Sandor Kisfaludy and his wife Roza Szegedi. The house has a wine museum and a restaurant with the most superb views.

Castles, stalagmites and Tokay: Northeastern Hungary is on fewer tourists' maps than Lake Balaton and the *puszta*, yet it has major attractions in historic towns like Eger and Sarospatak, the extraordinary Aggtelek caves and a wine district as famous as any in the world. The **Tokay** region is characterised by the gentle, thickly-wooded mountains which are the southernmost outcrops of the Carpathians. A lot of Hungarian history has been written in the valleys.

In the valleys of the **Cserhat Hills**, to begin with, are a people known as the Palots. Ethnographers are still not sure where to place them in relation to the

Bodrog River, near Tokay, in flood.

main body of Magyars. In the meantime, everything possible is being done to preserve their distinctive culture and Holloko, their most pristine village (albeit rebuilt after a fire in 1909), is on the UNESCO list of the "Cultural Heritage of the World". Ironically, most of the medieval houses are now occupied by Budapest intellectuals while the original inhabitants have gratefully moved into modern accommodation.

East of the Paloc lands are the **Matra Mountains**, a volcanic group which although not rising to any great heights (not much more than 3,200 ft/1,000 metres) are sufficient to give Hungary its winter sports facilities. The discovery of lignite deposits in the 1960s has resulted in some industrial intrusion. A strategic valley separates the Matras from the Bukk range, and this has given the city of **Eger** its special role in history. It was settled by some of the first Magyars and was one of the five bishoprics founded by St Stephen. Its turbulent existence since has left 175 listed historic monuments.

Eger castle was built after the Mongol invasion. Its heroic defence against the Turks in 1552 is the subject of a popular novel, *The Stars of Eger* by Geza Gardonyi, which has been translated into several languages. The story is that a garrison of 2,000 commanded by Stephen Dobo successfully saw off a Turkish force of 100,000. When at last the castle fell to the Turks in 1596, the city of Eger became one of the most northern outposts of Muslim power. They left behind an impressive minaret, improvements to the castle and, as always, some baths.

The bishop's palace beneath the castle is of particular interest to art historians. It was designed in the mid-18th century by Jakob Fellner as four huge wings around a central courtyard and 10-storey tower. Part of the complex is now a teacher training college which for unexplained reasons bears the name of Ho Chi Minh. **Kossuth Lajos utca** is probably the most impressive street in the city as everything in it is either baroque or Rococo. Notice particularly

Badacsony.

the wrought-iron gates and balconies on the Lesser Prior's House at No. 4. The **Minorite Church** in Stephen Dobo Square, the medieval market-place, is the work of the great baroque architect Kilian Ignaz Dientzenhofer.

One aspect of Eger must not be missed because this is the home of the legendary Bull's Blood. There are any number of wine bars in the city, and cellars on the outskirts, which serve this full-bodied red, known locally as Bikaver. The Leanyka white and the local sweet dessert wine are also well worth trying.

Horse-fanciers would like to know that one of the famous Lipizzaner stud farms is to be found a short distance away at **Szilvasvarad**, the former estate of the Margrave Pallavicini. The farm has a museum showing the history of the breed and it is possible to hire horses for riding. The rides are through a wonderful landscape of deep valleys, waterfalls and streams full of fish. Motorists will need prior permission, cheerfully given, to use the narrow road from Szilvasvarad to Lillafured and Miskolc.

Miskolc, Hungary's second city, has little of interest to offer tourists apart from the castle of **Diosgyor**, which is itself almost lost among high-rise apartment blocks. From Angevin times onwards, it was the property specifically of the reigning queen. The last to occupy it, however, was Maria of Habsburg, the wife of Louis II, who drowned at the battle of Mohacs.

Far more rewarding are the **Aggtelek caves** hard on the Slovak border, so hard in fact that some of them burrow well beyond it. These are some of the most impressive limestone caves to be found anywhere in the world. The biggest is the Baradla, more than 15 miles (24 km) long. A full tour takes all of five hours, but there are shortened versions which include the biggest stalagmite in the world, a monster called the Observatory which is 82 ft (25 metres) high and 26 ft (8 metres) across at its base. One of the chambers has been turned into nothing less than a concert hall capable of holding 1,000 people. Needless to say, the acoustics have a rather special quality

Left, Calvinist churches are well attended. **Right**, Nyirseg village.

and, better than any air-conditioning, the pleasantly cool temperature never deviates an iota.

Some 30 miles (50 km) east of Miskolc is the village which gave its name to the "King of wines, and the wine of kings", **Tokay**. The grapes in fact come from an area of some 12,000 acres (5,000 hectares) which incorporates a total of 28 villages. The altarpiece in the village church of **Tallya** captures the spirit of the area by showing St Wendelin and a bevy of angels all pitching in with the harvest.

It seems the Celts recognised the wine-making potential of this singular combination of volcanic soil and climate. The pressings of the best grapes, the "essence of Tokay", are matured for at least 12 years in a deep cellar, during which a black mould forms on the bottles. Attempts to reproduce the wine elsewhere have never come up to scratch. The whole story is told in the **Museum of Local History**.

The lesser but still very good Tokays, the dry "Szamorodni" and the sweet "Aszubor", are sold at quite reasonable prices at the government outlet at Tolcsva and a number of private cellars. As far as the Aszubor is concerned, the number of butts on the bottle-neck denotes the sweetness and purity. A higher number is generally a more important indicator of quality than the year.

Esterhazy Fertod Palace: The feudal system did not properly end in Hungary until 1945. The lives led by the great titled land-owners until then was opulent beyond belief. The post-war socialists naturally took an exceedingly dim view of all this. The magnates were chased out and their property confiscated, either to be left to rot or, in one case, turned into a museum of mining, of all things.

Many of the great estates are now being rehabilitated, but we shall concentrate here on the most magnificent, that of the Esterhazy family at Fertod, near Lake Ferto. The barons of Esterhazy were made princes of the Holy Roman Empire for their help in securing the kingdom of Hungary for the

Left, wife of a Calvinist chats to a pensioner. **Right**, Vezseny.

Habsburgs. At one point the Esterhazys owned 21 castles, 60 market towns, more than 400 villages, various castles and lordships in Austria, and the whole county of Bavaria.

In 1720, Prince Nicolaus Esterhazy, who affected a diamond-studded coat and was called "the Magnificent", was not satisfied with the palaces he already owned. He chose to build Fertod in what was then a swamp, not the most convenient place but near one his favourite shooting lodges. The draining of the swamp and construction of the palace cost more than 10 million florins, which happened to be a hundred times more than all the money in the Habsburg treasury at the time.

The palace had 126 guest rooms, two state ballrooms, a parade hall, vast kitchens supplied by ice-houses holding enough meat to feed a regiment, gardens and hothouses filled with exotic vegetables and fruit. The estate was guarded by 150 hand-picked grenadiers, all over 6 ft (1.8 metres) tall, drilled to perfection and kitted out in blue and scarlet uniforms, white waistcoats and trousers, and black bearskins.

The showpiece, however, was the **opera house**. The Esterhazys were music lovers and patrons in particular of the son of serfs on a neighbouring estate, Josef Haydn. The young Haydn was installed in the fully-equipped opera house which stood in a chestnut grove apart from the main buildings. It could seat 400 in boxes furnished with fireplaces, divans, mirrors and clocks. The adjoining puppet theatre was smaller but by no means trifling.

The Empress Maria Theresa was a frequest guest at the palace. When once she stopped to praise a newly completed Chinese pavilion crammed with priceless treasures, her Esterhazy host protested that it was "a mere bagatelle!". By 1790, however, the Esterhazys had grown bored with Fertod. The family moved back to one of their other palaces and Fertod was simply closed down. The palace was badly damaged in World War II but has since been splendidly restored. The Chinese section is still there to be seen.

Puszta: Hidden behind the Carpathian mountains, the Hungarian *puszta* is a semi-detached extension of the Northern Plain across which the Great Migrations flowed from the steppes of Central Asia into Eastern Europe. It is easy to see why the steppe-bred Magyars felt absolutely at home when they crossed the Carpathians and descended on to the plain. Unfortunately for them, the *puszta* was equally familiar terrain to the 13th-century Mongols who, each with two or three ponies in tow, could gallop across vast distances at astonishing speed.

Puszta actually means "ruination" or something to that effect and it applies not to the result of the Mongol invasion but that of the Turks in 1526. The Turks conducted a scorched-earth offensive against guerrilla resistance and, anticipating the defoliation tactics in Vietnam, destroyed forests and anything else that might provide cover for the enemy. The difference from Vietnam is that, technology aside, Turkish defoliation went on for 150 years.

The population deserted the area for

Reeds drying in the sun.

264

the safety of towns and it became a malarial swamp inhabited only by outlaws and undesirables. A miracle was required, and that's what happened in the 19th century as the unplanned result of flood control which caused the alkaline level of the soil to soar. Presto – a sea of grassland.

Viewed from Bucharest, the puszta stretches endlessly towards Romania. It is dotted with towns and cities, but romantic eyes prefer to dwell on cowboys – *cskikos*, to give them their local name – cracking whips over huge herds of cattle or wild horses roaming a vast emptiness. John Wayne in this context wears a wide-sleeved linen shirt and a broad-brimmed flat hat and is accompanied everywhere by working dogs. His family lives in an isolated single-storey homestead which he visits rarely for a change of clothing and to collect food specially dried for another long spell in the saddle. Some of the cattle drives went all the way to markets in Hamburg, Milan and Paris.

Mechanised agriculture after World War II ultimately transformed the puszta, but two chunks have been roped off and preserved as they were, even if closer inspection reveals that the odd isolated homestead now offers visitors bed-and-breakfast. The smaller of the two, **Bugac**, is 60 miles (100 km) from Budapest. **Hortobagy** is twice as far but offers the bonus of nearby Debrecen, historically (although not aesthetically) one of the most important cities in the country.

The centre of Hortobagy is the nine-arched bridge across the Hortobagy River, where a bridge market is held every year on 19 and 20 August. The **Herdsmen's Museum** in a converted toolshed gives a good idea of what life on the plain once was. Apart from honest herdsmen, the *puszta* was the notorious haunt of Betyars, originally men dodging military service. Crossing the *puszta* in 1852, Bismarck was given an imperial escort "as a protection against the Beytars, robbers on horseback, wrapped in great furs, whose leaders wear black masks".

Everything is now highly organised.

Village artist in the puszta.

Coach parties set off at advertised times and there are *cskikos* ready to exchange the jeans and wellingtons they normally wear for the traditional outfits in which they proceed to give shows of dazzling horsemanship.

Debrecen is "the Calvinist Rome". Protestantism took root here in the early days of the Reformation and never relinquished its hold. This was a thorn in the side of the Catholic Habsburgs, and Debrecen was in turn the centre of agitation for Hungarian secession and independence. It was here that Kossuth declared Hungarian independence in the 1848 revolution. The principal places of interest are the Calvinist College, the hotbed of rebellion, and the Arany Bika (Golden Bull) hotel, an establishment grand enough to have survived over-enthusiastic refurbishment in the 1970s.

Szeged is the principal town on the southern plain and, lying on the **Tisza River**, is the main producer of paprika. It has a very long history which includes the curious claim – the evidence being not at all clear – that Attila the Hun once camped here. The town was almost destroyed by a flood in 1879. When locals talk about old times, things are either before or after the flood, rather as other people use BC and AD.

Not many buildings survived the flood, but among those which did are some soda factories which used alkaline crystals that formed naturally because of the special properties of the earth. Szeg, reflected in the town's name, refers to the kind of earth. The boulevards laid out after the flood were named after the cities that rallied round with donations – hence London, Paris, Brussels.

Szechenyi Square has four statues which are supposed to keep an eye on the river, telling it what to do and what not to do. The main square is dominated by a mighty neo-Romanesque cathedral with twin towers which serve as the backdrop to the open-air Summer Festival of opera, dance and theatre staged here every year. It is worth popping into the **cathedral** for a sight of the organ which with 11,000 pipes is one of the largest in the world.

Debrecen.

Probably the most interesting church is **Alsovarosi templom** (Church of the Lower Town), built on the remains of a temple dating back to Arpad's time. Not to be missed either is the **New Synagogue**, designed by Lipot Bauhorn at the turn of the century. The interior has marvellous stained glass and an ark of the covenant made of Egyptian cedar.

Mora Park near the northern bridgehead has the ruins of a castle built by Bela IV as part of the defensive network thrown up in case the Mongols came back. As a prison in the 19th century, it held Italians captured by the Austrians in the 1848–49 uprising and also, for 12 years, Sandor Rossza, who was regarded as a kind of Robin Hood.

Szeged has a famous son, Albert Szent-Gyorgi, a Nobel Prize winner in 1937 for discovering that paprika contains vitamin C. "I owe a great deal to paprika," he said solemnly, "for this modest fruit has made the fulfilment of my scientific dream possible. Also, the good health of a not insignificant number of my people is based on this plant."

The paprika is not native to Hungary. Legend has it that a Magyar girl escaped from a Turkish harem with some paprika seeds, but that would not explain how the Turks got hold of it because it grew wild only in Central and South America. The "heathen pepper" was first used as a decorative garden shrub and not considered fit for eating, being part of the poisonous nightshade family. According to a 17th-century manuscript, a wreath of paprika worn round the neck was the best protection against bloodthirsty vampires. It was first used to liven up boring food by peasants; gentrification followed much later.

Although Szeged is called the paprika capital – and every restaurant in town has a special paprika dish – the title perhaps ought to be given to **Kalocsa** on the Danube where 3,000 people are employed in growing and processing it. It has a research institute, as closely guarded as a weapons development plant, devoted to the creation of new and superior strains of Szent-Gyorgi's "modest fruit".

Szeged.

In 1978, President Nicolae Ceausescu of Romania was still being feted as the Communist head of state who had dared to condemn the Soviet invasion of Czechoslovakia a decade before. He was in a motorcade on his way to a meeting with President Jimmy Carter in the White House when some Romanian exiles set up a chant of "Dracula! Dracula!"

Ceausescu knew whom they meant – not Bram Stoker's creation, the chap with an opera hat, black cape and unusual teeth who was reputedly the result of a dream after Stoker had "a too generous helping of dressed crab at supper one night", but a previous ruler of Romania who in a reign of just six years literally skewered as many as 20 percent of his subjects. He was Vlad Dracula or Vlad Tepes, generally known as Vlad the Impaler. Being tarred with the same brush made Ceausescu recoil. According to an intelligence officer travelling with him, he actually threw up in the car.

The Romanian tourist industry pragmatically accepts that a large proportion of its business is generated by the two heads of state at whom long-suffering Romanians would be least likely to point with pride. The Transylvanian castles which Bram Stoker fans faithfully file through are associated with the real, ghastly Vlad Dracula, not his perversely lovable, fictional namesake. To these attractions have been added, since Christmas Day, 1989, a certain ghoulish interest in Ceausescu's legacy, like the House of the Republic in Bucharest which he and his wife Elena planned as the biggest building in the world.

These twin pillars of Romanian wretchedness unfairly over-shadow the other attractions the country has to offer, although it has to be said that Romania will have to demonstrate considerable powers of recovery before Bucharest will be called, as it was before World War II, "the Paris of the Balkans", or, as one travel writer put it with a tinge of admiration, "the most immoral city in the world". Happily, broad boulevards, brasseries, pavement cafés and a miscellany of historic monuments managed to survive Ceausescu's vandalism. As the Romanian countryside has traditionally been almost as fertile as the Nile valley, it is to be hoped that the culinary spreads which once took guests' breath away as they entered the dining room of the Athenee Palace Hotel will one day reappear. In the meantime, the local wine and beer are both drinkable and cheap.

There are numerous tours on offer which, in pursuit of the Dracula story, take visitors out of the capital and into Transylvania. Perhaps it is time to look farther afield, and in the following pages we suggest other possibilities in less familiar parts of Wallachia as well as in generally neglected Moldavia.

Preceding pages: gypsies from a village near Bucharest; Sighisoara, birthplace of Vlad the Impaler. **Left**, Romanian peasant.

THE MAKING OF ROMANIA

Romania's name is itself a clue to what sets the country apart from its neighbours. The self-conscious connection is with Imperial Rome, and flowing from that is a language which sounds like Italian, if not vernacular Latin, and the use of the Latin alphabet where one might expect, Romania being Orthodox by religion, the Cyrillic script. The country, about the size of Great Britain, has a population of 23 million, of whom 90 percent are Romanians who view the Emperor Trajan as something of a father figure.

The 10 percent who constitute Romania's ethnic minorities are Hungarian, German, Serbian, Turkish, Ukrainian, Jewish and gypsies, survivors of Nicolae Ceausescu's fanatical campaign to make them shed their cultural identities. Many were forcibly repatriated – if "repatriation" applies to those who were the fourth, fifth or sixth generation born in Romania – yet those who remain probably wear peasant costume more proudly and naturally than anywhere else in Europe.

The scenery is varied: mountainous areas with summer and winter resorts, a marvellous stretch of the Danube as it descends towards the Iron Gates and the Roman Emperor Trajan's famous 3rd-century bridge, castles and palaces galore, monasteries with frescoes leaving no room for doubt about the wages of sin, Teutonic towns with well-preserved roots buried in the 13th century, Black Sea beach resorts, and the astonishing bird-life of the vast Danube delta.

If everything proves too much, there is a safety-net in no fewer than 160 spas collectively offering cures for practically every ailment known to man. According to legend, Hercules took advantage of the therapeutic waters to cure the wounds he suffered in his duel with the Hydra.

Real origins: Romanians vociferously distance themselves from their Balkan, Slavic and Magyar neighbours. They speak a language which sounds a bit like Italian, and they use the Latin alphabet, as explained above, because most are Orthodox by religion. They claim to be Roman by descent

and place much emphasis on this pedigree. But what are their real origins?

Carbon-dating of finger-bones found near Hunedoara suggests human activity in the Danube marshes at a very early date, and the Hamangia and Cucuteni cultures were producing works of considerable artistry at roughly the same time as the earliest pharanic dynasties in Egypt. In due course there were waves of Scythians, Cimmerians and other tribes common to all southeastern Europe, but at some point they were shouldered

aside to make room for the Getae, later known as the Dacians, who carved out what has been called "the greatest barbarian empire ever known in this part of Europe".

The Dacian empire reached its peak under King Burebista, a contemporary of Julius Caesar, and included not only modern Romania but Bulgaria, Moldova, Bohemia and parts of Hungary. Roman expansion forced the Dacian empire to contract, and in due course it occupied an area roughly corresponding with modern Romania. Trajan, elected Roman emperor in AD 98, enlarged his empire to incorporate Dacia, his victory over the Dacians celebrated by the famous

Left, Vlad the Impaler, the real Dracula. **Right**, Bram Stoker's Dracula as seen by Hollywood.

Trajan's Column in Rome, a copy of which stands in the Bucharest History Museum.

Trajan's bridge below the cataracts of the Iron Gates, near what is now Turnu Severin, provided the link between the Danubian provinces on either bank. Dacia was then colonised with a view to developing the extensive gold, silver and salt deposits. Herein lies the genesis of the claimed descent from Rome, because there seems to have been a large measure of integration and intermarriage between the colonists and the locals.

In 271, however, the Emperor Aurelian decided that Trajan's expansion across the Danube had stretched Roman defences too thin and, under pressure from Germanic tribes

in the west, he withdrew the army to face the more dangerous threat. But some retired veterans and members of the civilian workforce chose to stay put. Between them and the native population, a distinct Daco-Roman culture was consolidated.

Almost nothing is known about the fate of the Daco-Romans in the seven centuries or so following Aurelian's withdrawal. If they had stayed where they were, they would have been in the thick of vast barbarian migrations which swallowed up most smaller groups standing in their way. Ceausescu's team of tame historians attributed their survival to "superior forms of political and socio-economic organisation", but other historians suspect they found a bolt-hole in the Carpathian mountains, or possibly even in the Pindus mountains in northern Greece.

The argument, which has contributed to more than one war, is particularly heated when focused on Transylvania, which was absorbed into the kingdom of Hungary in the 11th century. The Hungarians say that when they and their Magyar kinsmen the Szekels moved in, the Romanians were nowhere to be seen. Nonsense, say Romanians, the Magyars stole their land. After nine centuries of Hungarian possession, Transylvania was awarded to Romania after World War I.

What is indisputable is that in the 13th and 14th centuries, when Wallachia and Moldavia rejoined recorded history after a prolonged absence, there were still Romanians or Daco-Romans around who spoke a kind of Latin that had served as the *lingua franca* of Rome's Eastern Empire. This language has subsequently fallen under other influences, and experts say it is now about one quarter Slavonic. There are frequently mutually unrecognisable Romanian, Slavonic and Hungarian for one and the same place, a conundrum for visitors and sometimes even for locals.

Terrible tyrants: Wallachia and Moldavia emerged from obscurity under a succession of native princes whose names alone point to an unhappy tradition of rotten rulers: John the Cruel, John the Terrible, Aron the Tyrant. There were a few exceptions, notably Mircea the Old, Alexander the Good and, the legendary John Hunyadi, whom both Hungary and Romania claim as one of their own. He was actually born in Transylvania but became Hungarian by adoption. The blot on Hunyadi's otherwise distinguished career is the prince he assisted on to the Wallachian throne, none other than Vlad Dracula.

This real Dracula was born in 1431 in Sighisoara, Transylvania, the grandson of Mircea the Old and the son of Vlad, known as Dracul because he was a member of the Order of the Dragon (*draco* in Latin) dedicated to fighting Turks and heretics. Dracula ("son of Dracul") spent most of his early manhood on the run from various family feuds, eventually receiving the protection of the great John Hunyadi. At 25, he was elected to the throne of Wallachia, a position previously held by his ancestors.

"He was not very tall," says a description,

"but very stocky and strong, with a cold and terrible appearance, a strong and aquiline nose, swollen nostrils, a thin and reddish face in which the very long eyelashes framed large wide-open green eyes; the bushy black eyebrows made them appear threatening… Swollen temples increased the bulk of his head. A bull's neck connected his head, from which black curly locks hung on his wide-shouldered person."

According to Romanian oral tradition, Vlad once gave a banquet for the region's poor, elderly, cripples and vagabonds. The supply of food and wine was unlimited, and Dracula waited until they were all in a stupor before springing his little surprise. The doors were locked and the place burnt down. "These men live off the sweat of others," he commented as his guests went up in smoke, "so they are useless to humanity."

Bram Stoker would appear to have taken his villain's most notorious trait from an account of the real Dracula sitting down to a meal to enjoy the spectacle of some prisoners being dismembered. He asked for their blood to be collected and brought to him as a dip for his bread. "Watching human blood flow," one of the chronicles comments, "gave him courage." While he was always ready to experiment with ways of making the death of his enemies ever more excruciating, Dracula knew he could always fall back on impaling. His most spectacular single atrocity in this respect was to impale 20,000 Turkish prisoners and leave them to rot. The over-generous view taken of this incident by Ceausescu's historians was that the victims were prisoners and anyhow Turks. On the whole, they conclude, Dracula was "a remarkable statesman and leader who defended the independence of his country".

In common with the other Wallachian and Moldavian princes of the period, Dracula was technically subservient to the sultan of Turkey. The cruel punishment was meted out to Turkish troops who were generally carrying out orders issued by the sultan when he felt that the princes had overstepped the mark. From time to time, the princes tried to break away from Turkish rule altogether, a notable case being Michael the Brave who united the three Romanian principalities in

1600 in his bid for genuine independence.

As the native princes became increasingly unreliable subjects, the sultans were receptive to a suggestion put forward by Greek entrepreneurs living in the Phanar or Lighthouse district of Istanbul that they should be allowed to rule the Romanian provinces on short-term contracts. The idea was that they would tender for the title and the highest bidder would pay the sultan in advance. It was then up to him to recover his investment as quickly as possible. This was clearly not the recipe for stable government or sound fiscal policies, and it showed. In the course of the 18th century, the thrones of Wallachia and Moldavia changed hands 41 and 36 times respectively. The only element of sta-

bility was that the thrones were passed around among members of the same 12 families. "What is remarkable about these despots," said one report, "is that all their riches, money, jewels, hordes and furnishings, are always in trunks and travelling coffers, as if they had to leave at any moment."

The sultans were not over-concerned about what the so-called Phanariots got up to as long as their payment for so doing came in. When the payments became irregular, the principalities were leased on more or less the same basis to the Russian tsar. The first Russian administrators were welcomed by the long-suffering "tenants", but compul-

Left, peasant girl in typical 19th-century costume. **Above**, Romanian solider, also 19th-century.

sory unpaid labour and deportation to Siberia for the slightest misdemeanour rapidly cooled the welcome. The arrangement with Russia ceased with the Crimean War, in which Russia and Turkey were on opposing sides. The principalities reverted to nominal Turkish rule but they were formally united and allowed to choose a single prince.

"Gentlemen," said Alexander Cuza, who was duly elected "Prince of the United Moldavia and Wallachia", "I fear you will not be satisfied with me." In some respects they were, in others not. He won approval for nationalising the enormous wealth of the Greek monasteries, introducing compulsory education and initiating agrarian reforms.

He disappointed his supporters with a disgusting private life, and in the end the liabilities outweighed the assets. Alexander was obliged to abdicate. Pessimistic about finding anyone locally who would not be swayed by private interests, the popular representatives decided to offer the throne to a foreigner. Their choice fell on Prince Charles of Hohenzollern Siegmaringen, the son of the Prussian premier (one before Bismarck) and a cousin of Napoleon III of France.

Unsavoury period: Before examining the reign of the new prince, it may be worth switching attention to Transylvania which, throughout the unsavoury period of the later

princes, Phanariots and Russians, had been part of Hungary, albeit the part of Hungary – much the greater part – which was itself within the Ottoman Empire after Turkey's victory at the battle of Mohacs in 1526. An important change occurred when a Habsburg victory over Turkey in 1699 saw Hungary, and Transylvania, surrendered to Vienna.

Under both the Ottomans and the Habsburgs, the Magyars remained very much in charge of the administration of Transylvania, and that amounted to the ruthless Magyarisation of all ethnic minorities. The Magyars were willing to concede the Szekel and Saxon minorities the status of "Recognised Nations", but no allowance whatever was made for the Romanians, who outnumbered all others by three-to-one. Romanians consequently could not own land, were required to do as much as six days a week of unpaid labour on a landlord's estate and all in all, says one account, "their backs were always at the mercy of the lash".

These policies produced a Romanian backlash. A certain Horia led an uprising in 1784, dubbing himself "King of Dacia". About 230 castles and manors were sacked and about 100 nobles killed. When Horia was eventually captured, he was broken on a wheel and disembowelled alive. The Magyar attitude towards such shows of defiance was contained in a widely circulated tract: "You, unhappy Wallachs (all Romanians being regarded as 'Wallachs'), there is no trace in human memory or in the pages of history of a free national life on your part. You were slaves under the Romans, slaves under the migrant peoples, slaves too in the last 1,000 years, and only the Magyars have extended to you… the dawn of liberty."

The Romanians rose again in the 19th century and this time it was outright racial war. They massacred Magyars, and the Magyars reciprocated in kind and with interest through the "Kossuth Hussars", as the forces loyal to Lajos Kossuth were known. The Romanians appealed to the Habsburg Emperor Francis Joseph, who was ultimately the ruler of Hungary as well, but were ignored. It was in the aftermath of this uprising and its brutal consequences that the Romanians of Transylvania learned that the United Principalities of Moldavia and Wallachia were about to receive Prince Charles of Hohenzollern Siegmaringen, but there was no reason to believe that it would make any difference to them.

Prince Charles's first impressions of his new domain were poor. "My sole task," he said, "is to revive by good administration a country that has been utterly ruined, morally and financially." He was not exaggerating. There were as yet no railways, and communications generally were poor. Agriculture had been wrecked by a succession of bad harvests and an outbreak of cholera. The army was in a mess, and Charles determined to reorganise it, and the country as a whole, along Prussian lines of efficiency.

Prince Charles became King Carol by a unanimous vote in 1881 and was crowned in

tended, the Sulina Canal was opened and the bridge at Cernavoda came into operation across 12 miles (19 km) of the Danube and its marshes. Constanza on the Black Sea was converted into a modern harbour, and Bucharest acquired many imposing public buildings. Agriculture was still vulnerable to a bad season, but Romania was one of the most fertile countries in Europe and recovery was swift. Optimistic economic forecasts overlooked the fact that little of this prosperity was filtering down to the peasants.

Illusions were abruptly stripped away on 15 March 1907. The disturbances began with the plundering of Jewish homes near Botosani and quickly developed into attacks on large

Bucharest Cathedral, the new crown pointedly made out of the metal of a captured Turkish cannon. Twelve years later the heir apparent, his nephew Prince Ferdinand, was married to Princess Marie of Edinburgh or "Missy", the grand-daughter of both Queen Victoria of England and Tsar Alexander II. It was a pragmatic rather than romantic union, typical of the times.

During the last decade of the 19th century, Romania made spectacular economic progress. The railway system was greatly ex-

Left, a reluctant Bessarabian subject of the tsars.
Above, Transylvanians on parade.

tenant farms and the estates of absentee landlords all over Moldavia. Rioting broke out in Jassy, now Iasi, and soon 4,000 peasants were marching on Bucharest.

The government passed emergency legislation meeting some of the peasants' demands but not soon enough to prevent pitched battles between troops and bands of insurgents now 10,000 strong and armed with guns, axes, knives and scythes. About 10,000 peasants were killed in a three-day period, and the government was shocked into putting real substance into the reforms which had so far only been cobbled together.

While discontent in Wallachia and Moldavia boiled over into agrarian revolt, the lot of the Romanians in Transylvania was unchanged. When a Romanian deputy attempted to make a speech in the Roman language in parliament, he was given the bluntest possible warning: "Don't provoke us to employ towards the other nations the methods of total extermination employed by the Anglo-Saxons towards the Red Indians of North America."

One proposal was that Romanian children should spend their first three years of schooling doing nothing but speaking, reciting and singing in Magyar. The Romanian tricolour and national colours were banned and all non-Magyars were under pressure to

Magyarise their names. While most Slavs, Saxons and Jews were ready to do so, Romanians resisted by giving their children names that could not be Magyarised. A name like Julius all too easily became Gyula, but not much could be done about Virgil, Ovid, Tiberius, Hortensia and so on.

The Transylvanian Romanians hoped they had a powerful ally in the Archduke Franz Ferdinand, the heir to the Habsburg throne, who endeared himself to them with remarks such as: "It was bad taste on the part of the Magyars ever to come to Europe." His assassination at Sarajevo in 1914 was a blow to their hopes, but his disappointment was of course lost in the explosive chaos of events which followed his death and resulted in World War I.

In Romania proper, the outbreak of war put Carol into an awkward position. His family were German and he felt under an obligation of loyalty to Austria, but as far as most of his subjects were concerned the only criterion was to fight alongside whomever was against Hungary. "Gentlemen," sighed Carol, "you cannot imagine how bitter it is to find oneself isolated in a country of which one is not a native." His discomfort was all the more acute because, unknown to all but a handful of top officials, he had secretly concluded a pact with the Triple Alliance – Germany, Italy and Austria-Hungary – in 1883 and had been quietly and regularly renewing it every 10 years.

Whether they liked it or not, and while Romania was still officially on the fence, about 400,000 Romanians found themselves in the Austro-Hungarian army. Of these, 50,000 were captured by the Russians on the Eastern Front and 20,000 deserted to join the forces of the Anglo-French Entente. King Carol never had to make up his mind. He died in the opening months of the war, ending what the historian R.W. Seton-Watson called "the most prosperous and pacific era in all the troubled history of the Romanian race…"

Ferdinand I, Carol's diffident nephew, prevaricated as long as possible before in August 1916 plumping for the Entente, but in so doing he declared war specifically on Austria but not on Germany. The Berlin newspapers, for one, were not deceived. "The Latin traitors," one screamed, "have proven their descent from ancient Rome's deported criminals." Bucharest had to wait only until 5 September to feel its first Zeppelin air raid.

The Romanian forces advanced against skeletal Austrian defences in Transylvania before having to turn around to face a combined German and Bulgarian push from the south. It was not soon enough. Bucharest was in grave danger, so government decamped to Jassy (Iasi), the historic Moldavian capital, while the country's gold reserves were sent to Moscow for safe-keeping. The Germans entered Bucharest on 6 December and, as for the gold reserves, they were never seen again after the Bucharest take-over.

Germany's ultimate defeat coupled with the emergence of a Communist regime in

Hungary under Bela Kun gave Romania the excuse to unleash a re-formed and re-trained army. It invaded both Transylvania and Hungary proper, settling old scores with venomous relish and indulging in an orgy of looting. Private houses were stripped bare and if factory plant was too big or awkward to be moved, it was blown up. Romania lost considerable goodwill at the Paris conference by refusing to evacuate Budapest when asked to do so, but the prize of a Greater Romania including Transylvania was within reach and next to that nothing else mattered.

Greater Romania was realised and survived in this form for 20 years, but the preceding half-century of competent and honest government was over. The rot set in at the top in the person of Crown Prince Carol, coldly called "the most unsavoury member of all European royalty". In 1926, he abandoned his wife and baby son to disappear with his mistress Elena Lupescu. When his mother tracked him down and protested that heirs to thrones could not simply vanish, his advice was to say that he must have drowned somewhere. He suggested Lake Maggiore.

King Ferdinand died the following year and Michael, the infant son whom Prince Carol had abandoned, was proclaimed his successor. Within three years, Carol had reconsidered his position and won support for a coup from Lord Rothermere, the British newspaper magnate. Flying from Paris with a forged passport, he landed in Bucharest and was proclaimed King Carol III the next day, his son being demoted to Crown Prince. Carol was ostensibly reconciled with his wife for the sake of respectability, but after a few weeks Elena Lupescu slipped surreptitiously back into Bucharest determined to assume a role in Romanian affairs.

In no time, the Romanian crown was back in disrepute. The king surrounded himself with "as unscrupulous a bunch of toughs as ever swaggered down the Calea Victoriei (Bucharest's main street)," according to *Life* magazine. These toughs were the nucleus of what emerged as the Legion of Archangel Michael, soon to be changed to the more forthright Iron Guard. It was Fascist, virulently anti-Semitic and made a fetish out of displaying the corpses of their martyrs, as

they saw it, in a flood of anarchy of which they themselves were the main promoters.

In 1938, sensing that the Iron Guard was out of his control, Carol rounded up 13 of its leading members and had them shot. Through some misunderstanding, Carol thought Hitler would approve of his action, but the Fuhrer was furious and put the Iron Guard's new leader, Horia Sima, under his personal protection. Carol decided that further opposition was hopeless and moved his own politics to the far right so that he became for all practical purposes a royal dictator.

As World War II drew nearer, Romania was trapped between the opposing sides as it had been in the previous war. The Nazi-

Soviet Pact of 1939 included a secret protocol to the effect that the USSR would get the Romanian province of Bessarabia, now "Moldova". Three weeks after Dunkirk, Molotov, the Russian Foreign Minister, gave Romania 24 hours to surrender Bessarabia and northern Bukovina. Hitler advised Carol to do as he was told. A month later, Germany lent its support to Bulgaria's seizure of southern Dodrudja. Then Hungary demanded Transylvania, although it won only the northern half of it. Greater Romania, which had been created after World War I, was undone.

In September 1940, Carol appointed General Ian Antonescu as Prime Minister with

Left, Romanian oil, a factor in both world wars. **Above**, King Ferdinand I of Romania.

unlimited powers, and within a week the general formally quoted these powers in ordering the king into exile. Scooping up money and Elena Lupescu, Carol barely escaped an assassination attempt as he took a fast train to the Yugoslav border. His son Michael succeeded him but was never more than a figurehead to Antonescu, who assumed the title of "Conducator", the Romanian equivalent of the Italian "Duce". Horia Sima, Hitler's pet, became his deputy and most of the other government positions went to members of the Iron Guard.

Readers of Olivia Manning's Balkan trilogy will be familiar with the mood in Bucharest during these ominous days, the hotels

Antonescu applied his "final solution" to Romanian Jews and gypsies. About 150,000 Jews living in Transylvania were murdered while 200,000 in Bessarabia were deported to a part of Ukraine which Romania was looking after on Hitler's behalf. Most were killed on arrival. A veil is usually drawn over Romania's role in the Holocaust. Instead, the spotlight is focused on Antonescu's change of heart in 1942 when he cancelled plans to sent the remaining Romanian Jews to the death-camps in Poland. As a result, some 300,000 Romanian Jews survived the war.

Romanian troops were given a major role in the German attack on Stalingrad and bore the brunt of the Russian counter-attack. The

crowded with shadowy figures including British agents hoping to blow up the Ploiesti oil fields before they were taken over as a vital part of the Nazi war machine. Carol died in Portugal in 1953 leaving Elena, whom he had married some years before, to spend the rest of her days there in comfort.

Back in Romania during the war, there was nothing King Michael could do as the Iron Guard went about massacring political opponents and Jews. Antonescu agreed to send Romanian troops on Hitler's invasion of the Soviet Union in exchange for the promise that Bessarabia would be returned to Romania. Now utterly beholden to Hitler,

huge Romania's losses were, for King Michael and even for Antonescu, the writing on the wall: Romania began to sound out the Allies about a surrender, or even a switch of sides. Stalin agreed to go along with the negotiations on condition that Romania surrendered its claim to Bessarabia and Bukovina. It might be necessary for Soviet troops to occupy Romania, said Molotov, but he gave an undertaking that there was no wish to impose Communism.

At the last minute Antonescu baulked and was put under arrest. An armistice was concluded, the Red Army marched across Romania into Hungary and Bulgaria, and the

Romanian army was sent to fight the Germans. It lost a further 170,000 men.

When Eastern Europe was divided up at the end of the war, Churchill's "naughty" scrap of paper accorded Russia 90 percent of post-war influence in Romania. As matters stood in 1944, however, the Romanian Communist Party was minuscule. Its leaders, few of whom were actually Romanian, were either in prison or in exile. Molotov's assurance about leaving the existing social order alone was revealed for what it was worth in 1945 when Red Army tanks surrounded the royal palace and King Michael was ordered to form a pro-Soviet government.

Elections were arranged for 1946 to quieten British and American misgivings about the coup. The arrangements extended to rigging the ballot so that it showed an 89 percent vote for the Communists, who ran as the "National Democratic Front". All non-Communists were immediately purged from the government, and on 30 December 1947 King Michael flew into exile.

Gheorghe Gheorghiu-Dej emerged as the Communist strong-man. The tempo of purges increased, and it is estimated that in the following decade as many as 60,000 people were executed. Romania's famously resilient agriculture collapsed under blundering collectivisation. "Complete the Five-Year Plan in Four Years!" was the slogan of the day, and 80,000 peasants were arrested for failing to show sufficient enthusiasm.

Gheorghiu-Dej supported the Soviet suppression of the 1956 uprisings in Poland and Hungary, although soon afterwards he started edging towards a line which was more independent of Moscow but no less loyal to the precepts of Stalinism. He died suddenly in March 1965 and was replaced by a seemingly grey little man who had worked his way up the Communist Party ladder by never rocking the boat. This was Ceausescu.

The new man was one of three sons of Andruta Ceausescu, a peasant farmer of Scornicesti in Wallachia, who were all named Nicolae because the father was too drunk to think of any other. In later life, Ceausescu certainly made up for the deficiency by assuming a formidable array of titles, including "Giant of the Carpathians" and "Builder of the Outstanding Stage in the Millennia-old Existence of the Romanian People". Titles and distinctions were showered on him from abroad, among them an honorary British knighthood and the "Great Girdle of the Mauritanian National Merit".

Elena Petrescu, the farmer-cum-shopkeeper's daughter whom Ceausescu married, also tried to make amends for the setbacks of childhood. Almost illiterate when she left school, she ended up a self-proclaimed scientific genius, the purported author of majestic works on subjects like macromolecular experimental chemistry. There was hardly a work of genuine Romanian scientific scholarship that she did not put her name to.

Self-effacement was not the Ceausescus' strong suit. His birthday tribute in 1988 included references to "the most beloved son of the people, outstanding revolutionary militant, hero among the nation's heroes, architect of modern, socialist Romania…" She was "Academician Elena Ceausescu, DSc, luminous example of a revolutionary and politician, of a remarkable scientist of world repute…" The personality cult was akin to that of Kim Il Sung of North Korea.

The realities of life for ordinary Romanians under this couple have been unfavourably compared with George Orwell's *Nineteen Eighty-four*. The Thought Police were

Left, overcrowded World War I observation post. **Right**, blessing the colours before battle.

reputed to have bugged every single telephone in the country. Apart from the usual security implications, the illustrious academician and remarkable scientist was said to have a predilection for eavesdropping on conjugal capers, especially those of her political enemies. All typewriters had to be registered with the police, so that the peculiarity of each typeface could be registered like fingerprints and traced if used to produce unauthorised documents.

Ceausescu's economic policies, especially his obsession about paying off the national debt, caused immeasurable hardship. He exported absolutely everything that could fetch hard currency, including food, and corre-

There could be no AIDS she said, in the socialist Utopia of which she was the foremost architect.

Astonishingly, the world at large remained unaware of what was going on in Romania. In 1983, George Bush, then Ronald Reagan's Vice-President, was still referring to Ceausescu as "the good communist", and his reputation in the United States soared when he challenged the Soviet boycott of the 1984 Olympic Games. At home, people knew better, but it was more than their lives were worth to say a word. Romanian television routinely devoted two hours to coverage of the Ceausescu's activities that day. When the Conducator addressed a political rally,

spondingly slashed imports. The result was that no room in a house was allowed more than one light bulb, 60 watts being the maximum, and in any case the power supply was cut off for much of the day.

Women were ordered to have five children each in order to reach a target population of 30 million by the year 2000. Birth control was banned and they were required to be examined every three months so that pregnancies could be registered and not surreptitiously aborted. The repeated use of hypodermic needles because they were so scarce led to an epidemic of AIDS whose existence was denied at Elena Ceausescu's insistence.

the prolonged standing ovation was screened in its entirety.

Scattered public protests began to surface in 1987, and in Brasov that year they amounted to a riot. Another followed in Timisoara a few weeks later when the Securitate, the dreaded political police, tried to arrest a Protestant Hungarian pastor, Laszlo Tokes. Ceausescu's orders were that in the event of any repetition police were to shoot to kill. Demonstrations in Timisoara continued and the killings commenced.

On 21 December, Ceausescu summoned a mass rally in Bucharest to demonsrate his popularity. It was broadcast live, and what ensued was powerfully reminiscent of what had happened in Washington in 1978 when demonstrators brought up the name of Dracula. Ceausescu was in full flow, Elena sitting grim-faced beside him, when students at the back of the crowd started booing. The booing spread quickly, and in no time the whole crowd was chanting in unison: "Ceausescu," they cried, "assassin. Ceausescu, assassin!" Ceausescu's jaw dropped in disbelief. He called for quiet but the chant grew louder and more insistent. Television screens suddenly went blank, nervous technicians having pulled the plug. Viewers therefore did not see the hundreds of demonstrators who were shot that night.

had fled, and the opposition National Salvation Council went on television to announce that it was taking over. Its leader was Ion Iliescu, once a Ceausescu aide but in disgrace since the 1970s for criticising him. On Christmas Day, Ceausescu and his wife were taken to an army barracks near Tirgoviste to stand trial on a long list of charges including genocide and embezzlement. "I do not recognise you," snarled Ceausescu, "I do not recognise this court."

The trial lasted 55 minutes and was filmed for showing on television later. Even Ceausescu's most implacable enemies would concede that the proceedings were a travesty. "Are you mentally defective?" the prosecu-

Huge crowds gathered the following morning and, just before noon, stormed the Central Committee building. Ceausescu and his wife were lifted off the roof by helicopter and taken to one of their country houses outside Tirgoviste, about 60 miles/100 km away. They tried to drive back to Bucharest but were intercepted by an army patrol and held prisoner in an armoured car which kept on the move for three days in order to foil any rescue attempt by the Securitate.

In Bucharest, word got out that Ceausescus

tor asked him at one point. "This is outrageous," shouted his wife.

At the end, four soldiers bound their wrists and escorted them along the corridor. Ceausescu was humming the "Internationale", apparently confident that they were about to be flown to Bucharest, which perhaps in his mind raised the hope of rescue. "Stop it, Nicu," Elena said. "Look, they're going to shoot us like dogs." They were faced up against a wall, without blindfolds. Instinctively, they began to turn around, and with that the four soldiers each pumped 30 rounds of automatic fire into them. It was Christmas Day, 1989.

Left, Bucharest, "Paris of the Balkans", between the wars. **Above**, Ceausescu and wife Elena.

ROMANIA: WHAT TO SEE

Wallachia: The rump of Romania is Wallachia, an ancient principality sheltered by the Danube to the south and the Transylvanian Alps to the north. To the east lies the Black Sea; to the west, the human wall of traditionally hostile Serbs and Magyars. Wallachia is the point at which Imperial Rome abandoned for a couple of centuries or so the general policy of pulling in its horns at the Danube. The result was that Romans and their cosmopolitan imperial personnel mixed with the Dacians north of the river to produce the Romanised culture which makes Romania so different from its Slavic and Balkan neighbours.

The mind's eye can quite easily see how the components of modern Romania – basically Wallachia, Moldavia and Transylvania – were brought together. Snow and rainfall in the Transylvanian Alps gravitated south through the forested lower slopes and across the broad Wallachia plain, then the Danube. The effect of this seasonal flow of water was like a tame version of the Nile's celebrated inundation. The marshes were soggy but wonderfully fertile, in need only of some kind of drainage.

The Romans, past-masters of hydro-engineering, would have recognised the potential at once, not that they did much about it. Their primary interest was the mineral wealth beyond the Transylvanian Alps, in Transylvania itself. The Romans could hardly have one without the other, hence the historical ties between Wallachia and Transylvania. Moldavia to the east, on the other hand, was Wallachia's window to the Black Sea. There are a hundred other considerations, but these factors are the genesis of the centripetal pull of Romania as a single nation.

In 1431, Joan of Arc was burnt at the stake in distant Rouen. In that same year, Vlad Dracula, or Vlad Tepes, was born. In his childhood, Bucharest was at most a village surrounded by a wooden

Left, Dracula's Castle.

palisade, as it had been since the Middle Ages. It had not developed further because being so close to the Danube was a decidedly mixed blessing: fine for practical purposes in peace-time; a liability when the river was used by marauders on the prowl, as the Ottoman Turks then were in the 15th century.

Tirgoviste, away from the river and close to the mountains, was a better defensive proposition, and it had grown up as the capital of a principality which was then about the size of New York State and had a population of about 500,000. Even so, Tirgoviste, to which we shall return in due course, was not much more than a small town. Wallachia was an agricultural society. The most imposing edifices then in existence were not the work of locals but of the crusading orders of Teutonic Knights who, before they finally made up their minds to settle along the Baltic coast, in and around Prussia, had considered putting down their roots in this region.

Bucharest: The town cannot have been much fun in Vlad Dracula's day, but Olivia Manning's *Balkan Trilogy* paints a tantalising picture of the city before World War II, when it was known as the Paris of the Balkans. Pavel's, a popular restaurant, prided itself on a mouth-watering presentation of its wares: "The heart of the display was a rosy bouquet of cauliflowers. Heaped extravagantly around the centre were aubergines as big as melons, baskets of artichokes, small coral carrots, mushrooms, mountain raspberries, apricots, peaches, apples and grapes. On one side there were French cheeses; on the other tins of caviar, grey river fish in powdered ice, and lobsters and crayfish groping in dark waters. The poultry and game lay unsorted on the ground."

Another visitor of the period describes a no less evocative scene of horse-drawn cabs, garden restaurants and cafés, charcuteries selling "wonderful hot meat and mushroom patties", gypsy flower-sellers, "Lagondas and Hispano-Suizas swerving to avoid ox carts" and "the hungry smell of corn-on-the-cob cooking over street braziers". It would be

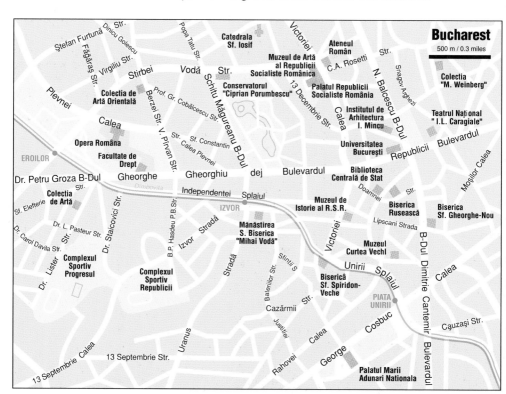

unfair to expect as much of Bucharest these days. Twenty years of grim post-war Communism, followed by as many years again of Nicolae Ceausescu, are considerable handicaps to overcome, but there is just enough left of old Bucharest to serve as a reminder of what the city once was, and perhaps just enough of a revival to indicate what it may yet again become.

Pavel's rosy bouquets of cauliflowers, the Lagondas and Hispano-Suizas are, alas, no more. The restaurant in the Athenee Palace Hotel and the Capsa are the strongest doses of nostalgia currently available, but don't expect to find the floor knee-deep in unsorted poultry and game. As for motor-cars, the ubiquitous Dacia is a double dose of nostalgia. The name is taken from the ancient kingdom which was Latinised by Imperial Rome; the hardware is Latin-ish too – recycled Fiat.

Architecturally speaking, Bucharest has grown up in fits and starts. Isolated from mainstream Europe for most of its existence, it was not exposed to great cultural surges like the Renaissance which shaped classical cities. The old part, known as **Lipscani**, is the best reflection of Bucharest as a staging-post on the trade route between Central Europe and Constantinople. Narrow alleys packed with small shops – heresy under Communism, of course – evoke visions of a semi-Byzantine bazaar.

There is then a gap until the Brincoveanu period, which was a curious hotpotch of neo-Romanticism, Romanian folk art and Byzantine extravagance. Judging by his output, Brincoveanu must have worked day and night all his life. After another gap, King Carol I arrived in the late 19th century bent on creating a modern European capital, and the influences are distinctly French. Ceausescu did his best to ruin the lot, releasing a fleet of rampaging bulldozers to make room for rectangular concrete.

The logical starting-point for a tour of Bucharest is the palace that Vlad Dracula built, the **Princely Court**. The thickness of the walls suggests that he might have brought in Saxons to do the building. The oldest sections were clearly made out of shaped river stones; the brickwork came later. Dracula's private quarters are distinguishable in the ruins, as is the large hall where he held court.

Vlad's younger brother Radu seems to have had a hand in expanding what began as a modest fort, but became the most powerful fortress in the land. The cellars are a good indication of the size. They cover a much wider area than the superstructure, and many of the shops and restaurants in the surrounding area are actually part of the palace complex.

In due course, a city grew up around the palace. The **Curtea Veche Church** next door was founded in the 16th century and is still favoured by women seeking a divine cure for their domestic difficulties. The **Hanul Manuc** opposite is early 19th-century and is one of the city's better hotels. It was grand enough in 1812 to be chosen for the signing of the peace agreement by which Turkey ceded Bessarabia to Russia.

While in the area, it is worth looking into **La Carul cu Bere**, a picturesque

Orthodox church, Bucharest.

old beer hall serving reasonable food, as well as the half-hidden **Stavropoleos Church** opposite. The church was built in 1742 by a Greek monk and is a good example of the Byzantine flavour of the Phanariot period.

Calea Victoriei, the famous street running between the Piata Natiunile Unite and the Piata Victoriei, is living evidence of the swing away from Byzantium to all things French. The early 19th century saw nascent nationalism all over Europe. Romanians were spellbound by the rediscovery of their Roman origins; instead of turning to Rome, however, the educated classes flocked to Paris. Their passion for the French language, literature and social habits was such that Romanian culture was in danger of being swamped. There were some who even hoped that Romania would become a French colony.

The **History Museum** and the **Savings Bank**, facing one another next to La Carul cu Bere, are unadulterated copies of the grandiose style of 19th-century Paris, complete with columns, stairways and domes. The History Museum was once the Post Office. It has a magnificent collection spanning Romania's history from prehistoric times: gold and precious stones, weapons, ornaments, royal regalia, and so on. The most famous item is the 5th-century *Hen with Golden Chickens*, 12 pieces carved out of gold and weighing nothing less than 45lb (20kg). **Trajan's Column**, commemorating the Roman emperor's victory over the Dacians in the 2nd century, is of course a copy of the famous original in Rome.

Going north along the Calea Victoriei, the streets running down to the left used to lead to the river marshes. These have now been reclaimed but there is still the popular **Cismigiu Garden** as a slight reminder of what the area must once have been. **Revolution Square**, farther on, was previously known as Palace Square and is the spot where Ceausescu's madness reached full fruition and his last days were played out. The gigantic **Palace of the Republic** was the late tyrant's conscious effort to create the biggest building in the world. The scars of the struggle in December 1989 are still plainly visible.

The **National Art Museum**, housed in the palace, was badly damaged, while the University Library was completely destroyed. The **Athenaeum concert hall**, home of the Romanian Philharmonic, escaped, and so did the metaphorical cause of all the trouble, the Communist Party headquarters. It was from the roof of the party headquarters that Nicolae Ceausescu and his wife were lifted by helicopter.

Readers of John Le Carré and his ilk should make a special point of visiting the aforementioned **Athenee Palace Hotel** next to the Athenaeum. This is where foreign dignitaries were put up, and it is said that even the ashtrays were bugged. They have now been removed, or at least disconnected, and even the odd chap wearing a coat with the collar turned up is probably a bona-fide guest expecting rain. Both the Athenee Palace and the Bucuresti Hotel nearby lay on cabaret and stay open late.

For other forms of entertainment, try

Learning to be capitalists.

the Bulandra, Nottara and National Theatres, the Comedia or the Variety Theatre Tanase. Discos are still relatively few in number and not particularly exciting, but this is an area in which Bucharest will undoubtedly be quick to catch up. In the meantime, the best places for informal entertainment are the beer and wine gardens, albeit only during the warm months.

The stretch of the Calea Victoriei running between Revolution Square and Victory Square includes a number of interesting buildings, among them the **Muzeul Colectiilor**, to give it the local name, the home of art collections which were once privately owned. The **George Enescu Museum** contains various memorabilia of the distinguished violinist and composer.

The streets beyond Victory Square head out of town, although the Parisian theme continues to play along Soseaua Kiseleff on its way to the **Arc de Triomphe** honouring the Romanian casualties in World War I. It was designed by Petru Antonescu and incorporates work by a number of Romanian sculptors. The **House of the Press** near the arch is a copy of the Lomonossov University in Moscow. Until March 1990, it was graced by a statue of Lenin. The red marble pedestal remains; the rest was sold off to someone who said he had a curio business in the West.

The **Village Museum** (Muzeul Satului), with its entrance on Soseaua Kiseleff, is a godsend to visitors who are going no further than Bucharest. It brings together more than 70 examples of indigenous architecture from all the corners of Romania, not merely houses with authentic period furnishings but churches, workshops and windmills. The adjacent Herestrau is an immense park dotted with lakes where it is possible to do a spot of fishing, hire a boat or eat *al fresco* in a wide choice of restaurants.

The lake which Dracula fans would not want to miss is **Snagov**, about 22 miles (35 km) north of Bucharest. It, too, has restaurants and sports facilities, but the special interest is focused on a chapel on an island in the lake. The

Today jeans, tomorrow McDonald's?

chapel was once part of a fortified monastic complex which covered the whole island, a town in itself with a royal palace, cloisters, a mint (the national treasury was stored here in times of danger) and a prison, the last with features designed by Dracula personally. He would invite his intended victims to enter a small cell and kneel before a small icon of the Blessed Virgin. The floor of the cell was in reality a trap door, which Dracula would then open at the appropriate moment, sending the worshipper hurtling downwards on to his specialities, a bed of sharpened stakes. The state of skeletons recovered at the site lend some credence to the story, as it happens.

It is popularly believed that Dracula's headless body was buried at Snagov after his decapitation by a Turk, but thorough-going searches have not yet produced conclusive evidence. The problem is not finding a headless body: there are plenty of them, Dracula made sure of that. It is really a question of which one, if any at all. Whatever the truth of the matter, a beautifully carved door, said to have come from the monastery in Dracula's day, is on display in the Bucharest Art Museum.

The two-hour drive from Bucharest to Tirgoviste, the earlier capital of Wallachia, passes **Ploiesti**. J. R. Ewing of *Dallas* fame would be impressed, but a gigantic petro-chemical works disgorging smoke and flames is unlikely to tempt ordinary tourists. Without stopping, it is still possible to appreciate that Ploiesti was the Kuwait of Eastern Europe long before oil became synonymous with the Persian Gulf. Control of these oil fields was uppermost in Hitler's mind when he planned his Balkan strategy, and readers of Olivia Manning's *Balkan Trilogy*, which ought to be every visitor's travelling companion in Romania, will recall the caricatured collection of British agents and enthusiastic amateurs plotting to blow them up before he could get to them. **Pitesti** is Ploiesti's twin oil-producing centre but it does not have quite the same colourful history.

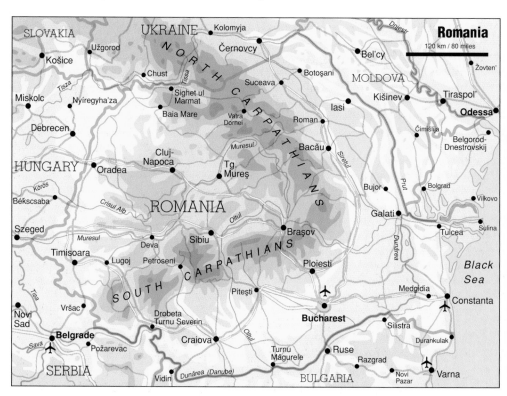

Tirgoviste was built by Mircea the Old, Vlad Dracula's grandfather, who reigned from 1386 to 1418. A reign of 32 years is almost without parallel in Romanian history, and Mircea managed it in the face of a constant Turkish threat. He threw up a string of forts along Romania's northern and south-eastern frontiers, the most powerful being the island fortress of Giurgiu. With his defences in place, he sat back and revelled in the title of "God's anointed and Christ's loving autocrat Ioan Mircea Great Voevod and prince, with God's help ruler over Ungro-Wallachia and parts of the country beyond the mountains, the Tatar lands, the duchies of Amlas and Fagaras, ruler of the Banat of Severin and of both banks of the Danube up to the Black Sea".

He was crowing too soon. He lost some of these territories to the Turks and had to submit to the Sultan in 1417. In exchange for a tribute of 3,000 golden ducats, he was allowed continued autonomy and it was agreed, for example, that no Turks would settle in Wallachia,

a concession with far-reaching consequences. Mircea is buried in the **Cozia Monastery** on the Olt River.

The ancient capital was a sizeable town which spread beyond the limits of the city walls. The location in the foothills of the Carpathians had a number of advantages. It was the centre of a wine-producing area known as the *podgorie*, and there may well have been a wooden monastery called St Nicholas of the Wines where there now stands the **Dealu Monastery**. Here many members of the Dracula family were buried and the head of Michael the Brave resides. The network of surrounding lakes evidently provided Tirgoviste with an abundance of fish.

Most of what Mircea the Old built was buried under Dracula's improvements, the most prominent of which is the **Chindia Tower**, which now houses a **Dracula Museum**. The tower was not merely a look-out for approaching enemies but a private platform which gave Dracula a clear view of the atrocities he laid on in the courtyard below.

Hitching a ride.

The throne room, whose outline is still visible, is reputed to be where Dracula, early in his reign, showed that he meant business. Some 200 prominent citizens were given a banquet in the room, little suspecting that Dracula thought they had been implicated in his grandfather's death. As soon as they were finished, Dracula had the elderly men and the women impaled. The able-bodied men, however, were chained together and marched 50 miles up the Arges River to turn a dilapidated fortress into what became **Curtea de Arges**, or Dracula Castle, and whose ruins may still be visited today. The chronicles don't bother to say what happened to them when the job was done.

Curiously, this castle happened to be at the epicentre of a series of earthquakes which rocked Romania at 30-year intervals from 1741, the blame for which was laid firmly at Dracula's feet. Not so long ago, peasants living in the area went nowhere without a Bible to ward off the forces of darkness. The 16th-century **Episcopal Church**, built

by Prince Neagoe Basarab, has a legend attached to its fountain which is a variation of the story told of countless places around the world, that the patron kills the architect or builder to prevent him from building anything so beautiful for anyone else. In this version, the unfortunate builder was a certain Manole, who was bricked up in the roof. He managed to escape but then had to jump. The tragic ending is that he fell to earth and was killed on the spot where the fountain came forth.

Wallachia is ribbed with valleys running from the Carpathians down to the Danube. Roads follow these valleys and generally make for scenic motoring, especially as they start climbing the foothills. The road running north from Ploiesti to Brasov passes through **Sinaia** with its famous monastery of the same name. A certain Mikhail Cantacuzino visited Mount Sinai in the 17th century and built the monastery to commemorate the trip. Sinaia used to be the hill station of the Romanian aristocracy, many of whose villas are now open to visitors.

Not so, unfortunately, **Peles Castle**, which was the royal summer palace of King Carol and his eccentric queen, better known as the plump, pink-faced pantomime dame Carmen Sylva. There are tales of her wandering around the grounds of the castle wearing diaphanous clothes and a helmet, waving a napkin at cows. King Carol died at Sinaia. According to Carmen Sylva, his last words were "Oh! What is this?" as he toppled into her arms, the victim of a heart attack.

Carmen Sylva was comforted shortly before her death in 1916 by discovering that she had a direct line of communication with the Archangel Raphael. They were in regular conversation until the very end. Sinaia has since been developed into a summer and winter resort with several good hotels. The ski slopes are some distance removed but may be reached by cable-car.

Moldavia: Moldavia and what used to be called Bukovina tend to take third place, behind Wallachia and Transylvania, on many tourist itineraries,

The Ceausescus' former villa

and this is a sad misjudgement of many fine attractions. Tucked away in the northeastern corner of Romania, Moldavia looks remote, and in fact the road journey from Bucharest is rather boring, but it is possible to fly from Bucharest to Bacau and then go by road to Suceava, which is not only one of the very oldest centres in the region – it was attacked by the Mongols in 1241 – but also the most practical hub from which to get the best out of northern Moldavia, or Bukovina, the most picturesque part.

Like Wallachia, Moldavia has a pivotal figure who stands as a landmark in its history and helps to put monuments into a meaningful perspective. He is Stephen the Great, no paragon of virtue but nevertheless a different kettle of fish from his loathsome contemporary, Vlad Dracula. Ironically, it was Dracula who helped Stephen depose his brother Peter Aron, whose thirst for blood would almost have stood comparison with Dracula's own.

Constantinople fell to the Turks in 1453 and there seemed nothing to stop them from sweeping right across Eastern Europe. Various Danubian and Balkan countries assume the credit for saving Europe from the Turkish yoke; Stephen the Great of Moldavia's claim is probably as good as any and better than most.

As visitors to Moldavia will run into memories of Stephen everywhere, they might like to consider an assessment of his character by Miron Costin, who has been called Romania's first serious historian: "Stephen was not tall of stature: he was irascible, cruel, prone to shed innocent blood, often at meals he would order people to be put to death, without legal sentence. But he was acute of judgement, sober, not proud, but a stubborn defender of his rights, in war always on the spot, well versed in military science, generally favoured by victory, never depressed by misfortune: ever expecting a better turn to affairs. The Moldavians think of him in political respects, with that veneration with which one holds a saint in religious honour."

The most popular sights in Moldavia

Gypsy village.

are monasteries which have frescoes inside and out. The astonishingly durable paint used on the exteriors evidently included ox bile, soot and egg yolk. The monasteries are built in cruciform with three rounded apses and conical tops which have been compared with witches' hats. The exteriors were painted for the benefit of people who were not allowed into the monasteries, and their purpose was propaganda. It would be impossible to exaggerate the impact the Siege of Constantinople had on society at the time and for generations afterwards, so it was a natural subject for the artists.

The equally ubiquitous depictions of the Day of Judgement were warnings – in as much sadistic detail as artists could bring themselves to imagine – of the grave consequences of flirting with, let alone joining, infidel religions, particularly Mohammedanism as it was then called. Religions competed fiercely for converts, and the unforgiving Day of Judgement was a powerful weapon in Christianity's armoury. The third sub-

ject to be seen everywhere, unsurprisingly, is Stephen the Great engaged in various heroic activities.

The Citadel in **Suceava** is Stephen the Great's work, albeit around the shell of an earlier fortress. Moldavians and Turks fought over it on numerous occasions, and it became such a symbol of Moldavian resistance that in 1675, having established their suzerainty over the Moldavians, the Turks blew it up. They no doubt put a supernatural interpretation on the fact that a few years later an earthquake pushed the demolition process one stage further.

Nevertheless, there is enough left to constitute an impressive ruin in a commanding position over the city. In Suceava itself, there are a number of excellent museums which provide a vivid insight into the life and times of Stephen the Great as well as the ruins of one of his several Princely Courts. The St Ioan Nou and St Dumitru churches in the city are both 16th century.

Of the dozen or so painted monasteries in Moldavia, a reasonable cross-

Moldovita's painted monastery.

section is within striking distance of Suceava. The example at **Moldovita**, badly weathered on one side, has some unusual additions to the almost obligatory Siege of Constantinople, in this case stones raining down on the infidel attackers while the icon of the Virgin and the Holy Shroud is being taken in solemn procession around the walls. Aristotle, Socrates, Pythagoras and Plato lend a touch of intellectual gravitas to the apses, while there is a saint each for 365 panels inside.

The convent still functions as such, and the adjacent museum contains a chair belonging to Peter Rares, Stephen's illegitimate son and definitely not a chip off the old block. "The kaleidoscopic character of his perfidy," it is said, "is almost unique even in the annals of the sixteenth century." He once warned the Saxons of Transylvania that he was looking forward to roasting them alive.

Stephen built the **Voronet Monastery**, his portrait inside commissioned by Peter Rares in a flash of filial piety. Peter may also have had a say in this particular Day of Judgement message, whose bluntness may be compared with that of the nearby monastery of **Humor**. In this instance it is the fate of the infidel to be devoured by wild animals and then regurgitated. David, inexplicably dressed as a troubadour, plays the mandolin while the just and unjust file off to their respective fates. The condemned ones are all too obviously Turks, Tartars and even Christian enemies.

The most revered of all the monasteries is at **Putna** because it was both built by Stephen and, more importantly, is his burial place. "I am surrounded by enemies on all sides," he wrote shortly before his death, "and have fought 36 battles since I was lord of this country, and of these won 34 and lost two." He is reputed to have built a church after each of his victories, Putna being his thanksgiving for a defeat of the Tartars which earned him the coveted title of "Athlete of Christ" and a carved ivory cross, supposedly containing a fragment of the True Cross, which had once been the property of Alexander the Great's mother.

Iris Iasi in Eastern Moldavia is perhaps better remembered as Jassy, the former capital of Moldavia and the provisional capital of Romania during World War I when Bucharest was evacuated. It was in the thick of Moldavia's violent history from the start and consequently had extreme swings of fortune.

It experienced something of a renaissance in the 17th century which produced, for example, the Golia monastery and the beautiful Trei Ierarhi church, but in the 18th century it was back in the doldrums because of the rapacious Phanariots. In 1764 a British diplomat complained that he "could not enter Jassy till daybreak, because of the deep mud which surrounds it". Duckboards were laid across the streets; the houses, he said, were "low and miserable and little better than in the scattered villages built of earth". Iasi bounced back and is now one of the more attractive cities in the country.

Iasi has a long intellectual tradition best personified by Demeter Cantemir, who wrote – in Latin – the first European history of the Turks. The Turks installed him on the Moldavian throne but he rebelled against what they expected of him and offered Moldavia to the Russian tsar, "esteeming it better to suffer with Christ than wait for the deceitful treasures of Egypt". The city also produced Mihai Eminescu, Romania's national poet. Appropriately, then, Iasi has first-rate museums of history, art, science and ethnography in the Palace of Culture and a separate Museum of Old Moldavian Literature.

Transylvania: The number of books specifically about Transylvania in the library of the Bruckenthal palace in Sibui is an astounding 100,000 or so. Werewolves, vampires and witches, the staple of Transylvanian legend, are of course well represented in this literature, but it is principally an extraordinarily controversial history which accounts for such an outpouring of words.

The cross-currents of Transylvanian history have produced all sorts of oddities, such as pockets of fair-haired, blue-eyed people conspicuous against a generally swarthy population, and towns which are decidedly German in character. Never has map-reading or asking directions been so fraught, because every place seems to have at least three names and even the locals may have to think twice before deciding which goes with which.

The historical arguments still raging today are fairly well covered in the preceding general article on Romania. What may bear repeating here is the question-mark over the whereabouts of the ethnic Romanians between the withdrawal of the Romans in AD 274 and the arrival of the Szekels, a Magyar splinter-group some seven centuries later. If the Romanians never left, their uninterrupted occupancy of the land would strengthen Romanian claims to Transylvania. The Hungarian argument is that they and their Szekel kinsmen inherited empty space; the fact that the Romanians later outnumbered them is not the critical issue. Neither side will yield the point; the impasse sparked ethnic warfare twice in the 20th century and has not been resolved yet.

One of the other points to bear in mind is the invitation that brought a considerable number of "Saxon" settlers – in reality, they were Germans from the lower Rhine, not Saxony at all – in the 12th and 13th centuries. They and their skills were needed to repopulate and reconstruct a landscape after the massacres and destruction of the Mongol invasions. It was these "Saxons" who formed the commercial classes and established the Sieben Burgen, or Seven Fortresses, which were virtually self-governing city states in an otherwise almost exclusively agricultural society. Sieben Burgen is what the Saxons called Transylvania as a whole.

"Transylvania" itself means "Across the Woods", and it brings to mind the reference in one of Saki's works, "those mysterious regions between the Vienna woods and the Black Sea".

Transylvania was part of the kingdom of Hungary from the 11th century until the Turkish conquest in 1526, whereupon there was an interlude during which Transylvania was ruled by a variety of princes, some with Polish connections, who were ultimately answerable to the Sultan of Turkey. This ended in 1699 when Turkey ceded Transylvania to Vienna, but Austria in turn ceded it to a virtually autonomous Hungary under the terms of the Dual Monarchy as established in 1867.

Broadly speaking, Hungarians (or assimilated Hungarians) formed the land-owning aristocracy, the Romanians were virtually landless peasants, and the "Saxons" maintained their position as a caste of town dwellers serving the needs of the wealthy upper classes. The manufacture of heavy cannon was a Brasov speciality, while Sibui produced the gunpowder. The German merchants maintained close contacts with the Hanseatic League.

The festering antagonism between Romania and Hungary boiled over at the end of the World War I. Hungary, facing defeat and dismemberment because of its involvement with Austria and Germany, was briefly a Soviet republic under Bela Kun. A Romanian invasion put an end to that, although not

Tiles brighten many village houses.

without the kind of vicious blood-letting that came to be known as the White Terror. Romania was rewarded with Transylvania after the war by virtue of the Romanian majority, but that turned the considerable Hungarian minority – not to mention the Szekels and Saxons – into an isolated and vulnerable enclave.

As things turned out, the Romanians treated the minorities reasonably well but, for Hungarians, Hitler's offer of Transylvania in exchange for their support in World War II was irresistible. Hungary actually jumped the gun in 1940, but was able to seize only northern Transylvania. It was restored to Romania after the war. Romania once again pursued a fairly liberal policy towards the minorities and in 1950, for example, set aside an autonomous district for the Szekels.

Under Ceausescu, however, all this was reversed. His bulldozers notoriously flattened ethnic Hungarian villages and West Germany was cajoled into "repatriating" some of the descendants of the 12th-century "Saxons" – and paying a substantial sum in hard currency for the privilege. What the present-day visitor sees in the way of fair-haired "Saxons", Szekels, German towns and ethnic variety generally is, therefore, a measure of Ceausescu's failure to achieve his objectives. That still leaves a multiplicity of names.

The most brain-teasing example of multiple names is **Alba Iulia**, about 45 miles (72 km) northwest of Sibui, where the recorded history of Transylvania begins. The Romans built their local capital around the ancient Dacian settlement of Apulon, renaming it Apulum. There are still traces of the Roman colony, but the more substantial monuments jump ahead to the 15th century, notably **St Michael's Cathedral**, by which time the Slavs had taken to calling the town Balgrad ("the white town"), while the Saxons preferred Weissenburg and the Hungarians Alba Julius.

The second barrel of the Hungarian name was in honour of a 10th-century Hungarian prince. Romanians stuck to "Balgrad" before finally adopting "Alba

Carpathian panorama.

Iulia", by which time the "Saxons" were calling it Karlsburg in honour of the Emperor Charles VI, who built the local fortress between 1716 and 1735. A Romanian uprising against Hungarian rule later that century ended with the two ringleaders being broken on the wheel outside the castle.

The original Romanesque cathedral was badly damaged by the Tartars and rebuilt in the Gothic style by John Hunyadi in 1443. He is buried in it, as is his son Ladislaus, who was beheaded in Buda in 1457.

Adjoining the cathedral is the **bishop's palace**, built in the 18th century, and nearby is the great library given to the city by Bishop Count Batthyany, said to contain one of the earliest manuscripts of the Nibelungenlied. Unless they have undergone a change of heart, the library staff are curiously reluctant to admit visitors.

Alba Iulia became Michael the Brave's capital when he briefly united Wallachia, Moldavia and Transylvania in 1600, and it was in commemoration

of this that King Ferdinand and Queen Marie chose Alba Iulia for their belated coronation in 1922 in the Orthodox church specially built for the occasion. The second unification of Romania, after World War I, was signed on the site of the present Museum of the Union, opposite the History Museum.

Between Alba Iulia and **Sibui**, or Hermannstadt, or Nagy-Szeben, is the plain where John Hunyadi defeated the Turks in 1442. Sibui, also a former capital of Transylvania, is situated on a hill above the Cibinul River and is one of the seven Saxon towns, some of the original 14th-century defences still clearly visible. The old city is built on two levels linked by steep staircases, and everywhere there are what are known as "the eyes of Hermannstadt". These are narrow slits in roofs which serve as windows, giving those below the sensation of being under constant surveillance.

The old town is a patchwork of small squares like one called **Dragonerplatz** after the cavalry officers who were billeted here during the wars against the Turks, and another named after the goldsmiths who set up shop in it. Few of the streets are paved, and as cars are rare and there is nothing to interrupt football matches in the road, the old town seems a long way from modern Europe.

The most illustrious name in Sibui is Bruckenthal, the governor of Transylvania from 1777 to 1787 in the reign of the Habsburg Empress Maria Theresa. The picture gallery in the palace has a collection of Old Masters unparalleled in this part of the world, including works by Titian and Van Dyck. These are complemented by the works of 19th-century Romanian artists, and the influence of French culture on young Romanians of the period is all too plain to see. The palace also includes the library alluded to above. The nucleus of the collection was Bruckenthal's own library; the later additions, as previously noted, are primarily books about, or at least containing reference to, Transylvania.

Next to the library is the **Bruckenthal Museum**, probably the best ethnographical collection in Romania.

When the state ran the markets, flowers and fruit couldn't be sold on the same stall.

Str. N. Balcescu is the busiest street in Sibui, a picturesque promenade lined with attractive houses. The **Hotel Imparatul Romanilor**, or Roman Emperor, at No. 4 is a curiosity. At one time or another Johann Strauss, Franz Liszt and the Emperor Joseph II all stayed here. The food is comparatively good and it can be an amusing place to pass an evening.

The main **Lutheran church** is a 14th-to 16th-century Gothic building on the site of a former Roman basilica, the bell-tower dating from 1499. The vaulted interior has a 15th-century fresco by Johannes of Rosenau. The "New Church" annex is actually 16th-century and contains the tombs of a number of Saxon counts, as well as that of Petrus Haller, the merchant whose imposing house stands on the piata Republica.

Brasov, or Kronstadt, grew up around a castle built by the Teutonic Order of Knights in the 13th century to become the most important commercial and manufacturing city in modern Transylvania. The local history is well represented in two museums, one in the former town hall, the other in the citadel south of the city centre.

Brasov's proudest possession is the **Black Church**, so-called because it was covered in soot when Austrian soldiers set fire to the city in 1689 to put down a revolt. There is still some evidence of the fire damage, but the sooty appearance has long since gone under the effect of extensive restoration. Built between 1385 and 1425, the church has choir-stalls which are magnificent examples of medieval carving. It is also noted for the rich oriental tapestries over the seats of the guilds and a massive organ.

About 7 miles (11 km) from, or perhaps above, Brasov is **Poiana Brasov**, one of Romania's most popular resorts with lifts up the nearby Postavarul mountains and the chance to ski back all the way to the doorstep of any one of a dozen hotels. There are also numerous summer sports facilities, so the place keeps going all year round.

The biggest attraction on the 90-mile

Old folks at home.

(145-km) stretch between Sibui and Brasov is, however, **Bran Castle**. Of all the castles in Romania, this is the one most closely identified with Dracula, both the ghastly Vlad Dracula of real life and Bram Stoker's creation. Local traders and even tourist guides are happy not to draw a rigorous distinction between the two, so it may be worth sorting out a few facts here.

Bran Castle, built in 1377 by the Teutonic Knights, guards one end of a narrow pass through the Carpathian mountains, a strategic route between Transylvania and Wallachia. Castle Dracula near Curtea-de-Arges was actually Vlad Dracula's stronghold. It was at the other end of the pass, in Wallachia, and in the Wallachian section of this book we have seen him rebuilding it with the help of some men whom he had invited to dinner. Their wives and children, we know, were impaled on this ill-starred occasion.

One early owner of Bran Castle was Vlad Dracula's grandfather, but otherwise the connections with him are tenuous. He certainly marched past it on occasion; it is less certain that he was held prisoner in it by Mathias Corvinus of Hungary. The castle had stood empty for centuries when it was given to Queen Marie as a present after World War I. Enchanted with the romantic setting, she decided to turn it into a holiday home. Her interior decoration was, by all accounts, an erotica innuendo.

The castle contains a museum of medieval life and is well worth visiting even if the Dracula connections are somewhat spurious.

Travellers arriving in Transylvania from Hungary by road or rail will first come across **Oradea**, just across the frontier. It was known as Grosswardein under the Habsburgs, while Hungarians call it Nagy Varad. It is a pleasant town with a brightly coloured central square. A tree-lined avenue leading from the square to the Crisul River passes an opera house by Helmer and Fellner, an indefatigable pair who seem to have built theatres in half the cities of Central Europe.

Bran Castle.

A park-like area north of the square includes the former palace, now a district museum, a baroque cathedral and an arcade known as **Cannons' Corridor**. There are two hotels in the town, although those planning an overnight stop might also like to consider one of several spas within easy reach. The best known of these is the **Baile Felix**, about 5 miles (8 km) distant.

Cluj-Napoca, or Clausenberg, is about 90 miles (150 km) into Transylvania. "Napoca" is the clue to Roman origins, although the date usually given for the founding of the city is 1272. It is perhaps most famous as the 1458 birthplace of Mathias Corvinus, Hungary's celebrated king but a Romanian by birth nevertheless. The house where he was born is at No. 6 Corvin strada, which runs at right-angles to the Piata Libertea, or Liberty Square. His equestrian statue in front of the Roman Catholic cathedral of St Michael is relatively new – 1902, by Fadreuz – whereas the church was started in the 14th century and rebuilt after a fire in 1689. The nearby **History Museum of Transylvania** has some Roman relics including an altar fragment of AD 104 with "Napoca" inscribed on it.

Liberty Square is the hub of the city. The Hotel Continental was until recently one of the few places in town where visitors could legally stay, a near-monopoly resulting in high prices and food which one visitor summed up as "vile".

Not far away are the altogether more pleasing **Botanical Gardens**, laid out for the town in the 19th century by Count Mika, a Hungarian nobleman. Trees of many varieties are planted over a large area broken up by ravines with little streams and wooden bridges. The **Ethnographic Museum**, within walking distance, is in the Reduta Palace and has a selection of Transylvanian peasant costumes.

A further 70 miles (110 km) east, on a turning off the road to Brasov, lies the least-visited and most resiliently Teutonic of the seven Saxon fortresses, **Sighisoara** or Schassburg. It is also the birthplace of the real Vlad Dracula, although with questionable judgement the

house where he was born has been turned into a restaurant. It is therefore possible to dine comfortably over the square where some of Dracula's atrocities were staged, just as he did in an incident recounted earlier.

The pinnacles and towers of the upper town, straddling a hill-top, make up for this gruesome note by providing a Disneyland-ish setting. Narrow paths wind between quaint houses and courtyards, and it is worth climbing the 14th-century clock tower of the town museum for the view. The museum's collection consists of old maps, furniture, and a selection of chemists' bottles!

It is worth exploring beyond Sighisoara itself. There is almost no traffic bar carts and horses on the small roads leading sooner or later to a Saxon village. **Sarosu**, or Schass, is about 5 miles (8 km) away; **Medias**, or Meivdiasch about twice as far. Sundays are best because of the strains of Bach coming from the churches – this is definitely Protestant country – and the fact that there seems always to be a wedding

Statue of Hungarian king Mathias Corvinus in Cluj-Napoca.

going on. Beer and schnapps flow and the colourful costumes look better in the flesh, as it were, than in the museums.

Banat was originally merely the name given to an area controlled by a military officer known as a Ban. Ironically, the southwestern corner of Romania known by this name never had a Ban of its own. It was captured by the Turks in the 16th century and retaken two centuries later by Prince Eugene of Savoy, on behalf of the Habsburgs, and Count Palffy.

The capital is **Timisoara**, whose fame as a centre of the Boicil method of treating rheumatism was overshadowed in 1989 when it was the scene of the demonstrations which led so swiftly to Ceausescu's overthrow. It was not the first time Timisoara rose on behalf of Romania: in 1514 it was the pivotal point of John Hunyadi's campaign against the Turks. On that occasion, however, the uprising failed and the Turks were in residence for the two centuries following. The city still has remains of the fortifications built by the Turks some four centuries after Iancu de Hunedoara built his castle, subsequently restored and now housing the Banat Museum.

The Danube flows through the area south of Timisoara down to the **Iron Gates**, the site of Trajan's famous bridge, whose remains are still to be seen. With the bridge close by, it is not surprising that the area has many Roman connections. The Romans founded the spa of **Baile Herculane**, and according to legend it was here that Hercules slew the Hydra and afterwards bathed his wounds in the mineral spring. Some of the original Roman baths were uncovered during the construction of the appropriately named Roman Hotel, and many Roman artifacts are on display in the nearby local history museum. The replica of the Roman statue of Romulus and Remus is in **30 December Boulevard**.

The spa was very much in vogue during the reign of Emperor Franz Joseph and his wife Elizabeth in the late 19th century. They brought their own furnishings from Vienna for the Villa Elizabeth where they customarily **Cormorants.**

stayed, although it seems they generally crossed the Cerna River to take the waters at the Neptune baths. The cubicles they used are preserved as they were then. The facilities, including the Moorish-style Hotel Traian, are in the process of being upgraded to first-class standards.

The **Danube**, in so many places a rather dull industrial watercourse, is spectacularly beautiful as it makes its descent from the Carpathians to the Iron Gates. As previously mentioned, the remains of some of the 25 pillars which Trajan drove into the river bed to support his bridge are still standing. This prize archaeological site also bears evidence of the later Byzantine occupation, the whole history imaginatively presented in the Iron Gates Museum at **Drobeta Turnu-Severin**.

Danube delta and Black Sea resorts: As the Danube approaches the Black Sea, it splits into three channels, each assuming a certain purpose. The northern channel, known as the Chilia, becomes the frontier between Romania and what used to be the Soviet Socialist Republic of Moldavia before it become Moldova. Romanians, however, tend to think of it as their long-lost province of Bessarabia. The centre channel is a conduit to the port of Sulina, while the southern one leads to the small port of Sfintu Gheorghe. Shipping no longer needs to use any of these because the 40-mile (64-km) Danube-Black Sea canal now slices directly across from Constanta to Cernavoda, cutting the corner as it were to the tune of 250 miles (400 km).

It is the land between the three channels which are of primary interest to visitors, because it is more than 1,500 sq. miles (4,000 sq. km) of forest, marshes and flats interspersed with small lakes and streams which combine to provide Europe with one of its finest wild-life sanctuaries. Moreover, it is accessible by paddle-steamer or hydrofoil, tickets obtainable in **Tulcea** where the three channels converge.

Tulcea is the logical starting-point because it is an interesting place in its own right apart from its good connec-

Residence on the Danube delta.

tions not only with the delta but also the roads leading to the Black Sea resorts to the south. The **Natural History Museum** has specimens of many, if not all, of the 300 species of birds and 60 of fish which inhabit the delta area. The pelicans are probably the most popular stars among the birds, but there are also large numbers of heron, egret and ibis. The biggest colonies of pelican are to be found on a chain of small lakes – **Rosca**, **Matita** and **Merhei** – in the southern part of the Letea nature reserve. Letea's vegetation is unusual considering the climate: lime trees, poplars, oaks, ash trees, willows and sandthorns.

Private expeditions in small boats known as *lotca* are easily arranged through local fishermen. The inhabitants of the area are a mixture of Ukrainians and Lipovanians (or Lipovans), descendants of one of the Old Believer sects who fled Russia when it was decreed, for example, that the sign of the cross would be made with three fingers instead of two. They live in isolated villages built on sandbanks, known as

grinds, where the water laps at the fence posts at the bottom of the garden. They are approachable and know every inch of the water whether for bird-spotting or fishing – the sturgeon will appeal to anglers – so their boats are much the best way of getting around.

More and more evidence is being found of early settlements in these parts. The Greeks were certainly here as early as the 6th century BC. They were followed by Romans, Turks and all the other parties with a vested interest in controlling access to the Danube. The **Ethnographic and Art Museum** sheds light on new discoveries.

Sulina, the port on the centre channel, has relics of former Byzantine and Genoese occupants. It is possible here to book day trips or overnight stops at hotels and campsites in the area. One can drive to Sfintu Gheorghe by car, but if time permits it would be a pity to miss the chance to do the trip by *lotca* along waterways which narrow suddenly and open up on lakes.

Histria, a derivation or corruption of Istros, the Greek name for the Danube, is a major archaeological site. Although it was founded by Greeks in the 6th century BC as a port, it now lies some distance inland, presumably an indication of how far the sea has receded. Its distance from the sea has nevertheless been its saviour: anything within range was bound to be bombarded by pirates. The walls were put up by the Romans, obviously in a hurry and using anything that came to hand. The same Romans were more particular about the construction of their baths, temples and villas; characteristically they built an aqueduct to bring fresh water from the distant hills.

About 40 miles (65 km) further south is the first of the Black Sea resorts, **Mamaia**, beyond which are Constanta and **Mangalia**, Romania's chief ports and also 6th-century BC Greek colonies, called Tomis and Callatis respectively. Following the general pattern, they were taken over by the Romans in the 1st century AD and held for three centuries or so.

The ruins of the fortress at Mangalia

Traditional musicians travel the country.

and the beautiful sculptures now in the museum at Constanta paint a picture of luxurious Roman living that is hard to reconcile with the fact that Ovid was exiled to Tomis from Rome. A terrible thing? A statue was erected to him in the city for his pains. Byzantine Greeks gave Tomis the name Constanta in honour of Constantine the Great. The old lighthouse in Constanta was built by the Genoese in 1300 while they were running a trading post here. As usual, the Turks were right behind them, and they have left their mark, too.

With this kind of background, one would expect the **National History and Archaeological Museum** in **Constanta** to be out of the ordinary, and so it is. The exhibits cover an enormous range: two Hamangian statuettes are at least 5,000 years old. Equally outstanding is the excavated Roman commercial centre, an entire complex of shops and warehouses with a vast mosaic floor.

The dozen or so modern resorts around these old Greek and Roman sites were built in the 1960s and 1970s to exploit the miles of sandy beaches, the inland lakes, mineral water springs and therapeutic Sapropel mud. These centres are clusters of hotels with swimming pools, tennis courts, riding schools and special features like the aquarium and dolphinarium in Constanta. Discos, cabarets, bars and cinemas keep up the tempo after the sun goes down; the sea sometimes does its bit by assuming a phosphorescent nocturnal glow which tempts many visitors into taking a late dip.

Restaurants make a special feature of local food and the wine produced a few miles inland. Murfatlar is the best-known of these vineyards, and it is possible to pay a convivial visit. The other inland attraction is a reproduction of **Trajan's column**, the one he erected to commemorate his hard-won victory over the Dacians. It is an enormous thing, 100ft (30 metres) or so in diameter and a third again higher, and it not only depicts scenes of the battle but the names and personal details of the 4,000 Roman soldiers who lost their lives. It is situated in the village of **Adamclisi**.

Sun sets on the Danube delta.

BULGARIA

Bulgaria's international image has come a long way since the dark days of 1978 when a secret service agent plunged a poisoned umbrella tip into the exiled dissident Georgi Markov as he was crossing Westminster Bridge in London. Three years later, the agents were at it again, lending their questionable talents to a conspiracy to murder the Pope. The arrival and phenomenal success of Bulgarian wine on Western markets in the 1980s was for many people the first intimation that anything to do with Bulgaria was not necessarily sinister and possibly lethal.

Still, there was no discernible movement on the political front in a country which seemed not to have adjusted to the fact that Stalin was dead. The large Turkish minority, 10 percent of the population, was subject to Stalinist assimilation and, having been forced to adopt Bulgarian names, was said to have ceased to exist. The change, when it came, could not have been more abrupt. On the very day after the opening of the Berlin Wall, President Todor Zhivkov was dismissed and free elections were announced. Zhivkov was soon put on trial and eventually jailed for corruption. The rehabilitation of Bulgaria was neatly rounded off when his successor, Zhelyu Zhelev, took time off on an official visit to Britain to pay his respects at Georgi Markov's grave.

Westerners who were thus inclined to visit Bulgaria in considerable numbers inherited facilities which had made Bulgaria's Black Sea coast the Riviera for Soviet bloc trade unionists. While 50 or more hotels in a single purpose-built resort may sound off-putting, bringing tourism to the Soviet masses had actually been executed with commendable style, and Bulgaria has since brought its resorts up to more discerning Western standards, notably through a full repertoire of watersports, with the same determination that has sold so much wine. In addition to the major hotels, the spirit of free enterprise has opened private houses to paying guests in villages so unspoiled that they have never had a hotel. While many hotels tend to suppose that Westerners will eat only "international" food and come up with a pale imitation of it, the local ingredients are excellent and it is getting easier to discover just what local recipes can do with them. For the moment at least, prices are very low.

Bulgaria's excellent ski slopes complement the Black Sea resorts to keep the tourist business going all year round, but there are many less obvious attractions. The country abounds in antiquity, not merely the relics of Greek Black Sea trading stations and outposts of the Roman Empire, but monasteries where the inmates really did cultivate contemplation of the navel. There are also, as we shall see in the following chapter, ancient cities belonging to what one historian has called "a vague and ill-known period, whose very name falls as a surprise on most Western ears".

Preceding pages: a cluster of folk costumes; Plovdiv. **Left,** stiff upper lip.

Bulgaria is knee-deep in antiquity. On reflection, it is not hard to work out why this should be so. The Danube, Bulgaria's northern frontier, was also once the frontier of the Roman Empire, which explains the number of Roman sites. The geography of the south similarly explains Greek, Byzantine and Ottoman relics.

A puzzle arises, however, over the ruins of entire cities which are not connected with any of these. The facts that emerge are of kingdoms and empires which most outsiders have never heard of. The historian Steven Runciman refers to "a vague and ill-known period, whose very name falls as a surprise on most Western ears".

The excellent National Museum in Sofia answers some questions but immediately raises even more. For a start, it has a priceless collection of gold artifacts from a necropolis at Varna on the Black Sea which was only uncovered in 1972. Dating them caused a sensation. At 4000 BC, they were the product of a civilisation which was obviously flourishing 1,500 years before the pharoahs got round to building their pyramids and all of 3,500 years before the Athenians thought of the Parthenon.

Scholars are inclined to think that the story of Jason and the Argonauts was a romantic interpretation of Greek entrepreneurs entering the Black Sea simply in search of new business opportunities. The Varna treasures imply that it may have been gold, if not the Golden Fleece itself, that they were after.

We shall here skip lightly over the early Thracian population, the conquest by Philip II of Macedon and the Roman period. The last was in most respects an adjunct of what is dealt with in the Romanian section of this book, and it concluded when the Romans abandoned the Eastern Danube at the end of the 4th century to meet the barbarian threat closer to home.

Specifically Bulgarian history begins with the unobtrusive influx of Slavs to fill the vacuum left by the Romans. The Byzantine emperors to the south were not alarmed until

Left, detail from the treasure-trove contained in Bulgaria's innumerable monasteries.

the 7th century, when the Slavs were joined by Bulgars who by their deeds gave credibility to their claimed descent from Attila's Huns. Emperor Constantine IV's attempt to drive them back beyond the Danube failed. Curiously, the emperor said he was thwarted by sore feet, which sounds like the original lame excuse. The Bulgars under the Sublime Khan Asperuch exacted the right to settle south of the Danube and founded their capital at Pliska in 680. At this stage both Sardica (Sofia) and Philippopolis (Plovdiv) were within the Byzantine Empire.

Relations between Bulgars and the Slavs who had preceded them were reasonably cordial. The Bulgars were essentially a military caste, but it would be wrong to think of the Slavs as serfs because they had a fairly orderly system and chieftains of their own. Tervel, Asperuch's successor, destroyed the *modus vivendi* with Byzantium by interfering in its politics – he helped to restore to the imperial throne Justinian II, whose nose had been slit when he was deposed. The result was a series of wars during which an attempt to conscript Slavs into the Bulgar army caused 200,000 to decamp to Byzantium.

Under the demands of these wars there were times when the First Bulgarian Kingdom was in danger of going under. Its salvation was evolving to the west where other Bulgars in what is now Hungary and Transylvania were able with help from Charlemagne to conquer the Avars. A merger of the two Bulgar khanates produced a much more substantial kingdom. The capital was in the east, Pliska, but the Sublime Khan came from the west, the formidable Krum. The Byzantine Emperor Nicephorus watched these developments and concluded that they meant war. He was right: the war broke out in 807.

One of Krum's main objectives was to take Sofia. He was busy doing so when Nicephorus advanced behind his back and took Pliska. While Krum massacred the 6,000-strong Byzantine garrison in one, Nicephorus plundered the other and, for good measure, had the Bulgar babies shoved through threshing machines. "Lo, thou hast conquered," cried Krum. "Take what thou wilt and depart in peace." Nicephorus was in no mood to do so and instead went after the Bulgars as they took to the mountains. The chase was a tactical error. The imperial troops were trapped between hastily erected barricades in a narrow defile and butchered, Nicephorus included.

If Krum appears in history books at all, it is for what he did to Nicephorus's head. It was exposed on a stake for a few days before being hollowed out and lined with silver to become Krum's favourite goblet.

Krum was now determined to take Constantinople itself. As a preliminary he took Nesebar, now one of the most picturesque spots on the Black Sea but then, when it was known as Mesembria, one of the wealthiest and most important ports in the Byzantine Empire. Constantinople was an altogether different proposition. It was as much as he could do to devastate the surrounding countryside while intimidating the defenders on the walls with a show of force, which involved human sacrifices on heathen altars. When Krum met the new emperor Leo the Armenian to discuss terms, Leo sprang concealed assassins on him, and Krum was lucky to escape with his life.

Krum's feelings about this treacherous act were robust. The force he assembled for an assault on Constantinople was so big that the Holy Roman Empire in the west was asked to send help against it. In the event it was not needed. On Holy Thursday, 814, the excitable Krum burst a blood-vessel in his head and dropped dead. He left Bulgaria as the greatest military power in Eastern Europe.

Krum's son Omortag concluded a 30-year peace with Constantinople, the terms of which were inscribed on a column in Pliska. He built a palace whose ruins are still visible at the site. A second palace followed at Preslav mainly as a show of force for the benefit of Slavs, Greeks and Byzantines alike. He proposed to deal with the growing popularity of Christianity among the Franks in Croatia with a full-scale invasion. His death in 831 brought this campaign to a halt. Like Krum, Omortag left a considerably stronger state than he had inherited.

Christianity took hold, it is said, when Khan Boris, who succeeded in 852, was terrified by a Greek painting showing the fate of infidels at the Last Judgement.

The other Khans were not as convinced, so he had them rounded up – 52 khans plus their wives and children – and put to death. This, according to a chronicle, was "shocking in so new a devotee of Christian meekness".

Boris chose to align himself with Byzantium rather than Rome at a time when the two branches competed fiercely for converts. Bulgaria became very Greek. The nobility sent their sons to be educated in Constantinople and had their houses built by Greek artisans. As the trend developed to the degree that it threatened to overwhelm Bulgarian culture, Boris was relieved to make the acquaintance of Methodius who, with his brother Cyril, had written books in the Slavonic language using the alphabet they had invented. Their texts were more accessible

to the population as a whole than were the Greek, and the result was the development of Slavonic Christianity. The same Cyrillic alphabet is used unchanged in Bulgaria today.

Boris's son and successor Symeon made Slavonic the official language of the Bulgarian church without lowering his admiration of Byzantine grandeur and the desire to emulate it. Pliska, battered in the wars between Krum and Byzantium, was replaced by a new capital, Preslav.

Symeon's ambition soared. Encouraged by victories over the Magyars and Serbs, he set out to conquer Byzantium with a view to becoming Emperor. But Symeon was unable to realise his dream and settled instead for the title of "Emperor of the Romans and the Bulgars", which for practical purposes was shortened to tsar. An interesting point is that there was a Bulgarian tsar long before the title appeared in Russia.

Many of Bulgaria's numerous monasteries were built in the next 40 years of relative peace in a surge of religious enthusiasm. Bulgaria's patron saint, Ivan Rilski, a herdsman who became a hermit, lived at this time. His tomb is near the great Rila Monastery.

The preoccupation with piety seemed to cause standards in other respects to lapse. Bulgarians were derided at the imperial court as "filthy beggars, and their tsar, not an

emperor, but a prince clad in skins". Nevertheless, Constantinople was wary of risking another war using Imperial troops. The alternative was to find a surrogate, and there was one waiting in the wings. He was a Varangian Russian, Prince Svyatoslav, and a bribe of 1,500 lbs (680 kg) of gold persuaded him to take on the Empire's dirty work.

Svyatoslav's army swept through Preslav and on to Plovdiv where 20,000 of the inhabitants were promptly impaled. The ensuing panic forced Tsar Boris of Bulgaria to abdi-

Left, Boris, the country's first Christian khan.
Above, the redoubtable Khan Krum.

cate. His unfortunate brother and potential heir Romanus was captured and castrated, a literal as well as symbolic end to the house of Krum. Romanus put a brave face on his sorry state and found work as a eunuch.

In due course, a new state took shape with its centre near Lake Ochrid in Macedonia, but first there was a poetic ending to Svyatoslav which might have been scripted from the grave by Krum himself. On his way home to Russia, he was ambushed and killed by the wild Petchenegs. They lopped off his head and presented it to their chieftain as a souvenir goblet. It was much cherished.

The exiled Bulgarians in Macedonia rallied under Tsar Samuel for what was to be a fight to the death with the Byzantine Empire. At first, Samuel concentrated on the Greek peninsula and once led his troops through Thermopylae, the pass where the Spartans put up their immortal defence against Xerxes and the Persians and the one used by the Germans in World War II. The challenge was taken up by the young Emperor Basil, who put aside a dissipated life to become "a terrible figure, chaste and severe, eating and sleeping sparsely, clad in unrelieved dark garments, never even wearing the purple cloak nor the diadem on his head".

A rejuvenated Bulgarian army managed to regain Pliska and Preslav and even stretches of the Black Sea coast for a while, but these successes merely raised the stakes for what was to be a final showdown at Cimbalongus on the Vardar River. Samuel himself did not take part in the battle which resulted in the capture of 15,000 Bulgarians and one of the more ghoulish episodes in military history. All but one in a hundred of the prisoners had their eyes put out. The exceptions were left with one eye each so that they could lead the blind home. The sight of the crippled army groping their way into his capital was too much for Samuel. He fell to the ground in an apoplectic fit. A glass of cold water revived him for a moment or two, but he then fainted and did not regain consciousness before dying two days later, 6 October 1014.

Basil was determined to end the Bulgarian menace once and for all. In the Macedonian highlands he blinded every Bulgarian he could find. Some of those captured in other areas were shipped off to Armenia. One of the few Bulgarians to be treated leniently was the last scion of the house of Krum, the enterprising eunuch Romanus, who had worked himself up to the position of governor of Skopje. Basil created him a patrician and he ended up as the governor of a province in Egypt. Basil's massacre of the Bulgarians earned him the title of Bulgaroctonus – "Basil the Bulgar-Slayer".

For nearly two centuries afterwards, Bulgaria was simply a province of the Byzantine Empire. Basil proved to be more generous in victory than in battle. The surviving Bulgarian aristocracy took happily to luxurious imperial service, and the only peasants who apparently cared one way or the other were the followers of "Pope Bogomil", who were totally opposed to government of any kind.

When the Byzantine Empire grew weaker, Bulgaria, as if obeying the rules of symmetry, was reborn under two boyar brothers, Peter and Asen, founders of what became known as the Asenid dynasty, with a new capital at Veliko Turnovo.

The Asenid dynasty did not have an easy passage. Both Peter and Asen were murdered, and it is hard to find very many among their successors who died in bed. The Crusaders were a constant scourge. In spite of the not inconsiderable influence of the bizarre Bogomils, Bulgaria was considered a Christian country. That no more swayed the Crusaders than did Constantinople's tower-ing position as the head of the Eastern Church. They sacked it too, in 1204.

The Bulgarians came to Byzantium's defence against the Crusaders and a year later captured Baldwin of Flanders, the Crusader leader and first "Latin Emperor" of Constantinople. He was held prisoner and died in the tower named after him in Turnovo.

Medieval Turnovo now lies in ruins but enough survives to fire the imagination. "It is as if ancient plays were staged here a long time ago," wrote a 19th-century Russian, "after which the actors and spectators died, leaving behind only the setting of this fairytale city, overhanging the precipitous, meandering ravine of the Yantra." In spite of the difficult times, the Second Bulgarian Kingdom produced an outpouring of architecture and the arts not merely in the capital but throughout the country. It proved to be a swan-song because in 1393 Turnovo fell to the Ottomans and with that, as far as Bulgarians are concerned, the Dark Age descended.

If an objective history of the nearly five centuries of Ottoman occupation has been written, it would not be found on sale in Bulgaria. The popular accounts are exclusively in terms of rape, looting and savagery, yet there is plenty of evidence of flourishing intellectual life in monasteries which presumably could all too easily have been closed down if the Turks had so desired. There are also intriguing glimpses of a tapestry richer than convention allows in a certain Osman Pazvantoglu who in 1792 proclaimed Vidin an independent city state and with French backing seceded from the Ottoman Empire. This bold enterprise lasted until 1807.

In general, the Turks put minarets on many churches to make them mosques and, when Bulgaria regained its independence in the 19th century, these minarets came off to make the mosques churches again. The Ottomans did allow some new churches to be built, but usually on condition that they were at a lower level than any mosques in the vicinity. The result is the number of churches, in the centre of Sofia and elsewhere, that are in holes in the ground.

The Bulgarian nationalist uprising against the Turks is the one aspect of the Ottoman era that is liberally covered. The most ubiquitous name in this respect is Vassil Levsky, a guerrilla leader whose cult has elevated him to the status of martyr, saint and apostle rolled into one. Levsky was undoubtedly a hero and necessarily mobile in his campaign against the Turks, although visitors may wonder whether there is a cave anywhere in the country or a monastery without a room where Levsky did not stay at some time.

Guerrilla attacks provoked severe Turkish reprisals, the most notorious being the "Bulgarian Atrocities" of 1876 when Turkish irregulars massacred 30,000 men, women and children. Europe as a whole was horrified. Russia was the first to act, and while a massive invasion might have been primarily in defence of "our Orthodox Slav brothers", it also fitted in neatly with Russia's desire to control the Black Sea and Bosporus and

wards were sufficient to produce 17 church bells, the largest weighing 12 tons. Russia's intervention, and in particular the enthusiastic role taken by Tsar Alexander II, were to colour Bulgarian foreign policy for generations to come.

Once independent, Bulgaria needed someone to occupy its throne. Bulgarian nationals were not considered suitable; it was thought essential to bring in a foreign prince with family connections where it mattered. Under the terms of the peace concluded with Turkey, however, the prince would remain the Sultan's vassal. The choice fell on Prince Alexander of Battenberg ("Sandro"), who was the tsar's favourite nephew and godson

hence access to the Mediterranean. The chief architect of this strategy was Count Nikolai Ignatieff, the Russian ambassador to Constantinople, who was content to cloak selfish Russian ambitions under the fashionable cause of "Pan-Slavism".

The ensuing war was a bloody affair. One of the more celebrated engagements was at the Sipka Pass near Pleven where 6,000 Bulgarians and Russians successfully held off a Turkish force of 27,000. It is said that the spent bullets found on the pass after-

and also acceptable to Germany and Britain. He was elected Prince of Bulgaria in 1879.

"Can you believe it when I tell you that in the few days I have been here I have aged by 10 years?" he wrote to his father from Sofia. "All the scum of Russia has taken refuge here." His task was made even more difficult when Tsar Alexander II, his benefactor, was murdered. He was succeeded by Alexander III who detested the struggling prince, whom he referred to as "that German".

With the prospect of "Sandro" becoming engaged to Victoria of Prussia, the tsar advised her by devious means that her prospective husband habitually entertained whores

Left, Vassil Levsky, hero of the revolt against Turkey. **Above**, the anti-Turkish uprising, 1868.

in the palace, had a penchant for "Turkish practices" and was riddled with venereal disease. The wedding was postponed pending further enquiries. While the rumours were untrue or at least exaggerated, it never took place.

Nevertheless, the prince soldiered on and achieved a stunning victory over the Serbs in a campaign lasting just two weeks. The tsar was not appeased. He first engineered an attempt to poison Sandro and then, when that failed, instigated a kidnap-cum-murder plot using a Russian army captain and a Montenegrin priest. When that also failed, he staged a full-blown coup. When the deposed prince refused to abdicate, he was spirited away to

candidate in question later denied that he had initiated the contact. He claimed that he was catching butterflies on the Vienna railway line embankment when he was surprised by a tap on his shoulder and out of the blue was offered the throne of Bulgaria.

Whatever happened, the news that Prince Ferdinand of Saxe-Coburg-Gotha had been selected was greeted with incredulity. "Totally unfit," stormed Queen Victoria, his cousin, "delicate, eccentric and effeminate." According to Tsar Alexander, who nursed hopes of becoming the "Grand Duke of Bulgaria" himself, "the candidature is as ridiculous as the individual".

Ferdinand's appearance worked against

Russia virtually as the tsar's prisoner.

A quick counter-revolution masterminded by the Bulgarian nationalist Stefan Stomboloff got the prince back, but he had lost his appetite for the job. With Russia threatening to declare Bulgaria a Russian protectorate under General Nikolai Kaulbars, the search for a royal replacement became urgent.

On 13 December 1886, the Bulgarian delegates scouring Europe for the right candidate took time off to see an opera in Vienna. There they were tipped off during the interval that there was in Vienna "a young prince of great family, related to all the courts in Europe" who was keen to take the job. The

him: tiny eyes and a colossal nose which, by his own admission, made him look like an elephant. He liked to think this amazing nose had its advantages. "Why should I not admit to myself that the enormous intake of air of which this gigantic nose is capable might not contain odours which would remain undetected by other, ordinary noses?"

With so much opposition to his selection, Ferdinand prudently travelled to Bulgaria locked in a lavatory on the Orient Express. He was sworn in at the ancient seat of Turnovo. Almost at once, the Russians tried to get rid of him, paying a certain Franz Maktich 6,000 French francs to blow him up.

Ferdinand thereafter wore a chain-mail vest everywhere and issued deliberately misleading information about his movements, which caused havoc with people who were supposed to meet him.

Russian determination to secure Bulgaria by any means and Germany's equal determination to prevent that from happening elicited a prescient warning from Bismarck. "Bulgaria, that little country between the Danube and the Balkans," he said, "is far from being of adequate importance for which to plunge Europe, from Moscow to the Pyrenees, and from the North Sea to Palermo, into a war whose issue no man can foresee."

Ferdinand had his own ideas about what needed to be done. Deciding that an heir was essential, he quickly married Marie-Louise, the daughter of Duke Robert of Bourbon-Palma and Prince Boris was born exactly nine months later. Stamboloff, the Prime Minister who had put him on the throne to begin with, was perceived as a hindrance and was hacked to death by men wielding Turkish cutlasses as he was leaving his club.

Austria's annexation of Bosnia and Herzegovina in 1908 was Ferdinand's opportunity to make a break with Turkey and become a king instead of a mere prince. He read out his proclamation of independence in the Church of Forty Martyrs in Turnovo, by which time a crown inscribed with "Tsar of the Bulgarians" was ready and waiting in Munich. He was unabashed by the prospect of war with Turkey. It would be, he said, "a struggle of the Cross against the Crescent". Even Kaiser Wilhelm was impressed by the speed with which the Bulgarian forces converged on Constantinople in what became known as the Balkan War: "The Bulgarians have been led in a masterly fashion and have engaged brilliantly... Perhaps we shall see Ferdinand I as tsar of Byzantium?"

If anything, Bulgarians at the walls of Constantinople alarmed European leaders otherwise predisposed toward Ferdinand. "I have 80 million Mohammedan subjects," wailed the King of England. Kaiser Wilhelm was the exception. "Rubbish!" he snorted. "The Bulgarians shall and must enter! Old Kiamil (i.e., the Turkish sultan) can die in peace; he is practically 100 years old!"

Ferdinand camped outside the walls of Constantinople in the story of Krum and Simeon all over again. In the event, though, the Bulgarians lost 10,000 men (with another 20,000 side-lined by cholera and dysentery) in the first two days. To add to his discomfort, Greece and Serbia, his nominal allies, were taking advantage of his preoccupation by scooping up lightly defended parts of the Turkish Empire. The prospect of a quick settlement receded when the Young Turks rose in rebellion and would not countenance any compromise.

Bulgaria earned a footnote in military history when hostilities resumed by being the first to use aircraft to drop bombs. They were

not bombs in the modern sense but grenades mixed with water-melons. The explosion of the melons' pink flesh on impact was intended to have a psychological effect.

Just as peace seemed within reach, Ferdinand did a complete about-face by ordering an attack on his supposed allies Serbia and Greece without even informing his own government. The idea backfired catastrophically. While the Bulgarians were tied down by the Serbs and Greeks, 150,000 Romanians crossed the Danube and captured Sofia with no resistance.

Bulgaria and Ferdinand personally paid heavily for this misjudgement at the subse-

Left, the Bulgarians take revenge for Turkish atrocities. **Above**, King ("Foxy") Ferdinand.

quent peace. The territorial awards after campaigns which had cost Bulgaria a total of 140,000 dead and wounded were all at Bulgaria's expense. Winston Churchill allowed the Bulgarians a note of sympathy: "They saw large districts inhabited largely by the Bulgarian race newly liberated from the Turks pass under the yoke – to them scarcely less odious – of Serbians and Greeks."

Victory emboldened Serbia to make moves towards the liberation of Serbs living under Habsburg rule in Bosnia-Herzegovina, Croatia and southern Hungary. If Serbia were to act rashly in any of these, the British ambassador predicted, Austria would retaliate by attacking Serbia and this in turn would

The Bulgarian line was broken within three days, and only then was Bulgaria invited to send a delegation to negotiate an armistice.

"Was anything said about me?" Ferdinand asked his Bulgarian delegation on its return. "I do not wish to discuss that subject," was the reply. "But the Allies spoke in terms of admiration about the Crown Prince." Ferdinand caught the drift and abdicated. The Crown Prince succeeded as Tsar Boris III and married Princess Giovanna of Savoy.

From the start, Boris was vulnerable. Alexander Stamboliski, his prime minister from 1919 to 1923, was murdered. In 1925, an unsuccessful attempt was made on Boris personally. In the same year, an "infernal

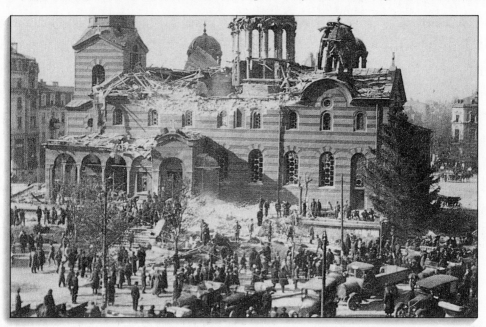

lead to "war with Russia, and possibly to a general conflict in Europe". With hindsight one can fill in the details: the Serbs would have a hand in the assassination of the Archduke Franz Ferdinand in Sarajevo, an Austrian ultimatum would follow – and so on to World War I.

Ferdinand waited until 6 September 1915 to throw in his lot with Germany and Austria, believing then that they were most likely to win. By January 1917 he was not so sure and began to look for ways to wriggle out. The Entente were not prepared to listen to him and an offensive against Bulgarian positions in Macedonia was accordingly launched.

machine" exploded in the roof of the old cathedral of Sveta Nedelja during a service for a general who had himself been assassinated. Most of these outrages were connected in one way or another with Macedonians, and evening gun battles in the cafés of Sofia were a common occurrence.

"In private life, the average Bulgarian is an excellent fellow," a contemporary visitor noted, "honest, hard-working, and hospitable. It is in the political arena that he still displays, beneath the thin veneer of 20 years' civilisation, the effect of five centuries of Turkish rule." Bulgaria made reasonable economic progress but King Boris's stringent attempts to maintain some kind of order eventually amounted to a royal dictatorship.

Boris was genuinely anxious to remain neutral as the storm clouds of World War II gathered and then broke, but he could hardly refuse Hitler's request to allow German troops to pass through Bulgaria en route for Greece. Bulgaria's Russophiles objected only when the Nazi-Soviet Pact collapsed, and by then Hitler had forced Romania to cede Southern Dobrudja to Bulgaria. Jews were forbidden to live in Sofia and were obliged to wear the yellow star of David, but Boris refused to let them be deported.

In August 1943 Boris was called to a meeting with Hitler. On leaving, he reached for his oxygen mask as the aircraft gained altitude – and died. Officially the cause of death was a heart attack but many believed that he was poisoned.

Prince Simeon succeeded at the age of six with a three-man regency. On 5 September 1944 Bulgaria broke off relations with Germany, an action which should have pleased the Soviets. Instead, a Soviet declaration of war followed within hours and an invasion was launched in support of a Soviet-backed coup. One of the first people to be tried by the hastily convened "People's Courts" was Prince Cyril, Boris's brother. He was literally forced to dig his own grave before being shot. Thousands of Bulgarians were murdered in a purge. On 8 September 1946 the monarchy was abolished on the strength of a somewhat suspect plebescite. Little Simeon, his mother and sister, were sent into exile.

The Bulgarian Communist party had been formed in 1919 by Georgi Dimitrov. The membership after World War II stood at only 8,000, but the presence of the Red Army ensured that nothing interfered with a systematic purge of opposition politicians, army officers and clergy. The official figure of 2,000 executions for "war crimes" is thought to be only 10 percent of the true figure, and in 1990 the existence of 85 or more concentration camps was admitted.

One of the most controversial aspects of Communist rule began in 1950 with the explusion of 150,000 ethnic Turks. The government line thereafter was that there were no more Turks in Bulgaria. In fact, there may still have been as many as a million, but the pretence was maintained by requiring all citizens to adopt Bulgarian names. The bluff was called when the border with Turkey was opened in 1989 and 320,000 people fled, shedding their Bulgarian names and reverting to Turkish ones as they crossed the frontier. Many of them subsequently went back.

The Bulgarian Communists faithfully shadowed every shift in Moscow: pro-Stalin then anti-Stalin, pro-Khrushchev then anti-Khrushchev and so on. Bulgarian troops took their part in the Soviet invasion of Czechoslovakia in 1968. When Gorbachev announced his first reforms in Moscow, Presi-

dent Todor Zhivkov announced that the same thoughts had occurred to him. If only out of force of habit, however, the police beat up a crowd of 5,000 who turned out in support of an international environmental conference which the government itself had organised.

Zhivkov was dismissed in 1989 by more reform-minded leaders who thought they were better able to keep up with the quickening pace of *glasnost* and *perestroika*. The Communist Party became the "Socialist Party", but the disclosure of secret orders for the use of tanks against an anti-government demonstration indicated that the leopard had not quite changed its spots.

Left, aftermath of a **1925** bombing of Sofia's Sveta Nedelja Cathedral. **Above**, King Boris of Bulgaria meets Adolf Hitler in **1943**.

BULGARIA: WHAT TO SEE

Sofia and environs: Even Alexander of Battenberg's gloom in 1877 on first seeing the ramshackle wooden houses that represented his new capital was lifted by Sofia's wonderful setting in a ring of mountains dominated by Mount Vitosa. The mountain now lends more than a pretty face to the capital: it brings winter sports right to its doorstep. The city was laid out by Alexander's successor Prince Ferdinand with a view to creating a capital fit to entertain European royalty. The unexpected bonus was that building works uncovered a city of great and splendid antiquity.

Sofia was called Serdica after the Thracian tribe, the Serdi, who originally built it. The Romans retained the name in making it the capital of their Thracian province. It was destroyed by the Huns in the 5th century and rebuilt in the 6th by Justinian, the Emperor of Byzantium. Sofia remained part of the Byzantine Empire while, farther east, the Bulgars and Slavs created the First Bulgarian Kingdom with its capital at Pliska.

The city has grown in two distinct phases since Ferdinand's time. The Dresden town-planner Alfred Mussman was responsible in 1935 for one of these; the Soviet school took over in the mid-1950s, its most visible monuments being the gargantuan **National Palace of Culture** and the former headquarters of the Bulgarian Communist Party.

To get the history into perspective, make a bee-line for the **National History Museum** on the Boulevard Vitosa and allow, if possible, a whole day to see it. The showpieces are arranged in the central hall; after this glittering introduction, it is possible to follow Bulgaria's development chronologically. Only a sample of the amazing gold artifacts found in the 4000 BC Chalcolithic necropolis at Varna are displayed here; the bulk of the find remains in Varna in a local museum. The Panahjuriste gold

Preceding pages: interior of Sofia Cathedral.
Left, Sofia "grows but does not age".

treasure, however, is all here: nine solid-gold drinking vessels probably made in the Dardanelles in about the 4th century BC, which allows the possibility that they were in Philip II of Macedonia's baggage train when he passed through in a campaign against the Scythians.

After the museum, Lenin Square is probably the logical place from which to plan forays into the city. The south side of the square is taken up by the 19th-century **Sveta Nedelja Church**, built on top of a Roman praetorium. It was blown up by terrorists in 1925 during the funeral service for a general whom the same people had murdered the day before. The death toll was 125, and the result was the "white terror" in which the army pursued the Communists who were thought to be responsible. The church was rebuilt 10 years afterwards.

The **Church of St Peter of the Saddlers** nearby is an example of the Ottoman ruling which required new churches to be built at a lower level than mosques out of deference to Islam. Low as it is,

there is nevertheless a 12th-century necropolis below and beneath that an even older Roman structure.

The church crouching in the courtyard of the Balkan Sheraton Hotel is similarly layered. A 4th-century Roman temple on the site was destroyed by the Huns. The Byzantines replaced it with a church in honour of St George the Dragon-Slayer, the Turks later converted it into a mosque with a minaret, and in the late 19th century it became a church again – without, of course, the minaret. The 11th-century frescoes managed to survive these changes but not without some wear and tear which is now in the process of being repaired.

One of the few minarets that did survive modern independence is the one gracing what in 1879 was Mehmet Pasha's Great Mosque and is now the **National Archaeological Museum**. The underpass outside the mosque preserves parts of the wall which surrounded the fortress from the 2nd to the 14th centuries. The empty **mausoleum** near the mosque used to contain the em-

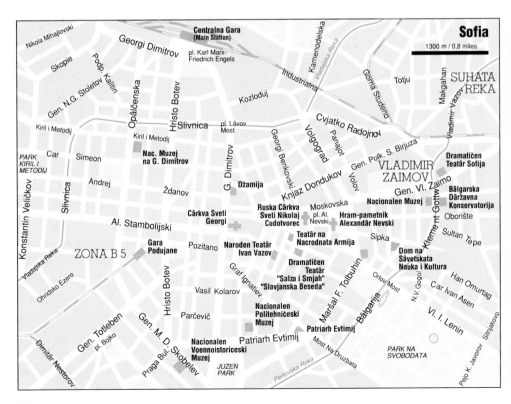

balmed body of Georgi Dimitrov, the founder of Communist Bulgaria. With the passing of the old regime, the body was removed and cremated. The future of the mausoleum has yet to be decided.

The present **National Art Gallery** nearby is the former Royal Palace. Questions about its royal past used to be met with stony stares, but this seems to be changing too.

Amid all this chopping and changing, it is curious that the **equestrian statue** in Ruski Boulevard has sailed through unmolested. It is of Tsar Alexander II (1818–81), and statues of recent tsars were lucky to survive anywhere in the Communist world. Alexander II's special dispensation in Bulgaria was because he committed huge numbers of Russian troops to the war of independence against the Turks, hence the **Monument to the Liberators** over which he now stands guard.

Visible from the Liberators' Monument is the **Alexander Nevsky Memorial Cathedral** (1904), named after the 13th-century hero of Novgorod in western Russia. He was not remotely connected with Bulgaria, but he was a personal hero of the idolised Tsar Alexander II, and any hero of his was good enough to be commemorated in Bulgaria. The cathedral is part-museum, part-gallery and part-concert hall. The throne it contains was ordered by Foxy Ferdinand but it seems he never sat on it. The pictures are mainly by East European artists, the singing often by members of the national opera.

The **St Sophia Church** across the square was built in the 6th century and even so is the third church on this particular site. The fate of the first is uncertain, but the second was destroyed by the Huns with just a mosaic to show for its existence. The Turks converted the present church into a mosque but then decided to leave well alone when an earthquake brought down the minaret. The eternal flame to the Unknown Soldier burns outside, and not far away is the grave of Vassil Levsky, probably the most famous of the rebels who took up cudgels against the Turks. He has

Vitosha Boulevard, Sofia.

also given his name to the vast sports stadium in nearby **Freedom Park**.

Behind the **Hali covered market** (a contrast with the Central Department Store, known as TsUM) is the synagogue built in 1909 when Bulgaria's Jewish population was about 50,000, the majority of whom lived in Sofia. There are the ruins of a 2nd-century synagogue at Oescus, the town near Gigen built by the Roman Emperor Trajan, so clearly the local Jewish roots run deep. Their numbers increased dramatically with the exodus from Spain in 1492. Under pressure from Hitler in 1943, the government served deportation orders on Jews, allowing them three days to reach the Danube ports. It is said that this was a deliberate ploy to foil the arrangements that would otherwise have sent them to extermination camps. The vast majority of Jews emigrated to Israel after the war, leaving the present population of about 5,000, of whom 3,000 live in Sofia.

The biggest attractions around Sofia are on and around **Mount Vitosa**, which can be reached by bus from the city centre. At the half-way point, in other words about 5 miles (8 km) from Sofia, where the city suburbs give way to country villas, is **Bojana**, the country retreat of medieval boyars. The ruined tower of **Maiden's Rock** (Momina Skala) marks what was once a fortified complex of houses, stables and kitchens.

A special point of interest is the **Bojana Church** with 13th-century frescoes by, and in some cases of, the artist Sebastocrator Kaloyan and his wife. There are 89 scenes in all, a marvellous evocation of Bulgarian feudal life. The originals are undergoing a lengthy restoration, but copies of the outstanding examples are on display.

The 14th-century **Dragalevski Monastery** is on a hill above a village of the same name and is linked by chairlift to the Aleko resort complex on Mount Vitosa, which is also accessible by a chairlift from Simeonovo (and of course by road). If Sofia were ever to realise its dream of holding the Winter Olympics, this is where the action would take place,

Sunny day in Sofia.

an indication of the quality of what is on offer. The ski centre is equipped to handle 35,000 skiers per day, so there is nothing half-hearted about it. The views alone would justify a trip to the numerous hotels and restaurants. In any case, the meals are good.

One of the most popular excursions from Sofia is – by road or rail – along the **Iskar River Gorge** north of the city. The river winds through the mountains and all the way on to the Danube; the scenery is magnificent and there are monasteries galore. One worthy alone claimed to have built 300 churches and 15 monasteries in the region. Two worth looking out for are the **Monastery of the Seven Altars** and the **Cherepishki Monastery**.

Sightseers travelling by train may wonder at the most un-Bulgarian name of **Thompson** given to one of the railway stations. He was a British Army major who was killed nearby while working with Bulgarian partisans against the Germans in 1944. The most spectacular part of the gorge is the stretch north of Kurilo with the so-called **Kutino Earth Pyramids** and, vertigo permitting, an opportunity to do some rock-climbing at Lakatnik. **Svoge** is a popular holiday resort.

Beyond the end of the gorge – probably too far for a day-trip but relevant to travellers going on to the Danube – are the **Magura caves** near the village of **Rabisha**, not far from Dimovo. The caves are among the deepest in the country (about 2 miles/3.5 km) and in addition to impressive stalactites and stalagmites there are Early Bronze Age paintings rendered in bat dung. The so-called Hall of the Roman Girl is named after the skeleton of a 1st century BC woman which was found surrounded by animal bones, suggesting that she met her end in some sacrificial ceremony.

The caves were opened to the public only in 1961 although their existence was certainly known to locals long before then. World War II partisans holed up in them and used the "Hall of Destruction" for weapons training. The humidity in the caves remains constant

Youth culture crosses all boundaries.

at 90 percent and is so beneficial to asthma sufferers that at one time beds were set up inside for them. They got in the way of 100,000 visitors per year filing through so the experiment was abandoned.

The Danube: In the extreme north-western corner of the country on the banks of the Danube is **Vidin**, where a ferry crosses to Romania (the only road crossing is at Ruse). The original settlement at Vidin had the Celtic name Dunonia before the Romans renamed it Bononia. Its strategic position made it an early target for the Huns as they came pouring across the Danube. It was attacked thereafter at regular intervals by – well, by everyone who ever approached the Danube with the slightest aggressive intent. The huge stone fortress, known as the Baba Vida Fortress and now a **museum**, was built by Khan Tervel in the 13th century.

Vidin's assigned role in the Communist Five-Year Plans was to manufacture synthetic fibres and motor-car tyres. Visitors are more likely to enjoy an

entirely different local product going back to Thracian times. It is full-bodied, has a good nose, and could pass as a glass of fairly decent claret. The label to ask for is "Gumza".

Bulgaria's stretch of the Danube, running east from Vidin is nearly 300 miles (470 km) long. Hydrofoils run regularly up and down the river and are the most practical way to see this famous northern boundary of the Roman Empire. The first place of real interest east of Vidin is an island at the mouth of the Iskar River where in Roman times a bridge spanned the Danube. The substantial remains are those of the Roman town of Ulpia Oescus. The magnificent mosaic recovered from the site is now in the Pleven museum.

Ruse is on the site of the Roman fortress of Sexaginta Prista, which later became a busy 17th-century port and is now Bulgaria's fourth largest city with a population of 190,000. The Friendship Bridge is the only road crossing between Bulgaria and Romania. It was built in 1955 but there has long been access to, and a love-hate relationship with, Giurgui on the other side. The Orient Express used to drop its passengers at Giurgui. They took a ferry across, took another train from Ruse to Varna, and then completed the journey to Istanbul by ship. All of this, and much more, is amply covered in the **National Transport Museum** in the city.

Fragments of the Roman ramparts are still visible. In medieval times, life on the river was considered so hazardous, that the entire town was moved inland to **Cherven**, the "city of bishops". The Turks razed Cherven and sent the inhabitants back to Ruse to work the port. They were a minority of 1,000 among 15,000 Turks who ruled here with a singularly light touch. Midhat Pasha, a 19th-century Ottoman governor, encouraged Turkish-Bulgarian bilingualism and nursed hopes of turning his city into a Balkan Vienna or Paris. He did remarkably well. The bourgeoisie invested in large houses and Ruse reverberated to the strains of Viennese music and opera. In his time Ruschuk, as the Ottomans called Rusa, was considerably

Melnik is famous for its wine.

larger than Sofia. It still has a relatively high proportion of ethnic Turks among the population.

Later development rather stressed political and military glory. Hence the **Freedom Monument** (1908), the **Monument to the Soviet Army** (1949) and a **Pantheon of Martyrs**. The local heroine is Baba Tonka ("Granny Tonka"), who sheltered anti-Turk revolutionaries in her house, now a museum.

The road from Ruse to **Silistra** completes the Bulgarian stretch of the Danube. Thereafter it is Romania on both banks. The road which follows the river is the obvious choice for bird-watchers, especially the nature reserve at **Sreburna** which Unesco has taken under its wing. The best months, at least for pelicans, are March to August, but there are hundreds of other species and points from which to observe them. Among the most popular attractions are goshawks, kestrels, owls, kingfishers, cranes and hoopoe.

The rival attractions on the inland route via Kubrat include the royal Thracian tomb at **Svestari** discovered in 1982. A covered corridor leads into a triple-chambered tomb, the vault above supported by 10 caryatids. The king in question lived in the 3rd century BC and probably ruled over the Getae. In any case, he was buried with his wife and five horses.

Three ancient capitals: Our general introduction to Bulgaria traced the arrival of the Bulgars from north of the Danube in 680 and the founding of the state with its capital at Pliska. The capital was at Preslav from 893 to 972, after which there was a hiatus during which Bulgaria was transplanted to Lake Ochrid in Macedonia. When the Bulgarians returned to their traditional land in 1185 the new capital was at Turnovo, where it remained until the Ottoman take-over at the end of the 14th century. All other things being equal, it would make sense to visit these in chronological order, using Sumen as a base for Pliska and Preslav and taking in the famous Horseman of Madara at the same time.

Pliska: The remains of the capital

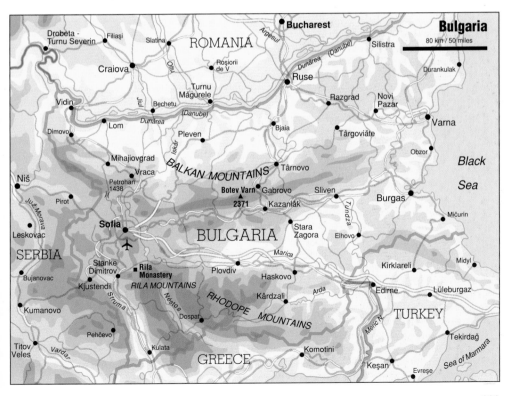

founded by Khan Asperuch are spread over several square miles. It is difficult to tell how the fragments once fitted together because the city was razed several times by the Byzantines, including the unhappy occasion, recounted previously, when the Bulgar babies were shoved through threshing machines.

It seems most likely that the surviving layout of the ruins corresponds with the reign of Omortag, son of the redoubtable Krum. He took advantage of a 30-year (815–845) peace with Byzantium, the terms of which are inscribed on one of the columns. The full extent of the capital seems to have covered some two miles by four (3 by 6 km), but within this area there was a citadel and at the heart of that a Great Hall and heathen temple. Omortag was wary of the influence of Christianity spreading north from Byzantium and any of his subjects suspected of harbouring Christian sympathies were forced to eat meat during Lent. His successor Boris, who is reputed to have become a Christian after seeing a Greek artist's interpretation of

what infidels could expect at the Last Judgement, turned the temple into a church, but that was only after victory over the anti-Christian mobs outside his palace.

The site museum is more concerned with the bric-a-brac of ordinary lives than royal finery. It seems the pre-Christian inhabitants were polygamous, wore turbans and trousers and, contrary to expectation says the historian Steven Runciman, "liked to wash themselves quite often". Their brand of paganism worshipped the sun, moon and stars and entailed the sacrifice of humans, horses and dogs. There was no moral code to speak of. Law enforcement amounted to the death penalty for almost everything, with only the most trifling offences qualifying for lenient mutilation.

Preslav: The ruins of Bulgaria's second capital are about 12 miles (20 km) southwest of Sumen. Modern Preslav has a population of 10,000 and is worth popping into at the right time of year to pick up a bunch of local grapes. Ancient Preslav was founded in 821 by Omortag, whom we met in Plioska, as a show of force for the benefit of the Byzantines. It became the capital in 893 in the reign of Symeon, a pious Christian whose education in Constantinople imbued him with a love of Aristotle and Demosthenes. His desire to make the works of his favourite Greeks available in the Slavonic language greatly accelerated the adoption of Cyrillic in Bulgaria.

Symeon radiated magnificence from his throne in the palace of the new capital. He is said to have worn "a garment studded with pearls, a chain of medals round his neck and bracelets on his wrists, girt with a purple girdle, and a golden sword by his side". No one had seen a city like it. John the Exarch described the sensation that overcame the visitor: "The sight of heaven adorned with stars, sun and moon, earth with the grass and trees, and the fishes of the sea of all sorts, come upon him, and his mind is lost. He comes back despising his own home and wishes to build himself as high as heaven."

Alas, little remains of the city which Symeon hoped would eclipse Constan- **A bike built to last.**

tinople. The Turks used it as a quarry; the Tombul mosque in Sumen, it seems, was built with materials removed from Preslav. Some restoration has been done on the walls and palace. The most complete building is Symeon's round church with a gilded cupola and interior mosaics – enough to give an impression of Symeon's architectural leanings.

Horseman of Madara: The "Horseman of Madara" on the main road east of Sumen is a copy of the original a few miles away at the village of Madara. The artist who chiselled this extraordinary work high in the cliff above the village – so high that even from the viewing platform it is best appreciated through binoculars – was possibly an Armenian. The horseman, accompanied by his dog and caught in the act of spearing a lion, is Khan Tervel, whom we have already briefly met. The work was commissioned by Omortag.

The warren of cells in the cliff-face was once part of a monastery. They are reached by a long flight of stairs, and there are paths along the top leading to a medieval rock chapel and the remains of a fortress and royal palace. The views from the top alone make the arduous climb worthwhile. If, as is thought, the origins of the fortress are 5th century, it precedes the Bulgars, although they took it over and it was improved over the centuries until finally put out of commission by the Turks.

Finds from the cells, and from the Great and Small Caves, are on exhibit in the Madara museum. The remains of Roman villas are to be found near the fortress and just outside the village.

Sumen, central for trips to Pliska and Preslav, is mainly an industrial town now but can remember the days when the local theatre staged the first performances of plays regarded as milestones in Bulgaria's post-Ottoman National Revival. These plays unfortunately have not travelled far from their native shores, their chances of commercial success abroad possibly handicapped by titles which at least in translation do not arrest: "An Unhappy Family", for example, or the even more

Splendid monasteries can be found around Veliko Turnovo.

thoughtful "Civilisation Misunderstood". The local intelligentsia are invariably at the bar in the Hotel Madara, so that is the place to seek enlightenment on such matters.

The Tombol mosque is the finest in Bulgaria, built in 1745 by Sharif Pasha. The town also has ethnographical and regional history museums and a Turkish quarter. A tiny footnote: the house at 35 Tsar Osvoboditel Street was a temporary refuge for the Hungarian Lajos Kossuth en route to Turkey after the defeat of his nationalist uprising in 1848.

Veliko Turnovo is Bulgaria's cultural jewel. The Yantra River doubles back on itself four times as it winds through the city, and the salients thus created each have a character and a history of their own. Evidence has been recovered of occupation from Neolithic times. The Romans manned a fortress on one of the hills, and the Byzantines built another in the quarter known as Tsarevets.

Among the ruins of the royal palace and lesser imitations built by the boyars in the Tsarevets salient in Turnovo is the tower in which Baldwin, the crusader who hijacked Constaninople, was imprisoned and died. The Church of Saint Dimitur is on the spot where the brothers Peter and Asen proclaimed Bulgarian independence from Byzantium before being chased across the Danube.

The Church of the Forty Martyrs, built by Ivan Asen II in the 13th century, incorporates a pillar with Omortag's inscription when he founded Turnovo. It reads: "The Sublime Khan Omortag is divine ruler in the land where he was born. Dwelling in the camp of Pliska, he made a palace on the Tutsa and increased his power against the Greeks and the Slavs... May God grant the divine ruler that he press down with his foot the Emperor so long as the Tutsa flows and the enemies of the Bulgars are controlled; and may he subdue his foes and live in joy and happiness for a hundred years."

The third notable church with well-preserved 14th-century frescoes is **Saints Peter and Paul**. The demolition

Veliko Turnovo.

of an outer wall in the 17th century during alterations exposed the secret library of Patriarch Euthymius, who had hidden it away from the Moslems. It was destroyed not by them but by Greek Orthodox bishops.

The city's **Varusa** quarter was built by the Ottomans after their conquest and later was an important centre of the National Revival after the Turks left. A prominent Revival architect was Nikola Ficev, responsible for the Konak which houses the **Bulgarian State Museum**. It was in this building in 1879 that the Constituent Assembly elected Alexander "Sandro" Battenberg Prince of Bulgaria and in which his successor Ferdinand took his oath in 1887.

The area around Turnovo has many monasteries. The story behind the name of the **Monastery of the Virgin of the Prisoners**, is of an unhappy Empress Theodora who was ushered in and compelled to take vows when her husband, Tsar Ivan Alexander, wished to marry a Jewish girl named Sarah.

There are three hotels in "new"

Turnovo and a number of restaurants. Most of the room at the Veliko Turnovo and the Yantra have superb views.

Valley of Roses: The famous Valley of Roses is on the main Sofia-Burgas road between Klisura and Kazanlak, but there is a lot to be said for combining the valley with a trip to Turnovo. The road running south from Turnovo to Kazanlak through Gabrovo is both scenic and interesting. The **Drjanovo Monastery** is in an area famous for its vineyards and silk industry. It was the scene of a pitched battle in the 1876 uprising between rebels under the command of a monk, one Hariton, and a larger force of Turkish troops sent up from Sumen. The monastery was gutted in nine days of fighting but has since been restored.

The pretty village of **Bozenci**, often overcrowded with visitors who have come to see its collection of National Revival houses, is said to have been founded by a boyar's widow after the fall of Turnovo to the Turks. Of the several flocks of sheep she had roaming around, one in particular always came

The museum village of Etar, 9 km from Gabrovo.

back looking remarkably well-fed. In following them to discover their secret, she came upon these fertile pastures and decided it was just the place to build a new house for herself and one for each of her sons.

While the living in Bozenci is supposedly easy, it could be a trial in **Gabrovo** because Gabrovians, one and all, are expected to be funny all the time. There are millions of Gabrovian jokes, although most seem to suffer terminal damage in translation. Such is the pressure on Gabrovians to be permanently amusing that in 1972 they opened a House of Humour which contains more than 110,000 objects which are intrinsically humorous, although by what criterion visitors must judge for themselves. An International Festival of Humour originally held every fourth year proved so popular that it is now held annually.

Between Gabrovo and the beginning of the Valley of Roses is the **Sipka Pass**. This is to Bulgarians and even to many Russians what Thermopylae means to Greeks. The fight for control of this pass in the Russo-Turkish war cost tens of thousands of lives commemorated by an imposing monument and a church by the same architect who did the Alexander Nevsky Church in Sofia. The church bells were cast from the bullets collected from the battlefield.

While the Sipka Pass controls movement north and south, the **Valley of the Roses** runs laterally. If its famous product, attar of roses, seems scandalously expensive, the defence offered is that it takes 2,000 petals to make a gram or, put another way, something like 5 cwt (5,000 kg) of petals to make two pints (just over one litre). The harvesting is done in May or early June, but only until 8am. because the petals lose half their oil when the sun is any higher. The industry was started by the Turks in the 1830s and with 70 percent of production going abroad is now an important export-earner. **Kazanlak** has a Museum of Rose Production and also a Bulgarian Rose factory which makes use of the side-products of the attar process to make liqueurs, rose-water, jams and a kind of Turkish delight. An annual Rose Festival is held in the first week of June.

The Black Sea: International flights to Bulgaria's Black Sea coast land at either Varna or Burgas. Varna is a considerable attraction in its own right and, with boat and hydrofoil services to all points along the coast, is an ideal base for exploring the coast. **Burgas**, on the other hand, is a busy port and industrial centre and is unlikely to detain tourists. Its Thracian and Macedonian past is so far buried that even the Museum of Archaeology looks distinctly light on exhibits. The city could possibly make something of its version of Alcatraz, a converted monastery on Bolshevik Island in Burgas Bay, but getting to the island is still almost as difficult as leaving it would have been in the past when it was a notorious prison.

Varna, now Bulgaria's third city (population: 300,000), was a thriving port in Thracian times, 3,000 years ago. The Greeks turned it into the city of Odessos in 585 BC and the Romans built on that. A chance discovery uncovered by excavations for a new canal

Village life in the Pirin Mountains.

in 1972, however, pushed the clock back even farther to 4000 BC in the form of a Chalcolithic necropolis of inestimable archaeological importance.

A new **Museum of Art and History** was opened to house these finds and others from the region. The collection fills 40 halls and cannot be done justice here. One would have to go to Colombia or Peru to find anything comparable in the way of gold death-masks and exquisite jewellery from the necropolis in question. A visit to this museum could easily occupy a whole day – but not Monday when it is closed as are most museums in the country. If Varna is not on the itinerary, there is some consolation to be had from representative samples of the necropolis treasures in the museum in Sofia.

The discovery of the necropolis came shortly after another exciting find, the 2nd-century Roman baths in **Khan Droum Street**. The grand scale rivals the best baths in Rome and leaves no doubt about the importance of Odessos as then was. The area around the baths is one of Varna's most picturesque, with the church of St Anthanasius hovering on a precipice above an old street restored and sympathetically brought up to date with restaurants, bars, etc.

Varna is the rare place in Bulgaria that continued to prosper and expand through Ottoman rule. It was, as it had been from ancient times, a key staging-post for trade between the Black Sea and central and western Europe. There is a fascinating Naval Museum near the popular Aquarium *cum* "Dolphinarium" in the Marine Gardens.

The city is a lively cultural centre, too, with the baroque **Buchvarov National Theatre**, a **National Art Gallery**, a summer international music festival and, every two years, an interntional ballet competition.

About 10 miles (16 km) from Varna on the road to Sofia is the strange "**Stone Forest**" (Pobiti Kamuni) which puzzled a British naval officer when he came across it during the Crimean War. Stone pillars up to 20 ft (6 metres) high and half as thick are, it transpired, marine stalagmites formed during the time this area was the bottom of the Lutsin Sea.

North of Varna: The pair of resorts just a few miles north of Varna are a contrast. **Golden Sands** (the signs read "Zlatni Pyasutsi") is a mammoth complex built since 1956: almost 100 hotels, numerous restaurants (which usually accept hotel meal vouchers), water sports, tennis, riding, nightclubs, discos, a "gypsy camp" and so on. If this sounds intimidating, younger visitors seem to enjoy the challenge.

Druzba, nearby, is more sedate, and in the Swedish-built Grand Varna Hotel has probably the best accommodation on the coast. It is a wooded area with sandy coves, a particularly good restaurant in a converted monastery (Manastirska Izba) and natural mineral water said to be good for rheumatism.

Albena with its 4 miles (7 km) of beaches was a late 1960s attempt to bring the "National Revival" style of the 18th and 19th centuries up to date. The result was dozens of hotels resembling futuristic pyramids. The effect is not disagreeable, and the recreational

Bulgaria's resorts are booming.

facilities are almost as comprehensive as those at Golden Sands. After a game of volleyball, it is worth looking for a small road marked "Skalen Manastir" because at the end is an establishment with connections which caused Edward Gibbon, of Roman Empire fame, to splutter one of his celebrated epigrams.

The **Alaja Monastery** with cells carved out of a cliff-face was home to the Bulgarian followers of Gregory of Sinai. The creed was Hesychasm, and its principles can be summed up in the words of a certain Simeon: "When thou art alone in thy cell, shut thy door and seat thyself in a corner. Turn thine eyes and thy thought towards the middle of thy belly, to the region of the navel. At first, all will be comfortless and dark, but persevering by day and night thou wilt feel ineffable joy, and no sooner will the soul discover the place of the heart, than it shall be involved in mystic and ethereal light." This, then, is the origin of navel contemplation. "The production of a distempered fancy," said Gibbon, "the creature of an empty stomach and an empty brain." The chapel is locked, but the cells are accessible.

Another religious curiosity nearby is the Arat Tekke at **Obrochishte**. A "tekke" is a monastery with a difference: Moslem, not Christian, and home specifically to Whirling Dervishes, a sect as energetic as the Hesychasts were immobile. An 18th-century visitor found 26 dervishes resident here. He reported that they had given up whirling in favour of making walking-sticks for sale to passing pilgrims.

Balchik is different yet again. In Greek times it was called Dionysopolis and devoted to orgiastic feasting. When it was destroyed by a tidal wave in 544, the indefatigable residents rebuilt the town high above sea level. As there was no repetition of the tidal wave, the town gradually worked its way down to sea level again. This region was in Romania until World War II and a fashionable resort whose tone was set by the Romanian royal family. King Carol I's eccentric queen, who wrote fanciful stories under the name Carmen Sylva, used to roam around waving her handkerchief at cows. The next queen, the former Princess Marie of Edinburgh, was especially fond of the royal villa. Today it is a rest home for retired members of the Union of Bulgarian Writers, Composers and Poets but the gardens are open to the public.

South of Varna: The coast immediately south of Varna is picturesque and relatively undeveloped until one reaches **Sunny Beach** (Slancev Brjag), a resort area which in the days of the Soviet Union was the last word in exotic excitement for Polish and Russian trade unionists but may have less impact on more widely travelled visitors.

Nesebar, a short distance away, is another proposition altogether. Situated on a peninsula and reached by a causeway, it is the kind of place that gets cameras clicking away. To complete the contrast with the large resorts, accommodation is available in private houses authentically restored by conscientious owners. Nesebar was a Thracian settlement in the 6th century BC: the ramparts visible from the cause-

The purpose-built Sunny Beach resort.

way are later – 4th century BC. Both Greeks and Romans went to town on temples here.

The town has associations with several of the colourful characters who crop up in Bulgarian history. It seems likely that the Emperor Constantine IV came here to cure his sore feet, or gout, after failing to drive the early Bulgars across the Danube. A grave found in 1947 is thought possibly to be his. The volatile Khan Krum was here in 812 to remove Nesebar from Byzantium and incorporate it into his empire.

The coast south of Burgas has caught the imagination of foreign writers and artists who now form small colonies in unspoilt ports like **Sozopol**, built on a cape like Nesebar. It was founded at about the same time as Nesebar by Greeks who naively picked a fight with Rome. As a result they lost their statue of Apollo, which was carried off to the Capitol in Rome where it remains.

There are plenty of campsites and private lodging between here and the Turkish border but, as yet, few hotels.

The construction of another large resort area just south of Sozopol is slightly worrying, although in fairness it must be said that Bulgaria has managed to put a lot of beds along the Black Sea already with a minimum of unsightly obtrusion.

Thracian Plain – the South: The fact that in 341 BC Philip II of Macedonia chose to rename a Thracian town called Pulpudeva after himself (Philippopolis) is a clue to the military importance of a route which followed the Marista River on to the Thracian Plain. The Romans in turn strengthened the garrison, which they called Trimontium, and built a road which at present is being converted into the A1 motorway from Sofia to Turkey. The Crusaders and others used this route on their way to the richest prize in the world, Constantinople, but of course the Ottoman Turks saw the situation in reverse. To them it was the road to the conquest of Europe: Sofia, Belgrade, Vienna; ultimately, Rome itself. In 1877, **Plovdiv**, to give this old garrison town its present name, was the scene of some of the worst "Bulgarian Atrocities".

Sozopol.

Plovdiv is a modern industrial centre and Bulgaria's second city. The **National Archaeological Museum** in Ploshtad Suedienenie is the best introduction to its action-packed past. The Panagjuriste treasure (Sofia has the originals, these are copies) consists of nine marvellously ornamented drinking vessels made out of solid gold. They are thought to have been made at Lampsacus in the Dardanelles in Philip of Macedonia's time or thereabouts. The Roman poet Lucian made reference to "the most splendid, the largest and fairest town, whose beauty shines from afar". There are many Roman sites, but none quite as evocative of the city in Lucian's time as a superb amphitheatre uncovered by a freak landslide in 1972. It is now used for operatic and theatrical productions.

The streets below the amphitheatre are strongly representative of "National Revival" architecture associated with the rise of the independence movement in the 19th century. The **National Ethnographic Museum** building is a clear example of what came to be known as

the Plovdiv style. Another, the **Balabanov House** at 57 Matanov Street, is furnished in the style of the period. The bride of the Armenian merchant who built the house was tragically killed on their wedding night when a chandelier collapsed on to the nuptial bed.

While the main road out of Plovdiv continues across the Thracian Plain to Turkey, another goes south into the Rhodope Mountains. This route is outstandingly beautiful as the road burrows along the Cepelarska River gorge. The **Asenov** fortress perched precariously above the road was the scene of Asen II's triumph over the Byzantine army.

A short distance beyond is the **Bachkovo Monastery** founded in 1083. It was first under the direct authority of the Patriarch of Jerusalem before passing to a succession of Georgian abbots who until the 17th century would not allow Greek monks on the premises. During the course of repeated destruction and reconstruction, the monastery acquired a curious roll-call of saints and heroes on its walls. In spite of the strong anti-Greek tradition, Aristotle, Socrates and even the comedian Aristophanes have been given places.

Farther into the mountains is **Smolyan** with a chairlift to the **Pamporovo** ski resort, a going concern for the past 50 years. West of the Rhodopes is Bulgaria's most famous mountain resort, **Borovec**, much loved and largely developed by Tsar Ferdinand. He built three palaces and a hunting lodge, the last reached by the Yastrebets chairlift.

A little further south is the **Rila Monastery**, the most famous in the land not least because it served as a repository of Bulgarian intellectual life and culture during the Ottoman centuries. The original building was a hermitage a couple of miles from the present site, now marked by the small church of St Luke containing the tomb of the founder, Ivan of Rila. The main monastery complex was repeatedly destroyed by war, avalanche and fire, and most of the present buildings were put up after a fire in 1833, the most notable exception being a tower built by Hrelju, a feudal overlord, in the 14th century.

Left, Sozopol. **Right**, folk dancers.

TRAVEL TIPS

GETTING THERE

GENERAL INFORMATION

Like the political and economic scene generally, the rules of travel in Eastern Europe have been in a state of flux, not to say turmoil, since the collapse of the old Communist order. Tourism used to be part of the centralised-command economy, the same masterplan which told the regional components just what they had to contribute to the Soviet imperial kitty. While one was required to keep all 15 Soviet republics and the "independent" Communist countries of Eastern Europe in tractor tyres, another applied its undivided attention to the manufacture of, say, light-bulbs.

In the matter of tourism, Moscow and Leningrad (as it then was) were supposed to supply foreign tourists with as much as they really needed to see of Russia, while Bulgaria's Black Sea beaches provided summer holidays for millions of Soviet trade unionists plus any foreigners who cared to rub shoulders with them. Foreigners did as they were told: they arrived, stayed, saw the sights and went home in supervised groups. The rare independent traveller who presumed to ask a policeman for street directions was likely to be met with a look of incredulity and the blunt question: "Where is your group?"

In the old days, travel within the Soviet Union (for the purposes of this book, Russia, Ukraine, Belarus, and the three Baltic States) was the monopoly of Intourist – a travel agency, transport company and hotel chain combined – and to some extent of Aeroflot, the Soviet airline. The satellite states – Poland, Czech, Hungary, Romania and Bulgaria – had their own scaled-down versions of Intourist, known as Orbis, Cedok, Ibusz, ONT and Balkantourist respectively, as well as their own national airlines.

One of the marked features of the new order is that Intourist has been broken up and, so to speak, privatised. The rump of Intourist remains as a specifically Russian agency, but it now has various semi-independent branches catering for independent travellers, special interest activities and so on. Most of the hotels in Russia remain under at least indirect Intourist ownership or management, but the different branches of Intourist (under various names) are not obliged to keep all business within the former family or to book all flights with what's left of Aeroflot. In short, the operation has been decentralised and thrown open.

In the meantime, Ukraine, Belarus and the Baltic States (Estonia, Latvia and Lithuania) have established their own state tourist agencies, together with their own airlines and, for that matter, their own currencies. The tourist agencies are roughly the equivalent of official tourist bureaux in the West and operate alongside, if not actually in competition with, the private sector. Unsurprisingly, both the state agencies and the private sectors are still feeling their way, some more successfully than others.

Representation abroad is decidedly skimpy; three years after the Berlin Wall came down, the newly-independent states were still struggling embassies and consulates in major foreign capitals.

The main implications of decentralised tourism industries in Eastern Europe are paradoxical. On the one hand, the scope for independent travel is very much greater. It would have been inconceivable in the old days to demonstrate one's dissatisfaction with a hotel by checking out and finding another. While large chunks of territory may previously have been out-of-bounds to tourists for supposedly dark security reasons, it was often the case that the bureaucrats had simply decided by their own mysterious criteria that the areas in question were of insufficient interest or too much bother. Tourists can now generally make up their own minds.

The paradox is that, having made up their own minds, tourists may find that the old state apparatus for shuffling them around is still relatively the most efficient, more so than private operators waiting for a telephone to be installed. In other words, there is a lot to be said for arriving and being processed through airport formalities as a member of a group. With hotel accommodation in acutely short supply in some areas, a group booking may be not merely convenient but essential.

The silver lining, we suggest, is a compromise: exploit group travel for all it's worth, which includes competitive rates, and then exercise the liberty to break away from the group and pursue independent interests as one feels so inclined.

The classified information which follows is as up-to-date as the practicalities of our production deadlines permit. That is to say, unfortunately, that some of it will inevitably be out-of-date before the proverbial ink is dry. Things are changing so fast throughout Eastern Europe – just think of disgraced leaders' statues being carted away and the renaming of cities, let alone streets – that nothing short of an hourly radio bulletin could realistically aspire to keep abreast of events.

That, we dare to say, is the best reason for going, but it does but a premium on a traveller's initiative. The visitor's best friend, in the circumstances, is the specialised travel agent in constant touch with the state of flux or turmoil, as the case may be.

BY AIR

The former Soviet Union operated the airport "hub" principle long before it was adopted in the West. International flights landed in Moscow and, after due immigration and customs procedures, passengers flew on from there. No-one flew from abroad direct to Kiev in Ukraine or the Baltic capitals although, in common with the general rules of tourism behind the Iron Curtain, there were a limited number of direct flights to satellite states such as Poland and Czechoslovakia.

All this has changed. The independent states are now serviced directly from neighbouring Western states, in most cases by their own brand-new airline as well as foreign carriers. In the course of time, it should be possible to fly direct from, say, Alaska to Russia's Pacific coast without the 10,000-mile detour via Moscow. Helsinki is emerging as a popular gateway to the Baltic States, Frankfurt and Vienna to Belarus and Ukraine. Plans are in hand for airlines to expand their East European networks from London, Paris, Amsterdam and other major terminals for transatlantic flights. Dates and other details are yet to be announced: specialised travel agents will be among the first to hear.

BY ROAD

Much the same rules used to apply to visitors arriving by road. It was a question of gaining the Soviet Union by one or other of the very few recognised border crossings, like Brest, on the Polish-Belarussian frontier, and driving along an approved route to Moscow in order to pick up another approved route going somewhere else.

The independent states are now free to admit visitors across their borders wherever they like, which has meant that even some minor roads now have passable border posts instead of barbed wire and minefields. The potential snag is that not all border posts are authorised to issue visas on the spot and, if they are, the cost may be exorbitant. The golden rule is to have visas in advance for all countries one proposes to enter, if only in transit.

SPECIALIST AGENCIES

The search for the right specialised travel agent may be more complicated than a flip through the local Yellow Pages. Household names like American Express and Thomas Cook will have East European experts buried somewhere in their bureaucracy, but they obviously have a vested interest in selling their own tours and, if there is a conflict of interest, can hardly be expected to recommend rivals. The same applies to Intourist, ORBIS, CEDOK etc.

We provide below a list of the some of the agents who specialise at least in part in East European travel. It is as well to remember that there are two kinds of agents. One represents the buyer, in other words the prospective traveller, and if any good will find the other kind of agent who has put together and is selling a package involving flights, hotels and so on. They have ways of splitting the commission, so don't feel inhibited about asking an agent to do the legwork on your behalf.

Readers doing their own legwork ought to be aware that airlines opening up new destinations in Eastern Europe will very likely be putting together deals with specialist operators, so the airline may be the place to start looking for interesting packages. Virgin, the British airline normally associated with the Atlantic run, not only operates to Crimea in Ukraine but has turned a previously sloppy socialist hotel into a showpiece.

UNITED STATES

NEW YORK

Uniontours. Tel: 212-683 9500; fax: 212-683 9511.
General Tours. Tel: 212-685 1800; fax: 212-685 2011.
Russian Travel Bureau. Tel: 212-986 1500; fax: 212-490 1650.
American Travel Abroad. Tel: 212-586 5250; fax: 212-581 7925.
Globus-Gateway Cosmos, Rego Park. Tel: 718-268 7000; fax: 718-520 1735.
ORBIS (Poland), 342 Madison Avenue, NYC 10173. Tel: 212-867 5011; fax: 212-682 4715.
CEDOK (Czech), 10 E 40th Street, NYC 10016. Tel: 212-689 9720.
IBUSZ (Hungary), 1 Parker Plaza, Fort Lee, New Jersey 07024.
ONT (Romania), 573 3rd Avenue, NYC 10016. Tel: 212-697 6971.
Balkantour (Bulgaria), 161 E 86th Street, NYC 10028. Tel: 212-722 1110; fax: 212-996 3316.
Intourist (Russia), 630 5th Avenue.

GEORGIA

American Express, Norcross, GA. Tel: 404-368 5202; fax: 404-368 5391.

ILLINOIS

Vega International Travel, Chicago. Tel: 312-332 7211; fax: 312-332 3811.

MASSACHUSSETS

Globetrotters, Cambridge. Tel: 617-621 9911; fax: 617-577 8480.

OHIO

Shipka Travel Agency, Cleveland. Tel: 216-351 1700; fax: 216-351 0610.

TEXAS

ITS Tours & Travel, College Station. Tel: 409-764 9400; fax: 409-693 9673.

WASHINGTON DC

Academic Travel Abroad. Tel: 202-333 3355; fax: 202-342 0317.

WASHINGTON

Eastern Europe Tours, Seattle. Tel: 206-448 8400; fax: 206-728 0836.

UNITED KINGDOM

Barry Martin Travel, Linen Hall, 162 Regent Street, London W1R 5TB. Tel: 071-439 1271. Specialists in business travel, exhibitions, etc.
Independent Travel Dept, Intourist Travel Ltd, 219 Marsh Wall, London E14. Tel: 071-538 5965.
Russkies, 236 Psalter Lane, Sheffield S11 8UT. Tel: 0742-583591.
Exodus Adventures. Tel: 081-675 5550.
Explore Worldwide. Tel: 0252 319448.
Goodwill Holidays. Tel: 0438 716421.
ORBIS (Poland), 82 Mortimer Street, London W1N 7DE. Tel: 071-636 8204.
CEDOK (Czech), 17 Old Bond Street, London W1X 4RB. Tel: 071-629 6058.
Danube Travel Agency (Hungary), 6 Conduit Street, London W1. Tel: 071-493 0263.
ONT (Romania), 17 Nottingham Street, London W1M 3RD. Tel: 071-224 3692.
Balkantour (Bulgaria), 18 Princes Street, London W1R 7RE. Tel: 071-499 6988.

GETTING TO RUSSIA

BY AIR

Moscow's Shermetyevo-2 Airport is still the first port of call for air travellers to Russia whether they fly Aeroflot, scheduled Western airlines or on special charters. Foreign operators used to be subject to bi-lateral (albeit insane) arrangements with Aeroflot, but tentative moves towards an "open sky" policy have introduced all sorts of lightly disguised discounting. These do not affect package tourists, who ought to be getting a pretty good deal anyway, but independent travellers can seek advantages by flying dog-legs. Instead of flying direct from, say, London to Moscow, it may be possible to make a substantial saving by flying from London to Warsaw on LOT, the Polish airline, and connecting with a second Lot flight to Moscow. Alternatively, it may be on Finnair via Helsinki, Austrian Airlines via Vienna and so on. American travellers may have to get themselves to Europe first to take advantage of these possibilities.

Bucket shops (cut-price travel agencies) have applied their customary ingenuity to Russian travel, but doing business with bucket shops carries a customary warning. Those who have fixed addresses and have been in business for some years are probably semi-secret conduits for an airline's surplus tickets and can be trusted. Those who operate from post office box numbers and ask for money upfront should be avoided.

The principle that rules the discount ticket industry is that national airlines are reluctant to sell discounted tickets to their own nationals who would quite likely fly with them anyway and pay the normal price. The prospect of seducing passengers from outside their normal catchment area makes them inclined to deal. They will fly these passengers in and out on the dog-leg for less than the advertised price of the second leg alone. Russia has now been drawn into this system, so independent travellers may plan their strategy accordingly.

BY SEA

The practical sea routes to Russia are crossings from Scandinavia to St Petersburg or to the Baltic ports for onward land travel from there. It is also possible to enter Russia via the Black Sea, in which case it is technically possible to reach Russia by sailing east across the Mediterranean. The only sailing most visitors would contemplate in Russian waters would be cruise ships, and that is another matter.

BY RAIL

It is still possible to stroll into London's Victoria Station and by a ticket to Moscow or for that matter Vladivostok, but these days it would be sheer masochism except for rail enthusiastics, and they would not need any of the information we could provide here. By all means sample rail travel in Russia – especially Moscow-St Petersburg – or even between Russia and neighbouring countries, but first get roughly where you want to go by air.

BY ROAD

The question of driving to Russia is covered by the general notes above on driving in Eastern Europe.

UKRAINE

BY AIR

Any competent travel agent should be up-to-date on scheduled flights directly into Kiev. Lufthansa were quick off the mark with flights from Frankfurt and Vienna, and Ukraine is setting up its own national airline using aircraft inherited from Aeroflot. Virgin Airlines pulled off a major scoop with its concession to fly parties in from Britain to the Crimea and its "own" hotel in Yalta.

BELARUS

BY AIR

Lufthansa was again first off the mark with flights into Minsk from Frankfurt and Vienna. For historic and geographical reasons, flights from Poland and the Baltic region ought to follow soon.

BY RAIL

In addition to the traditional rail connections with Russia, there is now overnight train from the Tallinn in Estonia.

ESTONIA

BY AIR

Lufthansa, Finnair and SAS operate in and out of Tallinn together with Estonia's fledgling Estonian Air. The direct foreign connections are with Helsinki, Stockholm, Copenhagen and Frankfurt. The most frequent of these are with Helsinki, just a 30-minute flight away. Discounts are available.

BY SEA

Tallinn port has come alive with passenger services across the Baltic, with services to Helsinki as frequent as some urban bus routes. Several hydrofoils belt across in about 90 minutes. The conventional ships (with cabins, bars, restaurants etc) take between three and four hours depending on sea conditions. Passengers from Stockholm may be able to save money by sailing to Helsinki and switching to one of the regular ferries than going direct.

Estonian New Line: in Tallinn, tel: 428 382; in Helsinki, tel: 90-680 2499
Estline: in Stockholm, tel: 08-667 0001; in Tallinn, tel: 666-579 or 443 524
Helta: in Helsinki, tel: 90-664 141; in Tallinn, tel: 428 701
Tallink: in Helsinki, tel: 90-602 822; in Tallinn, tel: 442 440.

BY ROAD

Long queues at Estonia's frontier posts with Latvia; the Russian border at Narva is not as busy.

Weekly coach from Warsaw via Riga.

Daily bus service to Riga and St Petersburg, and a painful overnight service to Vilnius.

BY RAIL

Overnight trains to Riga, Minsk, Moscow and twice daily to St Petersburg.

LATVIA

BY AIR

SAS flies direct to Riga from Helsinki, Stockholm and Copenhagen, the most convenient but also the most expensive flights. Lufthansa, Hamburg Airlines and Baltic International Airlines have regular flights from Frankfurt, Dusseldorf, Hamburg and Munich. CSA (Czech Airlines) flies direct to Prague. Homegrown Latvian Airlines went into business with services to Stockholm, Copenhagen, Helsinki, Frankfurt, Dusseldorf and Vienna. Finnair flies from Helsinki.

BY SEA

Regular ferry services between Riga and both Stockholm and Norkopping. Information from Riga passengers terminal, tel: 0132-329 514.

BY ROAD

For anyone driving from the West, the main problem lies outside Latvian territory at the Lazkijai crossing from Poland into Lithuania, where it is a question of coughing up a bribe or being stuck possibly for days. This problem is avoided by entering either Estonia or Lithuania by ferry, because formalities within the three Baltic states are comparatively relaxed, which is not to say that there won't be a long wait there as well.

A "luxury" thrice-weekly bus service has been inaugurated between Helsinki and Warsaw which stops in Riga.

BY RAIL

The busy Berlin-St Petersburg line is via Riga. Latvia visas available at the border for $20 (but check this, because such matters are fickle).

LITHUANIA

BY AIR

Lithuania quickly established direct flights to major European cities on gaining independence, and the list is likely to grow. The first were: Berlin, Budapest, Copenhagen, Frankfurt, Hamburg, London, Vienna, Warsaw, and Zurich with Paris and Amsterdam in the pipeline. The old connections were maintained through frequent flights to Moscow, Kiev and St Petersburg.

Lithuania's own airline is known as Lietuvos Avialinijos and is found at 12 Ukmerges Str, Vilnius, tel: 75-25-88 or 75-32-12.

The following airlines now fly into Lithuania: Austrian, SAS, Swissair, Estonian, Hamburg, LOT (Polish), Lufthansa and Malev (Hungarian).

BY SEA

A weekly ferry runs between the Lithuanian port of Klaipeda and Kiel in Germany. The voyage takes 30 hours and should be booked well in advance; for westerners, it cuts out the drive across Poland. A second ferry plying between Klaipeda and Mukran has very limited passenger accommodation.

Information from: Schnieder Reisen, Harkortstr. 121, 2000 Hamburg 50, tel: 4940-38 02 06 71. In Klaipeda, tel: 261-57 849 or fax: 261-53466.

BY RAIL

The main rail link between Vilnius and Warsaw still goes through Belarus, which means foreigners need a transit visa. The "historic" link, which uses the narrower European gauge rather than the Soviet, has been opened up between Sestokai in Lithuania and Suwalki in Poland.

BY ROAD

Daily coaches do the circuit around Warsaw, Gdansk, Bialystok (and/or Riga and Tallinn) and Vilnius.

POLAND

BY AIR

A new terminal was added to Warsaw's Okecie International Airport in 1992 to handle the increasing number of flights both by LOT, the Polish national airline, and international carriers. With the large Polish-American population, it is not surprising that travel from the United States is straightforward. Indeed, there are regular direct non-stop flights to Warsaw from New York and Chicago, and services from other cities may be laid on, if less frequently, in due course. Domestic flights link Warsaw to at least 11 cities and towns within the country. Virtually all the major European carriers fly to Warsaw from their home bases.

BY SEA

Ferries cross throughout the year to Swinoujscie and Gdansk in Poland from Scandinavian ports, and the Polish Ocean Line runs an trans-Atlantic crossing from Montreal and New York via Southampton and Copenhagen.

BY RAIL

The main international rail services into Poland are via Vienna and Berlin. The "East Pass" which is valid in Poland as well as neighbouring countries cannot be bought within Poland. American travellers should buy one before leaving home. Information from Rail Europe on 1-800-345-1990. Warsaw has several stations, and some "through tickets" may not make it absolutely clear that a switch from one to another is required.

It is possible to take a train to Poland from the Hook of Holland and Ostend (both with cross-Channel connections with Britain) as well as Paris, Cologne, Frankfurt and Basle. The London connection for the Hook-Warszawa Express begins at Liverpool Street station and goes via the Harwich-Hook of Holland ferry. The journey from Liverpool Street would start at about 0900 and arrive in Warsaw (in summer) at 15:40 the following day.

The service from Ostend in known as the Ost-West Express (connecting with the cross-Channel ferry from London-Victoria); the service from Cologne is named after it ultimate destination, the St Petersburg Express.

BY CAR

The main European routes across Poland are the E12 from Germany through Prague to Wroclaw, Lodz, Warsaw and Bioalystok, the E14 from Austria through the Czech Republic to Swinoujscie and on to Sweden, and the E8 from Germany through Poznan and Warsaw on to Russia. Border formalities between Poland and Lithuania can be a nightmare.

CZECH REPUBLIC

BY AIR

Prague is firmly on the international air grid, so many airlines now fly from New York to Prague and in the case of CSA, the Czech national carrier, the flight is non-stop. CSA also flies from Chicago via Montreal. Prague is directly linked to virtually every European capital.

BY RAIL

Prague is on the international train route beween Berlin and Vienna. Generally speaking, "Eurorail" and such passes may be used only on the Czech sections of international routes, not on the domestic network. There is no through service from the Channel ports.

The service from Paris is known to the French as the Paris-Praha Express and to the Czechs as the Zapadni Express. It leaves from the Gare de l'Est at 11pm and goes via Frankfurt and Nurnberg, arriving at Prague at 5.53pm the next day. The Donau Kurier from Cologne leaves at 7.58am, requires a change at Nurnberg, and reaches Prague at 9.55pm.

SLOVAK REPUBLIC

The full implications of the split in the former federation of Czechoslovakia are still to be seen, but it will probably be harmonious as these things go. No announcement has yet been made as to whether CSA, the Czechoslovak national airline, will be broken up.

BY AIR

Bratislava was served by a limited number of international flights before the split, and these will presumably increase. As long as Czechs and Slovaks remain on speaking terms, most international visitors will probably continue to filter in via Prague. Historically speaking, however, Bratislava has been more closely connected with Budapest.

BY RAIL

The international train services between Budapest and Vienna and points west run through the Slovak Republic.

BY BOAT

Bratislava is, of course, neatly placed for the river ships plying between the Danube cities. From April to October, a daily hydrofoil service runs between Vienna and Bratislava. At other times of the year it runs only on Thursday, Friday and Saturday.

For boat services from Vienna, contact: DDSG-Danube Cruises, Handelskai 254, A-1021 Vienna. Tel: 21-75-00.

HUNGARY

BY AIR

Malev, the Hungarian national airline, and international carriers provide a non-stop service several days a week from New York to Budapest's Ferihegy Airport, and there are also flights from Los Angeles and Chicago. All the major European carriers fly into Ferihegy as well. A second international airport is under construction at Sarmellek, near Lake Balaton, principally for tourist traffic.

BY RAIL

Four rail services run from various parts of Western Europe to Budapest all year round and are supplemented in summer by a fifth. The ordinary Orient Express (as opposed to the luxurious Venice-Simplon Orient Express from London to Venice) leaves the Gare de l'Est in Paris at 11.15pm and spends the following day passing through spectacular scenery in Bavaria and Austria in order to reach Budapest at 8pm. This is the famous train that used to go on to Istanbul; it now goes only as far as Bucharest.

The Oostende-Wien Express waits for the 9am connecting train from London Victoria (via Dover/Ostend) and then runs via Brussels and Cologne to Vienna, arriving at 9.10am the following morning in time to connect with the Wiener Walzer (from Basle) to Budapest.

The aforementioned Wiener Walzer leaves Basle at 8.27pm and passes through Zurich before picking up the Oostende-Wien passengers in Vienna and depositing all of them in Budapest at 1.05pm the next day. The Lehar from Vienna (at 7.45am) is a Eurocity express that cuts the travel time to Budapest down to less than three hours.

Fourth of the year-round trains is the 10.55pm from Rome which takes almost exactly 24 hours to reach Budapest after passing through Venice, Ljubljana and Zagreb.

The supplementary summer train (June to October) is the Rapide Paris-Vienna/Rosenkavalier which takes passengers from Paris as far as Vienna for the connection to Budapest.

Train connections with Eastern Europe are from Cracow, Warsaw, Prague and Berlin.

Rail Europe (in the United States on tel: 1-800-345 1990) can advise on the various Flexipasses, Eurorails, East Passes and so forth that are valid in Hungary and represent a considerable saving.

BY BOAT

River journeys down the Danube begin at either Passau in Germany or Vienna in Austria. These range from luxurious cruises (in the warmer months) to utilitarian travel. Details of cruises are available from CTC Line, 1 Regent Street, London SW1Y 4NN. All the countries along the Danube are cashing in on this traffic, so there is a rich choice including Bulgarian and Romanian lines.

A regular hydrofoil service from Vienna to Budapest runs daily and takes about 4œ hours. Details from DDSG-Danube Cruises, Handelskai 254, A-1021 Vienna.

ROMANIA

BY AIR

TAROM, the Romanian national airline, and other European airlines fly to Bucharest. There is a limited direct service from Frankfurt to Timisoara, and charter flights from a number of European starting points to Constanta in the summer.

The independent traveller who strolls into an airport and buys an ordinary scheduled ticket pays a hefty premium. STA Travel, 74 Old Brompton Road, London SW7 3LH, usually have a better idea.

A number of specialist agencies in or near New York put together packages with varying degrees of emphasis on the deplorable Count Dracula. Try: **ETS Tours**, 450 Harmon Meadow Boulevard, Box 1568, Secaucus, New Jersey.

Health and Pleasure Tours, 165 W 46th Street, New York, NY 10036. Tel: 212-586 1775.
Litoral Travel, 124 E. 40th Street, Suite 403, New York, NY 10016. Tel: 212-986 4210.
Victory Tours, 49 W. 45th Street, New York, NY 10036. Tel: 212-840 5964.

BY RAIL

The Orient Express and the Wiener Walzer from Paris and Basle respectively terminate in Bucharest. See the rail notes under Hungary (*on previous page*).

BY ROAD

The direct motor route from Western Europe is Germany, Austria and Hungary.

BULGARIA

BY AIR

The Bulgarian national airline is known as Balkan Airlines and operates out of three international airlines at Sofia, Varna and Burgas, the last two handling tourists bound for the Black Sea resorts. Balkan Air has been talking about starting New York-Sofia flights, but in the meantime it is possible to fly by Lufthansa and Swissair and change planes in either Frankfurt or Zurich. Sofia has long been a "backdoor" route between Western Europe and Greece, so if it is possible to get to Athens reasonably the remaining leg should not be too difficult.

BY RAIL

The only train which runs all the way to Sofia is the Istanbul Express from Munich via Venice, which runs daily all year round although at different times in summer and winter. The summer timetable means leaving Munich in late afternoon and arriving in Sofia about 26 hours later. As the trains run through Serbia, it would be as well to assess the security situation.

BY ROAD

Unless the roads through Serbia, Croatia, etc. are quiet, getting to Serbia from the West will require a lengthy detour.

TRAVEL ESSENTIALS

CUSTOMS

This is now a matter of common sense rather than former shocks like learning that a copy of the Bible or a thoughtful work on free-market economics – should one travel with either – was equated with hard-core pornography. Anything which would obviously command a high price locally, like video cameras or fancy watches, may be entered in your passport to make sure you bring the items out again. An inordinate number of designer jeans still in their original wrapping would be examined with interest but would no longer cause a sensation.

The worst thing to be caught with these days – always excepting illegal drugs of any description – is local currency. The whole point of Eastern Europe's tourism push is to earn foreign currency. Severe questions may be asked, therefore, if there is any suspicion of exporting foreign currency. If it was yours to begin with, a declaration on entry will enable the unspent balance to be brought out without hindrance.

The other point to watch on departure is carrying anything that may be taken as a valuable piece of the national heritage, such as an icon. No country likes to see its heritage disappearing into tourist suitcases to adorn the mantelpieces of the West. Generally, it is safe to assume that, if it's old or culturally significant, you might not be able to take it with you. If in doubt, have an export licence ready or something official – at least a receipt – to indicate that one is not necessary.

VISA REGULATIONS

GENERAL

The official position is that all the countries of Eastern European will now readily issue tourist visas. That said, the problems begin with the fact that the former members of the Soviet Union have hardly any embassies abroad to issue them.

The former Soviet embassies now represent Russia exclusively and can be disarmingly at a loss to offer any information about their recently departed cousins. We have quoted elsewhere in this book the case of the Ukrainian ambassador to London who, one year after Ukraine's independence, was still using his car as his office. If an embassy *can* be located – telephoning Directory Enquiries may be the simplest solution – visa applications may generally be made by post.

Locating an embassy is not the end of the story. Old habits die hard in the case of Russian embassies, which will almost certainly insist on application being made not by the individual concerned but by an accredited tour company.

Another shadow from the past is the need to provide a full itinerary. In practice, the application simply for "Moscow" will automatically include a radius of 100 miles (160 km) and without too much trouble can be extended to include other places on getting there.

The other countries tend to be more flexible, but in every instance allow for bureaucratic delays. The Russian Embassy in London, for example, charges £5 for a visa if there is no hurry; the price rises to £40 if it is needed within three days. Be sceptical, too, of airy assurances that a visa can be picked up on arrival at the airport; in the case of Ukraine, a border visa costs more than US$50.

Motorists should note that, while they will be allowed into Ukraine and the Baltic States with the documentation normally required in western Europe – a national or, preferably, international driving licence, the vehicle registration certificate and "Green Card" (international) insurance, they will need a special "Autoturist" in order to allowed into Russia.

FOR RUSSIA

All nationalities travelling to Russia require visas in advance. As stated above, the application is supposed to be made by an accredited tour company so that the proposed trip is laid out in every detail. This requirement is to some extent through force of habit: the trick seems to be to go along with the formality and then on arrival in Russia obtain permission to change one's itinerary.

The former Soviet embassies are now Russian embassies, and of course they are to be found everywhere. There is not much point in approaching them personally for a visa. Embassy staff are these days quite friendly and chatty, however, so if there is any difficulty getting hold of an Intourist office or the specialist travel agencies mentioned above, they may mention an agent with whom they do regular business.

Visa prices seem to be linked to inflation: they are multiplied several times over if the visa is needed quickly.

UKRAINE

A separate visa is now required for Ukraine. At the time of going to press, the position was that Ukraine had so little in the way of diplomatic representation abroad that visas would be issued on arrival. The regulations will probably become tighter as Ukraine

obtains the means to administer them. Until then, airlines flying passengers into the country are bound to known what's required of them, if only because they may be held financially responsible for repatriating visitors who are not admitted.

BELARUS

The position with regard to visas for Belarus is roughly the same as for Ukraine.

ESTONIA

Available on arrival ($20), but cheaper and less time-consuming if obtained in advance. British and Irish citizens do not need visas; Americans are issued them free. The three Baltic republics said in 1992 that a visa for any one of them would be recognised by the others. Long may that last.

LATVIA

Available on arrival, but again cheaper and less time-consuming if obtained in advance. 1993 prices: $20 for a single entry, $100 for a multiple. British and Irish citizens exempt. Hungarian citizens get visas free.

LITHUANIA

British, Irish and Danish citizens do not need visas. In theory, $20 will buy others a transit visa on arrival, but they may be problems on the Polish border.

POLAND

Valid visas in advance from Polish embassies and consulates. ORBIS or a competent travel agent would be able to handle the application. Transit visas are good for 48 hours; visitor visas for up to 90 days. They are valid for six months after the date of issue.

CZECH REPUBLIC

US and EEC passport holders do not require visas.

SLOVAK REPUBLIC

It is hoped that the Czech line will be followed, but nothing official as we go to print.

HUNGARY

US and EEC passport holders do not require visas.

ROMANIA

Required of everyone, in theory available on arrival, but more sensibly and cheaply obtained in advance.

Package tours sometimes include the cost of the visa, which in Britain is otherwise £20. Transit visas are for three days; tourist visas last 30 days but can be extended on the spot.

BULGARIA

Package tourists may not need visas, but independent travellers will certainly need them and they cannot be obtained on arrival. Allow 10 days for the processing of applications in Britain; two or three weeks in the US. An express visa (valid for fewer than seven working days) will be issued immediately to personal callers at the consulate but cost twice the going rate.

In the UK: 186–188 Queens Gate, London SW7 5HL. Tel: 071-584 9400.

In the US: 1621 22nd Street NW, Washington DC 20008.

MONEY MATTERS

This is another case of common sense. In the days when a Russian taxi driver would rather have a packet of Marlboro than the rouble equivalent of $20 on the meter, there is clearly scope for all kinds of imaginative kinds of exchange dealings. Black market transactions were risky then because *agents provocateurs* were everywhere.

The risk is practically nil now, but at the same time tourists can legitimately exchange their hard currency for realistic amounts of local money, it is hardly worth the bother. Nevertheless, locals would still much rather have hard currency, so it is as well to have small-denomination bills handy.

Hyperinflation has resulted in a rather different hazard. In Poland, for example, a 50-zloty note used to be worth US 20¢. Its value is now infinitesimal, but the notes are still in circulation. So, too, is the 1-million zloty note which, while a long way short of a king's ransom, is far too much to hand out through oversight as a tip. The issue of new and ever larger notes is another reason for not bothering with furtive black-market exchanges. The unsuspecting visitor may be landed with an impressive wad of notes which are no longer legal tender.

The well-known credit cards are widely welcomed throughout Eastern Europe. The convenience of paying by credit card is offset by the rate of exchange that may be applied to the transaction.

The most reliable clue to what is really going on is the degree of enthusiasm to which they are preferred to cash, even hard-currency cash. Hotels and restaurants in some instances may be obliged to demand payment in hard currency or by credit card, and the rate may be rather less attractive than the one available through banks. Quite often, though, the request for hard currency reflects a preference, not an obligation. It is difficult to imagine circumstances in which it would not be cheaper to pay with local currency if it is acceptable.

In changing money at an authorised outlet, find out whether a flat fee is payable in addition to the commission. The flat fee could make a nonsense out of changing only small amounts at any one time. Even without a flat fee, commissions may run at 10 percent or more.

Exchange rates are so volatile that to quote them as we go to press (in early 1993) would be no more than of historic interest. The following observations are therefore limited to countries that are in the process of introducing their own currencies and other points of more than transitory significance.

RUSSIA

Post-independence inflation has been so rampant that 1992 brought a succession of startling revelations. The first was that in the first six months of 1992 Russia had printed more bank notes than over the whole of the three decades preceding. A brief lull followed because, it was said, the treasury could not pay for any more notes to be printed.

Production was eventually resumed, but if only for economy's sake the notes remained of the old design with portraits of Lenin. In the meantime, the price of a Moscow Metro ticket was rising so fast (but only relatively so, because in real terms it remained next to nothing) that tokens were being rationed to prevent speculators from "buying forward" and hoarding.

UKRAINE

Ukraine was trapped between the old Soviet currency and plans for a new currency (to be called the grivna) that failed to materialise on schedule. The interim measure was a coupon system that was neither one nor the other and did not carry the convictions of even the most patriotic Ukrainian. Visitors might like a coupon or two as souvenirs but no more. Until things are sorted out, small denomination foreign bills remain the visitor's only viable currency.

BELARUS

The same situation as Ukraine but – we venture to predict – after the first flush of independence Belarussians were beginning to think that economic ties with Russia were inevitable and perhaps even desirable. If the Russian rouble regains respectability. it may end up as Belarus's alternative currency. The new national currency will be the taler.

ESTONIA

The Estonian kroon (abbreviated to "EEK" but pronounced "krone") has been the sole legal tender since 20 June 1992. Notes are printed in denominations of 1, 2, 5, 10, 25, 100 and 500. Coins are 5, 10, 20 and 50 "sents". At its launch, the kroon was pegged to the dollar, but the dollar and for that matter the rouble are not legal tender. It later floated with exchange rates set by the Bank of Estonia and posted daily.

Foreign currency (and in theory traveller's cheques) may be exchanged at the harbour, airport, major hotels, post offices, department stores and other specified points. Expect to pay a commission of around 2 percent.

LATVIA

Also on 20 June 1992, Latvia introduced the Latvian ruble, "LVR", at parity with the Russian (i.e. former Soviet) rouble, but the Russian rouble was quickly overtaken and within six months was worth only half the Latvian equivalent. Many stores and restaurants would still accept Soviet money in denominations of 200 roubles or more but at capricious exchange rates rather below the official one.

Exchange points have popped up all over Riga but are more elusive in other parts. Vendors compete over a narrow margin with their quoted rates; hotels offer the least attractive. US dollars and German marks command better rates than other foreign currencies.

LITHUANIA

Lagging behind the other Baltic republics, Lithuanian was still waiting six months later for its own national currency to be called the Lita. Coupons known as "talonas" were introduced as an interim measure in October 1992.

Lithuanians know the coupons as "Zveriukai", or "little animals", because Lenin's portrait has been replaced by politically neutral four-legged beasts. The 10, 50, 100, 200 and 500 "little animals" are smaller in size than the last generation of roubles (in denominations of 1 to 50) known as "Vagnorkes" after the former Prime Minister Gediminas Vagnorius who introduced them in 1991.

POLAND

The Polish currency is still the zloty, but meteoric inflation has meant that the largest denomination note has been getting bigger and bigger, although it may now settle down having reached the 1 million mark. There used to be hundreds of zlotys to the dollar; by 1993 the figures was more than 10,000. It's almost a case of waiting until after a meal to change one's foreign currency to pay for it, and of course 50- and 1,000,00-zloty notes should not be confused in the dark.

CZECH & SLOVAK REPUBLICS

The crown ("koruna" or "Kcs") was relatively stable; in the years bracketing the Soviet revolution, it dropped against the dollar by a factor of only three

or so, and the official rate was sufficiently realistic to make the black market only marginal. The Czech crown is unlikely to overwhelmed by the division of the Czechoslovak federation. It is not yet known whether the Slovak Republic will stay with the Czech currency or go it own way.

HUNGARY

Inflation has meant that the filler, of which there are 100 to the Hungarian forint, is all but extinct. Over the revolutionary period, the value of forint against foreign currencies dropped by a factor of about two. Realistic official exchange rates have marginalised the black market, although Hungarian currency is sold at a discount of about 25 percent. It is not worth the risk.

To be on the safe side, declare anything more than $200 in foreign currency on arrival and keep official exchange receipts. That will stop any arguments about foreign currency in your possession on departure. It will also enable a limited amount in surplus forints to be changed back into foreign currency on the way out.

ROMANIA

The Romanian unit is the leu, the plural of which is lui. Foreigners may be required to pay for petrol, hotel accommodation and some restaurant meals in foreign currency, which was partly the reason for dropping the earlier requirement to convert a minimum amount of foreign currency into lei in advance. Exchange bureaux are to be found in all tourist areas, and as some are run by licensed individuals (as opposed to banks), an element of competition has crept into the rates on offer. The devaluation factor over 1988–91 was about 30.

BULGARIA

The Bulgarian lev (plural leva) comes in notes in denominations of 1 to 20, with 100 stotinki (in coins) to the lev. The fact that Balkantourist offices have offered a conditional 80 per cent bonus on foreign currency exchanged through them is a tacit admission that the official rate is a nonsense. Beware. The Bulgarian police are notoriously humourless, and the glib stranger is more likely to be one of them in plain clothes or an outright crook than a sincere monetarist.

WHAT TO PACK

With regard to clothing, no generalisation would apply to the whole of Eastern Europe on any given day of the year. The short answer to filling up extra space in a suitcase is to look beyond obvious items such as camera film and medicine – absolutely any kind of medicine, down to humdrum aspirin – to little things that would normally be taken for granted. Gin and vodka drinkers, for example, may be appalled at the brutal power of some brands of Eastern European tonic water to inflict heartburn.

This is really a case for close scrutiny of little private joys, like peanut butter or biscuits. Whatever the outcome, anything left over at the end of the trip will be gratefully snapped up.

GETTING ACQUAINTED

DRIVING

The instinctive appeal of taking a private car into eastern Europe now that the borders are open may not stand closer examination. The Czech and Slovak Republics and Hungary have been relatively accessible for years, but the challenges mount in the remoter areas.

To begin with, fuel has become increasingly scarce and may be unobtainable. When and where it is available, the octane rating is abysmally low by western standards and unsuitable for high-compression modern engines. Unleaded fuel is unknown. These factors, combined with poor road surfaces, stray animals and locals who have not been driving long enough to perfect their technique at the wheel, conspire to make some kind of mishap a certainty.

While the improvisational ingenuity of rustic mechanics is beyond belief, they cannot manufacture spare parts. A broken-down car is a dreadful albatross around anyone's neck in these circumstances, and the compulsory repatriation of a wreck is both hugely expensive and time-consuming.

If these warnings fail to deter, an insurance policy that will pay for the repatriation of the car is imperative on top of the normal requirements of national and international driving licences, the vehicle registration certificate and the "Green Card" international insurance cover.

Observe the laws of the road as they are written, not as the natives of the country appear to observe them. This rule, of course, has many subsections. One of the most prominent concerns drink-driving. Don't do it. Most East European countries have a tolerance of zero alcohol in the blood. Another concerns speed limits. Generally these are 60 kph (37 mph) in built-up areas, 80 kph (50 mph) on country roads and 110 kph (68 mph) on motorways.

Specific national motoring information can be obtained from internationally recognised motoring organisations. They may also be able to provide you with up-to-date road maps and equipment for hire – such as snow chains and lockable roofracks for skis and bicycles.

HEALTH

Some countries have reciprocal health agreements with individual Eastern European nations. These are designed so that travellers can gain emergency health treatment wherever they go and merely pay the amount expected of the locals. A Frenchman in Poland, for example, can be hospitalised free of charge and will have to pay only 30 percent of the cost of medication. In Bulgaria, Romania and Poland, you will need to produce your national medical card.

Splendid though they are, these reciprocal agreements are not all-embracing, and include only emergency hospital treatment. If you arrive at the hospital and decide that you would rather be flown home, do not expect your government to come running with a personalised Lear jet. Take out some fairly comprehensive medical insurance as well.

Before travelling, stock up at your local pharmacy. Even the most elementary medicines are in short supply in Eastern Europe – headache pills, tampons, condoms, disinfectants.

No inoculations are currently deemed necessary for Eastern European travel. Rabies is present throughout the region, however, and if you are likely to come into contact with animals, an inoculation is recommended. Make sure that you are up-to-date with tetanus boosters and visit a travel clinic beforehand departing to establish whether there have been any flash outbreaks of typhoid or meningitis.

The water in most places is drinkable. The exceptions are where it has been heavily polluted by industry. Look around for big factory chimneys and trust your sense of taste.

When on your travels, should you need medicine in the middle of the night, check any pharmacist's window for a notice giving directions to the pharmacy on 24-hour duty.

The standard of health care varies from country to country and from place to place. Good treatment can be expected in any of the major capitals, while the tourists who find themselves in hospital in Azerbaijan can at least console themselves with the thought that they are probably pioneers in the field of local medical knowledge.

PETS

The best advice is leave them at home, but if visitors insist on the company of a dog or cat the minimum requirement is a valid veterinary certificate issued at least a year before travel. Notably in Russia, pedigree dogs are a status symbol and the number of arrogant hounds being led around by fawning owners is astonishing. If problems with travelling pets occur, they are more likely to be on the way home, in which case there could be tearful separations at the roadside. Do not even consider trying to get a pet across the channel into Britain: stringent quarantine regulations mean that it would be almost kinder to bury it at sea.

ELECTRICITY

The uniformly 220-volt power supply in Eastern Europe will blow up 110-volt American appliances without a transformer. The plugs are generally of the round-pin continental type, but some or the wiring is pre-war. It is easier to pick up a multi-adaptor in the West than on arrival: international airports routinely sell them. The power supply in many parts of Eastern Europe is erratic: it surges, fades, or goes off altogether, sometimes for extended periods. Battery-powered appliances are the answer, but be sure to bring enough batteries.

LANGUAGES

One of the features of east European independence has been the revival of national languages which were in most cases discouraged and in some all but extinct under the pressure of Russification. The revival will be apparent in signs that have been painted over, the previous Russian names either rewritten in the indigenous language or changed altogether.

Broadly speaking, the main languages of Eastern Europe are Slavonic (Russian, Polish, Czech, Ukrainian, Belarussian and Bulgarian), Indo-European (Latvian, Lithuanian) or Finno-Ugrian (Estonian and Hungarian), which leaves Romanian out on its own as a derivative of colloquial Latin *circa* 5th century.

The Slavonic languages are generally written in Cyrillic script, loosely based on the Greek alphabet, if for no other reason than that some of the Slavonic sounds are very difficult to convey in the Latin alphabet. The strings of consonants without vowels in Polish, and to a lesser degree in Czech (which has German influences) is an indication of what happens when one tries.

Western visitors will presumably be able to get their tongues around the Latin-alphabet languages for the purposes of, say, pronouncing a name on a map. The Cyrillic script may look formidable, but keeping a note of the key letters – "P" is pronounced like "R", "B" is like "V", and so on – will make place names quite readily recognisable and pronounceable.

PHOTOGRAPHY

Although every item of Soviet military hardware is now for sale at a knockdown prices with no questions asked, it cannot be assumed that tanks, military aircraft etc are open season for photographers. It is also quite futile trying to tell some officious corporal or self-appointed vigilante that satellites have already logged every airport, bridge, canal and so forth. Some of these characters may have purely private reasons for wishing to confiscate exotic camera equipment. Resist the temptation to photograph signs forbidding photography. Take with you as much film stock as you're likely to need.

Video cameras are not as commonplace as in the West and regarded as the smuggler's stock in trade. Don't volunteer to have the serial numbers written into the back of your passport – never appear too anxious to please – but this is ultimately the way to satisfy customs that the equipment will leave the country with you. If equipment logged in a passport is stolen, get some kind of verification that the theft was reported to the police.

STAYING IN TOUCH

Foreign radio broadcasts are no longer jammed, and a short-wave radio is indispensable for those who want to stay in touch, not least with the events that may be going on around them. The fact that Mikhail Gorbachev relied on the BBC World Service to find out what was happening to him while he was under house arrest during the short-lived 1991 coup is not as crazy as it sounds. The frequencies which give the best reception of the BBC or Voice of America tend to be in the lower wavebands (13 and 19 metres) during daylight, the higher ones (31 and 42 metres) at night.

CNN (Cable News Network) is available in some of the larger hotels. Many of the major Western newspapers are now available in Eastern capitals on the same day as publication, or at least the next.
Radio Frequencies
BBC World Service: Metres 17.01 19.91 31.88 48.54. In some areas, the BBC can also be picked up on medium wave.
Voice of America: Metres 25.06 31.02 49.67 50.04

GEOGRAPHY & POPULATION

RUSSIA

Russia was only one of 15 Soviet Socialist Republics that made up the former Soviet Union, albeit far the biggest with a population of about 150 million in an area covering 6,593,391 sq. miles. Its nearest rivals in terms of population and territory were Ukraine with 52 million and Kazakhstan with 1,064,092 sq. miles. Detached from the Soviet Union and its somewhat tentative successor the Commonwealth of Independent States, Russia still stretches across 11 time zones from the Baltic to the Pacific and from the Arctic Ocean to the Black Sea.

Convention draws a distinction between European and Asian Russia, the dividing line being the Ural Mountains which, looking east, signal the beginning of Siberia, whose natural resources make

Russia the richest country on earth. European Russia is poor in natural resources apart from timber, but Siberia more than makes up the deficit with inestimable wealth in coal, all kinds of ferrous and non-ferrous metals including gold, diamonds, natural gas and oil. Russia is the world's largest oil producer.

The majority of the population, about 80 percent, are Slavs who speak a homogeneous Russian language, use Cyrillic script and are generally (by tradition if not in practice) members of the Russian Orthodox Church. Although of Asiatic origin, these Slavs are now considered European and are sometimes called Great Russians to distinguish them from Little Russians (Ukrainians) and White Russians (Belarussians).

There are at least 100 indigenous ethnic groups living in Russia, especially Asian Russia, who are anything but Great Russians, speak mutually incomprehensible languages and practise other religions. The exact number depends on how "national group" is defined. Some 6 million Tartars live in a defined area on the Volga with Kazan as its capital, while the Yukagirs of Siberia, who are in no doubt that they are a separate people, number just 600 or so.

The picture is enormously complicated if one considers ethnic groups whose origins may have been elsewhere but have been living in Russian territory for centuries. These include Bulgars who have never had anything to do with modern Bulgaria and Germans who centuries ago migrated to the Volga region and were then, so to speak, cut off. These Germans have never been conceded a national area of their own, nor have the Jews. The so-called Jewish national area of Birobijan, facing Japan, was purely a progaganda exercise and one part of Russia where few Jews had actually ever lived.

Russia becomes the Russian Federation, or "RSFSR" as it used to be known, with the addition of territories which were less than Soviet Republics in their own right. In British terms, they are not unlike the Crown Colonies which survived the general dissolution of the empire. They have a measure of autonomy but retain direct links with Moscow in most cases rather than be overwhelmed by larger neighbours. The majority are in the Caucasus, like the pocket of Ossetians who have chosen to distance themselves from Georgia, previously one of the 15 supposedly independent Soviet Republics. In the west, Kaliningrad, formerly Konigsberg when it was part of German East Prussia, is an enclave wedged between Lithuania and Poland, part of the Russian Federation but not of Russia.

Moscow's average winter temperature is 18°F (−8°C). Summers are relatively warm with temperatures around 68°F (20°C). Such is the size of Russia, however, that the variations across the country are enormous. Winters are ameliorated by the Baltic, Black and Caspian seas, so broadly speaking the temperatures drop from south to north and from west to east, reaching their nadir in Verkhoyansk in northeast Siberia where the mean January temperature is −59°F (−50°C), dropping on occasion to a bracing −90°F (32°C). The seas of course have the opposite effect in summer, holding temperatures down, and the Arctic Ocean does this so efficiently that even in almost constant sunshine temperates along the coastline seldom exceed 50°F (10°C).

UKRAINE

A population of 52 million made Ukraine the most populous Soviet Republic after Russia. It covers 233,144 sq. miles (604,000 sq. km) and has borders with Romania, Moldova, Hungary, Slovakia, Poland, Belarus and Russia. Ukraine has a large Black Sea coastline including Crimea, a contentious issue since the break-up of the Soviet Union. The Crimea was in Russia until 1954 when the Kremlin made a "gift" of it to Ukraine. A largely symbolic gesture at the time, Russia would now like Crimea back.

Separated for centuries from Russia proper by different political fortunes, Ukrainians speak a slightly different form of Russian and their religion, though fundamentally Orthodox, has rejected the Russian Patriarch's supreme spiritual authority in favour of historic ties with the Greek church and to some extent Roman Catholicism. These and other factors have contributed to grass roots anti-Russian nationalism which manifested itself in some pro-German sentiment in World War II and which the Soviets did their utmost to suppress.

Ukraine remained within the CIS after the break-up of the Soviet Union in spite of unresolved disputes with Russia over Crimea and the liquidation of the Soviet armed forces. Internally, there is friction between Ukrainian nationalists and 20 percent minority of Russian immigrants. There are smaller German, Jewish and Moslem minorities.

BELARUS

The former Byelorussia or "White Russia" covers 80,290 sq. miles (208,000 sq. km) and is landlocked between Ukraine, Poland, Lithuania, Latvia and Russia. Belarussians are ethnically akin to Russians and Ukrainians, but the essence of the Belarussian identity is that they grew up apart from them and were influenced by their Lithuanian and Polish neighbours to the west. Poland encouraged Jewish immigration so that Minsk became a predominantly Jewish city. Genocide by Hitler, persecution by Stalin and subsequent emigration to Israel has reduced the present Jewish population to around 100,000.

The physical parameters of Belarus are somewhat arbitrary. The countryside is flat and marshy but not unattractive owing to numerous forests and more than 4,000 lakes, a rich habitat for wildlife. Forever caught between warring neighbours, Belarus's featureless frontiers have waxed and waned, and at one stage the state consisted of little more than Minsk and its environs. For that reason, the country revolves around Minsk to a remarkable degree.

Polish influence resulted in widespread Roman Catholicism. Although Belarussian nationalists are a relatively benign lot, they are apt to resent Roman Catholicism and Russian Orthodoxy alike as ecclesiastical imperialism. Their remedy is to turn their backs on religion and promote their sense of identity through the Belarussian language, which is sufficiently different from Russia to be regarded as their own special thing. Next to the grass roots movement in Ukraine, Belarussian nationalism operates at a cerebral level and seems ready to acknowledge that economic ties with Russia will have to be retained and even developed.

ESTONIA

The most northerly of the Baltic republics covers an area of 17,413 sq. miles (45,100 sq. km) and has a population of about 1,573,000, of whom 30 percent are Russian and other minorities an additional 10 percent. Independence was only the first step in what Estonians regard as the recovery of their country from a history of foreign domination which began with Danes and Teutonic Knights in pagan times. They are ethnically related to the Finns and linguistically to the Hungarians.

Estonia is flat and well-forested. With a combination of marshes, 1,500 lakes and 500 rivers in such a confined area, it could almost be said to be waterlogged. There are also some 1,500 coastal islands.

Lutheranism is the predominant religion, a legacy of the German cultural influence which continued long after the Teutonic Knights were spent as a military evangelical force. These beliefs survived the Russian occupation which fitted in with Peter the Great's opening of a Window to the West.

Russians who immigrated in the 18th century are not a factor in the fraught relations between Estonians and their largest minority. It is Russians who arrived under Soviet sponsorship and now represent more than 90 percent of the population in the northeast, especially in Narva, that are the target of draconian citizenship qualifications based on literacy in one of the world's most difficult languages.

LATVIA

Of the present population of 2.6 million, barely half are Latvians with one-third made up of Russians and the balance divided among Belarussians, Ukrainians and Poles. The extent to which Riga, the capital, dominates national affairs is reflected in the fact that its population is approaching 1 million.

The basis of Latvian nationhood is the Lett language, which is Indo-European in origin and quite unlike Polish or any of the Russian languages. It is vaguely related to Lithuanian, although historically the Lithuanians went off with the Poles

while the Latvians were more closely with southern Estonia. Common experience with Estonia explains why Lutheranism is the most prevalent religion among Latvians. Roman Catholicism filtered in from Poland and Lithuania. There are also Baptist and Jewish minorities, but the religious statistics are of course heavily influenced by the presence of token Orthodoxy in the large number of Russians present. In any case, religion is not a burning issue.

The country covers an area of 24,704 sq. miles (64,000 sq. km), most of it low undulations among 700 rivers and lakes. About 2 percent of the land is under water despite the Soviets' draining of Lubans, Latvia's largest lake, to half its original 35 sq. miles (35 sq. km).

LITHUANIA

At 25,090 sq. miles (65,000 sq. km), Lithuania is the largest of the three Baltic states but still only a shadow of its earlier self when the Lithuanian empire extended to the Black Sea. The most famous fact about the Lithuanians is that they were the last pagans in Europe – and very proud of it. These days the majority are Roman Catholic because the country's subsequent history was closely tied to Poland.

Lithuania's aristocracy and bourgeoisie were once so closely associated with their Polish counterparts that the two could hardly be told apart, so Lithuanianism existed virtually as a peasant culture until the late 19th century. About 80 percent of the present population of 3.5 million would now unconditionally declare themselves as Lithuanian, the dissenters being either Russian or Polish. The same tendency has led to a revival of the Lithuanian language. The second most famous fact about Lithuania is that the language is as close as anything extant to ancient Sanskrit.

POLAND

Poles always say that their geography is their history: 120,694 sq. miles (312,680 sq. km) of flat land, most of it less than 600 ft (180 metres) above sea level and some of it – parts of the Vistula Delta – actually below. The point about Poland's terrain is that it only has natural frontiers to the south in the form of the Carpathian and Sudeten mountains, not enough to prevent invaders from charging through. The result has been extremely fluid boundaries, so "Poland" has forever been moving about and in the 18th century did not exist as a separate state at all. Modern Poland conforms to the specifications drawn up after World War I.

Poland's population of 37 million is unusually homogeneous: 98 percent Poles with just a scattering of Ukrainian, Belarussian and Jewish minorities. The greatest population concentrations are in the industrialised central and southern regions. Poles have always been ardent Roman Catholics and more than once presumed to conquer Russia in order to convert the tsar and all his subjects. Religion has been a surrogate form of nationalism in times of subjugation, and there are shrines in almost every village.

CZECH & SLOVAK REPUBLICS

The Czech and Slovak Republics have an area of 49,362 sq. miles (127,881 sq. km) and are landlocked. However, there are 265 miles (425 km) of navigable inland waterways with the rivers Elbe, Oder and Danube providing access to the North, Baltic and Black Seas respectively. It is a hilly region: to the north the Carpathians rise to a height of 8,737 ft (2,663 metres) on the Polish border. The Dunaj Plain lies in the south.

The combined population stands at 15.5 million and is made up principally of Czechs (31.5 percent) and Slovaks (30 percent). Germans, Hungarians, Poles, Ukrainians and Russians make up the other 6 percent.

CZECH REPUBLIC: The Czech half of what was between 1918 and 1993 the single country of Czechoslovakia is itself in two parts, Bohemia and Moravia. Topographically and culturally, Bohemia and Moravia blend imperceptibly into one another, but there is then a sharp distinction in both senses between them and Slovakia. Prague (population 1.2 million) in Bohemia is the capital of what is to be known as the Czech Republic; Brno is the regional capital of Moravia.

After the Magyar invasion of the 9th century, Bohemia and Moravia were drawn into the Germanic orbit of the Habsburg Empire, and for a while Prague was the Emperor's preferred capital. The Czech lands have therefore been in the mainstream of European cultural development, a course leading through the Reformation, Renaissance and industrialisation.

SLOVAK REPUBLIC: Slovakia is separated from Moravia (and hence the Czech Republic) by the White Carpathians and the Morava river. The mountain scenery in the north is some of the most spectacular in Europe. Going south, the land flattens into the remarkably fertile plains of the Danube which were once the granary of Hungary before and after it was part of the Austro-Hungarian Habsburg Empire. For a while, when the Hungarian court fled from the Turks, Bratislava was the *de facto* capital of Hungary. Accustomed to playing second fiddle to Prague in the days of Czechoslovakia, it is now capital of the Slovak Republic.

The split in the Czechoslovakian federation is, from the Slovak point of view, an exercise in restoring self-esteem. They were completely subjugated during 11 centuries of Hungarian direct or indirect rule, and they feel that they were treated as poor cousins under federation with the Czechs, which is ironic because three of the heroes of 20th-century Czechoslovakia, the Masaryks *père et fils* and Alexander Dubcek, were Slovaks.

Nevertheless, the Slovak nationalists who triggered the split in 1992 seemed bent on proving that they were not agricultural serfs, as they had been under the Hungarians until World War I, nor toadies to the Czech establishment in Prague afterwards. Slovakia cannot be divorced from its past, however, so it brings to independence a tradition of Hungarian-imbued Roman Catholicism and a sense of pristine Slavdom uncorrupted by Germanic influences to the west.

The fascinating point to look out for is how an independent Slovak Republic chooses between its Czech connections of recent memory and the former overlords across the southern border in Hungary.

HUNGARY

Hungary is a country of some 36,000 sq. miles (93,000 sq. km) with mountains to the north and west which level out into a great plain. It is divided by the Danube – here flowing from north to south – and has Europe's largest lake in Lake Balaton.

Of the population of 11 million, the vast majority are either Magyars or others who have been so assimilated as to be indistinguishable. The recognisable minorities are Germans, Romanians, Slovaks, Serbs, Croats, Jews and Gypsies. Budapest, the capital, has a population of more than 2 million.

As the bearer of King Stephen's Apostolic Crown, Hungary is traditionally a Roman Catholic country although there is a substantial Protestant Hungarian Reformed Church as well as Lutheran and Orthodox minorities. Fierce patriotism has kept shored up Hungarian culture and especially the language against the influence of powerful influences swirling all around.

ROMANIA

Romania is a country of some 92,000 sq. miles (238,000 sq. km) lying north of the Danube and with an outlet to the Black Sea between Ukraine and Bulgaria. Its present boundaries were largely set at the Paris peace conference after World War I when Romania was given Transylvania, the home of the legendary Dracula, which had previously been Hungary's. In World War II, however, Romania had to give up Bessarabia, which became "Moldavia" and more recently "Moldova".

The population is 23 million, of whom nearly 90 percent are Romanians claiming descent from Romans who married into the local Dacian population in the time of the Caesars. The minorities, now more or less integrated, are Hungarians, Germans, Serbs and Jews. The Gypsies, who number about 1 million, tend to keep to themselves.

Romania is an unusual case of a predominantly Orthodox population whose use the Latin alphabet (out of deference to their Latinate language) rather than Cyrillic script. Like the Ukrainian Church, Romanian Orthodoxy is, well, unorthodox.

BULGARIA

The topography of Bulgaria's 42,800 sq. miles (110,000 sq. km) is wonderfully varied, a mixture of mountains and open plain leading up to the Danube and the Black Sea. The amount of yogurt the inhabitants eat is supposed to account for amazing longevity. The purported regiments of sprightly centenarians never seem to have proper birth certificates handy, but there must be something in the food or air that has given Bulgaria an unquestionable Olympic gold-medal monopoly in pint-sized weightlifters. The climate in summer is tempered by Black Sea breezes and cool air in the mountains. Crisp winters provide good skiing conditions winter.

Bulgarian is a Slavonic language and uses a Cyrillic script. The population of 9 million is perhaps 88 percent ethnic Bulgarian, but the minorities question is vexed. Bulgarians have attempted to repeat what the Magyars did in Hungary, forcing minorities into line with compulsory name changes and so on. The chief targets have been the Turkish population, probably because the Bulgarians were Turkish subjects in Ottoman times. The other principal minorities are Romanian, Armenian and gypsy.

The Bulgarian Orthodox Church has its own Patriarch who resides in the Holy Synod in Sofia, the capital. The authorities have recently shown concern over the spread of Islamic fundamentalism among the Pomaks, an ethnically distinct group who live in the Rila-Rhodopen mountains in the southeast. There is some international concern that Bulgaria may be drawn into a dispute with Greece and others if it lays claim to Macedonia, in former Yugoslavia, which was once part of the Bulgarian Empire.

GETTING AROUND

RUSSIA

BY AIR

Internal Flights: Once mighty Aeroflot is in disarray with a large part of its fleet grounded by fuel shortages or mechanical disorder. In theory, it still flies to hundreds of cities and towns, but routes and timetables have been juggled around out of all recognition. Because of cancellations and delays, allow a whole day for any internal flights.

The only practical advice of any enduring value to visitors already in Russia is to ask Intourist to use its influence. For what private enquiries are worth, the main Aeroflot offices are at:
Moscow: 4 Frunzenskaya Naberezhnaya.
Tel: 245-002.
St Petersburg: 7/9 Nevsky Pr. Tel: 211-7980.

BY BUS

Buses for Moscow's three airports (Sheremetyevo for international flights) leave from the Central Air Terminal Building, 37 Leningradski Prospekt.

BY RAIL

By far the most sensible way of getting around Russia independently. Consider buying an ordinary ticket like any Russian and then upgrading it to an "Intourist ticket" either before departure or on the train itself. The savings are substantial. If that is not a primary consideration, Intourist tickets may be booked in advance either through the agency's normal offices or Intourtrans, 15 Petrovka, Moscow.

Moscow has nine railway stations, at time of writing still bearing their imperial names (Kiev, Riga, etc.) which give a rough indication of the direction in which departing trains leave but do not take too much for granted. The overnight train from Moscow to St Petersburg could be taken for the experience and not merely as the most satisfactory way of getting from one to the other. "Soft class", the proliterian euphemism for "first class" means two-berth compartments; the ordinary class has four bunks per compartment. Anything beneath that is at most a dormitory. If there is no restaurant car the railway stewardess attached to each car keeps a *samovar* brewing at the end of the corridor.

BY ROAD

By Car: Self-drive hire cars are not readily available, and in any case one would require a special motoring visa (different from the "Autoturist" visa) to drive one around. In short, forget about driving yourself around and, if necessary, hire a car with a driver. As always, have as little as possible to do with the cars that hang around tourist hotels. In practice, almost every car in Russia is available for private hire, but draw the line at police cars or military jeeps whatever cheerful assurances the driver may offer. Up-to-date motoring information is available from the Institutski Pereulok, Moscow. Tel: 101-496.

By Coach: Bumpy, over-crowded and inadvisable.

BY BOAT

Two river terminals in Moscow have sailings to cities as far away as Astrakhan, Perm, Rostov-on-Don, Ufa, Kazan, Kuibyshev, Saratov, Volgograd, Kasimov and Ryazan. Bookings can be made through Intourist or at the terminals themselves:

Northern River Terminal: 51 St Petersburg Highway. Tel: 457-4050.

Southern River Terminal: Yuri Andropov Prospekt. Tel: 118-7955.

In St Petersburg, information about the various river services may be obtained from Rechnoy Voksal, 195 Obukhovskoy Oborony, tel: 262-1318.

URBAN TRANSPORT

In Moscow and St Petersburg, look no further than the Metro, the stations recognisable by "M" in red neon. Admission is by inserting the fixed fare into an automatic barrier, which is a ticket to ride as much as you like, changing trains if necessary. The fares keep on going up, but finding out the current cost and having the appropriate coins is as much as you need to know in this department.

With a little note as a reminder of how cyrillic letters transcribe into the Latin alphabet, it is possible to make sense of the names on the Metro maps and also the signs that indicate exits to street level or transfers to other lines. As the doors close, a mystery voice announces the name of the next station, so progress can be followed on the map in the carriage. Do not be daunted by any of this. Mastering the system is really quite easy and gives a completely disproportionate sense of achievement.

UKRAINE

The practicalities of travel within Ukraine will be determined by the degree to which an independent Ukraine tries to extricate itself from the Soviet air and rail networks. Kiev, Kharkov, Lvov and Uzhgorod have internal airports, but the services depend on how much of the Aeroflot fleet the national airline inherits and can keep in the air.

KIEV

Most transport problems are solved by Kiev's Metro system.

Railway station: at the end of Komintern Street off Vokzalnaya Square.

Bus terminus: Avtovokzalnaya Square.

Boat terminus: main one at Pochtovaya Square; local services from the Prigorodnaya pristan pier in Naberezhnoye Road.

LVOV

Railway station: Privokzalnaya Square.

Bus terminus: Yaroslav Mudry Square.

BELARUS

In general, the remarks addressed above to internal travel in Ukraine apply as well to Belarus.

MINSK

Travel around Minsk is solved by the Metro system. The railway station is south of what was, and may still be, Lenin Square.

ESTONIA

BY AIR

The newly created Estonian Air has cobbled together a domestic service out of 12 ex-Aeroflot Tupolevs, installed a British Airways computer ticketing system and sent the air stewardesses off for training by SAS. The result is a domestic and Baltic network which, from Tallinn, takes in Tartu, Kuuresaare, Kardla, Riga and Vilnius. Unfortunately but perhaps understandably, foreigners are bearing a large part of the start-up costs by being charged 10 times as much as locals for the same flight. It is just as well, therefore, that the latter's fare are very low. Estonian Air has a Tallinn office at 10 Vabaduse valjak (tel: 446-382) but it is possible to pick up a ticket at the airport as well, space permitting.

BY RAIL

Frequent but slow service from Tallinn to all major towns within the country and points beyond. Until timetables are printed, the vital information is most easily obtained from boards at all stations.

BY ROAD *

By Coach: Unusually in Eastern Europe, coaches and buses are a reasonable alternative to trains, but they are crowded and there is no room for big pieces of luggage. Tickets can be bought in advance from the office at 19 Parnu mnt. behind the Palace Hotel. For some reason, they won't issue the second half of a return ticket at the point of departure. It has to be collected at the other end.

Car Hire: A reasonable proposition on lightly used roads for foreigners who are over 22 and have a valid national drivers licence.

Refit, 20 Magasini, Tallinn. Tel: 661 046 or their branch office at the Hotel Olympia.

Ideal, at Tallinn airport. Tel: 212 735.

Baltic Limousine Service, 10B Vabaduse valjak, Tallinn. Tel: 666 672; fax: 444 725.

LATVIA

BY AIR

There is a domestic air service, but Latvia is so small no flight takes more than 30 minutes, and most of that is devoted to taking off and landing. Nevertheless, details from Riga Airport. Tel: 0132-223 175.

BY RAIL

Short legs on the international trains are quicker and more comfortable than the electric commuter trains, but the latter are perfectly adequate and go everywhere. Buy the ticket before boarding at the central station closest to the big clock in Riga Town Square. Information: Tel: 007-232 134.

BY ROAD

By Coach: A choice between coaches and faster mini-buses to all destinations. The coach station is at Pragas iela; the mini-buses congregate outside the central railway station.

Car Hire: Hertz and Avis are at Riga Airport. Otherwise:

Auseklitis, 13 Dzirnavu iela, Riga. Tel: 0132-331 505.

Hotel Riga, 30 Aspazijas Boulevard, Riga. Tel: 0132-216 516. With or without a driver.

Ventus, Hotel de Rome. Tel: 0132-216 516.

LITHUANIA

BY AIR

The fledgling Lietuvos Avialinijos (Lithuanian Airlines), 12 Ukmerges Str (tel: 75 2588) has inaugurated its domestic service with flights to Palanga, the seaside resort near Kleipeda.

BY RAIL

Frequent trains from Vilnius to Kaunas (2 hours), Klaipeda (10 hours), Panevezys and other cities and towns. Advance bookings from Reservation Bureau, 3 Sopeno str, near the station (tel: 62 3044).

Tickets are available on the day of travel from the main station in Gelezinkelio str., but allow for up to two hours in the queue.

BY ROAD

By Coach: Cheap but not famously comfortable, coaches make up for the gaps in the rail services. The terminus is at 22 Sodu Str. (tel: 26 2482).

Car Hire:

Baltic Auto, 28 Zveju. Tel: 73 1385; fax: 73 2160.

Eva Garage, 14 Jacionu. Tel: 64 9428. Accepts American Express.

Litinterp, 10/15 Vokieciu. Tel: 61 2040; fax: 62 3415.

Balticar. Tel: 46 0998; fax: 75 8924.

POLAND

BY AIR

LOT, the national airline, operates a domestic service to 11 cities and towns. Book through ORBIS.

BY RAIL

The rail service is busy so advance booking is recommended if not essential. On some lines, steam engines are still used. Visitors may buy the Polrail Pass for hard currency abroad, but tickets can be bought locally with zlotys.

BY ROAD

By Coach: PKS, the state bus service, operates a number of long distance routes and local ones which serve as feeders for the trains.

Car Hire: Hertz and Avis at airports, local operators in town.

Orbis Rentacar, 27 Nowogrodzka ul, Warsaw. Tel: 211 360; fax: 293 875.

BY BOAT

From 1 May to 15 October there are regular services along the following coastal routes: Gdansk-Sopot-Hel; Gdynia-Jastamia; Gdynia-Helsowie-Szczecin-Swinoujscie-Miezyzdroje. Boats also operate on the Vistula between Warsaw and Gdansk, on the Masurian lakes and on the Elblag-Ostroda Canal.

CZECH REPUBLIC

In every respect as straightforward as any country in Western Europe except that non-express trains are painfully slow.

BY AIR

CSA, the national airline, has a very comprehensive domestic service. Bookings through CEDOK at 18 Na Prikope, 11135 Prague 1. Tel: 127 111.

BY RAIL

An extensive rail network throughout the country but it is worth the supplement to travel on the express trains. Long-distance trains invariably have restaurant cars.

BY CAR

A self-drive car in Prague would be a waste because the interesting parts of the city are mostly blocked off to private traffic. Use Prague's modest but efficient Metro instead. For journeys outside Prague (and especially to the Slovak Republic) a self-drive car is ideal. Centralised booking through Pragocar, 42 Stepanska, Prague 1. Tel: 235 2825.

SLOVAK REPUBLIC

The rules will only be different from the Czech Republic if the Slovak Republic decides to divorce itself from the former Czechoslovak networks, which hardly seems likely.

HUNGARY

Hungary is sufficiently small for everyone to get around satisfactorily on the ground, although small aircraft (generally 12-seaters) link the major towns.

BY RAIL

MAV, the state railways, run three types of train: *gyorsvonat* (express), *sebesvonat* (stops at major centres) and *szemelyvonat* (milk train). The network is laid out as a hub with Budapest at the centre.

Tickets are sold at the IBUSZ offices in stations up to 60 days in advance. The MAV information office is at 35 Nepkoztdarsasag utja, Budapest (tel: 22 7860). Two single tickets (*egy utra*) seem to cost no more than a return (*oda vissza*).

BY CAR

The familiar international hire companies are in business at the airport or have a presence in the major hotels.

For motorists using their own cars, it is as well to be aware of the Yellow Angels breakdown service. For general information contact: the Hungarian Automobile Club, 4A Romer Floris, Budapest 2. Tel: 11 52040; fax: 11 53089.

ROMANIA

BY AIR

TAROM and LAR run regular services (at least in summer) from Bucharest to Arad, Bacau, Baia Mare, Caransebes, Cluj-Napoca, Constanta, Iasi, Oradea, Satu-Mare, Sibiu, Suceava, Tirgu Mures, Tulcea and Timisoara. Flights may be booked through the National Tourist Office at 7 Magheru Boulevard, Bucharest.

Whereas international and some domestic flights use Otopeni Airport, it is as well to know that other domestic flights operate out of Baneasa Airport, which is about 5 miles from the city centre (Otopeni is about 12 miles).

BY RAIL

It is advisable to book well in advance at Romanian Railways Travel Office, 10–14 Domnita Anastasia str, Bucharest (tel: 132 644). Curiously, tickets must officially be bought from stations at least six hours before the (loosely) estimated time of departure, which is rather pointless because everyone knows that the ticket clerks always keep a few in reserve for later applicants. Trains marked "personal" sound rather grand but in fact are the slowest, wretchedly so. "Accelerat" trains are better, "rapide" the best.

BY ROAD

By Coach: Not even the Ministry of Tourism recommends the coach service.
By Car: The Romanian Automobile Club, 2 Cihovschi str (tel: 11 0408) is the best source of information for the current state of fuel rationing by coupons etc.

Car hire through ONT or ACR offices in Bucharest and major towns.

BY BOAT

Romanian and international vessels sail on the Danube. One of the most attractive stretches is between Cazane and Portile de Fier, the gorge between the Carpathian and Balkan mountains. Boats ply regularly between Orsova and Turnu Severin, and Tulcea is the main port for cruises on the Delta.

NAVROM, the Romanian shipping line, is at 38 Dinicu Golescu Boulevard, Bucharest (tel: 18 0290). Tickets bought in Romania are substantially cheaper than prices in advance abroad.

BULGARIA

BY AIR

Balkanair's services from Sofia to Varna, Burgas, Vidin and Ruse are only slightly more expensive than rail. Flights to the Black Sea take 50 minutes by turbo-prop or 35 minutes by jet.

BY RAIL

From Sofia there are five main routes: to Varna, Burgas, Plovdiv, Dragoman and Kulata. The overnight trains to the Black Sea have 1st and 2nd class sleeping cars with bunk beds and limited buffet services. Long queues at stations, so it is better to book in advance through the Rila Bureau at 5 General Gurko ul (tel: 87 0777). Tickets bought locally are cheaper than abroad. The train categories are *ekspres vlak* (express), *brzi vlak* (fast) and *patnicheski* (slow).

BY BOAT

Cruises operate along the Danube as well as between Black Sea ports. A regular hydrofoil service links Varna-Nesebar-Burgas-Sozopol. Boats ply between Varna-Druzba-Golden Sands-Albena-Balcik.

URBAN TRANSPORT

Tickets for all forms of transport cost 6 stotinki per trip. Buy them at kiosks in books of ten and have them punched on boarding the tram or bus. Tickets are only valid in the town in which they are bought.

BY CAR

Self-drive hire through Hertz, which has linked up with Balkantourist. As long as there are shortages, petrol can only be bought with vouchers paid for with hard currency through the Sipka Tourist Agency offices. If in trouble, dial the emergency number 146.

WHERE TO STAY

In the old days, all hotels were of course owned by the state, managed by bureaucrats and staffed by people who generally gave the impression that they would rather be doing something else.

The concept of a competitive service was unknown, although to be fair there were exceptions like the odd hotel manager who took pride in doing his best in unhelpful circumstances and old retainers who could regale guests with tales of the days when so-and-so – usually some forgotten prince – swung from the chandeliers. The engaging old retainers were shuffling about on their last legs, however, so the prospect of a new generation of dedicated hotel staff under the post-revolutionary economic order has come along in the nick of time.

The biggest change is that visitors now have a say in where they stay. They previously had to stick to establishments which were specifically for foreigners, which generally meant that the locals were kept out

and the telephones in rooms reserved for shady foreign correspondents and the like were bugged. The logistics of group travel in any case deprived visitors of any choice, and there never any question of packing up and leaving a place that did not come up to scratch.

In theory, hotel rooms in most East European countries, and especially Russia, are still supposed to be booked by an approved agent in advance. In practice, a traveller with magical hard currency can show up anywhere unannounced and if the reception desk is absolutely adamant that the hotel is full, it probably is. Therein lies the irony. With greater freedom of travel and all sorts of entrepreneurs arriving in search of new business opportunities, the hotel shortage in many areas is acute, so the surest way to have a room waiting is to resort to the old group travel arrangements that were previously such a pain.

Hotels run by Intourist and its counterparts in the other countries generally maintain reliable if uninspired standards. The "P" system of hotel classification is spreading, but of course it is easier to pin up a row of stars on the front door than to deserve them. The infallible difference between ☆☆☆ and ☆☆☆☆☆ is, dramatically, price. This is especially so in Moscow, and herein lies another irony. Visitors used to be shepherded into Intourist's most modern hotels whereas some of them, at least, would have preferred the more atmospheric National or Metropol with their faded tsarist trimmings. This puzzled well-meaning Intourist types: who would want to stay in an old place like that? Come the revolution, however, these exotic preferences were noted, with the result that the grand old places have been sympathetically done up and now charge the earth: up to $1,000 a night for the best rooms. Variations on this theme are played out in other East European capitals.

The intriguing newcomers on the scene as far as foreign visitors are concerned are the ☆ or ☆☆ establishments that were earlier not allowed to "accept" them. Do not enter these premises with unreasonable expectations. There will probably be running water in rooms, but running hot water could be asking for too much. Seasoned travellers have learned to cope with the missing bath plug, the international icon of budget-minded travel, but a hotel that has run out of food can take some getting used to.

A grassroots tourist industry – families who do up a couple of rooms and take in paying guests – has resulted in touts hanging around at airports, railway stations and (it may be worth remembering) tourist information bureaux, or what passes as such. Obviously, discretion is required. Have grave doubts about a glib young man who puts you in a taxi, mutters an incomprehensible address to the driver, and says he'll follow in separate taxi with all your luggage. The safer bet is to deal with landlords or landladies touting for themselves rather than agents.

That said, private homes could be the most rewarding accommodation, especially if there is enough of a common language to converse. De-criminalising such private enterprise has meant that visitors can now stay in villages and whole areas where previously there was no accommodation for them at all.

Youth hostels and campsites exist but not on the same scale as in the West. Camping in the wild is robustly discouraged.

HOTELS

RUSSIA

Tourists are supposed to have booked all the accommodation they will require in advance through an approved agent. This is tantamount to the Russians saying that they would still rather prefer their visitors to arrive in organised groups. The point is reinforced by the prices quoted to independent travellers, which are ridiculous next to group rates for the same facilities. The solution, as always, is to book through a group and then, if you like, abandon it.

MOSCOW
National, 14/1 Prospekt Marksa. Tel: 203-6539. Joint-best and most convenient hotel in Moscow, next to the Kremlin, but these days expensive. Worth a visit in its own right.
Metropol, 1 Prospekt Marksa. Tel: 225-6677. Joint-best with the National, and exactly the same comments apply. Recently done up.
Mezhdunarodnaya, 12 Krasnopresnenskaya. The hub of the foreign business colony, a complex of shops, offices and restaurants. Good for business, especially the world's oldest, but far from the centre and inconvenient for ordinary tourists.
Rossiya, 6 Ulitsa Razina. Tel: 290-5409. Dubious distinction of being the world's biggest hotel: quantity before quality.
Ukraina, 2/1 Kutuzovsky Prospekt. Tel: 243-3021. Not as big as the Rossiya, but it is one of the Moscow "wedding cakes" and looks heavier.
Intourist, 3 Ulitsa Gorkova. Tel: 203-4008. Formerly the Intourist flagship, now a bit tacky but perfect location.
Berlin, 3 Ulitsa Zhdanova. Tel: 925-8527. A leaf out of the National/Metropol book, a restored tsarist establishment.

ST PETERSBURG
Pribaltiyskaya, 14 Ulitsa Korablestroitelei. Tel: 356-5112. Big, brash, on the sea – and miles from anywhere.
Astoria, 39 Ulitsa Gartsena. Tel: 219-1100. St Petersburg's answer to Moscow's National, see above.
Yevropeiskaya (Hotel de l'Europe), 1/7 Ulitsa Brodskovo. Tel: 211-9149. Local answer to Moscow's Metropol.
Moskva, 2 Ploshchad Alexandra Nevskovo. Tel: 274-9505. On the river, commute by boat.

Leningrad, 5/2 Vyborgskaya Naberezhnaya. Tel: 542-9123. Reasonable, efficient and a walk, albeit a fair walk, from the prime sights

MUSCOVY: GOLDEN RING

There are "approved" hotels in only Yaroslavl, Vladimir and Suzdal among the towns on the Golden Ring route, which means a travel agent would not be able to make a booking in any of the others. Nevertheless, they do exist and are tolerable.
Yaroslavl: Hotel Yaroslavl, tel: 21275.
Vladimir: Hotel Vladimir, tel: 3042.
Suzdal: Intourist Hotel in the centre; the Suzdal Hotel and Motel (tel: 21137) in a suburban leisure complex which also includes the Pokrovskaya Hotel (tel: 20131) inside a former monastery.

Among the "unapproved" hotels (unless they have since been promoted) are the eponymous Pereslavl-Zalessky and Rostov-Veliky hotels.

NOVGOROD
Intourist Hotel, 16 Ulitsa Dmitrievskaya (tel: 750-89), and only if this is genuinely full should consideration be given to the alternatives, the Sadko (tel: 95170) or Volkhov (tel: 72498).

CAMPING: About 6 miles out of town on the Moscow road. Tel: 72448.
PSKOV
Rizhskaya, 2–6 Rizhskoye Shosse. Tel: 24301.

BLACK SEA

In Soviet times, the Crimea and Black Sea coastline was an uninterrupted Soviet Riviera, and the frontiers between Ukraine, Russia and Georgia were inconsequential formalities. With independence, however, the Riviera has fragmented into distinct national segments, with Ukraine robustly exercising its authority over the Crimea and the Georgian sector unfortunately caught up in civil war. Of the many resorts on which Muscovites used to descend, Sochi is the only major one that remains unequivocally Russian.

SOCHI
Zhemchuzhina, 3 Ulitsa Chernomorskaya. Tel: 934-355.
Intourist, 91 Kurortny. Tel: 990-292.
Camelia, 89 Kurortny. Tel: 990-398.
Numerous sanatoria will admit foreigners.

UKRAINE
KIEV
Rus Hotel, 4 ulita Gospitalnaya. Tel: 20-5091. Central, new and nothing to write home about.
Hotel Bratislava (Kiev and the Slovak capital are twinned), 1 Andrei Malysko. Tel: 57-7233. Also quite new. Better food than the Rus but out of town.
Dnieper, 1/2 Kreshchatik. Tel: 914-861. Recognises its limitations in its rate card.

Lybid, Pobeda Square. Tel: 742-066. An older hotel but tries harder.

CAMPING: At the Prolisok Motel and Camping Site about 8 miles west on the road to Lvov, which has a good restaurant.

Lvov

Intourist Hotel (which may be due for a name change), 1 Mickiewicz Square. Tel: 726-751.
Lvov Hotel, which is better, is only now being re-opened to foreigners.

CAMPING: Lvovsky camping site. Tel: 721-373. About 10 miles out on the Kiev road.

Zaporozhye

Zaporozhe Hotel, 135 Prospekt Lenina. Tel: 341-292.

Odessa

Foreigners used to be billetted in the three hotels mentioned below, but there are numerous others which will soon drop their discrimination clauses, if they have not done so already.
Chernoye More Hotel, 59 Lenin Street. Tel: 242-025.
Odessa Hotel, 11 Primorsky Boulevard. Tel: 225 019.
Krasnaya Hotel, 15 Pushkin Street. Tel: 227-220.

CAMPING: Delphin Camping Site. Tel: 36-212. About 12 miles north of the city; Kotovsky Park, in Luzabovka.

CRIMEA

Dozens of hotels catered for the Russians who used to throng here. With the Russians less welcome than before, foreigners with hard currency can expect open arms. Sevastopol and Balaklava, Crimean War drawcards, were virtually closed to foreigners because of arms shipments en route to the Middle East, among other sensitive activities. They are still tricky but no longer impossible.
Oreanda Hotel, 35/2 Lenin Embankment, Yalta. Tel: 325-794. A 19th-century hotel effectively taken over by Virgin Airlines and a revelation.
Yalta Hotel, 50 Drazhinsky Street, Yalta. Tel: 350-150. A huge place with windsurfing etc.
Tavrida Hotel, 13/2 Lenin Embankment, Yalta. Tel: 327-784.

BELARUS

While Belarus was a major manufacturing centre for Soviet industry, tourism was wholly neglected, so there is practically no infrastructure outside Minsk, the capital.

Minsk

Yubileinaya Hotel, 19 Masherov Prospekt. Tel: 29-8835 or 29-8024.
Minsk Hotel, 11 Lenina Prospekt. Tel: 29-2363.
Planeta Hotel, 31 Masherov Prospekt. Tel: 23-8416.

CAMPING: Minsk Motel and Campsite. Tel: 22-6380. About 12 miles out on the Brest road.

Brest

Intourist Hotel, 15 Ulitsa Moskovskaya. Tel: 51-073.

ESTONIA

Estonia's tourist industry traditionally drew on two sources: Russians in search of Olde Worlde Europe, and young Finns in search of an affordable weekend binge. Most of the action was and still is concentrated on Tallinn, the capital, which copes admirably. A floating hotel in the harbour should be in operation soon.

Tallinn

Viru Hotel, 14 Viru Square. Tel: 652-081. A venerable yet distinctly lively establishment on the edge of the Old Town.
Tallin Hotel, 27 Gagarinipuiestee. Tel: 444-264 or 441-504. Near the railway station.
Olympia, 33 Kingissepa. Tel: 602-436.
Kungla, 23 Kreutzwaldi. Tel: 421-460.
Palace, 3 Vabaduse Valjak. Tel: 443-461/444-761.
Sport, 1 Regati pst, Pirita. Tel: 238-598. Built for the 1980 Olympic yachting events.

CAMPING: Kloostrimetsa, on the coast east of Tallinn.

Narva

Hotel Narva, 6 Pushkini. Tel: 22-700.
Vanalinn, 6 Koidula. Tel: 22-486. In a quaint medieval building and the better bet.

Haapsalu

Hotel Haapsalu, 43 Posti. Tel: 44-847. Large, modern and comfortable.
Pension Pipi, 37 Posti. Tel: 45-174. Only 8 rooms and minimal.

Tartu

Park, 23 Vallikraavi. Tel: 33-663. Fine location, sauna.
Pro Studiorum, 13 Tuglase. Tel: 61-853. Converted apartment building.
Taru, Rebase 9. Tel: 73-700. Luxurious.
Tartu, 3 Soola. Tel: 32-091. Near the railway station as a last resort.

Viljandi

Sammuli, 28 Mannimae. Tel: 54 463. Large lodge on shores of Lake Viljandi. The Hotel Viljandi in town is best avoided.

Parnu

Victoria, 25 Kuninga. Tel: 43-412). Attractive and expensive *belle-époque* hotel.
Emmi, 2 Laine. Tel: 22-043). A mile from the centre, but preferable to the ghastly Parnu Hotel in town.

LATVIA

Latvia's paramount tourist attraction is its capital Riga, an old Hanseatic city which in its time has acted as a principal port for both Poland and

Sweden. Riga was not on any of Intourist's approved routes through the former Soviet Union, so this once busy place has been uncharacteristically quiet for most of the 20th century. As it was a cul-de-sac at the end of a flight path from Moscow, the demand for hotel rooms was slack. The situation is now improving.

RIGA

Latvia Hotel, 55 Elizabetes Iela. Tel: 212-503. Regular evening entertainment.

Fremad, 55 Elizabetes Iela. Tel: 221-611.

Riga Hotel, 22 Padomju Bulvar. Tel: 227-895. Popular with locals but surely not for its food. The Hotel de Rome and the Eurolink and are incorporated in it.

Metropol. Tel: 216-184. When completed, promises to be the best hotel in the Baltic.

Ridzene, 1 Endrupa Iela. Tel: 324-433. Prestigious and central.

The following are spartan, clean and cheaper:

Victoria, 55A Caka Iela. Tel: 272-305.

Baltija, 33 Raina Boulevard. Tel: 227-461.

Turists, 1 Slokas Iela. Tel: 615-455.

JURMALA

Jurmala Hotel, 47/9 Jomas Iela. Tel: 761-340.

Majori Hotel, 29 Jomas Iela. Tel: 761-380.

CAMPING: Sites are generally poor, but information can be had from Riga Bureau of Tourism, 10 Smilbu Iela. Tel: 224-903.

LITHUANIA

Under the Soviet regime, the capital Vilnius was the only city in Lithuania where tourists were allowed to stay overnight. Moreover, there was only one hotel allowed to take them in. This situation is bound to change, but new hotels are not the top priority in a country whose economy is almost inextricably tied to Russia.

VILNIUS

Hotel Lietuva, 20 Ukmerges Street. Tel: 356-016.

Astorija, 35/2 Didzioji. Tel: 62-9914.

Draugyste, 84 Ciurlionio. Tel: 66-2711.

Mabre, 13 Maironio. Tel: 61-4162.

Narutis, 24 Pilies. Tel: 62 2882. Popular with backpackers.

Neringa, 23 Gedimino. Tel: 61-0516.

Sarunas, 4 Raitininku. Tel: 35-3888.

Vilnius, 20/1 Gedimino. Tel: 62-4157.

TRAKAI

Book accommodation in private homes through Nakvyne Hotel Travel Service, Vilnius. Tel: 63-7732.

POLAND

Free-market economics notwithstanding, ORBIS is not inclined to loosen its monopoly on Poland's better hotels. Visitors may draw their own conclusions from the fact that if a kind Polish acquaintance

were to book a hotel room, the rate would be substantially lower than that demanded of foreigners. Poles are nothing if not enterprising entrepreneurs, so all sorts of possibilities are opening up in the private sector.

WARSAW

Victoria Intercontinental, 11 Ulica Krolewska. Tel: 279-291. Part of the Intercontinental chain, which manages to maintain remarkable standards in more difficult locations than Poland.

Warsaw Marriott, 65 Aleje Jerozolimskie. Tel: 283-444. Another chain visitors can bank on.

Europejski, 13 Krakowskie Przedmiescie. Tel: 255-051. Its shortcomings partly redeemed by the central location.

Zajazd Napoleonski, 83 Ulica Plowiecka. A private inn where Napoleon reputedly rested on his ill-judged trip to Moscow.

CRACOW

Forum Hotel, 28 Ulica Konopnickiej. Tel: 669-500. In the city centre, swimming pool and tennis courts.

Grand Hotel, 5 Ulica Slawkowska. Tel: 217-255. A new, smallish hotel in the heart of the Old City.

Holiday Inn, 6 Ulica Koniewa. Tel: 750-44). The first Holiday Inn in Eastern Europe.

Pod Roza, 14 Ulica Florianska. Tel: 229-399. A central hotel of historic character.

Cracovia, Aleje Puszkina. Tel: 286-66. Large but efficient.

GDANSK

Grand Hotel, 8–12 Ulica Powstancow Warszawy, Sopot. Tel: 511-696. Some distance out of town but well worth the extra effort.

Gdynia Hotel, 22 Ulica Lipca, Gdynia. Tel: 206-661. Also out of town but modern and good.

Marina Hotel, 20 Ulica Jelitkowska. Tel: 531-246. Another Baltic seafront hotel with good facilities.

Hevelius Hotel, 22 Ulica Heweliusza. Tel: 315-631. The most satisfactory hotel in central Gdansk.

CZECH REPUBLIC

Within weeks of independence, Prague was deluged with foreigners who came to see, liked what they saw, and decided to take up at least temporary residence. In less than a year, the expatriate colony was reputed to number some 40,000, and there has been a queue for hotel rooms ever since. In the case of the Three Ostriches Hotel, guests are advised to make their holiday bookings at least six months in advance. Demand all round is especially heavy during the mid-May/early-June Spring Music Festival.

PRAGUE

Three Ostriches, 12 Drazickeho Namesti, Prague 1. Tel: 536-1515. A 17th-century inn at the foot of the Charles Bridge.

Europa Hotel, 20 Vaclavske Namesti (Wenceslas Square), Prague 1. Tel: 236-5274. This hotel is the Three Ostriches' closest rival for atmosphere, but that does not make it a grand hotel. Only some rooms have baths.

Alcron Hotel, 40 Stepanska, Prague 1. Tel: 235-9296. Just off Wenceslas Square and should have been restored by the time this book comes out.

Palace Hotel, 12 Panska. Tel: 237-151. Recently renovated to its Art Nouveau glory. Close to Wenceslas Square.

Forum, Ulice Kongresova, Prague 4. Tel: 41-01-11. Probably the best bet for business visitors.

Inter-Continental, 43–45 Namesti Curieovych. Tel: 231-1812. A superbly run but being modern in a historic city it is, inevitably, away from the centre.

Panorama, 7 Milevska, Prague 4. Tel: 416-111. Another modern and also impressive hotel.

BOTELS: This is not a misprint. These are converted river boats moored on the Moldau in Prague.

Botel Albatross, Nabrezi L Svobody, Prague . Tel: 2-231-3634.

Botel Admiral, Horejsi Nabrezi, Prague 5. Tel: 2-547-445.

PRIVATE ROOMS: Bookings can be made through CEDOK offices or:

Buro Hello, 3 Namesti Gorkeho-Senovazne, Prague 1. Tel: 222-4283.

Czechbook, 52 St Johns Park, London SE3 7PJ. Tel: 081 853-1168.

Prices in 1993 were around $13/£8 per day.

YOUTH HOSTELS: CKM (Travel Agency for Young Czechs), 26 Zitna, Prague 2. Tel: 236-6640.

TABOR

Palcat Interhotel, just off the main square. Tel: 2235/229-01.

Slavia, near the railway station. Tel: 2235/228-28.

KARLSBAD
(Karlovy Vary)

Grand Hotel Pupp, 6 Namesti Mirove. Tel: 22-121. Looking its splendid 18th century self again after a comradely spell as the Grand Hotel Moskva.

Hotel Narodni Dum, 24 Ceskoslovenske Armady. Tel: 24952.

Hotel Adria, 1 Konevova. Tel: 23765.

MARIENBAD
(Marianske Lazne)

Some of the Edwardian nests of adultery are on their way to becoming hotels again after drab lives as therapeutic clinics. In the meantime:

Palace Hotel Prana, 67 Odboraru. Tel: 22-223. A fairly authentic period piece.

Golf Hotel, Zabud 55. Tel: 2712. Luxurious but reasonably priced hotel a little distance from the centre with an undemanding but agreeable golf course.

CESKE BUDEJOVICE

Gomel, 14 Miro. Tel: 27-941. Officially ☆☆☆☆.

Interhotel Slunce, Namesti Zazkova. Tel: 367-55.

Hotel Malse, opposite railway station. Tel: 276-31.

BRNO

Frequent trade exhibitions put a premium on hotel accommodation in the Moravian capital. If the hotels are full, a friendly word with the reception desks will obtain pointers towards private accommodation.

Hotel Continental, 20 Leninova. Tel: 75-3121.

Slovan Hotel, 23 Lidicka.

Metropol Hotel, 5 Dornych.

SLOVAK REPUBLIC

The Slovak half of the former Czechoslovakia drew the short straw when the country previously split in the 9th century and, to a lesser degree, under federation. A separate entity again in 1993, the Slovak Republic will gradually assume control of its own tourist industry. For up-to-date accommodation information, start with the former CEDOK office at 13 Sturova, Bratislava. Tel: 52-280.

BRATISLAVA

Hotel Kyjev, 2 Ulice Rajska

Forum Bratislava, 2 Namesti Mierove. Tel: 34-8111.

Palace Hotel, 1 Postova. Tel: 33-3656.

Hotel Carlton, 7 Namesti Hviezdoslavovo. Tel: 33-1851.

Sputnik ("Youth Hotel"), 14 Drienova. Tel: 23-4340.

LOW TATRAS

The most convenient base from which to plan excursions into the Low Tatras is Zilina.

Hotel Slovakia, in the centre. Tel: 465-72.

Hotel Polom, 1 Olomoucka, Zilina. Tel: 21151.

Enquire locally about availability in the small regional hotels and chalets, e.g. Interhotel Vratna, Chata na Gruni and Hotel Boboty.

HIGH TATRAS

Enquire at the tourist office in Poprad, the airport and rail terminus, about availability.

Hotel Park and Grand Hotel, Stary Smokovec.

Hotel Horec and **Grandhotel Praha**, Tatranska Lomnica.

Hotel Panorama and **Hotel Patria**, Strbske Pleso.

HUNGARY

Like the country as a whole, the Hungarian tourist industry turned its back on the Communist line a long time ago, so accommodation is available in as wide a range of hotels, pensions and private homes as one would expect in Western Europe.

BUDAPEST

Budapest Hilton, 1–3 Hess Andras Ter, Buda. Tel: 17-51800. Complete with 13th-century church.

Duna Intercontinental, 4 Apaczai Csere Janos Utca, Pest. Tel: 11-75122. On the river.

Gellert, 1 Szent Gellert, Pest. Tel: 18-52200. Probably the most evocative hotel in the capital.

Astoria, 29 Kossuth Lajos Utca, Pest. Tel: 11-73411. Moderately priced and well-run period piece.

Erzsebet, 11 Karoly Mihaly Utca, Pest. Tel: 13-82111. Another moderately priced and well-run establishment.

THERMAL: Thermal Aquincum and Ramada Grand Hotel are spa hotels on Margaret Island.

CAMPING: The Magyar Camping and Caravaning Club (MCCC) at 6 Ulloi Utja, Budapest 1085 (tel: 13-36536) publish details of the 280 campsites nationwide.

YOUTH HOSTELS: Express Youth and Student Travel Bureau, 16 V Szabadsag Ter, Budapest 1395. Tel: 11-11430.

SZENTENDRE
Pension Coca Cola, 50 Dunakanyar Krt. Tel: 26/10410. Sounds dubious, actually quite good.
Hotel Party, 5 Ady Endre Utja. Tel: 26/12491. Another good hotel.

VISEGRAD
Hotel Silvanus, "on the mountain". Tel: 361/28136. Has a bus connection from the boats' berth.

ESZTERGROM
Esztergom, Primas-sziget. Tel: 8168. Small and modern.
Hotel Furdo, 14 Bajcsy-Zsilinszky Utja. Tel: 292.
Hotel Volan, 12 Jozsef Attila Ter. Tel: 705.

LAKE BALATON
This is Hungary's premier resort area, so there are hotels, pensions and private rooms galore. Most of the big hotels close from mid-October to mid-April. The following are in the places highlighted in the preceding text.
Annabella, 25 Beloiannisz Utca, Balatonfured. Tel: 86-42222. Large lakeside hotel.
Marina, 26 Szechenyi Utca, Balatonfured. Tel: 86-43644.
Kastelyszallo, Nagyvazsony. Tel: 80/64109. Formerly the 18th-century stately home of the Zichy family.

EGER
Hotel Minaret, Harangonto Utca . Tel: 36-20473. Small and appealing.
Senator-haz, 11 Dobo Ter. Tel: 36-20466. Even smaller and equally appealing.
Park Hotel, 8 Klapka Gyorgy Utca. Tel: 36-13233.

SAROSPATAK
Hotel Bodrog, 58 Rakoczi Utca. Tel: 41/11744. Outwardly underwhelming but good food.

TOKAY
Hotel Tokay, 5 Rakoczi Utca. Tel: 4658.

SOPRON
Sopron Hotel, Forvenyverem Utca. Tel: 99/14254. Picturesque setting above the town.
Hotel Palatinus, 23 Uj Utca. Tel: 99/11395. In the historical part of town.
Lover Hotel, 4 Varosi Utca. Tel: 99/11061. In the woods out of town.

FERTOD
Kastelyszallo. Tel: 99/45971. Is the heavily-subscribed hotel within the Esterhazy Palace.

KECSKEMET
Harom Gunar,7 Batthyany Utca, Kecskemet. Tel: 76/27077. Restored historic hotel, excellent food.

Aranyhomok, 3 Szechenyi Ter, Kecskemet. Tel: 76/20011. In the centre of town.

SZEGED
Hotel Hungaria, 4 Komocsin Zoltan Utca, Szeged. Tel: 62/21211. On the river.
Hotel Royal, 1 Kolcsey Utca, Szeged. Tel: 62/12911. Long-established and central.

ROMANIA

Do not expect too much of Romania's hotels outside Bucharest regardless of the official "Deluxe" rating. The Ministry of Tourism used to own all hotels open to foreigners, but an increasing number are now owned by city or local councils, a sort of half-way stage to privatisation. Under Ceausescu, only party bosses and foreigners (for propaganda purposes) ate well; the rest of the country's famously prolific food supply was exported. There is not yet an abundance, but at least the distribution is more equitable, with the ironic but quite proper result that foreign visitors are relatively worse off.

BUCHAREST
Athenee Palace, 1–3 Episcopeiei Street. Tel: 14-0899. In almost every novel, film and set of memoires about Bucharest, this hotel is centre stage, rather like Raffles in Singapore.
Intercontinental, 406 N. Balcescu Boulevard. Tel: 14-0440. For which contemporary diplomats and VIPs have forsaken the Athenee Palace.
Manuc's Inn, 30 Decembrie Street. Tel: 13-1415. Originally a caravanserai, centrally located.
Lebada, 3 Biruintei Boulevard. Tel: 24-3010. Quiet but somewhat remote lakeside setting.
Bucuresti, 63–81 Victoriei. Tel: 15-4580. Ceausescu's idea of what Bucharest's premier hotel ought to be.

YOUTH ACCOMMODATION: Youth Tourist Bureau, Onesti Str.

TIRGOVISTE
Dimbovita. Tel: 926-13961. The point of interest being the ancient capital.

CURTEA DE ARGES
Posada, 27-9 Republicii Boulevard. Tel: 977-11800. Another former capital of Wallachia.

ALBA IULIA
Cetate, 41 Horia Boulevard. Tel: 968-23804. In the heart of Roman Dacia.

BRASOV
Carpati, in the city centre. Tel: 921-42840.
Postavarul, older but also central. Tel: 921-44330.

PLOESTI
Prahova, 11 Dobrogeanu-Gherea Str. Tel: 971-26850. For oil business visitors.

SUCEAVA
Hotel Bucovina, Ana Ipatescu. Tel: 1-7048. A roof over one's head.
Hotel Arcasul, 4–6 Mihai Viteazul. Tel: 1-0944. Basic.

SIBIU
Hotel Imparatul Romanilor, 4 Nicolae Balcescu Str. Tel: 1-6490. Impressively preserved relic of 18th-century Romania.

TIMISOARA
Continental, August Boulevard. Tel: 961-34145.

CRISANA
Hotel Lebada. Tel: 915-14720. Rendezvous for Danube delta explorers.

CONSTANTA
Hotel Palas, 5–7 Opreanu Str. Tel: 915-14720. Grand nostalgia above the port.
Continental, near archaeological site. Tel: 916-15660.

NEPTUN
Hotel Neptun, on the lake. Tel: 91-31020.

BULGARIA

The best hotels in Bulgaria can be very good, but the rate of decline thereafter is precipitous except on the Black Sea coast, where tourism has been longer established and standards are less erratic.

SOFIA
Sheraton Sofia-Grand Hotel Balkan, Sveta Nedelya Place. Tel: 87-6541. Central, excellent but expensive.
Novotel Europa, 131 Georgi Dimitrov Boulevard (due to be renamed). Tel: 31261. Convenient for business travellers.
Vitosha-New Otani, 100 Anton Ivanov Boulevard. Tel: 62451. Japanese-designed hotel at foot of Mount Vitosha.
Grand Hotel Sofia, Narodno Subranie. Tel: 87-8871. Central, nightclub, etc.
Bulgaria, 4 Ruski Boulevard. Tel: 87-1977. Good value for its moderate prices.

VIDIN
Bononia Hotel, near the river.

RUSE
Riga and **Dunav**, both Interhotels.

PLOVDID
Hotel Trimontium, Kapitan Raycho Ul. Tel: 22-5561. Conveniently central to the sights.
Novotel Plovdiv, 2 Zlatju Boyadjiev Street. Tel: 55171. Across the river.

SUMEN
Hotel Madara, originally a Turkish hotel, popular local rendezvous.

VELIKO TARNOVO
Hotel Veliko Tarnovo, 2 Emil Popv Ul. Tel: 30571. Splendid views of the old city.
Yantra, 4 Velcova Zavera Street. Tel: 20391. Also panoramic.

GABROVO
Balkan and **Jantra** hotels in Bulgaria's joke capital. Etur Inn outside town.

KAZANLAK
Hotel Kazanlak in Bulgaria's rose capital.

BOROVETS
Samakov, modern hotel in the Rila Mountains.

BLACK SEA REGION

BURBGAS
Bulgaria, Interhotel near the Maritime Park.

VARNA
Cherno More, 35 Georgi Dimitrov Boulevard. Tel: 22391. Near the Marine Gardens and open all year.
Odessa, 4 Cernoarmiejski Boulevard. Tel: 25653. Also near the gardens and also year-round.

DRUZBA
Grand Hotel Varna. Tel: 86-1491. 736-room Swedish-built resort hotel. About 8 miles from Varna and open all year.

ZLATNI PJASACI
Golden Sands)
Gdansk, **Pliska** and **Veliko Tarnovo** are the three pyramids with a snack bar but no restaurant. Numerous other hotels, some open all year.

ALBENA
Dobrudja is the newest among the complex of hotels.

BALCHIK
Beljat Brjag motels about 4 miles out of town.

SLANCEV BRJAG
(Sunny Beach)
Globus is probably the best in the main resort; villas for rent at Zora, a couple of miles away, and self-catering at the Elenite further out.

FOOD DIGEST

RUSSIA

On his first morning in Russia, a veteran foreign correspondent who made a proud point of eating local dishes wherever he went airily ordered "a typical Russian breakfast" in his Moscow hotel and ended up wondering how to react to a large bowl of cold beetroot. There was a breakdown of communication somewhere because beetroot is by no means the usual Russian breakfast – bread with either jam or a slice of cold meat is more likely – although there is an awful lot of beetroot about in Russian cuisine, beginning with various kinds of borsch soup.

Drawing up a list of authentically typical Russian dishes would in any case be an academic exercise. Chicken Kiev, which until recently would have been considered quintessentially Russia, is if anything Ukrainian, and these days that difference is a political issue. Just as there are now more Indian restaurants in London than New Delhi, the Soviet empire attracted the regional variations of a large chunk of the world to the Moscow centre, with the result that ethnic restaurants probably outnumber exclusively Russian establishments.

In any case, the dishes on the menu are almost irrelevant to the traditional concept of a Russian restaurant, which was of a place with the charisma of a factory canteen doling out food that served no greater purpose than to keep body and soul together for another 24 hours. On the other hand, a Georgian or Uzbek establishment a few doors away might be alive with lip-smacking bon viveurs. The problem was getting into either: it was a case of using advanced psychological techniques to paralyse the doorman long enough to barge past.

While it is as true today as it ever was that the food served to guests in an ordinary Russian home surpasses the fare in an ordinary restaurant, the blurring of the distinction between hard- and local-currency restaurants together with the birth of privatisation and Russian yuppiedom has meant that the range of choice and prices is moving closer to Western norms.

Beetroot aside, the unremarkable offerings for breakfast in hotels these days can be Russified by the addition of *tvorog* (deep-fried curds), *kefir* (a kind of yogurt) or *kasha* (porridge). Lunch and dinner menus are as interchangeable as they are in the West, and either can be major productions with *zakuski* (appetisers) followed by a hot or cold soup substantial enough to be regarded as a main course.

Curiously, many restaurants refuse to serve soup after 4pm, presumably to urge customers on to the main courses proper. These are a choice between fish, poultry and meat followed by a pudding. The accompanying drinks begin with a vodka or two to put the world right, followed by wines in the conventional order, with perhaps champagne standing in for the white, and brandy to round things off. It is acceptable, and indeed expected, even in the most genteel company – to leave the table worse for wear. Russians tend to get jollier as things progress, not morose.

The specialities to look out for in these various courses, accompanied by the many kinds of Russian bread, are as follows:

Zakuski (appetisers)
The big treat is of course caviar (*ikra*), with the distinction drawn between *chornaya*, the black variety from the sturgeon, and *krasnaya* from the salmon. These are normally served with toast, but they are even better with the famous bliny pancakes, preferably with sour cream (*so smitanou*).

The array of cold fish is likely to include smoked salmon (*kapchonaya syomga*), sturgeon (*osetrina*) and lesser varieties in aspic. The hot dishes are generally chicken (*stolichny*) in thin strips in a white sauce, or mushrooms in sour cream (*griby v smitane*).

Salad (*salat*) comes in numerous combinations, the classic Russian version containing a bit of all of them, like ham, chicken, egg, carrot, peas, onion and cucumber. Because of the climate, Russians of necessity perfected the art of pickling vegetables, although a whole head of pickled garlic may put off the faint-hearted.

Soups
Beetroot is accompanied in the celebrated borsch by a meat stock, cabbage and sour cream with a little pasty (*pirogi*) on the side. *Shchi* puts the emphasis on the cabbage content, *pelmeni* has the distinction of pasta balls or dumplings, and *ukha* is a fish soup. *Okroshka* is a thin vegetable soup served cold, the predominant flavour being provided by the ubiquitous beetroot.

Fish
The presence of Russian fishing fleets off countries like Mozambique indicates how low the more convenient stocks have run. Stock fish are generally nondescript catches from the Arctic. Sturgeon (*osetrina*) may be served either fried (*free*) or in a casserole with tomatoes and vegetables (*pa-russki*). Trout are *faryel*, while the *soodak* which crops up on menus is pike.

Meats
Steaks and roasts are certain to disappoint or at least taste unfamiliar. With the exception of Beef Stroganov, evidently of Siberian origin, the most palatable meat dishes are ethnic imports: kebabs (*shashlik*), a tangy Georgian chicken (*tsiplyata* or *kuritsa tabaka*) and various meat-and-rice pilafs (*plof*). Interesting things can be done with duck (*ootka*) and goose (*goos*).

Puddings
Russians eat ice cream (*marozhenoye*) at any time in any weather and after a meal with or without rum baba (*romovaya baba*), jam pancakes (*blinchiki s'varyenyem*) or rather sickly cakes in ostentatious hues.

DRINKING NOTES

The traditional Russian drink is of course vodka, swallowed ice-cold, neat, at a gulp and after a toast to anyone or anything. The crackdown on alcoholism by Gorbachev in 1985 will not affect visitors with access to hard-currency shops and bars except that they might wish to postpone lunch until 2pm, when alcohol sales officially commence. The flavoured vodkas less familiar to Westerners are generally not drunk with meals.

The best wine-producing areas, Georgia and Crimea, are outside Russia proper, and the break-up of the Soviet Union may persuade these producers to pay more attention to non-rouble markets, as indeed Bulgaria has done. If this were to happen, Georgia and Ukraine would probably follow the Bulgarian example and continue to ship Russia the inferior stuff. This would not concern Russians too much because they tend towards wines which are sweeter than Westerners would normally drink.

Tsinandali and Gurdjiani are among the drier Georgian whites; the reds to look out for are

Mukuzani and Kaketi. Soviet "champagne", which can no longer be called that, is a fairly common tipple, about a third of the cost of a bottle of vodka, but Westerners would probably find most of it too sweet. There is a "brut", but it is not as widely available.

Georgian and Armenian brandies are not at all bad, and the quality improves noticeably with the number of stars on the label, a progression duly reflected in the price.

Russian beer (*pivo*) is cheap but insipid. The hard currency bars sell foreign brews, in one or two places on draught.

Ordinary coffee is hard to come by; the usual offering is the thick, sweet Turkish type. Tea (*chai*) is the everyday drink, served in tall glasses with metal holders. Milk is never added and the sweetening ingredient is a blob of jam.

RESTAURANTS

RUSSIA

One of the great heroes of perestroika is a certain Andrei Fyodorov, who in 1987 opened Moscow first "co-operative" restaurant in Kropotkinskaya. Within a year there were more than 100 in Moscow alone. As one might expect, some are better than others, but it among their number that visitors are most likely to find satisfaction. Most of them are officially dry, so it is a case of bring your own.

Although McDonald's has hogged the limelight, Russian fast food is sold through a number of different outlets: *shashlichnaya* (kebabs), *pyelmennaya* (pasta balls stuffed with meat), *sosiskaya* (sausages), *blinnaya* (blinies) and *pirozhkovaya* (pie stalls). Cafés are not exactly fast food: they fit a slot between restaurants and cafeteria (*stolovaya*).

Moscow

The restaurant scene, especially the "co-operative" sector, is so fluid that we can only suggest visitors find out whether those listed below are still functioning or whether there are any newcomers which have clearly overtaken them. The special number to call for information about new co-operatives is 929-3762.

Ulitsa Kropotkinskaya 36. Tel: 201-7500. Was the pioneering co-operative specialising in northern Russian dishes, mainly meat and dumplings.
Rasgulyai, Ulitsa Startakovskaya. Tel: 267-7613. Quickly set the standard to which other co-ops aspire with classic Russian dishes.
Kolkhida, 6 Sadovaya-Samotyochnaya. Tel: 299-6757. Specialises in Georgian cooking.
Atrium, Leninsky Prospekt. Tel: 137-3008. Is part Caucasian, part Byzantine.
Gunaya, opposite Park Kultury metro, Georgian specialities.
Bely Lebed, 3 Sivtsev Vrazhek. Tel: 203-1283. Russian and Armenian.

Of the older city-run restaurants, two used to stand out and it remains to be seen how they respond to the competition.
Aragavi, 6 Ulitsa Gorkovo. Tel: 299-8506. Was the best place in Moscow for years, a Georgian hang-out.
Uzbekistan, 29 Ulitsa Neglinnaya. Tel: 294-6053. The attraction being not the food as much as the regulars, homesick Uzbekis whose nostalgia late at night brought on a certain resemblance to Genghis Khan.

The hotels with the best restaurants are:
Praga Hotel, 2 Ulitsa Arnat. Tel: 290-8171.
National Hotel, 1 Ulitsa Gorkovo. Tel: 203-5595.
Metropol Hotel, 1 Prospekt Marksa. Tel: 225-6677.

St Petersburg

With the same qualifications about their counterparts in Moscow, these co-operatives are worth considering:
Azerbaijani Café, Ulitsa Gavanskaya, convenient to the otherwise remote Pribaltiskaya Hotel.
Aist Café, 79 Karl Marx Prospekt.
Brik Café, 22 Ulitsa Kolokolnaya.
Iveria Café, 35 Ulitsa Marata.
Classic, 202 Ligovsky Prospekt.
Restaurant Na Fontanka, 77 Fontanka Embankment.
Uralskiye Pelmeni, 12 Ulitsa Blokhina.

Of the city-owned restaurants, the following have secure reputations:
Kavkazky, 25 Nevsky Prospekt. Tel: 146-656. Serves imaginative Georgian dishes.
Astoria Hotel restaurant, 39 Ulitsa Gartsena. Tel: 219-1100. Popular with the military brass.
Dubrava and **Neva restaurants**, Pribaltiyskaya Hotel, 14 Ulitsa Korablestroitelei. Tel: 356-0158.
Yevropeiskaya Hotel (formerly Hotel de l'Europe), Ulitsa Brodskovo. Tel: 211-9149. The top floor Art Deco restaurant.

MUSCOVY: GOLDEN RING

Yaroslavl
Moskva Restaurant, 1 Ulitsa Komosomolskaya.
Chaika, Ulitsa Lenina.
Rossiya, Ulitsa Chkalov.

Vladimir
Traktir Restaurant, 2 Ulitsa Stolyarova.
Golden Gates Restaurant, 17 Ulitsa Tretyego Interntsionala.

Suzdal
Pokrovskaya Hotel in the Motel Suzdal complex.
Trapeznaya, in the town kremlin.

Novgorod
Detinets Tourist Restaurant, in the kremlin tower.

BLACK SEA REGION

Kurortny Prospekt in Sochi is lined with restaurants, but it is worth looking farther afield than this main tourist track. In the town itself, two are worthy of special attention:

Primorsky Restaurant, 21 Primorskaya.
Goluboy Restaurant, 8 Voikov Street.

Out of town:
Akhun Restaurant on Bolshoi Akhum mountain.
Kavkazski Aul Restaurant in the Agura valley.
Staraya Melnitsa Restaurant on Bytkha Hill.
Gorskaya Derenya at the Agura waterfalls.

UKRAINE

Ukraine can without too much argument claim Chicken Kiev as a national speciality among "Russian" dishes, but it always wants the credit for borsch. The local cooking goes in for liberal use of garlic, pepper and vinegar, and the stews and casseroles are often accompanied by small pastries. Dumplings come with various stuffings. One of the national dishes may strike foreigners as a slightly odd combination: pork and beetroot. *Kartoflia solimkoi* are deep-fried potato matchsticks.

KIEV
Dubki, 1 Ulitsa Stetsenki.
Kureni, 4 Parkovaya Alley.
Mlyn, Trukhanova Island in the Hydropark.
Vitryak, in the Pirogovo Museum.
A number of restaurants are grouped around Ulitsa Kreshchatik.

LVOV
Apart from the restaurants in the Intourist and Lvov Hotels, the most reliable seem to be:
Moskva, 7 Mickiewicz Square.
Pervomaisky, Lenin Prospekt.

ZAPOROZHYE
Dnepro, 202 Lenin Prospect.
Zaporozhye, 135 Lenin Prospect.
Teatralnaya, 23 Chekista Street.

ODESSA
Outside the previously listed hotels, consider:
Ukraina, 12 Karl Marx Street.
Chernomorsky, 23 Karl Marx Street.
Yuzhny, 12 Khalturin Street.
Volna, down at the harbour.

CRIMEA
There are predictably places to eat all along the Ukrainian Riviera, but the more serious restaurants are concentrated in and around Yalta. Apart from the hotels listed in the appropriate section above, consider:
Sitil co-op, 35 Ulitsa Balaklavskaya.Gurman co-op, on the seafront.
Hispaniola Schooner, moored near Oreanda Hotel.
Gorka and Gorny Ruchei, at the top of the cable-car on Darsan Hill.
Lesnoi, on Lake Karagol, especially for wild boar among other game dishes.
Vodopad at the Uchan-Su waterfall.
Yakor, in the port area.

BELARUS

If, for example, Hungary is the land of the paprika, Belarussian cooking is all about mushrooms, a characteristic shared with neighbouring Lithuania. Belarussians go hunting for mushrooms as French pigs go after truffles or Scottish lairds after grouse. With or without mushrooms, dishes are likely to liberally dosed with garlic and caraway.

Local specialities also include *mokanka*, a multifarious and mountainous salad usually served as a starter, and dumplings called *galushki* or *kletski*. A herbal drink known as Belovezhskaya Bitter may be too medicinal for many palates, but give it a try.

On the whole, however, it would be misguided to arrive in Belarus with high culinary expectations. Nowhere even in the capital can be singled out as a joyful experience, but it may be worth trying three outside the previously listed hotels:
Neman, 22 Lenin Prospekt, Minsk.
Kamenny Tsvetok, 12 Ulitsa Tolbukhin, Minsk.
Teatralnoye, 34 Ulitsa Gorkovo, Minsk.

ESTONIA

Tallinn, the capital of Estonia, was traditionally regarded as the culinary capital of the Baltic if not of the former Soviet Union. It remained a Soviet capital nevertheless, and that meant the accolade was relative rather than absolute. Outside a few expensive establishments, the food in private homes was generally better than in the public places that ordinary people could afford to eat in, which amounted to a stand-up bar serving a piece of meat with potatoes and one other vegetable. On special occasions, Estonians might have gone up-market to an establishment serving a rich soup (*soljanka*) as a starter and ice cream (*jaatis*) for pudding.

New restaurants are appearing all over the place and standards are rising appreciably, even if they have some way to go. Given the freedom to experiment, it is interesting to see the old historical influences at work. Fruit soups and the cakes served with afternoon coffee point at the German Balts, and variations on the theme of salted or pickled fish probably came from the Danes and the Swedes across the sea.

TALLINN
Linda, a restaurant in the Palace Hotel. Tel: 666-702. Is widely acknowledged as the best and most expensive in the city.
Sub Monte, 4 Rutli, behind the Niguliste church. Tel: 666-871. Attractive setting in a medieval cellar, good food and also pricey.
Toomkooli, 11 Toomkooli, in the ramparts of Toompea castle. Tel: 446-613. Huge menu, Saaremaa beer on draught, and reasonable prices.
Astoria, 5 Vabaduse valjak. Tel: 448-462. "Roaring Twenties" atmosphere keeps the customers awake but perversely seems to send the staff to sleep.
Miker, 3 Kuninga, Old Town. Guilty of the

pernicious practice of quoting the price of meat and fish dishes on the menu as so-much per 100 grammes, which of course is only a shadow of what one gets and is charged.

Vana Toomas, 8 Raekoja plats, Townhall Square. Tel: 652 093. Convivial and cheap; in other words, most of the customers leave, if they do not arrive, drunk.

As ever, the best bars and cafés are crowded with locals, a good omen with certain practical drawbacks.

TARTU

Gildi Frahter, 7 Gildi. Not as good or expensive as the flashy decor implies.

Tarvas, 2 Riia. Tel: 32 253. Haunt of the *nouveaux riches*.

Poossirohukelder, 28 Lossi. Tel: 34-124. In a former powder cellar.

In Narva and other towns, stick to the main hotels unless locals recommend restaurants of 1993 or later vintage.

LATVIA

Latvian food is mild and light on spices, the preference being for dairy products – notably cheeses and curdled milk – and various preparations of potatoes served in a separate dish. Among the specialities are pearl-barley soup with dried mushrooms, smoked pork with "grey" peas, and whipped cream on bread. Most characteristic of all, perhaps, are *piragi* – little rolls with bacon and onions. In the more serious restaurants, look out for *Riga Tel'noe* (deep-fried fish fillets stuffed with mushroom and anchovy) and hare cooked in mushroom, cheese, wine and herbs. Latvian Aldaris beer puts Russian beer to shame.

RIGA

The hotels previously listed have good or indeed very good restaurants. In addition to these, try:

Astoria, 16 Audeju Street (near the Riga Hotel), above the department store.

Straburags, 55 Suvorov Street, for fish.

Kaukazs, 8 Merkela Street, near the railway station.

Scecina, 260 Maskavas Street, a Polish restaurant about 3 km up-river.

Riga, 22 Aspazijas Boulevard.

Put vejini (literally "Blow, wind!"), 18 Jauniela (off 17 June Square).

Of the numerous cafés and bars, try:
Apollo, **Café of Thirteen Chairs** and **Petercailis**.

SIGULDA

Senite Restaurant, near the Sigulda and Turaida Castles, is a distinguished exception to the rule that restaurants outside Riga hardly had a chance to establish a track record under the Soviets. No doubt this situation will change rapidly in 1993 and afterwards.

LITHUANIA

As far as Lithuanian cuisine is built around one single factor, it is the noble cabbage. Wonderful things happen to the cabbage here: as *golubtsy* it has a meat stuffing, otherwise it appears with bacon or apples. When the cabbage is rested, the potato steps in as *cepelinai* – mashed, rolled, filled with meat and annointed with a bacon-butter sauce – or as *bulvinai blynai* (pancakes), *vedarai* (with a sausage) etc. Game dishes rule the top of the culinary scale.

VILNIUS

The best restaurants in Vilnius, a relative term, are found in the Old Town. The new generation of private restaurants usually open in converted basements.

Stikliai, 7 Gaono. Tel: 627971. To which visiting dignitaries are invariably whisked.

Medininkai, 4 Ausros Vartu. Tel: 61-4019.

Lokys, 8 Stikliu. Tel: 62-9046. Wild boar and elk in season.

Senasis Rusys, 16 Sv. Ignoto. Tel: 61-1137.

Bociu, 4 Sv. Ignoto. Tel: 62-3772.

Literatu Svetaine, 1 Gedimino pr. Tel: 61-1889.

Viola, 3 Kalvariju, Armenian food.

Zaliasis, 43A Jankiskiu. Tel: 65-3233.

TRAKAI

Kibinine Café, Melnikaite, for Crimean specialities.

KAUNAS

Gildija Restaurant, Old Town Square.

Ugne Café, Old Town Square.

POLAND

Poland has retained a distinctly national cuisine to an unusually high degree. It is generally heavy and filling, the overall flavour provided by dill, marjoram, caraway seeds and wild mushrooms. There is a considerable gap between restaurant food and what Poles eat at home, the latter influenced by the fact that Poles start work early (6 or 7am) and come home for a main meal at about 3pm.

Hotel breakfasts are very substantial. No fooling about with coffee and a croissant, Polish hotels send their guests into the world bursting with salami, cheese, ham, pickles, eggs, sausages, several kinds of bread and so on.

The main meal of the day, half-way between conventional lunch and dinner, has starters (*przekeska*) which may include smoked fish (*ryby wedzone*), fish marinated in sour cream. fish in aspic, stuffed fish and herring (*sledz*) in various guises, pig's knuckles (*golonka*), spicy sausages and cheese spreads, different pâtés (*pasztety*) and smoked bacon and ham (*szynka*). Hot starters include beef or lamb pieces in bouillon (*kolduny*) and mushroom and cabbage pasties (*kulebiak*), at which point a Pole is ready for the *sine qua non* of every meal, soup.

Not, for Poles, a watery soup but one that will hold a spoon upright. Sour cream provides the thickening for pearl barley, noodles, dumplings or suet balls. If clear soups do appear, they are accompanied by stuffed hot pasties.

Main dishes make use of pork (*wieprzowina*), beef (*wolowina*), duck (*kaczka*), goose (*ges*), hare (*zajac*) and venison (*sarnina*). The main course might equally be fish, however, like trout (*pstrag*) or pike with horseradish (*szczupak w sosie chrzanowym*) or sweet and sour carp (*karp w galarecie*). Cabbage leaves stuffed with beef and rice are *golabki*. Two noteworthy favourites are *flaki*, which is seasoned tripe, and *pierogi*, stuffed noodles. If Poles were to nominate a national dish, however, it would probably be *bigos*, which is sauerkraut, cabbage and onions supplemented by whatever meat comes to hand plus sausages and smoked bacon.

Poles drink vodka as heroically as Russians, but they are also partial to beer (*piwo*) with meals and to mead (*miod*). Wine is imported and therefore expensive. As in Russia, tea is drunk without milk.

WARSAW

Bazyliszek, 7–9 Rynek Starego Miasta, Old Town Square. Tel: 31-1841. The perennial favourite with visitors and has a good spread of game in season.
Canaletto, Victoria Intercontinental Hotel, 11 Krolewska Ulica. Tel: 27-8011. Generally recognised as Warsaw's best.
Klub Swietoszek, 6/8 Jezuicka Ulica. Tel: 31-5634. A co-op that has soared to become the Canaletto's closest rival.
Kamienne Schodki, 26 Rynek Starego Miasta. Tel: 31-0822. Widely admired duck dishes.
Wilanow, 27 Wiernicza Ulica. Tel: 42-1852. Near the Wilanow Palace.
Kuznia Krolewska, 24 Wiernicza Ulica. Tel: 42-3171. Also near the palace.
Lers, 29 Dluga Ulica. Tel: 635-3888. Near the Old Town and moderately priced.

Cafés:
Krokodyl, 19 Rynek Starego Miasta. Tel: 31-4427.
Bombonierka and **Fukier**, in the same square.
Telimena, 27 Krakowskie Przedmiescie, literary watering hole.

CRACOW

Wierzynek, 16 Rynek Glowny, Town Square. Tel: 22-9896. Reputed by many to be the best Polish restaurant in the world. King Casimir III (1310–70) used it, as did his contemporary Emperor Charles IV. To the restaurant's immortal credit, prices are not at all steep.
Hawelka, at number 24 in the same square. Tel: 22-4753. Will not disappoint those who cannot get into Wierzynek.
U Wentzla, at number 18, completes a distinguished triumvirate.
Starpoloska, 4 Ulica Sienna. Tel: 22-5821. Simple but honest with some respite for vegetarians in a generally non-vegetarian society.

ORBIS hotel restaurants are reliable.

Cafés:
Jama Michalika, 45 Florianska Ulica, a famous Art Nouveau rendezvous.
Noworol, Old Cloth Hall, Rynek Glowny.
Ratuszowa, basement, Town Hall tower, Rynek Glowny.

GDANSK
Summer brings tables and chairs out on pavements all over Gdansk. Serious restaurants include:
Pod Lososiem, 11 Szeroka Ulica, for fish in the Old Town.
Pod Wieza, 51 Piwna Ulica, also central, excellent stews.
Kaszubska, 76 Kartuska Ulica, fish specialities.

ZAKOPANE
Obrochtowka, Kraszewskiego Ulica, a pleasant little place just out of town.
Siedem Kotow, also on the outskirts.

SZCZECIN
Jubilatka, 41 Wojska Polskiego.
Chief, 16 Swierczewskiego Ulica.

WROCLAW
Polonia, 68 Gen Swierczewskiego. Tel: 31021.

CZECH REPUBLIC

The underlying cause of the former federation of Czechoslovakia was the deep cultural division created by Habsburg-Germanic influence on the Czechs and Moravians as opposed to Magyar-Hungarian influence on the Slovaks. The division is reflected in the food: Czech food – hearty helpings of pork, goose and dumplings – washed down with beer versus a Slovak preference for goulash and wine.

The typical cold starter in Czech cuisine is thinly sliced Prague ham, and it's meat all the way thereafter, ideally roast pork with sauerkraut and dumplings or goose or duck with the same trimmings. Expect hare, venison and game birds when the shooting season opens in autumn. When fish appears on a menu it is usually carp. The rich sauces served with the meat dishes are mopped up with dumplings. Fresh vegetables are usually murdered when they put in a rare appearance.

In the absence of vegetables, the abundance of home-grown fruit is perhaps surprising, although it is less likely to be served whole than in apple strudels and the like.

Restaurant tables were hard to come by even for lunch before the post-independence tourist inundation, so booking is almost essential. Failing that, lighter meals are served in wine bars and beer halls.

Czech beer is more famous than American visitors may realise. Their Budweiser takes its name from the Bohemian city of Ceske Budejovice whose name, in German, was Budweis. The original is sold in the country of origin as Budwar in various strengths, most rather more powerful than their American counterparts. The other celebrated local brewery produces Pilsen Urquell. The power of some forms of plum brandy, *slivovice*, is awesome.

Three Ostriches Restaurant in the hotel of the same name near the Charles Bridge at 12 Drazicheho namesti. Tel: 53-6151. Is with good reason heavily over-subscribed, so book as far in advance as possible.

Europa Hotel, 25 Wenceslas Square, has unremarkable food but is the best people show in town.

Hanavsky Pavilion, 173 Letenske sady. Tel: 32-5792. The river terrace in summer, especially.

Klasterni Vinarna, Narodni trida. A former convent, close to the National Theatre.

Opera Grill, 24 Divadelni. Tel: 26-5508. Gracious.

Pelikan, 7 Na Prikope. Tel: 37-4546. Elegant and reasonable.

Rotisserie, 6 Mikulanska. Always busy.

Staroprazska Rychta, 7 Vaclavske namesti. A dreamy place.

U Kalicha, 12 Na bojisti. Tel: 29-6017. Not a restaurant at all but a beer hall famous as the watering hole of Jaroslav Hacek, creator of *The Good Soldier Schweik*. The food hardly matters.

U Fleku, 11 Kremencova. Tel: 29-2436. Another beer hall where Hacek would have been equally at home.

Outside Prague: the best restaurants are invariably in the hotels shown in the earlier hotel listings.

SLOVAK REPUBLIC

For a general idea of Slovak cooking, please refer to the notes on Hungarian food below.

BRATISLAVA

Arkadia, 3 Beblaveho. Tel: 33-5650. "Hungarian" specialities including goose-liver.

Vel'ki Frantiskani, 10 Dibrovovo namesti. Tel: 33-3073. The Magyar theme is taken a step further with gypsy violinists.

The hotels and mountain lodges in the Low and High Tatras provide the kind of food which keeps long-distance hikers striding purposefully forwards.

HUNGARY

Hungary is a bit like France in that any restaurant serving really evil food would soon go out of business. Hungarians love to eat well, and the cuisine is by no means as insular as the language. It has borrowed from countries all around, so to think purely in terms of goulash is a grotesque oversimplification. The belief that practically everything is laced with paprika is not far from the truth.

Landlocked Hungary would not automatically make one think of bouillabaise, but that would be to overlook Lake Balaton. The result is *halaszle*, which comes either clear or thick and creamy.

Porkolt or *tokany* is closest to the general idea of goulash, a pork stew served with sour cream and dumplings. In Hungary, the *gulyas leves* is rather a soup than a stew. The Transylvanian variation (reflecting the days when Transylvania was part of the Hungarian kingdom) adds extra cabbage among other things.

Kolozsvari rakottkaposzta is a kind of lasagna with layers of cabbage instead of pasta, the filling made up of smoked sausage and pork with rice and eggs. Cabbage leaves are the shell around minced meat in a tomato sauce in *toltott kaposzta*; in its perhaps more familiar form, with peppers forming the shell, the dish is known as *toltott paprika*. Steak, onions, paprika and potatoes go together as *serpenyos rostelyos*, and there is a Hungarian version of Wiener schnitzel called *becsi szelet*.

When chicken has been given the paprika treatment it emerges as *paprikas csirke* (with a sour cream sauce and a cucumber salad on the side), a dish in which turkey or duck are sometimes substituted. King of the poultry dishes is *liba maj*, or fried goose livers at a regal price.

Sweets are taken very seriously indeed, eaten as a pudding or bought from a pastry shop at other times. *Retes* are flaky pastry filled with ground nuts; *dobostorta* are the layered cakes with a hard, sugared top.

"Bull's Blood" is to Hungarian wine what goulash is to the food. It is a full-blooded variety (Egri Bikaver) able to hold its own against all the paprika, but there are also lighter wines, including whites. Tokay is of course legendary.

BUDAPEST

The state-ownership of restaurants under Communism did not weigh as heavily on the quality of the food and service as in most other East European countries. Liberalisation has improved the already good standards and also opened up the gap between the most expensive and cheapest establishments. One gypsy violinist strolling about with a fiddle under his chin won't necessarily increase the bill, but a whole orchestra undoubtedly does. The list of good or even excellent restaurants is too long to be fitted in here, so we have excluded hotel restaurants and many other worthy contenders in order to mention those with some notable speciality.

Alabardos, 2 Orszaghaz utca. Tel: 156-0851. Goose liver at a price.

Arany Hordo, 16 Tarnok utca. Tel: 156-6765. 14th-century building on Castle Hill, fish specialities.

Café Hungaria (New York Café), 9 Erzsebet korut. Tel: 122-3849. Once famous, it went into a decline but is now poised for a renaissance under new owners.

Paradiso, 40a Istenhegyi utca. Tel: 156-1988. Private villa in Buda Hills within reach of South Station.

Gundel, 2 Allatkerti korut. Tel: 122-1002. Founded by the author of a famous 1910 cookbook (Karoly Gundel) but unequal for the past 40 years to the standard he set. It may be in for a renaissance as well.

Kiskakukk, 12 Pozsonyi utca. Tel: 132-1732. Game dishes at moderate prices.

Legradi Testverek, 23 Magyar utca. Tel: 118-6804. A treat, albeit extravagant.

Margitkert, 15 Margit utca. Tel: 135-4791. Traditional Hungarian dishes and gypsies in full song.

Regi Orszaghaz, 17 Orszaghaz utca. Tel: 175-0650. Historic inn on Castle Hill

Szazeves, 2 Pesti Barnabas utca. Tel: 118-3608. Charming location and some rare fish dishes, at a price.

This list regrettably makes no mention of numerous very good "ethnic" (i.e. non-Hungarian) restaurants.

EGER

Feher Szarvas, 8 Klapka utca. Tel: 1322-23. Renowned for wild game dishes.

ESZTERGOM

Uszo Halaszcsarda, Esztergom Island. Tel: 230. Specialises in fish.

PECS

Elefant Sorozo, 6 Jokai ter. Tel: 134-49. Quaint.

SZEGED

Alabardos, 13 Oskola utca, cellar restaurant.

Halaszcsarda, 12 Roosevelt ter. Riverside fish restaurant.

ROMANIA

Romanian cuisine was a big factor in Bucharest's pre-war celebrity as the "Paris of the Balkans", but the post-war years emphatically put paid to that. The stable these days is a kind of corn mush known as *mamliga* and the most readily available biscuits, *pogacsa*, are made out of baking powder. Eating has improved since Ceausecu's policy of exporting all foodstuffs was halted, but it is still rather basic. Breakfast in hotels is substantial – cold meats, cheese, fried eggs, bread and jam, etc – so it is sensible to emulate the camel by filling up for what could turn out to be a barren time ahead.

Romanian starters are generally little skinless sausages, grilled and served hot, and vegetable purees, usually spinach or beans with other ingredients to enliven the taste. Pork or chicken in aspic makes *piftie*. Soup is a good standby. Practically anything qualifies as an ingredient, but with a sure touch the results are both tasty and filling.

While *mamliga* (possibly enhanced by meat pieces in a garlic sauce) remains the reality for most people, traditional main dishes include pork stuffed with ham and cheese under a rich sauce (*muschi ciobanesc*) and beef stuffed with mushrooms, bacon, peppers under a tomato and puree sauce (*maschi poiana*). Moldavian dishes are generally chicken-based.

Some of the sweets are obviously of foreign origin (e.g. baclava), but Romanians have a line of their own in excellent doughnuts, some with a cheese filling.

Romanian wines are appearing all over Western Europe these days in an attempt to emulate the remarkable export record of Bulgarian wine. The wine that stays behind is perfectly drinkable. It goes down easily enough, but a second bottle (per head) may result in remorse the following morning. Tuica, a fruit brandy made mainly from plums, demands respect. The beer is good.

BUCHAREST

Capsa, 34 Calea Victoriei. Tel: 13-4482. The best glimpse of what Bucharest must have been before the rot set in.

Casa Lido, in the Lido Hotel, Magheru Boulevard. Tel: 14-4930. Good fish to gypsy music.

Doina, 4 Soseaua Kiseleff.

Hanul Manuc (Manuc's Inn), 30 Decembrie. Tel: 13-1415. Another nostalgic glimpse of Bucharest of old.

Parcul Privighetorilor, 3 Calea Dorobanti. Tel: 12-1743. Good local atmosphere.

ALBA IULIA

Crama Cetate, tavern in the citadel wall.

BRASOV

Carpathian Stag (Cerbul Carpatin), Republicii Street, in an old townhouse.

Cetatuia Fortress. Sometimes lays on an operetta while guests eat.

NEPTUN

Insula, on an island in the lake.

Calul Balan, in the Comorova forest.

SIBIU

Butoiul de Aur, Sibiul Vechi and Bufnita are all colourful taverns in the Old Town.

SIGISOARA

The Citadel. The associations with Dracula draw the crowds even if the food doesn't.

TIMISOARA

Bastion, 2 Hector Street. Tel: 13-3172. Restaurant in the Turkish fortifications.

CONSTANTA

Casa cu Lei, good restaurant with impressive decor.

BULGARIA

The pity in Bulgaria is that all too many restaurants aspire to be "international" when Bulgarian food can be delicious and all but the most timorous visitors would probably prefer to eat it. Like Greek food, Bulgarian cooking carries the hallmark of the "Ottoman Yoke" but manages it altogether better. The main ingredients are lamb, potatoes, tomatoes, onions, peppers and eggplant.

The Bulgarian equivalent of a Greek salad is *shopska salata*, a mixture of chopped cucumber, tomato, onion and red peppers with a sprinkling of sheep's cheese (*sirene*). Bulgarians, however, wash it down with a gulp of *rakiya* or plum brandy. The three most popular soups are *tarator* (yogurt, cucumber, garlic and walnuts served cold), *bob bobchorba* (bean soup) and *shkembe chorba* (tripe, garlic and red peppers).

The simplest main courses are spicy grilled meat balls made of veal or pork and kebabs. Casseroles are made up of meat and vegetables crowned with poached eggs, and both chicken and fish are done in a rich sauce of tomatoes and peppers. *Agneski drebulijki* is a kind of deluxe kebab made of grilled liver, kidney and other chunks of meat, while a *mesana skara* is to all intents and purposes a mixed grill. Meat is used as a stuffing in cabbage leaves (*sarmi*), peppers and eggplant. *Banitsa* is a cheese or spinach pastry; *sirene po sopski* a baked cheese dish.

Meals are rounded with a very superior yogurt made of sheep's milk or fresh fruit. *Lokum* is Turkish delight.

Oceans of Bulgarian wine, mainly red, have been sold in the West since the mid-1980s so many visitors will already be familiar with them. Those who are not may drink assured. Of the strong drink, the ubiquitous *radiya* is joined by *mastika*, which tastes like ouzo or pernod, and the more delicate liqueur made from rose petals.

Coffee is either Turkish or espresso; tea is usually taken black.

Sofia
Bulgaria is a curious inversion of the general East European rule that the capital is much better served by restaurants than the outlying areas. Outside the main hotels, the majority of Sofia restaurants are not as good as they ought to be. They seem to allow their attention to be lost in putting on folkloric shows, which are all right once or twice but not with every meal. Some of the exceptions are:
Koprivshtitsa, 3 Vitosha Boulevard. A popular tourist haunt.
Crystal, 10 Aksakov Street. Tel: 88-1172.
Ropotamo, 63 Lenin Boulevard. Tel: 72-2516.
Rubin, Sveta Nedelya. Tel: 87-2086.
Vodenicharska Mehana, at the foot of Mount Vitosha. Tel: 65-5088. Be ready for a folk show.
Pamporovo
Chevermeto-. Tel: 326. Decorated like, if it wasn't once, a mountain dairy.
Vodenicata, a converted water mill about five miles out of town.
Malina, lamb on a spit in traditional architecture.
Plovdiv
Kambanata, Pldin, Trakijski Stan and Riton in the Old Town.
Zlatnijt Elen, in the Hotel Bulgaria, for game specialities
Varna
Galata, Druzki ulitsa.
Starata Krusha, Druzki ulitsa.
Veliki Tarnovo
Rodina, 17 Dimitrov ulitsa. A National Revival house.
Boljarska Izba, Dimiter Blagoev Street.
Hadji Minco, Poborniceski Square,
Vinarna Tavern, 1 Gurko Street.

Useful Addresses

EMERGENCY NUMBERS

Fire   Tel: 01
Police   02
Ambulance   03
Gas emergency 04
These are the same throughout the old Soviet Union.

USEFUL NUMBERS IN MOSCOW

The following are all Moscow numbers:
Aeroflot international enquiries: Tel: 1568019
Sheremetievo international airport enquiries: Tel: 578-9101
Customs enquiries: Tel: 975-4584
Train enquiries in English: Tel: 921-4513
River boat enquiries: Tel: 457-4050
Intourist general enquiries: Tel: 203-6962
Dial-a-cab: Tel: 927-0000 or 457-9005
International telephone exchange: Tel: 8-194
International telephone enquiries: Tel: 8-190
Booking a call from your hotel room: Tel: 3334101
American Express: Tel: 2544495

CONSULATES IN MOSCOW

Argentina: Sadovaya-Triumfal'naya ul. 4/10. Tel: 299-0367.
Australia: Prechistenka (Kropotkinsky) per. 13. Tel: 246-5012.
Austria: Starokonyushenny per. 1. Tel: 201-7317.
Canada: Starokonyushenny per. 23. Tel: 241-5070.
China: Leninskie Gory, ul. Druzhby 6. Tel: 143-1543.
Czech Republic: ul. Fuchika 12/14. Tel: 250-2225.
Denmark: per. Ostrovskovo 9. Tel: 201-7868.
Finland: Prechistenka (Kropotkinsky) per. 15/17.
France: Kazansky per. 10. Tel: 236-0003.
Germany: B.Gruzinskaya ul. 17. Tel: 252-5521.
Greece: ul. Stanislavskovo 4. Tel: 290-2274.
Hungary: Mosfilmovskaya ul. 62. Tel: 143-8955
India: ul. Obukha 6-8. Tel: 297-1841.
Ireland: Grokhol'sky per. 5. Tel: 288-4101.
Italy: ul. Vesnina 5. Tel: 241-1533.
Japan: Sobinovsky per. 5a. Tel: 202-0061.

Luxemburg: Khrushchevsky per. 3. Tel: 202-2171.
Malaysia: Mosfilmovskaya ul. 50. Tel: 147-1415.
Netherlands: Kalashny per. 7. Tel: 291-2999.
New Zealand: ul. Vorovskovo 44. Tel: 290-3485.
Norway: ul. Vorovskovo 7. Tel: 290-3872.
Poland: ul. Klimashkina 4. Tel: 254-3612.
Portugal: Grokholsky per. 3/1. Tel: 230-2435
Romania: Mosfilmovskaya ul. 64. Tel: 143-0424
Singapore: per. Voevodina 5. Tel: 241-3702.
Spain: ul. Gertsena 50/8. Tel: 291-9004.
Sweden: Mosfilmovskaya ul. 60. Tel: 147-9009.
Switzerland: per. Stopani 2/5. Tel: 925-5322.
Thailand: Eropkinsky per. 3. Tel: 201-4893.
Turkey: Vadkovsky per. 7/37. Tel: 972-6900.
United Kingdom: nab. Morisa Toreza 14.
Tel: 231-8511.
United States: ul. Chaikovskovo 19/23.
Tel: 252-2451

AIRLINE OFFICES
IN MOSCOW

Air France: ul. Dobyninskaya 7. Tel: 237-2325,
237-3344. Monday–Friday 9am–1pm and 2–6pm.
Air India: ul. Dobryninskaya 7, korp.1 (ground
floor). Tel: 237-7494, 236-4440. Monday–Friday
9.30am–1pm and 2–5.15pm, Saturday 10am–3pm.
Alitalia: ul. Pushechnaya 7. Tel: 923-9840/56.
Monday–Friday 9.30am–1.30pm and 2–6pm,
Saturday 9.30am–1pm.
Austrian Airlines: Krasnopresnenskaya nab. 12,
fl.18, Office 1805. Tel: 253-8268, 253-1670/71.
Monday–Friday 9am–6pm, Saturday 9am–1pm.
British Airways: Krasnopresnenskaya nab. 12, fl.19,
Office 1905. Tel: 253-2492. Monday–Friday 9am–
6pm.
Finnair: Proyzd Khudozhestvennovo Teatra 6. Tel:
292-8788, 292-3337. Monday–Friday 9am–5pm.
Japan Airlines: ul. Kuznetsky Most 3. Tel: 921-
6448, 921-6648. Monday–Friday 9am–6pm.
KLM: (Royal Dutch Airlines), Krasnopresnenskaya
nab. 12, fl. 13, Office 1307. Tel: 253-2150/51.
Monday–Friday 9am–5pm.
Lufthansa: (German Airlines), ul. Kuznetsky Most
3. Tel: 923-0488, 923-0576. Monday–Friday 9am–
5.30pm.
Pan American: Krasnopresnenskaya nab. 12, fl.11,
Office 1102A. Tel: 253-2658/59. Monday–Friday
9am–5.30pm.
LOT: (Polish Airlines), ul. Dobryninskaya 7, Office
5. Tel: 238-0003, 238-0313. Monday–Friday 9am–
6pm, Saturday 9am–5pm.
Sabena: (Belgian World Airlines), Hotel Belgrade-
II, fl.7, kom.721. Tel: 248-1214, 230-2241. Mon-
day–Friday 9am–1pm and 2–6pm.
SAS: (Scandinavian Airlines), ul. Kuznetsky Most 3.
Tel: 925-4747. Monday–Friday 9am–6pm, Saturday 9am–noon.
Swissair: Krasnopresnenskaya nab. 12, fl.20, Office
2005. Tel: 253-8988, 253-1859. Monday–Friday
9am–6pm.

These airlines and others have also offices in
Sheremetevo-2 Airport.

AIRLINE OFFICES
ST PETERSBURG

Finnair: ul. Gogolya 19. Tel: 315-9736, 312-8987.
Pan-American: ul. Gertsena 36. Tel: 311-5819,
311-5820, 311-5822.

These airlines and Air France, British Airways,
KLM, Lufthansa and LOT also have their offices in
Pulkovo-2 Airport.

BELARUS

USEFUL NUMBERS

Customs office: 2a ul. Ostrovskogo, 220004 Minsk.
Tel: 203822.
Belintourist: 19, pr. Masherova, 220078 Minsk. Tel:
269840/260793.
**Society of Friendship and Cultural Relations with
Foreign Countries**: 28 ul. Zakharova, 220665
Minsk. Tel: 332781/331821.
German consulate: 26 ul. Zakharova, 220034
Minsk. Tel: 332409/330752.
International flight information: Tel: 973941/
973734.
Air and rail information: Tel: 233551/269233.
Taxi call desk for foreigners: Tel: 269832.

LATVIA

EMERGENCY NUMBERS

Fire	Tel:	01
Police		02
Ambulance		03
Gas emergency		04

USEFUL NUMBERS & ADDRESSES

Road accidents: Tel: 223074
Lost property: 219635
Train information: 007
Train tickets ordered by phone: 226002
Main bus terminal: 213611
Tourist information (English spoken): 212927
British embassy: 320737
Long-distance operator: 812
Long-distance information: 818

Long-distance calls, placed either through your
hotel switchboard or at the main post office on
Brivibas Bulvaris, are expensive. Direct dialling
doesn't exist.

The British Embassy, Elizabetes iela 2, Riga
226010. Tel: 320737/325287.
The American Embassy, Raina Bulvars 7, Riga
226050. Tel: 211572/228289/210005.

LITHUANIA

EMERGENCY NUMBERS

Fire   Tel: 01
Police   02
Ambulance   03
Gas emergency 04

USEFUL NUMBERS & ADDRESSES

Airport information: Tel: 630201/635560/669465
Train information: Tel: 630086
Dial-a-cab: Tel: 772929

The British Embassy, Antakalnio St 2, Vilnius 2055. Tel: 222070; fax: 357579.
The US Embassy, Akmemu St 6, Vilnius 2600. Tel: 223031; fax: 222724.

POLAND

EMERGENCY NUMBERS

The following essential phone numbers can be used free of charge:
Police   Tel: 997
Fire   998
Ambulance   999

USEFUL NUMBERS & ADDRESSES

Roadside assistance. Repairs carried out by PZM, the Polish motor society, ul. Kazimierzowka 66, 02/518 Warsaw. Tel: 981
More roadside assistance: Tel: 954
International airport: Tel: 469873
Main customs office: Tel: 6943587/6955596
International rail information: Tel: 204512
Domestic rail information: Tel: 200361
Polish Ocean Lines information: Tel: 248925
Polish Baltic Lines information: Tel: 302961
Long-distance operator: Tel: 900
International operator: Tel: 901

British Embassy, Al Roz 1, 00-556 Warsaw. Tel: 281001; tlx: 813694; fax: 217161.
German Embassy, Dabrowiecka 30, 03-932 Warsaw. Tel: 173011; tlx: 813455; fax: 173582.
US Embassy, Al Ujazdowskie, 00-540 Warsaw. Tel: 283041; tlx: 813304.

CZECH & SLOVAK REPUBLICS

EMERGENCY NUMBERS

Ambulance and doctor   Tel: 155
Fire   150
Police   158

USEFUL NUMBERS & ADDRESSES

Breakdown service: Tel: 154
24-hour rail travel information: Tel: 264930/2360565
Bus travel information: Tel: 221445
Dial-a-cab: Tel: 203941/202951
Information on boat trips: Tel: 293803

British Embassy, Thunovska 14, 12550 Prague 6. Tel: 533347; tlx: 121011; fax: 539927
German Embassy, Vlasska 19, 125 60 Prague 1. Tel: 532351; tlx: 122814.
US Embassy, Trziste 15, 12548 Prague. Tel: 536641; tlx: 121196; fax: 532457.

HUNGARY

EMERGENCY NUMBERS

Police   Tel: 07 (or 007 outside Budapest)
Fire   05
Ambulance   04

USEFUL NUMBERS & ADDRESSES

The Hungarian telephone system is antiquated and in need of modernisation. The following numbers might work:
Tourist information in English, German, French and Russian: Tel: 3611179800
Yellow Angels breakdown service: Tel: 220668/160183
Domestic train information: Tel: 429150
Information about the country's roads: Tel: 1227052/1227643
Information about Budapest public transport: Tel:1171173
American Express: Tel: 4943733

British Embassy, Harmincad utca 6, 1054 Budapest 5. Tel: 1182888; tlx: 224527; fax: 1180907.
German Embassy, Izso u.5, 1146 Budapest. Tel: 1224204; tlx: 225951; fax: 1601903.
US Embassy, Szabadsag te 12, 1054 Budapest 5. Tel: 1126450/ 392275; tlx: 224222.

ROMANIA

EMERGENCY NUMBERS

Police: Tel: 055
Ambulance in Bucharest: 061
Ambulance outside Bucharest: 06
Fire in Bucharest: 081
Fire outside Bucharest: 08

USEFUL NUMBERS & ADDRESSES

Breakdown service of the Romanian Automobile Club (ACR): Tel: 027

Breakdown service outside Bucharest: Tel: 12345
Railway information: Tel: 052
International flights: Tel: 333137
Domestic flights: Tel: 330030
Phone-a-taxi: Tel: 053
Operator for international calls: Tel: 071

British Embassy, Str. Jules Michelet 24, 70154
Bucharest. Tel: 111634; tlx:11295; fax: 595090.
German Embassy, Str. Rabat 21, 7944 9 Bucharest.
Tel: 792580; tlx: 11292; fax: 796854.
US Embassy, Str. Tudor Arghezi 7-9, Bucharest.
Tel: 104040; tlx: 11416; fax: 861669.

BULGARIA

EMERGENCY NUMBERS

Police   Tel: 166
Fire   160
Ambulance   150
Medical rescue service in the mountains:
Tel: 521605

USEFUL NUMBERS & ADDRESSES

Long-distance operator: Tel: 121
International operator: Tel: 123
Information on international calls: Tel: 124
National breakdown organisation (also accident
reports): Tel: 146
Information about road conditions: Tel: 829536
General travel information: Tel: 597187
International flight information: Tel: 451113
International train information: Tel: 311111
Sleeper reservations: Tel: 597124
International coach travel information: Tel: 525004
Call-a-taxi in Sofia: Tel:142
Call-a-taxi outside Sofia: Tel: 318045
Interpreter service: Tel: 833518
British embassy: Tel: 885361
US embassy: Tel: 884801
Cultural "what's on today": Tel: 171
Sporting "what's on today": Tel: 195

British Embassy, Boulevard Tolbukhin 65-67, So-
fia. Tel: 879575; tlx: 22363; fax: 656022.
German Embassy, Henri Barbusse Street 7, 1113
Sofia. Tel: 722127; tlx: 22590; fax: 718041.
US Embassy, Boulevard A Stamboliiski 1, Sofia.
Tel: 884801; tlx: 22690; fax: 884806.

ART/PHOTO CREDITS

Photography by

Page 286/287, 304, 307	Regina Maria Anzenberger
53	Bodo Bondzio
135	Contrast/Brissaud
124	Contrast/Shone
125	Contrast/Sumovski-Zoya
28/29, 30/31, 52, 63, 70	Fritz Dressler
59, 85	Gudenko
144/145, 156/157	E. Guerassimov
36, 50/51, 55, 56, 57, 58, 60, 61, 62,	Jimmy Holmes
66, 68, 69, 71, 72, 73, 74, 75, 76/77,	
78, 90/91, 93, 95, 96, 97, 99	
344	Alfred Horn
161	Hutchison Library
67, 104, 116/117, 130, 268/269, 290,	Impact Photos
291, 293, 294, 295, 300, 302, 305, 306	
14/15, 16/17, 18/19, 64, 88, 98, 101,	Jürgens Ost + Europa Photo
102/103, 109, 110/111, 112, 113, 120,	
150/151, 178/179, 180/181, 183, 191,	
211, 230/231, 256, 267, 270/271, 285,	
296, 312, 326/327, 329, 330, 331,	
335, 337	
12/13, 114/115, 118, 129L, 129R, 132,	Lyle Lawson
133, 136/137, 138, 140, 147, 148, 149,	
159, 160, 308/309, 343	
188	Christian Parma
185	Polska Agencia Interpress
7, 20, 21, 22, 23, 24L, 24R, 25L, 25R,	Tim Sharman
27R, 164/165, 166, 184L, 184R, 189,	
187, 190, 192, 193, 219L, 220, 223,	
224, 225, 226, 227L, 227R, 228, 229,	
232/233, 248/249, 252L, 252R, 253L,	
253R, 254, 258, 259, 260, 262L, 262R,	
263L, 263R, 264, 265, 266, 289, 298,	
299, 303, 310/311, 314, 332, 334, 336,	
338/339, 340, 341, 342	
27L, 242	Hans-Horst Skuppy
1, 26, 194/195, 198, 202, 214/215,	Tony Souter
216L, 216R, 218, 219R, 221	
246/247, 257, 261, 272, 301	János Stekovics
131, 152, 155	John Massey Stewart
92	Stin/Firson
301	Topham Picture Source
196/197, 212/213·	Karel Vlcek
200	Dieter Vogel

Maps	Berndtson & Berndtson
Illustrations	Klaus Geisler
Visual Consultant	V. Barl

INDEX

Lvov (*U*) 93, 96–97, 175 *also see* **Lviv**
Lvov, Prince 47

M

Maclean, Sir Fitzroy 57
Madara (*Bu*) 333, 335
Magura caves (*Bu*) 331
Magyars 26, 201, 227, 235, 237–239, 276, 278, 316
Malbork (*P*) 192–193
Mamaia (*Ro*) 306
Mangalia (*Ro*) 306
Manning, Olivia 282, 288, 292
Mansurian Lakes (*P*) 193
Marcus Aurelius, Emperor 256
Maria Theresa of Austria 132, 174, 205, 228, 42, 264
Marianske Lazne (*C*) 222
Marienbad (*C*) 222
Markov, Georgi 313
Marshall Plan 209
Marshall, George 209
Marx, Karl 35, 45
Masaryk, Jan 208, 209
Masaryk, Thomas 206, 207, 221
Matejko, Jan 170, 189
Matita, Lake (*Ro*) **306**
Matra Mountains (*H*) 261
Medias (*Ro*) **303**
Meinhard of Bremen 139, 146, 148
Merhei, Lake (*Ro*) **306**
Metternich, Clemens von 243
Michael, King of Romania 282–283
Michael, Tsar 41, 56, 63
Mieszko I, Prince of Poland 169
Mikulov (*C*) 227
Minsk (*Be*) 108, 112–113
Mircea the Old 276, 293
Miskolc (*H*) 262
Mniszek, Jerzy 40
Mniszek, Marina 40, 41
Modlin (*P*) 186
Mohacs (*H*) 241, 278
Moldavia (*Ro*) 273, 276–280, 294–297
Moldova 21, 24, 44, 281, 305
Moldovita (*Ro*) 297
Molotov 155, 281, 282, 283
Mongol Yoke 35, 36, 39, 60, 82, 105, 107, 121, 153, 169
Mongols 36, 60, 61, 82, 93, 112, 239, 249, 264 *also see* **Tartars**
Monomakh, Vladimir 35, 55, 82, 96
Morava River (*C/S*) 227
Moravia 26, 201, 208–209, 224–227, 241
Moscow (*Ru*) 22, 24, 36, 37, 38, 39, 40, 41, 42, 44, 48, 53–59
    Arbat 59, 60, 82
    Gorky Park 59
    GUM 56
    Kremlin and Red Square 53–56
    Lenin's Tomb 56
    Lubyanka 57
    Museums 59
    St Basil's Cathedral 57
Moscow River 53, 58
Moscow State Circus 59
Moussorgsky 39
Mozart 222

Mstislav, Prince 74
Muscovy (*Ru*) 36, 53, 60
Mussman, Alfred 327

N

Nagaya, Maria (also known as Marfa) 39, 40, 61
Nagyvazsony (*H*) 259–260
Napoleon 44, 54, 55, 68, 105, 111, 113, 158, 160, 174, 186, 205, 243
Narva (*Es*) 42, 121, 122, 123, 132–133
NATO 33, 35
Nazi-Soviet pact 47, 108, 119, 124, 155, 281, 323
Neapol Skifsky (*U*) 100
Nemunas River (*Li*) 156
Neris River (*Li*) 156
Nero, Lake (*Ru*) 60
Nesebar (*Bu*) 316, 340–341
Neva River (*Ru*) 36, 64, 65
Nevsky Prospekt (*St Petersburg, Ru*) 70
Nevsky, St Alexander 60, 70, 121, 129, 134, 329
Nicephorus, Emperor 315–316
Nicholas I, Tsar 35, 44–45, 56, 243
Nicholas II, Tsar 45, 46, 47, 55, 66, 72, 75, 100, 175
Niemen River (*Be/Li*) 44
Nikon, Abbot 41–42
Novgorod (*Ru*) 36, 39, 41, 73–74
Novotny, Antonin 210

O

Obrochishte (*Bu*) 340
Ochakov (*U*) 100
Odessa (*U*) 93, 100
Oescus (*Bu*) 330, 332
Oka River (*Ru*) 36, 53
Olga, Princess of Kiev 81
Oliva (*P*) 192
Olsztyn (*P*) 193
Olt River (*Ro*) 293
Olvia (*U*) 100
Omortag, Khan 316, 334, 336
Oradea (*Ro*) 302–303
Orsha (*Be*) 113
Otrepyev, Grishka ("Dmitri") 40
Ottokar I of Bohemia 201, 217, 226
Ottokar II of Bohemia 201, 217

P

Palach, Jan 210, 221
Pamporovo (*Bu*) 342
Pannonhalma (*H*) 257
paprika 235, 266, 267
Paris peace conference 23–24, 26, 27, 107, 119, 199 *also see* **World War I peace conference**
Paul I, Tsar 43, 69, 72
Paul, son of Catherine the Great 43–44
Pechori (*E*) 135
Peipus, Lake (*Ru/E*) 36, 121, 129, 134
Pereslavl (Pereslavl Zalesski) (*Ru*) 60
perestroika 49
Pest (*H*) 240
Peter III, Tsar 43
Peter the Great 33, 35, 42, 54, 55, 58, 60, 64, 65, 66, 67, 68, 70, 71, 73, 74, 97, 119, 122, 132, 133, 134, 140, 147
Pieskowa Skala (*P*) 190

Y

Z

INSIGHT GUIDES

COLORSET NUMBERS

You'll find the colorset number on the spine of each Insight Guide.

INSIGHT *Pocket* GUIDES

EXISTING & FORTHCOMING TITLES:

Aegean Islands
Algarve
Alsace
Athens
Bali
Bali Bird Walks
Bangkok
Barcelona
Bavaria
Berlin
Bhutan
Boston
Brittany
Brussels
Budapest &
Surroundings
Canton
Chiang Mai
Costa Blanca
Costa Brava
Cote d'Azur
Crete
Denmark
Florence
Florida
Gran Canaria
Hawaii
Hong Kong
Ibiza

Ireland
Istanbul
Jakarta
Kathmandu
Bikes & Hikes
Kenya
Kuala Lumpur
Lisbon
Loire Valley
London
Macau
Madrid
Malacca
Mallorca
Malta
Marbella/
Costa del Sol
Miami
Milan
Morocco
Moscow
Munich
Nepal
New Delhi
New York City
North California
Oslo/Bergen
Paris
Penang

Phuket
Prague
Provence
Rhodes
Rome
Sabah
San Francisco
Sardinia
Scotland
Seville/Grenada
Seychelles
Sikkim
Singapore
South California
Southeast England
Sri Lanka
St Petersburg
Sydney
Tenerife
Thailand
Tibet
Turkish Coast
Tuscany
Venice
Vienna
Yogyakarta
Yugoslavia's
Adriatic Coast

United States: **Houghton Mifflin Company, Boston MA 02108**
Tel: (800) 2253362 Fax: (800) 4589501

Canada: **Thomas Allen & Son, 390 Steelcase Road East**
Markham, Ontario L3R 1G2
Tel: (416) 4759126 Fax: (416) 4756747

Great Britain: **GeoCenter UK, Hampshire RG22 4BJ**
Tel: (256) 817987 Fax: (256) 817988

Worldwide: **Höfer Communications Singapore 2262**
Tel: (65) 8612755 Fax: (65) 8616438

❝ I was first drawn to the Insight Guides by the excellent "Nepal" volume. I can think of no book which so effectively captures the essence of a country. Out of these pages leaped the Nepal I know – the captivating charm of a people and their culture. I've since discovered and enjoyed the entire Insight Guide Series. Each volume deals with a country or city in the same sensitive depth, which is nowhere more evident than in the superb photography. ❞

Sir Edmund Hillary